★

EARLY TEXAS

PHYSICIANS

★

EARLY TEXAS
PHYSICIANS

1830-1915

INNOVATIVE ★ INTREPID ★ INDEPENDENT

---

edited by

R. MAURICE HOOD, M.D.

introduction by

T.R. FEHRENBACH

Published by

STATE HOUSE PRESS

Austin, Texas

for

THE TEXAS SURGICAL SOCIETY

San Antonio, Texas

1999

Library of Congress Cataloging-in-Publication Data

Early Texas physicians, 1830-1915 : innovative, intrepid,
independent / edited by R. Maurice Hood ; introduction by T. R.
Fehrenbach.
        p.   cm.
"Published by State House Press, Austin Texas, for The Texas
Surgical Society, San Antonio, Texas."
ISBN 1-880510-63-4 (alk. paper)
ISBN 1-880510-64-2 (limited deluxe)
        1. Physicians—Texas—Biography.
    2. Medicine—Texas—History—19th century.
    3. Medicine—Texas—History—20th century.
    4. Frontier and pioneer life—Health aspects—Texas—
History—19th century. 5. Texas—Biography.
    I. Hood, R. Maurice (Raleigh Maurice), 1924-
            II. Texas Surgical Society.

R335.E27 1999
610'.92'2764—dc21   99-12318
[B]

Printed in the United States of America

cover design by David Timmons

Cabeza de Vaca Insignia by Tom Lea

STATE HOUSE PRESS
P.O. Box 15247
Austin, Texas 78761

DEDICATED

TO

ROBERT S. SPARKMAN
B.A., M.D., L.L.D., F.A.C.S.

★

Dr. Robert S. Sparkman

DEDICATION

★ROBERT S. SPARKMAN WAS BORN in Brownwood, Texas, February 18, 1912, and died at his home in Dallas on March 22, 1997.

He moved with his family to Waco, Texas, when his father was chosen to head the Spanish Department of Baylor University. He was educated in the Waco public schools and received a combined B.A. and M.D. degree from Baylor University and Baylor College of Medicine in Dallas. He received a Distinguished Alumnus Award from each institution and the L.L.D. from Baylor University.

His post graduate training at Cincinnati General Hospital, Good Samaritan Hospital in Lexington and Baylor Hospital in Dallas was interrupted by five years of active duty in the Army Medical Corps during World War II, with over three years of service in Australia, New Guinea, and the Philippines. During his military service he was promoted from first lieutenant to colonel and moved from Ward Officer to Chief of Surgery at three different hospitals and to commanding officer of one of these.

He married Willie Basset on February 21, 1942. She was a loving companion and supporter in all of his research and writing.

He was interested in many things including rare books, art, literature, music, libraries, and the design and printing of books. He was particularly interested in the history of surgery and was the editor of *The Texas Surgical Society; The First Fifty Years* and *The Southern Surgical Association; The First 100 Years*. The history of surgery of the biliary system was the subject of much of his research, writing, and lectures.

Early in his career, the writings of such doctors as Pat Ireland Nixon, George P. Red, and George Cupples attracted his attention to the unusual abilities of early Texas doctors. As a result, he conceived the idea of this book, *Early Texas Physicians*. He assigned each chapter about a specific doctor to a colleague. Additional chapters and authors were added as interesting information was discovered.

In the months before his death, Doctor Sparkman's failing health prevented his completion of the book, so he wisely turned the project over to the talented surgeon and author Dr. R. Maurice Hood.

—Walter B. King, M.D.

TABLE OF CONTENTS

Introduction xi
   T.R. Fehrenbach
Preface xiii
   R. Maurice Hood
The Practice of Medicine 1830-1910 1
   R. Maurice Hood
John Wesley Carhart (1834-1914) 9
   Charles C. Tandy
David Cerna (1857-1953) 29
   Robert B. Krause
George Cupples (1815-1895) 41
   R. Maurice Hood
Ferdinand Eugene Daniel (1839-1914) 61
   R. Maurice Hood
Greensville Dowell (1822-1881) 79
   Joseph P. McNeill
James Fentress (1802-1872) 123
   R. Maurice Hood
John Salmon "RIP" Ford (1815-1897) 131
   R. Maurice Hood
Berthold Ernest Hadra (1842-1903) 151
   A.O. Singleton, Jr
Ferdinand Ludwig Herff (1820-1912) 171
   Vernie A. Stembridge
Anson Jones (1798-1858) 201
   Martin L. Dalton
Nicholas D. Labadie (1802-1867) 211
   William F. Hood and R. Maurice Hood
Gideon Lincecum (1793-1874) 227
   Howard R. Dudgeon, Jr
Frank Paschal (1849-1925) 247
   Arthur S. McFee

Amos Pollard (1803-1836) 273
   Richard J. Andrassy, Flora L. (von) Roeder
   and Anthony Shinn
Joseph Henry Reuss (1867-1919) 291
   James E. Pridgen
Jerome Bonaparte Robertson (ca 1813-1890) 311
   R. Maurice Hood
Nicholas T. Schilling (1845-1919) 321
   Drew Davis Williams
Ashbel Smith (1805-1886) 335
   Martin L. Dalton
James E. Thompson (1863-1927) 349
   Walter B. King
Index 367

INTRODUCTION

★ TODAY IT IS DIFFICULT FOR BOTH physicians and the public to grasp the realities of the practice of medicine in frontier Texas.

There are a number of reasons. First, Texas throughout the nineteenth century remained very much a frontier. Although Indian troubles had ceased by 1883, and although law and order was gradually becoming ascendant over most of the state, frontier conditions still prevailed. The population was overwhelmingly agrarian and rural, thinly scattered over vast areas; some of the most populous counties contained no towns or cities of significant size. For the most part, this population was part of the post-Civil War South, living in a commodity-dependent economy beset by falling commodity prices. Much of Texas, especially along the gulf coast, was subject to epidemic diseases such as yellow fever, malaria and typhoid, the causes of which were not understood. Doctors, or course, did not yet have answers to many afflictions such as carcinoma or heart disease, but the major concerns of today were then not so important as were the treatment of fevers and repairing of injuries.

It must be remembered that medicine was not yet an art supported by science, at least on the frontier, until after the turn of the century. Doctors had achieved professional status but were not yet licensed as such, and the doctors in Texas included both men possessing state-of-the-art medical educations as well as practitioners with only sketchy on-the-job training. The public does not seem to have discriminated; they sought other qualities than formal degrees in their doctors.

The practice of medicine and the role of the physician were thus quite different than they are today. Doctors were, and had to be, traveling men, often going great distances to treat patients. In pre-scientific medicine the qualities of patience, experience and caring were predominant. Probably more love, in both patient and physician, was present than in modern, science-based medicine. As ill-equipped as they were, doctors enjoyed great respect so long as they clearly cared; a few "good" or "bad" cases might make or break a doctor's career in small communities. Medical men also played a much greater public and civic role than today. They were less narrowly focused; many became community leaders with interests ranging far beyond the pure practice of medicine. Doctors were respected not merely as medical authorities but as moral authorities, a burden most bore well.

It is important that the stories of early Texas doctors be told. They are a vital part of the history of Texas and its society. While they tell us little about the advancement of medical science, these lives illuminate our pioneer days. Early Texas doctors struggled to heal the sick and ease suffering and pain on the frontier; they shared the frontier's hardships in those horse-and-buggy days, but they also did much to bring civilization to it. They often went where no medical men had gone before, and where few might choose to go today. If most were better at setting broken bones and fighting fevers than effecting seemingly miraculous cures, they laid the foundation for our imposing Texas medical edifice that now contains more Nobel Prizes than most nations and which ranks among the highest in the support it renders to its medical research institutions.

We have made enormous progress in a short hundred years. But as the lives of these true medical pioneers reveal, we may have lost something, too.

—T.R. FEHRENBACH

PREFACE

★SEVERAL YEARS AGO, Dr. Robert Sparkman asked me to be a participant in a book which he originally planned to title *Fabulous Physicians of Early Texas*. He assigned a number of the subjects to be included in the book to doctors in the Texas Surgical Society, and others of the subjects to doctors outside this organization. Dr. Truman Blocker was to share in the production but his death ended his participation.

It is my impression from all the material Dr. Sparkman sent me that the project was originally more ambitious and included chapters on Texas cities in the latter half of the nineteenth century and chapters on early Texas hospitals, but when the seriousness of his illness became obvious, these additional subject areas were dropped. He asked Martin Dalton and myself to assume the editorship and bring the project to completion.

The last year has been a busy one for me as I tried to bring this book to reality. Some of the physicians he had selected as subjects had no assigned authors and I have completed three of these. Three were dropped for lack of information and/or author. The final manuscripts describe nineteen early physicians. I am certain that my literary efforts fall short of Dr. Sparkman's standards, but I have made as good an effort as I am capable of. It is my hope that Mrs. Willie Sparkman, and those that read this volume, will be pleased and that it will serve as a tribute to Dr. Sparkman by the authors, all of whom have regarded him so highly.

—R. Maurice Hood, M.D.

The Practice of Medicine
1830-1915
by
R. Maurice Hood, M.D.

★The medical environment in which the physicians and surgeons of this volume lived and worked was greatly different to that with which the readers are accustomed. The nineteenth century has been termed "The Century of the Surgeon," "The Golden Age of Medicine" and the "Age of Discovery." More medical discoveries and developments were made prior to 1900 than after. Medicine has made great progress in the twentieth century, but few of these advances would have been possible had it not been for the monumental discoveries of the previous century. For the doctors of Texas during this period, however, the above statement would not have seemed true because they were practicing their art much as it had been practiced since the Middle Ages.

Before discussing medical practice, it is worth noting the different disease spectrum with which the physicians had to cope. Infectious diseases such as malaria, yellow fever, pneumonia, typhoid fever, erysipelas, cholera, dysentery, post partum infection, smallpox, tuberculosis, measles, and wound and soft tissue bacterial infections caused the majority of deaths and the disabilities common to the age.

The incidence of malaria in southern and eastern Texas is unknown but was probably as high as 50 percent. Even today, malaria accounts for more deaths than any disease in the world, although it is largely non-existent in the United States today. The cause of malaria is a protozoan parasite transmitted by mosquitoes, but the doctors did not know its cause or its mode of transmission.

Yellow fever was the devastating disease of the nation in the nineteenth century. Caused by a virus, also transmitted by the mosquito, it raged in epidemics in the summer months in coastal cities from Texas to New York. These epidemics varied in mortality from 30 percent to 80 percent. No less than fifteen epidemics in Texas were documented prior to 1900. Its cause was unknown and there was no treatment.

Pneumonia, caused by a number of bacteria, plagued all communities each winter. The pneumococcus was responsible for the variety known then as lobar pneumonia, which was fatal for up to 30 percent of its victims. Bacteria were unknown, and pneumonia was blamed on such things as having become chilled or wet or exposed to night air. There was no effective treatment. It was not until 1945 when sulfanilamide became available that this tragic disease was largely conquered.

Several varieties of dysentery or diarrhea, which we now know as cholera, shigellosis, salmonellosis and amebiasis, were always endemic because the water supply and waste disposal were grossly inadequate. Diarrhea, particularly cholera, was often fatal to adults, and in all forms was frequently fatal to infants and small children. Death was usually due to dehydration. Fluid replacement intravenously was largely unavailable until near the end of the century.

Tuberculosis was rampant and its cause and contagiousness were unknown until Koch discovered the etiologic bacteria in 1882. This discovery resulted in isolation of the victims until 1949 when streptomycin and isoniazid became available.

Postpartum infection, which was highly lethal, was a constant threat to young mothers. A young Hungarian doctor, Ignaz Phillip Semmelweis, became convinced that "childbed fever was caused by the unwashed hands of doctors" and began a life-long crusade to stop "this murder" as he called it. His pleas, beginning in 1844, continued to be almost totally unheeded by the time of his death in 1865.

The conquering of bacterial and viral infections has yet to be accomplished and probably never will be, but the antibiotic age has made an enormous difference.

The heroes of the century in the fight to conquer infection were Robert Koch, Louis Pasteur, and Joseph Lister. Koch, using a primitive microscope, discovered that the organism Mycobacterium Tuberculosis was the cause of human tuberculosis.

Pasteur first found that a microorganism caused the fermentation of wine. He suspected that cholera was caused by a bacteria and believed that many diseases were caused by microorganisms. His efforts gave birth to a new area of science—bacteriology. This genius has been regarded by many as the father of modern medicine, but his work would not affect the practice of medicine in the nineteenth century.

Lister's teachings in the eyes of most of the medical and surgical world were heresy and were scoffed at by the majority of doctors. Lister, basing his work on the work of Pasteur, believed that postoperative infection could be prevented by sterilization of instruments by phenol, the soaking of drapes by the same agent, and the vigorous washing of hands and rinsing with a phenol solution. He also atomized a phenol solution into the air of the operating room. Later he advocated sterilization of instruments, drapes, and sponges by steam and heat. He called this "asepsis" as opposed to "antisepsis," which the former method was termed. He would not be vindicated until the turn of the century. The American surgeon William Stewart Halsted, of Johns Hopkins, led the way in America after visiting Lister in England, but acceptance was still slow. Lister and his principles of antisepsis and asepsis opened the door to surgery inside the human body and stopped the inevitable post injury infections. He, more than any other person, paved the way for the rapid development of surgery.

Texas doctors in the last half of the nineteenth century benefited little from these monumental advances.

The control of pain had been a goal for most of the span of medical history. Surgical procedures with no anesthetic was practiced until 1844. An obscure dentist, Horace Wells, with Dr. John M. Riggs, proved that nitrous oxide (laughing gas) could produce sufficient unconsciousness to permit painless tooth extraction. Sir William Osler was later to call this discovery "the greatest single gift ever made to suffering humanity."

Dr. W.T.G. Morton, a Boston dentist and acquaintance of Wells', was a witness to Wells' successful cases and possessed sufficient influence at Harvard to convince the authorities to allow him to demonstrate the technique for a surgical procedure. Dr. John Collins Warren, professor of surgery, selected a patient with a tumor in the neck. The procedure was successfully accomplished using ether instead of nitrous oxide. Anesthesia was thus introduced to the world on October 19, 1846. Crawford Long in New Orleans had used ether for several years prior to Morton's case, but he did not publish his results until 1849. Apparently he, not Morton, was the first to use ether.

Ether had the negative characteristics of a disagreeable odor and was extremely flammable. Sir James Y. Simpson, a Scotsman trying to find a substitute, came up with chloroform, which was not a new compound. He successfully used chloroform for delivery on January 19, 1847. An American, Dr. Nathan Cooley Keep of Harvard Dental School, first used chloroform in America. His work was reported April 14, 1847.

The use of these agents was rapidly accepted and spread over the nation. They were in wide use by the time of the Civil War; unfortunately, the supplies of these agents were limited particularly to the Confederate surgeon. As a result, a great number of operations were performed without anesthesia. Despite the wide use of anesthetic agents, they were not widely used in Texas, particularly in rural areas, until well after the Civil War. The discovery and use of anesthesia along with those of Lister resulted in the birth of modern surgery.

Since the doctors in this volume cover the period of time from 1830 to about 1915, there is no point in discussing medicine prior to these times. Pat Ireland Nixon's excellent book *Medicine in Early Texas* adeptly covers the Indian, Spanish and Mexican periods.

The doctors of early Texas had severe limitations in the procedures, diagnostic methods and pharmacopeia. They could splint fractures, suture wounds, perform amputations and drain infections, but their limitations in physical diagnosis were many. Most had stethoscopes but little more. Readers will note that in the latter part of the century, doctors Cupples and Herff were able to perform many major surgical procedures because of their training and because anesthesia was available.

Physicians received their education in three ways. Some attended medical schools in the northeastern United States then immigrated to Texas. Some were trained by studying under another doctor for varying periods until their mentor decided that they were capable. Still others received their education in

European medical schools which were generally more advanced than their American counterparts. These men who came from Europe to Texas were some of the most advanced doctors of their time. The level of training and the expertise of doctors thus varied greatly.

Some methods of treatment dated back to the Middle Ages. The use of enemas and cupping are examples. Cupping, or the removal of variable amounts of blood, was based on the presumption that the blood contained harmful "humors" or other causes of disease and could be removed. There were a number of poultices or plasters where various agents were applied to a cloth, which was then applied to the chest or other affected part, sometimes with the addition of heat. These sometimes produced first and second degree burns which only added to the patient's problems.

Doctors could cast or splint fractures, and some were very skillful in reducing displaced fractures. They could suture wounds although they used unsterile methods. Some were adept at obstetrics, although also with unsterile techniques.

Medicines varied greatly, including herbs empirically selected without knowledge of the agent. There were many home remedies that were used by doctors probably because patients demanded them. Some agents were selected because they produced visible results that the patient could appreciate. Curative qualities have been ascribed to almost every known substance. Some of the agents or medicines used included calomel, quinine, blue mass pills, belladonna, ipecac, whiskey, various herbal concoctions, columbo, asafetida, boneset, squill, pokeweed, hog's foot oil, castor oil, digitalis, and many others. Most were harmless but not all. Outright quackery was widespread.

For a drug to be effective, it was believed that it had to be foul-smelling or tasting. Powders were thought to be superior to tablets and colored tablets better than white ones. Ointments were popular if they had a pungent odor or were known to contain some exotic substance.

Pain relief was sought by using opium usually as a tincture. Morphine (laudanum) was widely prescribed. Paregoric was widely used. The addicting qualities of these agents was vaguely understood. Alcohol was used in many instances.

There was another discipline termed homeopathy, which

was non-scientific but had many advocates, including physicians. Gradually the scientific form of medicine prevailed. Throughout the century, scientific advances slowly brought medicine to a solid profession based upon the experimental method.

The wars of the twentieth century resulted in enormous medical and surgical progress. Although the greatest medical event of the nineteenth century was the Civil War, this war was notable for resulting in almost no discovery or progress. Medical and surgical knowledge was still in the Middle Ages. Anesthesia was generally available to the Union surgeons but in very limited quantities to the Confederates. Over 530,000 persons were killed or died from illness during the war, about half from injury but many thousands from pneumonia, dysentery, typhoid fever, typhus fever, and epidemics of smallpox and measles that ravaged both armies. There were 1,213,685 cases of malaria reported in both armies during the war. As many as 30,000 cases were seen in one Union army. A Virginia unit sustained over 1,000 cases of small pox in three months. Amputation was the only treatment for wounds of the extremities associated with a fracture. Amputations were performed by multiple thousands with a mortality rate from 50 percent to 85 percent.

The discoveries of Pasteur and Lister were still in the future; therefore, post injury and postoperative infection was in excess of 70 percent. Pneumonia and other infections acquired in the hospital led some to say that a wounded soldier stood a better chance of survival if he were not taken to a hospital.

To put this into sharper focus, the famed Hood's Texas Brigade had 5,300 men who served in the brigade during the war. Some were taken prisoner and a few deserted, but only 617 survived to surrender at Appomattox. Over 4,700 had died of injury or illness.

Many Texas doctors, including several in this book, served in the Confederacy as soldiers or as doctors, some with great distinction.

From the foregoing it would be tempting to look upon physicians of this era as ignorant and incapable, but this would be in error. They have to be judged by the knowledge and reasoning of their time rather than in the light of modern medicine. They thought that they were practicing sound medicine and the majority were honest, intelligent and conscientious in their care of patients. They often had to work under very adverse circumstances and with inadequate equipment. They rarely had access to a hospital and its facilities. In fact, hospitals were essentially non-existent. The John Sealy Hospital, associated with the Texas Medical College, was the first modern hospital and did not exist until 1890 although it had been preceded by a small primitive hospital in 1847. Many physicians used one or more rooms of their office or home as a "hospital." At one time the Alamo was used as a hospital.

One of the principal contributions of doctors of this age was their physical presence and psychological support during illness and death. They could inspire hope and comfort in the patient, which has always been a major factor in recovery from illness. Because they were often the most educated in the community, along with the minister, lawyer and teacher, they had great influence outside of medicine.

REFERENCES

P.I. Nixon, *The Medical Story of Early Texas* (San Antonio: Molly Bennett Memorial Foundation, 1946), 284-300, 393.

Rene Vallry-Radal, *The Life of Louis Pasteur* (New York: Sun Dial Press, 1937), 227.

Jorgen Thorwald, *The Century of the Surgeon* (New York: Pantheon, 1937), 226-44.

Rhoda Truax, *Joseph Lister, Father of Modern Surgery*, (New York: Bobbs-Merrill, 1944), general reference.

H.R. Raper, *Man Against Pain, The Epic of Anesthesia*, (New York: Prentice-Hall, 1945), 75-77, 91-92, 98-99, 157-60.

P.E. Steiner, *Disease in the Civil War* (Springfield, Ill.: Charles C. Thomas, 1968), 20-22, 54.

S. Brooks, *Civil War Medicine* (Springfield, Ill.: Charles C. Thomas, 1966), 99, 118, 120.

H.B. Simpson, *Hood's Texas Brigade, Lee's Grenadier Guard*, (Waco, Texas: Texian Press).

John Wesley Carhart in his early years, published in *Four Years on Wheels; or Life as a Presiding Elder*, 1880.

JOHN WESLEY CARHART, M.D.
1834-1914

by

Charles C. Tandy, M.D.

★TEXAS HAS HAD BETTER DOCTORS. It has had none whose interests and activities were so varied. John Wesley Carhart, Methodist minister, author, inventor and physician, was born in Albany County, New York, near the rural village of Coeymans on June 26, 1834. His father, Daniel Sutton Carhart, was a tenant farmer. His mother, Margaret Martin Carhart, a deeply pious woman, wanted to instill in each of her seven children some of her own religious fervor. Because his family lacked many necessities, and also because he was the oldest of three sons, John Wesley was forced at a very early age to assume his share of farm work. Although his strength was often taxed almost beyond endurance, he believed in the importance of physical labor. Later in life he said that it had been a valuable part of his formative years.

The boy loved the country of his birth and described it with affection. In his autobiography, *Four Years on Wheels*, he described the slightly broken, rolling land "furnishing an almost infinite variety of scenery, and mapped out into beautiful and productive farms." Near his home grew huge pine trees, under which he spent as much time as he could, listening for hours to the wind as it whispered through their branches. The spell cast by his surroundings moved him emotionally, "Each tree, rock and shrub was dear to me, and the beauty of the scenery impressed my young mind."[1]

John Wesley's early education, received at a neighborhood school, only sharpened his desire to learn more. Wishing to satisfy his hunger for more knowledge, he went to work on a neighboring farm, performing the same kind of hard labor which he had known at home. For his work he received eight dollars per month, and from this amount he saved enough to enroll in the Union Seminary at Charlottesville, New York. When his funds were depleted, he borrowed fifty dollars from an elderly uncle to complete his studies. During the winter following his year of study he taught school, and in the spring he repaid his debt. His mother's influence determined his selection of what he believed to be his life career. At the age of seventeen he was preaching, at twenty he was ordained a Methodist minister, and at twenty-seven he received a D.D. degree. While performing his ministerial duties, John Wesley was developing interests in two apparently unrelated fields. He began to write—poetry, essays and biographies—on subjects of general and literary interest as well as religious subjects. At the same time, he became interested in machines and in the way they functioned. It is easy to understand his interest in the written word—a minister knows the power of words and that he must cultivate the ability to use them—but why machines? No doubt John Wesley shared the nineteenth-century fascination for inventions which were appearing in great abundance, inventions destined soon to change everyone's way of life.

In 1856 the Reverend Carhart was appointed to the pastorate in Richmondville, Schoharie County, New York. Illness and loneliness threatened to ruin his year until he met Theresa Mumford, daughter of John H. and Mary Mumford. By the following year the couple, now married, were living in Rutland, Vermont. John Wesley wrote more and more.

> I found, not only the natural atmosphere congenial to my physical nature, but the literary and moral atmosphere congenial to my mind and heart. The village itself, was beautiful and had an air of newness, and of smartness, that pleased me, while the natural scenery was unsurpassed by anything I had ever seen. Washington Irving says he considers it a fortunate thing to be born in sight of some great and noble object in nature, like the Hudson River, or the Catskill mountains. I was so fortunate as to be born in sight of both

of these great and noble objects in nature, and here in
my childhood I cultivated that love of nature and the
beautiful, that has continued with me thus far through
life, and has been an inspiration and will be a joy
forever![2]

Editorials, essays, poems and biographies—one, a life of the
Italian poet Torquato Tasso—were published in various newspapers, magazines and church publications. He arranged his
poems and published them in 1859 in an edition of one-thousand
copies.[3]

The Carhart family moved often. The year 1858 found them
in Fultonville, New York, "a pleasant little village in the valley
of the Mohawk, on the west side of the River . . . divided by the
Erie Canal."[4] Until this point the Carhart autobiography does
not mention the subject of medicine, but medicine was another
developing Carhart interest and at this point he wrote that the
leading physician of the place,

> frequently invited me to ride with him, which I was
> glad to do, as it gave me some recreation—chance to
> see the country and to make a great many acquain-
> tances. On one occasion he invited me to ride with
> him the following day. . .We had a delightful ride, over
> the hills and through the valleys, stopping here and
> there to dress a wound, treat a sore eye, look at and
> pity a helpless old lady, console a hypochondriacal
> middle-aged man, or to 'pull a tooth' for some farm
> hand.[5]

An article by Terese von Hohoff describes the practice of
medicine on the west bank of the Mohawk by a Dr. Carhart,
who was "a large, clean-shaven man with brown, protuberant
eyes." The doctor made a deal with the author's grandfather to
provide medical care in exchange for grain.

> The doctor and my grandmother, between them, took
> care of the sick and needy for miles around. In the
> absence of organized social workers, they made a
> pretty good substitute. He was cheerfully non-sectar-

ian, in a rabidly sectarian village. No church party,
from the Methodist to the Catholic, was complete
without him and he carved at the dinners in winter
and served the ice cream in summer.

One incident mentioned by the writer reveals the doctor's
questioning nature.

One of the berry pickers fell screaming in the straw-
berry bed, to die a few hours later of acute indigestion.
Dr. Carhart blamed himself. He said there was something he didn't know that could have saved her. Oh
yes, he admitted that acute indigestion was nearly
always fatal, but there was something—only he
couldn't put his finger on it. He found it awhile later
in a medical journal; removal of the vermiform appen-
dix.[6]

Was this man John Wesley Carhart? It could have been. The
first name of the Mohawk Valley doctor is lacking, and the
author gives no specific date to place him chronologically. There
are some similarities between the two doctors. The Reverend
Carhart lived in the Mohawk Valley area, and the curiosity to
question and to solve a troublesome problem fit his character.

John Wesley Carhart, who always seemed to have time for
activities outside his ministry, could have practiced medicine
informally and without a license in the Mohawk Valley on the
west bank of the Hudson. In the nineteenth century and earlier,
many physicians did so, beginning their careers as apprentices
or assistants to older, experienced doctors. Many of them continued to practice without medical degrees. Their grateful patients never knew the difference.

After two years in Fultonville, and another year in Stuyve-
sant Falls, New York, Dr. Carhart was appointed to a pastorate
in Pittsfield, Massachusetts, and received his Doctor of Divinity
degree in 1861. He also showed his first definite interest in
medicine and began to study it under the tutelage of Dr. Timothy Childs, a Pittsfield physician. Dr. Childs (1822-1865) had
attended Williams College (1841), and Berkshire Medical College where he obtained his medical degree in 1846. He became

Professor of Anatomy, Physiology and Medical Surgery in the Berkshire Medical College, a school which his father, Dr. Henry Childs, had helped to found. Dr. Carhart attended one session of lectures at this medical college. Although the school's faculty from time to time included such respected names as Elisha Bartlett, Alonso Clark, and Willard Parker, these men did not remain long in Pittsfield. The small town lacked material for good clinical instruction.[7]

More than twenty years were to pass before Dr. Carhart received his medical degree. In March 1883, after completing two courses of lectures at the College of Physicians and Surgeon's at Chicago, he was graduated with its first class of students. The next year he took a course of postgraduate study at the New York Polyclinic.[8] These courses completed his formal medical training.

While serving as minister in Cohoes, New York, his next pastoral home, Dr. Carhart had a preview of how industrial progress could affect communities and the people who lived in them. Cohoes was a town completely lacking the natural beauty it should have had. "There were no deep, dark, old forests into which one might rush from the busy cares of life and lose oneself in holy meditation. But the clank of the cotton loom was forever on the air and wearied, at times, my very soul..."[9] He had always enjoyed visiting with members of his church, but he soon discovered that after a day in the cotton mills, the workers were bone-tired and wanted no visiting—not even with their pastor. He felt frustrated.

On the morning of his arrival in Troy, New York, his next pastorate, he learned of President Lincoln's assassination. His first duty was to preach a Lincoln memorial sermon which he included in his autobiography. He continued to write, and in 1865 he published a book on Hebrew poets and poetry.[10] The *Troy Daily Whig* referred to the author as "a clergyman who is at once a scholar and an inventor, a poet and mechanic, learned and ingenious."[11] In Troy he also perfected and sold his first invention.

> I always had an irrepressible passion for mechanics, and during my stay in Troy I accidentally invented and subsequently perfected an invention in the form of an

oscillating valve for steam engines, which I patented and out of which I made a few thousand dollars. But, like most Methodist preachers, I had no great acquaintance with business matters and I was induced by sharper men than I was to invest what I had in unproductive property, which in the course of its development, called for more money, and still more, which together with my disposition to assist friends, brought me into business relations and complications, which afterwards resulted unpleasantly.[12]

After Troy came a pastorate in Mechanicsville, New York, another beautiful, little village on the west bank of the Hudson River about twelve miles north of Troy. Could this have been the place where he might have practiced medicine? If so, he now had some medical training although as yet no medical degree. Dr. Carhart had to abandon his preaching temporarily because of bad health. He sought less taxing work and took a position as agent for the State Temperance Society, "a moneyless institution, which expected me to work for nothing, take collections at my lectures, and forward to them to pay their salaried secretary."[13]

With his growing family he needed money. In 1871 he found it economically necessary to resume preaching, this time in Waterford, a town about three miles north of Troy. He lived here only a few months. In the fall of 1871 he transferred to Racine, Wisconsin. He gave no reason for his transfer, but his health and his unstable finances could have contributed much to his decision. The trip to Wisconsin was pleasant and he was optimistic, hoping for better days in a new environment. "The weather was delightful, nature was enwrapped in a soft, golden haze, the foliage of the forests had assumed a restful air . . . I had my family all with me, and we were starting out on a new departure, and were, in some sense, beginning life anew."[14]

In 1872 in Racine Dr. Carhart completed another invention, one for which he should be remembered today: he invented the first vehicle in the United States to travel under its own power. Modern histories of the automobile fail to credit him with this achievement. The "Spark," his clumsy, two-cylinder contrivance fueled with hard coal, resembled a buggy. Unlike the buggy,

John Wesley Carhart's steam vehicle, the first automobile in history.

it could rumble along Wisconsin country roads at approximately four miles per hour—all without the aid of a horse! It was the first of its kind. In 1903 Dr. Carhart reminded manufacturers to pay careful attention to "the operating features of the machines" so that accidents caused by speed or bad roads might be avoided. At the International Automobile Exhibition held in Paris in 1905, the inventor was acknowledged as the "father of the automobile" and was awarded a certificate of honor and a cash award.[15] Two historical associations in Wisconsin and Texas recognized the Carhart priority in the invention of the automobile,[16] but his steam-propelled vehicle was too slow. Later, petroleum-fueled versions of the automobile moved much faster, often leading to the accidents which Dr. Carhart had warned against. The "father of the automobile" was soon forgotten.

Several misfortunes befell the Carhart family in Racine. The youngest child, a baby, died and was buried there. John Wesley was plagued again with illness. He transferred to Oshkosh, and again he expected better days. Bad luck, like his shadow, followed him. His Oshkosh congregation needed a new church building and pledged money to build it. Some of the members pledged beyond their ability to pay; others had a change of mind and defaulted. A collector, employed to obtain the promised funds, was no asset; he told everyone the church would never meet its financial obligations. Everyone blamed the pastor.

At the next Conference, the Reverend Carhart was appointed Elder of the Appleton District, a position which he held for four years. The Carhart children, several now young adults, were beginning to make their own history. Two of them, Edward Elmer and his sister, Minnie T., embarked upon a career of their own and in April 1876 began publishing a newspaper, *The Early Dawn*. The following year, on January 4, 1877, they enlarged their paper to six columns. Two other Carhart children were drafted to assist them in their enterprise by setting type and handling some of the press work. Printing became a family affair. The proud father, with an office in the editorial room, wrote articles for the paper, and assisted his children in any way he could.[17]

In the meantime, one of John Wesley's brothers, the Reverend Louis Henry Carhart, founded the town of Clarendon, Donley County, Texas, better known to rowdy cowboys as "saint's roost."[18] At this time there were no newspapers in the Texas Panhandle, and the Clarendon minister wanted one. He could find no type available in the area, so he sent his newspaper copy to Oshkosh, Wisconsin, and there his brother's family printed the first Panhandle newspaper, not in Texas, but in Wisconsin![19] Before long the young Carharts sold their newspaper, which soon lost most of its subscribers and was discontinued. Edward Elmer moved to Carendon to become printer and publisher of the *Clarendon News*; Minnie T. obtained employment in Oshkosh.

In the fall of 1877, at a camp meeting at West Pensaukee, Wisconsin, the Reverend E.L. Alling, pastor at Sturgeon Bay, died and his newly wedded wife assumed his church duties. The majority of the congregation requested that she continue as her husband's successor, and in his capacity as Presiding Elder, Dr. Carhart appointed her to the Sturgeon Bay pastorate. She served a full year as minister, the first time a woman was reported to have held such a position in the Methodist Church. Methodist bishops disapproved. They ruled against licensing and ordaining women as ministers, and the General Conference sustained their decision.[20]

Dr. Carhart soon discovered Texas, and he liked what he

saw. His brother, the Reverend L.H. Carhart, Presiding Elder of the Denison District, invited him to participate in the dedication of a new church in Sherman, Texas. After the dedication, John Wesley spent four weeks traveling and observing different parts of the state around Sherman, Dallas, Ft. Worth, Austin, Houston and San Antonio. When he returned to Wisconsin he wrote, "I found the country more beautiful, the inhabitants, as a rule, more intelligent and enterprising and the products of the country more varied and abundant, and the internal improvements vastly in excess of what I had reason, from the reports, to expect."[21]

Dr. Carhart was disappointed with his work in Wisconsin. Bickering, malicious gossip, failure of church members to support church financing, rejection of his sermons against alcohol and tobacco, inadequate salary, and perhaps something in his own personality all contributed to his disillusion. His mental attitude and his way of life were not those of the robust Wisconsin frontier. They were more closely akin to the life styles of New York, Vermont, and Massachusetts.

The animosity of one man in particular pursued him, behind his back and using other men to accomplish his purpose.

> I was entirely ignorant of his plans to remove me from the District until our District Conference at Fort Howard, held September 9-12, 1878. I had scarcely reached the seat of the Conference, before brethren came to me with the intelligence that Rev. George C. Haddock, pastor of Algona Street church, Oshkosh, was organizing a movement to remove me from the district . . . false reports, damaging to my reputation, were industriously circulated, and every effort was made to awaken a public sentiment against me.

The Committee, appointed to investigate charges against Dr. Carhart, exonerated him completely. The verdict in his favor should have settled the matter completely, but the fight against him continued, vindictive, bitter, and often anonymous.[22]

The Reverend Carhart had had enough. He severed all relations with the Methodist Church and prepared to leave Wisconsin. For twenty-nine years he had served his church.

Now, at the age of forty-six he considered his life career ended. He wrote *Four Years on Wheels*, a partial autobiography, and moved to Texas.

After spending approximately a year and a half in the Texas Panhandle, Dr. Carhart moved to Lampasas, Texas, in late 1883 or early 1884.[23] The Methodist pastor who had devoted the early part of his life ministering to man's spiritual and moral life now directed his attention to man's physical needs. He began to practice medicine, and his writings now included subjects of medical interest—patient histories, medications, and patient response to medical care. All aspects of general medical practice won his attention, but he soon began to show a special interest in the medical problems of women and children. He believed that women should not be permitted to bear defective or diseased children, "When a woman's capability for producing children, healthy in body and mind, ceases, she should cease bearing them. No one has the right to project upon society a sickly or enfeebled offspring."[24] To insure the production of healthy offspring, he believed that marriage laws throughout the United States and its territories should be uniform. Qualified physicians should be required to examine all matrimonial candidates and should forbid the marriage of couples with diseases which could prove harmful or injurious to prospective offspring. Doctors "should be empowered to issue, or to withhold, license, which license, if granted, should be a matter of record with the Clerk of the District or county Court in which parties to the contract reside."[25]

Dr. Carhart believed that a young child should never be treated as an adult because of the physical and physiological differences which physicians should know and respect. When treating sick children, he cautioned that "we must begin to treat the child before he is born. We must begin when the mother is yet a child."[26]

Although he was a general practitioner, Dr. Carhart believed that medical specialization was sometimes necessary, and he made this point in an article on the role of physicians as witnesses in court, "A troublesome proposition, which almost invariably confronts the doctor—witness in cases of mental alienation, is the assumption, on the part of lawyers and judges, that all mental alienation is due to diseased conditions in the physical being. A doctor who has not specialized in the study of mental problems is not necessarily qualified to testify in trials involving criminal acts stemming from 'lunacy'."

> The only remedy, it seems to me, is . . . from some thoroughly competent specialist in the field of mental alienation to be attached to trial courts, as commissioner of lunacy, with coordinate powers as examiners of witnesses, and by every legitimate, scientific means, acquire all possible knowledge of the case, and give the court an opinion based on the ascertained facts. By the adoption of some such means will the character of the medical profession be maintained and the interests of the suffering and accused be subserved.[27]

Dr. Carhart could not forget his ministerial experience.[28] He reminded doctors that as healers of the sick they had moral responsibilities, "Multitudes of physicians are now, not only healers, but teachers; and the time will come when they will be the most potential moral teachers of the world."[29]

There were other responsibilities which doctors should accept. They should give patients the best care possible. In prescribing drugs, doctors should insist on quality, and not on price, ". . . I am fully convinced that our labors would be attended with far more satisfactory results if our druggists would purchase standard goods of tried and reliable houses. That desirable result will not be reached, until the medical profession insists that it shall be done."[30]

Above all, a professional physician should work for his own self respect as well as for the betterment of his profession. Dr. Carhart wrote that too many doctors place their own financial gain above their patients' welfare. Selfish and incompetent physicians should not be accepted by the medical profession. The conscientious doctor should encourage and promote better medical education, should support the publication of good medical books and journals, should promote actively the use of quality drugs, and should provide for himself an efficient, well-organized and comfortable office where he could meet with his patients during office hours. A dark cubbyhole in a crowded drugstore was not good enough. "Let physicians respect them-

selves and honor their calling, as individuals, and let every
worthy man join some Medical Society——take all medical journals he can read and pay for——do business on business principles,
and we shall all be more prosperous and happy."[31]

In more heavily populated areas, public health was beginning to emerge as a medical specialty. Dr. Carhart wrote several
papers on subjects which he felt demanded the attention of
doctors: the disposal of human excreta, the location of burial
grounds, and the management of smallpox and yellow fever
epidemics. His paper on graveyards was read in St. Louis at the
Seventeenth Annual Meeting of the Mississippi Valley Medical
Association in 1891.[32] In this paper Dr. Carhart encouraged all
physicians to assert their influence whenever they learned of
proposed new burial grounds. Doctors should try to direct the
location of new burial grounds to places where they would not
jeopardize the health of the living. When trying to influence the
general public in this matter, physicians should approach the
subject tactfully. Death and burial are surrounded in the popular
mind by a "pseudo-sacredness fostered by the profoundest sen-
timents of our nature. The method of disposal of the dead
should be founded on reason and not on custom or sentiment."
Whenever possible physicians should encourage cremation.

In February 1890 Dr. Carhart published the first of two
papers on the resort possibilities of Lampasas, Texas. This first
paper gives us an approximate dating of his arrival in Lampasas,
late 1883 or early 1884, "I have now practiced medicine here for
nearly six years."[33] This same paper describes the faults of
Lampasas as a health resort. In spite of the natural beauty of the
area, promoters had advanced false and misleading information
about the town. Lampasas was unsanitary, its streets rough and
unkept with no sidewalks or street lamps. Its drinking water,
piped from local springs, was polluted, and threatened the health
of its users. The town, formerly Burleson, had received the name
Lampasas at the time of its incorporation in 1874. By 1885 it had
a population of three thousand, seven churches, and two schools.
It had a planing mill, several flour mills, two iceplants and three
privately owned waterworks. By 1890 it had acquired two
newspapers.[34] In February 1894, four years after his first paper
on Lampasas, John Wesley Carhart published his second paper.
In it he overlooked or minimized many of the problems de-

scribed in the first paper and now emphasized only the positive, "The therapeutical effects of these waters are decided, and there is no doubt of their value in certain cases, when intelligently used." Had city fathers corrected the faults described earlier? Had John Wesley bowed to objections of the town's irate citizens? Had his wife's death robbed him of his interest in the town's public health problems?

Theresa Mumford Carhart had died on July 9, 1893. "after a painful illness." In May 1894 John Wesley moved to La Grange, Texas.[35] Although he never said so, he must have depended on his wife's help and support through the family's many moves with their eight children: Minnie T., Matilda, Edward Elmer, Nina B., Charles Wheeler, Agnus Gould (?), Hallie Rogers, and Ethel.[36]

After moving to Texas, Dr. Carhart continued to write poetry and fiction, now on subjects relating to Texas. *The Sign Rider*, with its subject of ranches and cowboys, was written in five serial installments to appear in the *Lampasas Leader*. It was probably based on some of the experiences of his son, Edward Elmer, in Donley County. He began to publish his own newspaper, the *Lampasas Teacher*,[37] and he wrote a series of short stories on the troubled lives of black people, all of them native Texans living in such Texas towns as Austin, Ennis, San Antonio and Lampasas. The black farmers, laborers, entertainers and convicts were all poor and all fighting to achieve their own personality and their own dignity. The author described them with sympathy and understanding. He collected his stories, but they were not for Texas readers, many of whom still harbored bitter memories of the Civil War and the Reconstruction period which followed it. He sent the stories to Cincinnati where they were published.[38]

His novel *Norma Trist* aroused the anger of Texas readers.[39] Norma, no ordinary fictional heroine, was portrayed as a resident of La Grange, Texas. Her story, resembling a dime novel both in theme and in format, dealt with a subject which shocked the squeamish reader of the 1890s. Norma was a lesbian, perhaps the first lesbian to be written about openly in American fiction. Her love affair with her music teacher was ended when the music teacher decided to marry a handsome young Mexican. Norma, enraged, tried to murder her faithless lover, but several sessions

The front cover of Carhart's novel *Norma Trist*

with an understanding "alienist" soon cured her of her unnatural passion. The story of Norma was based on a true case in Memphis, Tennessee. Alice Mitchell, the Memphis prototype of Norma, fell in love with a young woman named Freda Ward, and when Freda refused to return her love, Alice killed her. The resulting trial found Alice to be insane, and she was committed to the State Insane Asylum in Bolivia, Tennessee. She died there in 1898. Her case was reviewed in detail by the First Pan American Medical Congress.[40]

Dr. Carhart's novel, one of the earliest fictional treatments of homosexuality, would not shock today's readers, but in 1895 he felt that he had to justify his reasons for writing the story, "The principles involved are as broad as the human race, and will be of interest while abnormality of which we treat shall continue to mar the happiness of man."[41]

His reviewers, doctors though they were, did not agree. One of them commented,

> A feature worse than flaunting before the public a subject about which the average reader knows nothing is the exhibition of immoral and lustful passions, the making of no distinction between the lust and love. Such literature is hurtful to public morals, is prurient and salacious, and should be condemned by all good people.[42]

The general public agreed. The author was arrested at his home in La Grange and was charged with "sending obscene literature through the mails." Later he was released and his case dismissed.[43]

Little is known of Dr. Carhart's activities during the next nine years. In 1903 he published a paper on the effect of higher education on the lives of women as wives and mothers. In 1904 he wrote of the responsibility of the United States to help neighboring countries to control smallpox and yellow fever. He felt that such help, although prompted sometimes by selfish motives, could bring good results, not only to those countries which lacked the means to help themselves but also to our own country into which deadly epidemics could quickly spread.[44] In 1914 Dr. Carhart read a paper before the San Antonio Academy of Medicine on rocks and the minerals which contribute to man's diet and health. This paper, published in March 1914, was his last.[45] On December 21, 1914, at the age of eighty, he died in San Antonio, Texas.[46]

Carhart truly was a complex person, talented, restless and perhaps dissatisfied with himself. As a minister he allowed his

Portrait of Dr. Carhart in his later years, published in *Four Years on Wheels; or Life as a Presiding Elder*, 1880.

conscience to hold him to his "calling" for almost thirty years, even though his mind was focused on things other than the needs of his congregation, things such as oscillating values and steam powered engines. Even with his machinery he did not follow through or further develop his mechanical skill. As a writer he had original ideas, but he lacked the ability to express them in language better than that of the nineteenth-century dime novel. He never became a major author.

Perhaps if he had started his medical career sooner, he could have used his mechanical knowledge to improve or invent medical or surgical tools. It is unfortunate that he did not become a pioneer in medical engineering. Nevertheless, John Wesley Carhart is appropriately chronicled among significant early Texas physicians.

ENDNOTES

1. John Wesley Carhart, *Four Years on Wheels; or Life as a Presiding Elder* (Oshkosh, Wisconsin: Allen and Hicks, 1880), 1-10.

2. Ibid., 56-58.

3. J.W. Carhart, *Sunny Hours, Consisting of Poems on Various Subjects* (New York: Pudney and Russell, 1859), 233.

4. Carhart, *Four* Years, op. cit., 64.

5. Carhart, *Four* Years, op. cit., 68-69.

6. Therese Von Hohoff, "Hudson Valley Doctor." *New York State Journal of Medicine* 54 (June 15, 1954), 1814-15.

7. J.E.A. Smith, *History of Pittsfield* (1876) 369; Calvin Durfee, *Williams Biographical Annals* (1871), 527; Francis R. Packard, *History of Medicine in the United States*, vol. 2 (New York: Paul B. Hoeber, 1931), 767-68.

8. *History of Medicine and Surgery, and Physicians and Surgeons of Chicago* (Endorsed and Published under the Supervision of the Council of the Chicago Medical Society, Chicago, Illinois, 1922), 218-23; W. Morgan, Hartshor, ed., *History of the New York Polyclinic Medical School and Hospital* (New York, 1942), 1-3.

9. Carhart, *Four* Years, op. cit., 118.

10. J.W. Carhart, *Poets and Poetry of the Hebrews* (New York: Sheldon and Co., 1865), 195.

11. Carhart, *Four Years,* op. cit.., 133.

12. Ibid., 138.

13. Ibid., 139-41.

14. Ibid., 142-43.

15. J.W. Carhart, "An Early Doctor's Steam Engine." *Horseless Age* (January 14, 1903), 100; "Psychological Laws Operating in Running Automobiles." *Horseless Age* (January 27, 1904), 103; "J.W. Carhart, M.D." *Wisconsin Medical*

Journal 57 (September 1958), 344; "The First Automobile, a Description of the Vehicle Built and Operated by the Late J.W. Carhart." *Texas State Journal of Medicine* 10 (February 1915), 427.

16. *Handbook of Texas,* vol. 1 (Austin: Texas Historical Association, 1952), 296; *Dictionary of Wisconsin Biography.* State Historical Association of Wisconsin (1960), 67.

17. Carhart, *Four Years,* op. cit., 165-66.

18. Laura V. Hamner, *The No-Gun Man of Texas: A Century of Achievement, 1835-1929* (Amarillo: Privately Printed, 1935), 142-45.

19. Willie Newbury Lewis, *Between Sun and Sod* (Clarendon, Texas: Clarendon Press, 1938), 65-75, 81-82.

20. Carhart, *Four Years,* op. cit., 188.

21. Ibid., 215-16.

22. Ibid., 247-53, 279.

23. J.W. Carhart, "Grass Staggers." (Loco Weed). *Medical Record* 31 (January 1, 1887), 10.

24. J.W. Carhart. J.W., "Child-Bearing and Modern Civilization." *Texas Courier-Record of Medicine* 4 (November 1886), 97-104.

25. J.W. Carhart, "A Step Backwards; or, The Legal Control of Marriage." *Texas Medical Association, Transactions* 23 (1891), 141-50.

26. J.W.Carhart, "Necessity for Special Study, on the Part of the General Practitioner, of the Medicine and Hygiene of Infancy." *Texas Medical Association, Transactions* 22 (1890), 215-23.

27. J.W. Carhart, "The Average Practitioner of Medicine on the Witness Stand as an Expert Alienist." *Medical Progress* 22 (October 1906), 277-81.

28. J.W. Carhart, "Morality as a Therapeutic Agent; and Hygiene and Therapeutics as Factors in Moral Problems." *Texas Courier-Record of Medicine* 4 (1887), 498-504.

29. J.W. Carhart, "The Charities of Regular Medicine." *Texas Courier-Record of Medicine* 7 (February 1890), 152-54; "The Physician's Chief Wealth Is in What He Gives, and Not in What He Gains." *Texas Courier-Record of Medicine* 4 (1887), 303-309.

30. J.W. Carhart, "Substitution of Cheap Pharmaceuticals in the Filling of Prescriptions." *Texas Medical Association, Transactions* 23 (1891), 92-96; *Mississippi Medical Monthly* 1 (1891-92), 149-53.

31. J.W. Carhart, J.W., "What Is Lacking, If Anything, to Place the Medical Profession upon its Proper Footing?" *Texas Courier-Record of Medicine* 7 (July 1890), 299-301.

32. J.W. Carhart, J.W., "The Disposal of Human Excreta." *Texas Courier-Record of Medicine* 2 (July 1885), 602-607; "Influence of Graveyards on Public Health." *Medical Age* 9 (November 25, 1891), 694; *Journal of the American Medical Association* 17 (December 5, 1891), 901-902.

33. J.W. Carhart, "Lampasas, Texas as a Health Resort of Northern People." *Medical Age* (February 25, 1890), 77-80; "Lampasas a Health Resort." *Texas Sanitarian* 3 (February 1894), 135-41.

34. *Handbook of Texas,* vol. 2, op. cit., 17.

35. (News Note). *Texas Sanitarian* 2 (July 1893), 398; 3 (July 1893), 301; (May 1894).

36. Irving A. Watson, *Physicians and Surgeons of America* (Concord, New Hampshire: Republican Press Association, 1896), 755.

37. (News Note). *Daniel's Texas Medical Journal* 8 (June 1893), 575; *Texas Courier-Record of Medicine* 10 (May 1893), 267.

38. J.W. Carhart, *Under Palmetto and Pine* (Cincinnati, Ohio: The Editor Publishing Company, 1899), 228.

39. J.W. Carhart, *Norma Trist; or, Pure Carbon: a Story of the Inversion of the Sexes* (Austin, Texas: E. Von Boeckmann, 1895).

40. *Pan American Medical Congress, First, 1893, Transactions* vol. 1 (1895), 15; C.H. Hughes, "Erotropathia: Morbid Eroticism." *Pam American Medical Congress, First, 1893, Transactions*, vol. 2 (1895), 1830-1893; *Texas Medical News* 7 (April 1898), 252.

41. Carhart, *Norma Trist*, op. cit., 254.

42. (News Note). "Norma Trist." *Texas Sanitarian* 4 (October 1895), 518; "A Fishy Novel by a Texas Doctor. A Review." *Texas Medical Journal* 11 (November 1895), 247-51.

43. (News Note). *Texas Medical News* 5 (February 1896), 181.

44. J.W. Carhart, "The Effect of the Higher Education of Women on Wifehood and Motherhood." *Texas Medical Journal* 19 (November 1903), 155-60; "The Responsibility of the U.S. Government for the Sanitary Condition of Neighbor Nations." *Texas Medical News* 13 (February 1904), 220-24, February 1904.

45. J.W. Carhart, "Our Indebtedness of the Rocks." *Texas Medical News* 23 (March 1914), 415-20.

46. "John Wesley Carhart" (Obituary). *Texas State Journal of Medicine* 10 (February 1915), 438.

BIOGRAPHICAL SKETCH OF AUTHOR

DOCTOR CHARLES C. TANDY is a Clinical Professor of Anesthesiology at the University of Texas, Southwestern Medical School, Dallas, Texas. He serves as the Director of Ambulatory Surgery at Methodist Medical Center, Dallas, where he also is an anesthesiologist. He is a former Chairman of the Board of Trustees of the Wood Library Museum of Anesthesiology, Park Ridge, Illinois.

Portrait of Dr. Cerna made while he was a professor at the School of
Medicine in Galveston, probably about 1896-97

DAVID CERNA, M.D.
1857-1953

by

Robert Bernard Krause, M.D.

★DR. DAVID CERNA WAS BORN near San Buenaventura, Coahuila, Mexico, on his father's ranch in 1857. His descendants believe that his early education was under the Jesuits who were active in Mexico at that time. In 1871 at the age of fourteen, he was sent to Philadelphia to attend LaSalle College, which had opened its doors in 1863.

David Cerna learned English rapidly and won silver and gold medals for excellence in his studies. He then entered the Medical School at the University of Pennsylvania and was graduated in 1879. He was awarded a prize for his thesis, a requirement for an M.D. degree at that time. The subject of the thesis was a native plant of Mexico named Thevetia iccotli, a member of the oleander family of plants. His research was on the toxic effects of this plant rather than on its medicinal uses. In Mexico it was used as a sedative, a subject which he later discussed in a published paper entitled "The Pharmacology of the Ancient Mexicans." His research resulted in a manuscript of some ninety pages which is now in the possession of Dr. Cerna's descendants.

Later the same year he received a Doctor of Philosophy degree, and his dissertation was entitled "Phenol: Its Poisonous Effects and Its Antidotes." He also wrote and published several pieces of music while he was in school, one of which was dedicated to and played at his commencement exercises in 1879.

Dr. Cerna then returned to Mexico and practiced in the state of Coahuila. During this time he continued to write on literary

AN ESSAY ON

Thevetia Iccotli and its Glucoside

FOR THE

Degree of Doctor of Medicine,

IN THE

HOSPITAL   COLLEGIATE

MEDICAL

University of Pennsylvania.

BY

David Cerna   of   *Mexico*

County, *San Buenaventura* State, *Coahuila.*

Residence in this City, *3206 Chestnut Street*

Preceptor, *Thomas S. Butcher,*

Duration of Studies, *4 years*   Age, *22*

Presented, *February 7th*   *1879*

Title page of Dr. Cerna's thesis, written while a student at
the University of Pennsylvania in 1879.

subjects including a translation into Spanish of John William Draper's *History of the Conflict between Religion and Science.* Dr. Cerna's ability to speak English was of great benefit to him as there were many Americans living in Coahuila at that time. In 1884 he was elected to the state legislature, but the appointment by President of Mexico Porfirio Diaz of a military government ended his term.

In 1885 Dr. Cerna was married to Dolores De la Garza, who died in 1887. Two years later he returned to Philadelphia and was appointed to a position with the Department of Experimental Therapeutics at the University of Pennsylvania Medical School. He published several papers in this field and also gave lectures to the public on aspects of life in Mexico with particular emphasis on the native Indians of that country. One of his lectures was to the Alumni Society of the Philadelphia College of Pharmacy. During this period of time, Dr. Cerna was elected to the Philadelphia Pathology Society, the College of Physicians of Philadelphia, and the Philadelphia County Medical Society.

Matilda Lorenz of Philadelphia and Dr. David Cerna were married in 1891. A year later, in 1892, the University of Texas opened its Medical Branch in Galveston, and Dr. Cerna took a position in the Department of Therapeutics. He was one of eight professors on the staff of the Medical Branch at that time. He joined the Galveston County Medical Society, the Texas Academy of Science, and the Texas Medical Association, of which he was later elected a vice-president. He contributed to the *Texas Medical Journal* and edited a publication called *Notes on Newer Remedies, Their Applications and Administration*, a book of 177 pages which was published by W.B. Saunders in 1893.

During his time in Philadelphia and in Galveston, Dr. Cerna authored some forty-six articles and lectures. A complete list of these can be found in the P.I. Nixon Medical History Library at the University of Texas Health Science Center in San Antonio. His papers included studies on malaria, typhus fever, opium and belladona, chloroform, phenocal and phenacetine, as well as medical education and ethics. His interest in Mexico was reflected by the articles he wrote on Aztec medicine, the civilization of the Toltecs, phonetic arithmetic and pharmacology of the ancient Mexicans.

Dr. Cerna's active research and teaching career came to an

end in 1897, an event noted by Dr. P.I. Nixon in his book *The History of the Texas Medical Association* published in 1953.

> When Drs. H.A. West, A.G. Clopton, and David Cerna resigned, apparently under pressure, from the faculty of the Medical Department of the University of Texas at Galveston, there was a demand that these positions be filled by members of the profession in Texas.

It is believed that this was a political decision in order to assure that only native-born physicians were employed at the school. Dr. Cerna returned to Mexico and began the general practice of medicine. Very little is known about the next seventeen years of Dr. Cerna's life. Some papers and pictures that he brought from Mexico in 1914 because of the revolution there reveal that he was mayor of Monclova for a time and that his parents remained in Mexico and died and were buried on their ranch. It is interesting to note that Dr. Cerna's grandson, Daniel Cerna, discovered that the deeds to the ranch were still in the Cerna name when he visited the area.

The period of 1911 to 1914 was a disruptive and confusing time in Mexico, but no expressions of Dr. Cerna's feelings on the matter have been found. It was difficult to leave at the age of fifty-five, but leave he did with his wife and two children. He first went to Eagle Pass, and then to San Antonio where he again established a medical practice. He had an office in the old Frost Building on Main Plaza, and his residence was on Madison Street in what is now the historic King William area. He primarily practiced obstetrics and became a member of the Texas Medical Association and the American Medical Association.

Dr. Cerna continued to be involved in the field of literature, and he contributed often to the Spanish-language newspaper of San Antonio called *La Prensa*. He translated, with his wife, a pamphlet entitled "The Bronze Race" in defense of the Indians of Mexico, gave a talk to the working men of Monclova, addressed the Library Society of Mexico in Mexico City, wrote an essay on the history of philosophy and bought a Whippet automobile! These actions are not to be taken lightly. Most of these were done after he had quit practicing medicine when he

A group photograph made while Dr. Cerna was mayor of Monclovia, date unknown. Dr. Cerna is seated in the center. Courtesy Daniel Cerna, San Antonio, Texas.

Dr. Cerna standing beside his 1920 Whippit automobile. Courtesy Daniel Cerna, San Antonio, Texas.

was in his seventies and eighties and still living in San Antonio.

His essay entitled "The History of Philosophy" was printed by the Biblioteca Monclova in 1927. In this article, Dr. Cerna gave credit to Will Durant for a definition of philosophy and of science, "Philosophy is the hypothetical interpretation of the unknown or poorly understood. Science is analytical description, while philosophy is synthetical interpretation." Dr. Cerna added that the two were intimately linked----where one ended the other began. Essentially, he felt that it was impossible to separate philosophy from medicine. The philosophy of the Greeks had such influence on medicine in the past that the fundamental doctrines of philosophy are the bases of the theoretical principles of medicine. The medicine of the ancient Greeks possessed the essential character of philosophy until the time of Hippocrates who, using new methods, sent it down a new path more in keeping with clinical observation.

In 1932 Dr. Cerna wrote an essay for the *Annals of Medical History* called "Pharmacology of the Ancient Mexicans." He must have had a knowledge of their languages as he went into some detail about the sources of their medications. Of interest here is that he wrote that Thevetia was used as a sedative. The most useful drug that they had, opium, was from the poppy. One of its uses was to narcotize the prisoners being used in human sacrifice at which time the chest was opened and the beating heart was offered up to the gods.

On May 29, 1936, Dr. Cerna wrote an article for *La Prensa* with the title "Foods [Nutrients] and the Elements." It was also read at a conference given in Mexico City. He noted,

> The Greek philosophers who represented that illustrious race which, among the ancients, achieved the highest intellectual development concluded in their investigations that the physical and chemical nature of [human] bodies, organic and inorganic, originated from what they called the four primordial or primary elements: water, air, fire and earth. It isn't surprising that this idea of the four elements advanced by these intellectuals and accepted for many centuries would still be referred to in our modern times by many different writers of notable literary works, and espe-

cially by that greatest of all, the immortal Shakespeare, in his inimitable dramatic works.

He continued that the Greeks, and all those who blindly believed in the existence of the four elements, made a serious mistake in that air, fire, water and earth are not elements.

> Modern chemistry, a true science . . . has replaced the false alchemy of the ancients. In summary, let me repeat that the three principal classes of nutrients are albuminoids, carbohydrates, and fats. These are the true nutrients whose oxidation in the organism give vitality and energy to the individual. However, other substances besides these are added to the ordinary diet such as mineral salts, especially sodium chloride, and other almost equally important those mysterious substances which we call vitamins. So an ordinary diet is, or should be, composed of meat, eggs, milk, and various vegetable and fruits. It is in exactly these substances that we find vitamins in considerable quantity.

The article "Shakespeare and the Circulation of the Blood" was published in *Medical Records and Annals*, but the date is not known.

> It may be said that the myriad-minded genius of Stratford-on-Avon knew at least as much of the science of medicine as most of the learned physicians of his times.
>
> Modern investigators, among them reputable physicians, seem to have demonstrated that the great English poet entertained correct notions of anatomy, physics, surgery, obstetrics, internal medicine, hygiene, therapeutics, dietetics, legal medicine, insanity and even medical ethics.
>
> Shakespeare reveals this knowledge of blushing and pallor in the second part of "Henry IV," Act III, Scene ii; in "Romeo and Juliet," Act IV, Scene v; in the "Sonnets;" in "Measure for Measure" Act I, Scene iv and Act II, Scene iv; in "The Merchant of Venice," Act III, Scene ii; in "King John," Act II, Scene i. All these

contain expressions that show a knowledge of the movement but not the circulation of the blood.

In Shakespeare's time, arteries did not carry blood; they carried air. Only the veins were thought to carry blood. Servetes knew of pulmonary circulation, but his work *Christianismi Restituto* was published in 1553 and all copies but two were burned. Harvey's *Exertitatio anatomica de motu cordia et sanguinis in animalibus* was published in 1628. Shakespeare died in 1616 at the age of fifty-two.

Dr. Cerna believed that Shakespeare was lacking in the extensive knowledge of Latin, Greek and Hebrew that would have enabled him to read the "works of the ancients." He seemed to agree with Lafcadio Hearn that intuition gave Shakespeare his powerful creativity.

At the age of eighty-two Dr. Cerna wrote a "Tribute to the 'Ildefonso Fuente' Mutualist Society/Workers of Monclova." While this article was not concerned with medicine, it reflected his philosophy of life and his ability to express it, a trademark of his education and wisdom. His opening paragraphs are as follows.

Serene, satisfied, conscious of having faithfully completed your sacred duties, all of you have completed another year of life, free of any serious difficulties, lamenting only the eternal disappearance of various companions.

You have not suffered any discouragement in your work. On the contrary, your integrity, your strength, your enthusiasm, remain firm: you constitute an impregnable bastion, an inaccessible Gibraltar against all unjustified aggression. All you workers of heart and spirit, always willing to obey orders given to you, orders which translate into the noble task of earning a living through the sweat of your humble but honorable brows, you haven't failed, and undaunted you have gone forward with unbreakable faith in the present and the future. . . .

I well know that at heart your organization has always worked for your own interests, it is true; but

Portrait made during Dr. Cerna's later
years, before his return to Mexico.
Courtesy Daniel Cerna,
San Antonio, Texas.

at the same time, the undeniable fact is that he who
works for his own well-being, also necessarily works
for the good of humanity.

And, I, in spite of finding myself absent from my
beloved country, condemned to involuntary exile,
living a life of uncertainty,—but with my head high,
I send to you all, from this hospitable land, my warm-
est blessings, ardently wishing that you continue to
enjoy, as you deserve, endless growing prosperity,
taking the liberty at the same time, of urging you to
continue your noble work boldly with your head held
high, always high.

In May of 1935 Dr. Cerna was honored by the Bexar County
Medical Society as one of eleven physicians who had been in the
practice of medicine for fifty years or more. He continued living
in San Antonio, Texas, until 1944, at which time he and his wife
moved to Mexico City to live with his daughter. His wife
preceded him in death. He died in 1953 in Mexico at the age of
ninety-five.

BIBLIOGRAPHY

Daniel Cerna. Personal Communication, San Antonio, 1997.

Lucas Cerna. Personal Communication. San Antonio. 1960.

Pat Ireland Nixon M.D. *A Century of Medicine in San Antonio: the Story of Medicine in Bexar County, Texas* (San Antonio: privately printed, 1936).

Pat Ireland Nixon M.D. *A History of the Texas Medical Association 1853-1953* (Austin: University of Texas Press, 1953).

Pat Ireland Nixon M.D. *The Medical Story of Early Texas 1528-1853* (San Antonio: Mollie Bennett Lupe Memorial Fund, 1946).

Irvina A. Watson, ed. *Physicians and Surgeons of America: a Collection of Biographical Sketches of the Regular Medical Profession* (Concord, N.H.: Republican Press Association, 1896).

PUBLICATIONS BY DAVID CERNA

"Actions and Uses of Pentol." Transactions of the Texas Medical Association, vol. 25 (1893).

"Alimentos y Elementos." *La Prensa* (29 de Mayo de 1836).

"The Antagonism between Opium and Belladonna." *Daniel's Texas Medical Journal*, vol. 8 (December 1892).

"Aztec Medicine." *University Medical Magazine*, Philadelphia (July-August 1892).

"Breves datos soblre historia de la filosofia." Biblioteca Monclova (1927).

"Civilization of the Toltecs." Spring Garden Unitarian Society of Philadelphia (1891).

"A Contribution to the Study and Actions of Chloral on the Circulation." *University Medical Magazine*, Philadelphia, vol. 4 (November 1891).

Notes on the Newer Remedies, Their Therapeutic Applications and Modes of Administration. Philadelphia: Saunders, 1893.

"The Pharmacology of the Ancient Mexicans." *Annals of Medical History*, vol. 4 (May 1932).

"Pharmacy among the Aztecs." *Philadelphia College of Pharmacy Alumni Association Bulletin*, vol. 1 (1865).

"The Phonetic Arithmetic of the Ancient Mexicans." Texas Academy of Science Transactions, vol. 1 (1896-1892).

"Phenacitin as a Toxic Agent." *Journal of the American Medical Association*, vol. 24 (1895).

"Phenic Acid: its Poisonous Effects and the Soluble Sulphates as Antidotes." PhD. Thesis. University of Pennsylvania (1879).

"Shakespeare and the Circulation of the Blood." Medical Records and Annals. n.d.

"Thevefia Iccotli and its Glucosides." Thesis. University of Pennsylvania (1879).

"Un Tributo a la Sociedad Mutualista 'Ildefonso Fuentes' Obreros de Monclova." San Antonio (Junio de 1939).

"The Bronze Race." With Mathilde Lorenz de Cerna, Translated from the Spanish of Amado Nervo. San Antonio (1920).

"Contributions to the Study of the Actions of Chloroform." With Edward Randall. *Transactions of the Texas State Medical Association*, vol. 26 (1894).

"The Effects of Drugs and Other Agencies upon the Respiratory Movements." With H.C. Wood. *Journal of Physiology*, vol. 13 (1892).

"A Research to Determine the Action of Nitrous Oxide, Nitrogen, Oxygen, and Carbonic Acid upon the Circulation, with Especial Reference to Nitrous Oxide Anaesthesia." With H.C. Wood. *Therapeutic Gazette.* s 3, vol. 6 (August-September 1890).

BIOGRAPHICAL SKETCH OF AUTHOR

ROBERT BERNARD KRAUSE, M.D. a sixth-generation Texan, was born in Burlington, Milam County, Texas, on June 16, 1923. He served in the U.S. Navy for four years during World War II as a medical corpsman attached to the U.S. Marine Corps in the South Pacific. After attending Texas A&M College, he was graduated from the University of Texas Medical Branch in Galveston in 1952. After internship, he was in general practice in south Texas before taking a residency in anesthesia at Parkland and Scott and White Hospitals. He was in the practice of anesthesia in San Antonio for over thirty years. He is a diplomat of the American Board of Anesthesiology, a fellow of the American College of Anesthesiology, a member of the Bexar County Medical Society, the Texas Medical Association, and the American Medical Association. He served as president of the Texas Society of Anesthesiology. He also held the office of president of the San Antonio Historical Society and of the P.I. Nixon Medical Historical Library. He has maintained an interest in history and in medicinal plants for a number of years. He is retired and living in Plano, Texas, and is the father of five children.

Portrait of George Cupples, presumably after the Civil War. From P.I.
Nixon, *The History of the Texas Medical Association,* University of Texas
Press.

GEORGE CUPPLES, M.D.
1815-1895
by
R. Maurice Hood, M.D.

★ONE OF THE TRULY OUTSTANDING surgeons of early Texas was George Cupples. His eighty years were filled with accomplishments, valor, foresight and honor which were unsurpassed in his time.

George Cupples was born in Berwick County, Scotland, October 13, 1815, the son of Robert and Camelia Cupples.[1] His father was a surgeon in the Royal Navy who also practiced privately. George was the oldest of nine children. Little is known of his early life and education. He was graduated from Edinburgh with honors in 1836, but further education was postponed when he traveled to Europe with his mother. During their stay in Europe he enlisted in the British Legion and served as a surgeon during assignments to Spain and Paris. He returned to England and entered specialty training in several London hospitals.

Cupples returned to Paris to attend the University of Paris where he met and married Alexia Bourland. At this same time he encountered Henri Castro who was recruiting a company of people to immigrate to Texas. He also met Ashbel Smith who was serving as minister of the Republic of Texas to France in 1843 and 1844. Smith was well known in the Paris medical community. It is generally conceded that Smith influenced Cupples to make the decision to go to Texas. The poor health of his wife was also thought to be a factor in his decision.

Ashbel Smith, who had already had an impressive career in Texas, was to become one of the most important figures in early Texas history. He was to serve in the War with Mexico on the

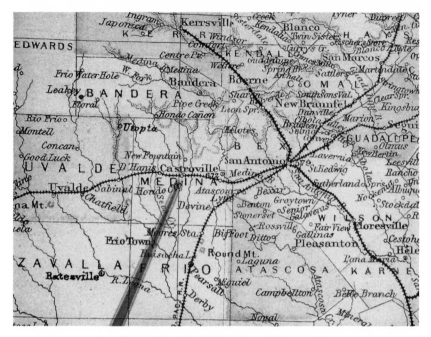

Detail map showing the location of Castroville.

staff of Zachary Scott, and he became an illustrious line officer in the Confederate Army, rising to the rank of brigadier general.

George Cupples and his wife sailed for the New World and arrived in the San Antonio area on April 27, 1844, with other members of the Castro Colony who would locate west of San Antonio. In his own words, "Without knowing it, I located the present townsite of Castroville and I cut the first brush here for the first clearing."

There is little known of the early village of Castroville and little of Dr. Cupples' medical practice there.[2] Cupples' mother and two other of her children, Charles and Jane, followed her son George to Texas in October 1846. Jane had married Joseph Guerin in Paris but he died of yellow fever in New Orleans in 1849; their daughter, Camille, lived in San Antonio the rest of her life and her descendants still reside there. Charles married Evelyn Jocelyn in 1861 and sired five children who carried on the Cupples' name.

The date of George Cupples' move to San Antonio is unknown as are his reasons for moving from Castroville. By 1850

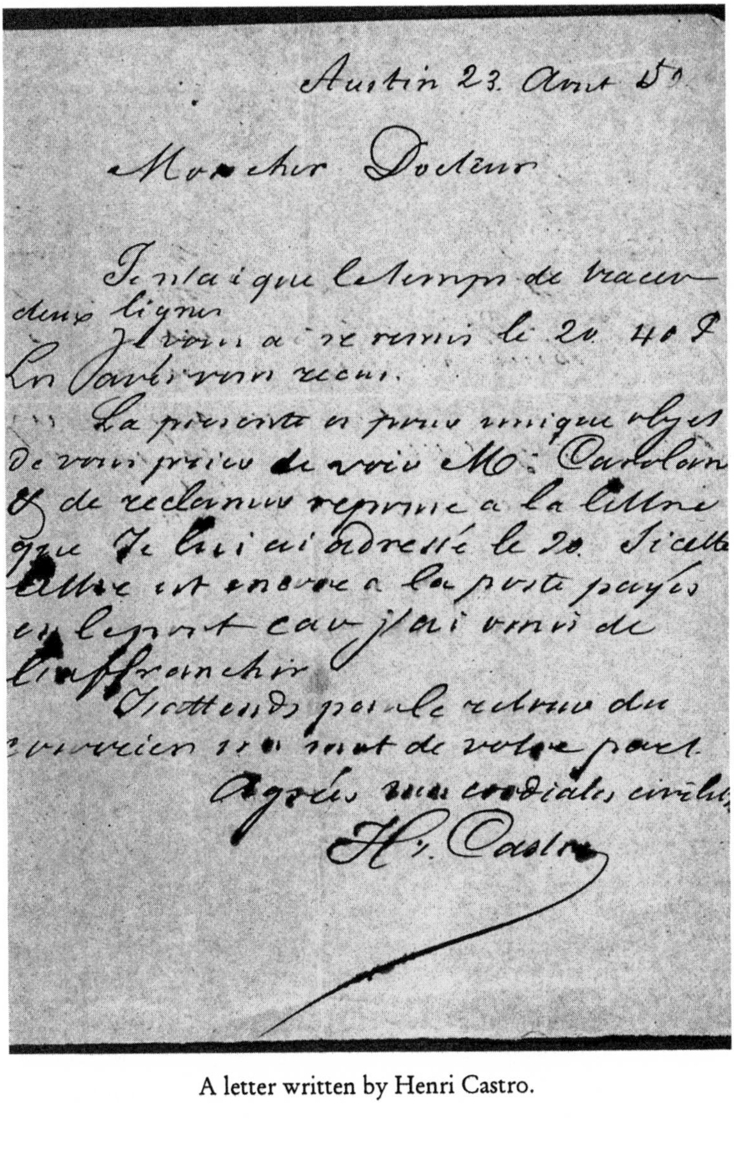

Austin 23. Avril 50

Mon cher Docteur

Je n'ai que le temps de tracer deux lignes
Je vous ai remis le 20. 40 $
Les avez-vous reçu.
La présente a pour unique objet de vous prier de voir M. [illegible] & de réclamer réponse à la lettre que je lui ai adressé le 20. Icelle lettre est encore à la poste payée en le port car j'ai omis de l'affranchir
J'attends par le retour du courrier un mot de votre part.
Agréez mes cordiales civilités
H. Castro

A letter written by Henri Castro.

he had established an office in the F. Kaltmeyer Drug Store and had his residence on Soledad Street between Houston and Rodriguez Streets. When he entered practice he was probably the second or third physician in the community. Very shortly, he interrupted his practice to volunteer for service in the Texas Cavalry under Colonel Jack Hays and was appointed the surgeon for the Second Texas Cavalry during the War with Mexico.[3]

San Antonio, at the time Dr. Cupples began practice, had a few more than one thousand inhabitants, about 90 percent of Mexican descent. There was a business section, the principal structures of which were the Catholic Church and the courthouse. West of the church was the Military Plaza of two dusty squares from which radiated unpaved streets for a distance of no more than nine hundred feet. Most of the houses at that time were adobe.

From the beginning Cupples had been interested and participated in community affairs. He had been serving as a Notary Public for Bexar County when he went off to war. Upon the doctor's return from the Mexican conflict, he resumed his practice and again became involved in community activities. He was elected County Commissioner and Alderman under Mayor J.S. McDonald, serving from January 1851 until 1852. He helped to establish the Bexar County Medical Society and was its first president in 1853. He served as the City Health Physician in 1854.[4]

Dr. Cupples was instrumental in organizing the Texas Medical Association but was not present at the organizational meeting held in Austin on January 7, 1853, at which Joseph Taylor of Harrison County was elected president.[5] A circular of the proceedings was distributed to all Texas doctors. A second and better-attended meeting was held also in Austin on November 14, 1853.[6] This meeting was principally an organizational meeting. The constitution and by-laws and the code of ethics were rewritten and adopted.[7]

Dr. Cupples was elected the second president.[8] Cupples took an active part in the organization and recommended that a diploma be issued for qualified members. He addressed the assembled group on the final night of the meeting and his speech ended with the statement, "The man . . . who regards his

ORIGINAL ARTICLES

ADDRESS

delivered before

THE MEDICAL ASSOCIATION OF TEXAS

At its first annual meeting, Nov. 16th, 1853.

BY

GEORGE CUPPLES, M. D.,

President of the Association.

SAN ANTONIO, TEXAS.

Gentlemen, Fellows of the Medical Association:

Of all the elements of progress to which the present age owes its unparalleled advance in every department of science and art, none is more marked, more characteristic of the times in which we live, than the spirit of association and concert of design in the attainment of results far beyond the reach of individual enterprise or of isolated exertion.

The co-operation of various associations in different parts of the world has diminished distance by improved modes of conveyance by land and sea. The whole extent of this Union and of the continent of Europe is harnessed by railroads conveying travelers with a rapidity undreamt of by the last generation. The whistle of the locomotive is the voice of civilization, and its shrill tones are now heard where a few years ago desolation reigned supreme and nought disturbed the silence save the occasional cry of wild beasts, or the rare footfall of the still wilder savage. Even now, in this city, is being agitated the greatest undertaking that man ever conceived in

Dr. Cupples' Presidential Address before the Texas Medical Association, November 16, 1853.

profession but as a means of earning a livelihood or of amassing a fortune ought not to practice an art so fraught with good or evil to his fellows."

Dr. Cupples' professional practice was interrupted again in 1861 by the beginning of the Civil War. Texas was remote from the war that was then apparently to be only in Virginia. Despite this fact, patriotic fever, identification with the Southern cause, and resentment against the North pushed the state into secession. It is difficult for most to understand the patriotism, the zeal, the determination and the optimism that characterized the Confederacy at that time. Regiments in numerous counties were easily recruited, officers were appointed, the procurement of uniforms and weapons was begun. Several units were sent to Virginia to be a part of what was to become the famed Texas Brigade in the Army of Northern Virginia. Others ended up in Tennessee and Louisiana in the Army of Tennessee under such generals as Pat Cleburne, Ben McCulloch, Sterling Price, Sul Ross, Hiram Granbury and Albert Sidney Johnston. These units fought hard with few victories, little glory and a series of defeats.

Henry Hopkins Sibley, an obscure general, obtained permission from Jefferson Davis to undertake a grandiose and ill-planned campaign to drive the Federal forces from New Mexico.[9] New Mexico at that time included what is now New Mexico, Arizona and part of Nevada. He hoped to invade and capture California as well. His plan captured the imagination of the Texas patriots including George Cupples. As a result, the 4th, 5th and 7th Texas Cavalry Regiments were recruited primarily from the San Antonio area. They were armed and underwent a four-month period of training. They were, in reality, mounted infantry or dragoons.

Sibley's Brigade, under their hopelessly incompetent and alcoholic leader, marched to Fort Bliss at El Paso and made ready for their ill-fated crusade. Dr. Cupples was appointed First Surgeon of the 7th Regiment under Colonel William Steele.

The small brigade marched up the Rio Grande valley where they encountered Union troops under the command of General E.R.S. Canby. Three engagements were fought: at Valverde, at Apache Canyon and Glorieta Pass just east of Santa Fe. Tactically, each battle was won by the Texians, but near Glorieta Pass a small detachment of Union troops captured Sibley's supply train. The loss of food and ammunition were fatal to the campaign. One of Sibley's presumptions, which proved to be false, was that the troops could live off the land. Sibley decided to abandon New Mexico and began a napoleonic retreat back to Texas, burdened by wounded and suffering terribly from lack of food and water.

More men were more disabled by illness than by wounds. Of the 2,300 men who began the campaign, five hundred died of wounds or disease and about five hundred were captured. There were ten medical officers, one of whom deserted. Cupples was the best trained and threw himself tirelessly into the battle against death. He was not a novice and, as one biographer stated, "He laid down his sword and took up the scalpel and cotton; no clearer head or braver man or steadier hand ever passed judgement on life or limb. No angel from above ministered more tenderly to the wounded." Working with inferior equipment and instruments, no hospital and with primitive transportation, his medical and surgical efforts were greatly hampered. Pneumonia and infections were the complications common to the injured of the Civil War and took their toll in deaths. Dysentery and an epidemic of smallpox also resulted in a number of fatalities.

Dr. Cupples was forced to abandon some of the wounded near Fort Craig for want of transportation during the hurried retreat. The rag-tag survivors struggled back to Fort Bliss but their needs for food and adequate water could not be met there and they were forced to march on to San Antonio before they were finally able to receive supplies. George Cupples walked and rode almost sixteen-hundred miles from San Antonio to the Santa Fe area and back, suffering along with the rest of the men and earning a well-deserved reputation for his surgical skill and for his conscientious care of the sick and wounded.

After the New Mexico campaign he was named Medical Director for the Eastern District of Texas and later became Medical Director and Inspector of Cavalry for the Trans-Mississippi Department. His name became legendary among the Southern soldiers for his surgical prowess; many owed their lives and limbs to his skill. He received many official commendations and accolades from his superiors including General Thomas Green. His brother, Charles, became a captain in the Confederate Army and was killed in action.

Dr. Cupples kept only scant records of his experience as a Confederate surgeon. Two letters survive and are in the Cupples collection of the Texas State Archives.[10] In one of these, a letter to his wife, Alexia, he gives an eye-witness account of the Battle of Galveston. Excerpts are quoted.

> I called at the (Urseline) convent (established in 1847) which I had selected for the hospital . . . they gave me very large rooms capable of accommodating forty men each . . . at five o'clock the firing opened and the heavens were in a blaze; musketry and heavy guns, pop, pop of the rifles and roaring, rushing and finally the exploding of shells in the air and on the vessels. The wounded began to come in very soon after . . . I had 28 prisoners in the hospital of whom two died. The remaining 26, with forty-four of our own men, made up the seventy in the hospital besides eight who died there. One of my ass't surgeons, Dr. Fischer, a German, was killed by grape shot . . . while attending the wounded . . . the shells rushed and roared handsomely over us, but though the houses were riddled by the shells and round shot, not a citizen was hurt. Indeed, the city is deserted.
>
> The Yankee officers say such a damnable cannonade and such fighting they never saw or heard of. It lasted a little over an hour. I have for my guests the surgeon of the Massachusetts regiment, A.J. Cummings. He was to have been Medical Director but who says he has had enough fighting in Texas, though he would like to come and settle here; and the Naval Surgeon, Thos. A. Penrose, a gentlemanly man. I house and provide for their wounded, but they attend them, and our relations are very agreeable. They say the best time of it is since being taken . . . we have a great deal of hard fighting yet to do. The Yankee Surgeon says 10,000 troops are coming to Texas, but that Jack Hamilton (appointed Military Governor of the state by Lincoln in 1862) will never show himself here nor would the Yankee troops if they knew how

Texans fight.

I have reason to be well satisfied with the efficiency of the medical staff though it costs superhuman exertion night and day. The wounds mostly from shells, splinters and grape shot are unusually dangerous. My paper is full and I am very tired. My travel bags stolen. I have not a shirt to change, my trunk's in Houston and I am going to bed. Goodnight. Love to all.

Dr. Cupples returned to San Antonio at the end of the war and resumed his surgical practice. In contrast to his experiences in the war, he kept a rather detailed journal of his surgical work. In this journal are a number of interesting cases and among them a number of surgical "firsts" which make him a truly remarkable surgeon for his time. His surgical achievements place him among the foremost of Texas surgeons and place him high on the list of America's pioneer surgeons.[11]

This was a time of momentous advances and changes in medicine and surgery, and George Cupples was an observer and a participant in many of these events. He was the first surgeon in Texas to use a general anesthetic. The patient was a sixty-year-old man who developed a gangrenous leg which required amputation. The operation was performed in May 1850 and Dr. Cupples recorded in his notes that "this is the first time chloroform has been used in Western Texas." A second patient, a nine-year-old boy who had sustained a gunshot wound of the hip and inguinal area, was operated on under chloroform. Amputation was performed easily and rapidly. The patient initially recovered from the anesthetic and appeared to be doing well when he suddenly died one and a half hours after surgery—the cause not apparent.[12]

A third example extracted from his surgical journal is testimony to Dr. Cupples' skill and innovative ability.[13] This was the case of a Confederate soldier who "while in the act of mounting his horse with both arms extended, had the left forearm traversed by a ten-pound Parrot shell which exploded in front of him lacerating the left arm up the joint. Below the axilla he had a coursing musket shot wound traversing the whole width of the thorax." An attempt at chloroform anesthesia was unsuccessful and Dr. Cupples, without anesthesia, disarticulated the right arm and the shoulder and amputated the left arm above the elbow. Recovery was complete and without incident.

Dr. Cupples was a courageous and innovative surgeon who performed several procedures for the first time. In addition to being the first surgeon in Texas to use ether and chloroform, he was the first in America to resect the tongue for cancer.[14] He performed the first resection of an ovarian tumor in a child (age six).[15] He was the first surgeon in Texas to employ Freund's procedure for removal of the uterus and ovaries.[16] He was the first surgeon in Texas to amputate an extremity at the hip joint and at the knee joint successfully.[17]

These procedures are particularly impressive when one considers that the first hospital in San Antonio was not built until 1869. All of his procedures up to that time had been performed in makeshift Civil War hospitals or in his office. Antiseptic surgery was not practiced in America until near the end of the century, although Semmelweis had been pleading for cleanliness and hand washing since 1845. Pasteur was still at work in his laboratory, the existence of bacteria was only suspected, and its relationship to human disease and wound infection was still only a theory. Cupples made the observation, as many Civil War surgeons had, that the more patients there were in a hospital the more wound infections there were. Cupples described scrubbing and cleansing of the operative site during his first operation under ether, a practice that would not be common until after 1880.[18]

George Cupples was certainly one of the most active and respected surgeons of early Texas. Another, Ferdinand Herff, also a San Antonio surgeon, was a contemporary of Cupples' and between the two of them they performed about one fourth of all of the surgery in Texas during their productive years.[19]

Cupples, as already mentioned, was active in establishing and improving organized medicine in the state. He attended every local and state meeting whenever possible and was an active participant. He was the second president of the Texas Medical Association and was elected president again in 1878, the only physician to be so honored.[20] He also became active in local community affairs and assumed a leadership role. He was a strong advocate of compulsory vaccination when this was a very unpopular position to hold. He, along with his contemporaries, labored through the multiple epidemics of cholera, yellow fever, and smallpox that plagued all American cities at that time.

He was instrumental in establishing a State Board of Examiners for the licensing of physicians in 1875.[21] The *Encyclopedia of American Biography* states that this was the first such board in the United States.

A Committee on Surgery of the Texas Medical Association was formed in 1886 and was composed of six surgeons with Dr. Cupples as chairman. This committee surveyed surgery in the entire state up to that time. The report was completed and presented at the annual meeting and published in the *Texas Medical Journal.* The summary is interesting in that it revealed only 138 doctors performing surgical procedures, of which George Cupples had performed 10 percent. Dr. Cupples made the following statement in the report which was of interest and prophetic.

> If the truth must be told, the writer of this report remembers to have read in the London Lancet some years ago, 'What good (professionally, that is) can come out of Texas?' and he has it very much at heart to answer the sneer of the great London journal by proving from a survey of their work, that surgeons of Texas, country doctors though they may be, though no long string of academic honors illustrate their names, are second to those of no country in the variety, the boldness, and the success of their operations; in practical skill, infertility of resources and in the self reliance founded on knowledge, without which no man can be a successful surgeon.

This report attained national recognition and much of it was reproduced in the *Journal of the American Medical Association.*[22] Dr. Frank Paschal who was his assistant and protege, said of him,

> Dr. Cupples was a master in his profession, laborious, careful in all his practices, his reports, his cases and private records. He was a man of broad culture, a fluid conversationalist. He was a friend of young physicians, kind, considerate, helpful. He was a constant

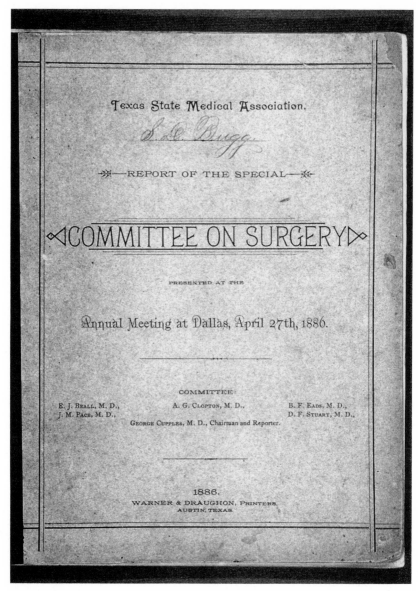

Texas State Medical Association.

S. C. Briggs

―REPORT OF THE SPECIAL―

◁COMMITTEE ON SURGERY▷

PRESENTED AT THE

Annual Meeting at Dallas, April 27th, 1886.

COMMITTEE:

E. J. BEALL, M. D.,   A. G. CLOPTON, M. D.,   B. F. EADS, M. D.,
J. M. PACE, M. D.,   D. F. STUART, M. D.,
GEORGE CUPPLES, M. D., Chairman and Reporter.

1886.
WARNER & DRAUGHON, PRINTERS,
AUSTIN, TEXAS.

Report of the Committee on surgery of the Texas Medical Association of 1886, presented by George Cupples.

were by the following surgeons:

	Number of cases reported
Acheson, Alex W., Denison, Texas	61
Beall, E. J., Fort Worth, Texas	30
Blackmore, T. M., Abilene, Texas	13
Carothers, A. E., San Antonio, Texas	60
Clopton, A. G., Jefferson, Texas	3
Cupples, George, San Antonio, Texas	221
Dowell, Greensville, Galveston, Texas	20
Eads, D. F., Marshall, Texas	20
Hadra, B. E., Austin, Texas	22
Herff, Ferd., San Antonio, Texas	214
Jordan, P., Beaumont, Texas	30
Loggins, J. C., Ennis, Texas	5
Paschal, Frank, Chihuahua, Texas	11
Reeves, W. W., Wills Point, Texas	22
Stinson, J. B., Sherman, Texas	20
Wilkerson, C. H., Galveston	69
Wooten, T. D., Austin, Texas	28

It will be impossible to review all the out-standing surgeons of these periods, and it is

From the Report of the Committee on Surgery

Dr. Frank Paschal, long-time protege and associate of George Cupples'.

Portrait of Hugh Hampton Young, who was delivered by George Cupples.

attendant of national, state and local medical society meetings, and until within a few months of his death, never failed to attend our county society meetings always taking an active part in its affairs and in the discussion of scientific subjects. There never lived in this state a member of our profession more entitled to recognition than the father of organized medicine, Dr. George Cupples.

The delivery of a baby boy by Dr. Cupples in September 1876 represented, although unknown to the good doctor, one of his greatest accomplishments. This child, named Hugh Hampton Young, became the legendary intern and resident surgeon of William Stewart Halstead, surgical genius and professor of Urology of the Johns Hopkins Medical School and Hospital.[23]

George Cupples died April 19, 1895, at the age of seventy-nine years. His funeral, according to accounts at the time, was the largest ever held in the city with numerous eulogies by a number of doctors and leading citizens. A memorial meeting of the West Texas Medical Association was held in San Antonio, and the San Antonio Druggists Association also held a special meeting. Many of the eulogies and other tributes were printed in their entirety. George Cupples was buried in the San Fernando Cemetery. Obituaries were printed in the *Texas Courier-Record of Medicine*, the *Texas Sanitarian*, the *Boston Medical and Surgical Journal*, and the *Journal of the American Medical Association*.[24]

The author has chosen to add the evaluation of Doctor Cupples by Doctor Pat Ireland Nixon[25] whose eulogy surpasses any other. Dr. Nixon writes,

> Doctor Cupples was president of the State Medical Association of Texas in 1854 and again in 1878. He was the first to introduce into Texas the use of anesthetics, ether first and chloroform afterwards. He was the first in the United States to perform the extirpation of the tongue for cancer, by Nunnely's method. The patient lived many years. He was the first in the U.S. to perform the operation for ovariotomy in a child under eight years of age and Freund's operation for extirpa-

N MEMORY
OF DR. CUPPLES.

EMORIAL SERVICES BY WEST TEXAS MEDICAL SOCIETY.

loquent Tributes Paid to the Life and Works of the Great Physician by His Professional Brethern and Friends.

The memorial services by the West Texas Medical Association in honor f the late Dr. George Cupples, the ounder of the association, were held 1st night in the Young Men's Christian Association hall. The hall was well lled with members of the medical profession and intimate friends of the deeased.

On an easel on the platform was a ife size portrait of Dr. Cupples, while on table near by were spread many rare pecimens of the great physician's skill n the operating room. On the table vas also the sword carried by Dr. Cupples during the Mexican war and the var between the States.

The meeting was called to order by Dr. D. Berry at 9 o'clock. He stated ts object and introduced Dr. Spring, he first speaker. Dr. Spring said:

"Mr. President, Ladies and Gentlemen: "In this tribute to the memory of Dr. George Cupples, our honored riend, whom all admired for his integriy and his never failing devotion to his hosen profession. I desire as a member and representative of the West

well and obeys the calls humanit a right to make upon him, is ju much a hero, entitled to recognit song and story and to have his inscribed on bronze and marble a deeds enshrined in the memory people. This assemblage is not in to eulogize a great military chiefta patriot, although in his long and career no call of country or of p ism was left unanswered by brav faithful service. An humble trib come to pay to the memory of on by long service in the cause of hur earned the right to be remembe one of the great men of his day an eration.

"Dr. George Cupples was bo Scotland Oct. 13, 1815, and died Antonio, Tex., on April 19, 1893 blood of the Campbells coursed t his veins and early in life he distinguished among his associa his intellectual superiority and for physical courage. Before finished his professional educat the University of Edinburgh he pointed surgeon in the English engaged in the Carlist war, and service he at once distinguished as capable professionally and bra sonally. After this service he v Paris and there renewed his sional studies. In 1844 he came Antonio. In those days, fifty yea imagine what San Antonio was village on a dangerous frontier, overrun by savages and out small English-speaking colony of in the wilderness. Think what quisition such a man was to th munity. None who knew him life can doubt that he at once a leader, not only as a physic surgeon, but as a citizen. In of 1846 he participated, giving adopted country his profession personal services as freely as ardor of youth he had entered vice of his native land. After he continued to reside in San and fought all battles with ev demic and every form of dise death which has ever visited ou with untiring courage, skill and

A photograph of the San Antonio newspaper with the account of George Cupples' funeral and of some of the eulogies given.

tion of the uterus and ovariless. He was the first in
Texas to amputate at the hip joint and knee with
success. The ovariotomy was performed in the summer of 1874, on the bed in which the child lay. The
pedicle was tied off and returned, an unusual procedure in those days. They were then treated extraperi-
toneally. The diagnosis was accurately made. The
tumor was an unilocular cystoma about the size of an
adult head. She lived to womanhood and became a
mother. The hysterectomy was performed October
14, 1878. The patient lived fifty hours. Then there was
no defined method of operating. The operation was
abdominal. The broad ligaments were tied off with
silk, piece-meal using for that purpose an aneurysm
needle. Today it is not a difficult operation but was a
very difficult one in those days. The operation, ovariotomy was performed in a boarding house with no
conveniences. There were no hospital in this city at
the time these operations were performed. I had the
honor of assisting him in the two latter operations.
Doctor Cupples was a master in his profession, labo-
rious, careful in all his practice, his reports, his cases
and private records. He was a man of broad culture,
familiar with every historic reference, with every royal
family and their traditions, a fluent conversationalist.
He was a friend of young physicians, kind, consider-
ate, helpful; he was a constant attendant of national,
state and local medical society meetings, and until
within a few months of his death never failed to attend
our county society meetings, always taking an active
part in its affairs and in the discussion of scientific
subjects.

This is not the proper time to eulogize one whose
deeds are more lasting than bronze or marble. In years
to come it may be that a monument will be erected to
his memory, for no physician could be more deserv-
ing. There has never lived in this state a member of our
profession entitled to recognition than the father of
organized medicine in Texas, Doctor George Cupples.

Left: George Cupples near the end of his life.
Bottom: The tombstone of George Cupples in the San Fernando Cemetery in San Antonio.

GEORGE CUPPLES
SURGEON
7 TEXAS CAV. C.S.A.
OCT. 13, 1815 – APRIL 19, 1895

One of the unattainable goals of the historian is to try to portray or recapture in an understandable way the personality, beliefs and the character of the subject and not just relate facts. George Cupples was a complex personality, possessing many interests, great surgical ability and with outstanding leadership capability. He held strong beliefs about his profession, ever seeking perfection and advancement of the surgical profession. He left behind a legacy of excellence and of compassion for his fellow man. A quotation from his presidential address in 1878 will serve to end this account of his life.[26]

> "YES, GENTLEMEN, GLORY AND PATRIOTISM HAVE HAD THEIR HEROES, RELIGION HER MARTYRS, BUT NEITHER ARE WANTING IN THE ANNALS OF SCIENCE, AND IF THEIR HISTORY HAS NOT YET BEEN WRITTEN, IT IS NOT BECAUSE THE MATERIALS ARE LACKING."
>
> GEORGE CUPPLES, M.D.
> 1815 - 1895

ENDNOTES

1. W.S. Spear (ed), J.H. Brown (rev ed). *Encyclopedia of the New West* (Marshall, Texas: Biographical Publishing Company, 1881), 339.

2. Julia Waugh. *Castroville and Henri Castro, Empressano* (San Antonio, Texas: Standard Publishing Company, 1934); S.J. Wright. *San Antonio de Bexar, Historical Traditional, Legendary* (Austin Morgan, 1916), 103.

3. Spear, op. cit., 340.

4. P.I. Nixon. *A Century of Medicine in San Antonio* (San Antonio, Texas: Privately Published), 98.

5. P.I. Nixon. *A History of the Texas Medical Association, 1853-1953* (Austin: University of Texas Press), 12,14,15.

6. *Circular to the Physicians of Texas* (Austin: Walker Printing Company, 1853).

7. George Cupples (ed). Constitution and By-laws of the Medical Association of Texas, *Texas State Journal of Medicine* 14 (1853), 7-13.

8. Nixon, *Texas Medical Association*, op. cit., 12.

9. Jerry Thompson. *Henry Hopkins Sibley, Confederate General of the West* (Nachitoches: Northwestern Louisiana State University Press, 1987)(multiple refs).

10. George Cupples. Two Battlefield Letters, D.H. Winfrey (ed). *Southwestern Historical Quarterly* V:XLV (October 1951).

11. George Cupples. Personal Journal 1850-1876. Pat Ireland Historical Library, University of Texas Health Science Center, San Antonio, Texas.

12. R.B. Krause. Unpublished Manuscript, Presidential Address to the San Antonio Historical Association; Cupples, Personal Journal, op. cit.

13. Cupples, Personal Journal, op. cit.; Spear, op. cit.

14. Spear, op. cit.

15. Krause, op. cit.

16. Spear, op. cit.; Krause, op. cit.

17. Krause, op. cit.

18. George Cupples. "Chloroform vs Ether." *Texas Courier Record of Medicine* 8 (1850), 9-11.

19. George Cupples. Report of the Special Committee on Surgery, Presented at the annual meeting of the Texas State Medical Association in Dallas, April 27, 1886.

20. Nixon, *Texas Medical Association, op. cit.,* 21.

21. Ibid., 98.

22. George Cupples. Report on Surgery in Texas, *Journal of the American Medical Association* 9 (November 5, 1887), 135.

23. Nixon, *Texas Medical Association*, op. cit., 372; Krause, op.cit.

24. *Texas Courier Record of Medicine* 12 (May 1895), 261; *Texas Sanitarian* 4 (May 1895), 301; *Boston Medical and Surgical Journal* 132 (1895), 148; *Journal of the American Medical Association* 20 (April 27, 1895), 650.

25. Nixon, *Texas Medical Association*, op. cit., 21-22.

26. George Cupples. Presidential Address State Medical Society of Texas, 1878.

BIOGRAPHICAL SKETCH OF AUTHOR

R. MAURICE HOOD was born at Lubbock, Texas, on July 25, 1924. He attended Lubbock public schools and was graduated from Lubbock Senior High School in 1941. Pre-medical education was obtained at Texas Technological College in Lubbock from 1941 to 1943. He was accepted into the freshman class of the Southwestern Medical College for the term beginning July 1, 1943, and was graduated in June 1946.

Internship was served at Baylor University Hospital, Dallas, Texas, 1946-47. Residency in general surgery was at the U.S. Naval Hospital, San Diego, California, U.S. Naval Hospital, Guam, M.I. and U.S. Naval Hospital, Oakland, California from 1947 through 1952. Graduate education in thoracic surgery was obtained at the University of Michigan 1952 to 1954. He is certified by the American Board of Surgery and The American Board of Thoracic Surgery.

Dr. Hood served in the U.S. Naval Medical Service from 1943 to 1958, rising to the rank of commander. He resigned from the regular Navy in 1958 to enter private practice in cardiothoracic surgery in Austin, Texas, and continued in the Naval Reserve retiring with the rank of captain in 1974.

He became Professor and Chairman of the Department of Thoracic Surgery at Texas Tech School of Medicine in 1972 and served there for two years before returning to private practice in Austin. In 1981 he accepted a position as Professor of Clinical Surgery at New York University and continued in this position until 1986 when illness forced retirement.

He was an active member of the staffs of Brackenridge Hospital, St. David's Community Hospital, Seton Hospital, and Holy Cross Hospital while in Austin.

In New York he served on the faculty of Bellevue Hospital, New York University Hospital and Manhatten V.A. Hospital. While in New York he was editor/author of four surgical textbooks and is the author of chapters in two surgical texts and the author of twenty-three publications including two original research papers.

He is or has been a member of: The American College of Surgeons, The American Association for Thoracic Surgery, The Society of Thoracic Surgeons, The Southern Thoracic Surgical Society, The American Trudeau Society, The Frederick Coller Association, The John Alexander Society, The Texas Surgical Society and is an Honorary Member of the Texas Medical Association.

Dr. Hood and his wife have served as medical missionaries on fifteen occasions at the Nigerian Christian Hospital in Nigeria.

Dr. Hood has been honored by being elected or named or having received:
Recognition Award, Residents of St. Joseph's Hospital
Outstanding Surgeon, Brackenridge Hospital, Austin, Texas
Attending Surgeon of the Year, New York University Medical Center
Most Worthy Citizen of Austin, Texas, 1976
Award for Meritorious Service, Austin Dental Society
President, Westchester, New York Civil War Roundtable
Honorary Plaque for Outstanding Service in Medical
Missions, African Christian Hospitals Foundation
Honorary Fire Chief Austin and Lubbock Fire Departments
Honorary Member Brackenridge Hospital
Tom Pinkney Award, Austin Fire Department 1976

Ferdinand Eugene Daniel, M.D.
1839-1914
by
R. Maurice Hood, M.D.

★FERDINAND E. DANIEL WAS BORN in Greenville County, Virginia, July 18, 1839, the son of R.W.T. Daniel and Hester Jordan Adams. The father was the principal figure in the Daniel family and was well known throughout Virginia. Ferdinand's mother was the daughter of Edwin Adams and granddaughter of Colonel Charles Adams, a prominent military figure in the Revolutionary War. He was also related to the Massachusetts Adams family of John and Samuel and John Adams, John Quincy Adams and Charles Francis Adams.[1]

The family moved to Mississippi in 1844 and to Vicksburg in 1852 where Ferdinand had his early education. At the wishes of his father he studied law in Jackson but soon became disenchanted with the legal profession and decided to become a doctor. He began to read medicine under Dr. T.J. Mitchell. The following year he enrolled in the New Orleans School of Medicine for the 1860-61 term. Three of his teachers were the two Flints and Dr. E.D. Fenner.

With the start of the Civil War, Daniel dropped out of medical school and enlisted in the Confederate States Army. He was assigned to Company K, 18th Mississippi Regiment and appointed orderly sergeant. After one year he reenlisted in Sanders Battalion, Jackson Cavalry, Wheelers Corps in the Army of Tennessee. He was sent to Virginia and became part of the Army of Northern Virginia. He took part in the Battle of Manassas, or Bull Run, in General Bee's Brigade. He was injured in the battle and was discharged for recovery.[2]

Daniel reentered the New Orleans School of Medicine for

the 1861-62 term[3] and was graduated February 3, 1862. He and many other students barely escaped capture by Union forces following the Battle of New Orleans. He immediately reenlisted in the Confederate Army as Acting Assistant Surgeon. On July 8, 1862, he was given an examination at the Headquarters of the Army of Tennessee at Tupelo. Based upon his superior grade in the examination he was formerly commissioned as Surgeon by the Confederate War Department. At only twenty-three years of age he was the youngest surgeon in the Army of Tennessee. Dr. Yandell of the examining board endorsed the appointment with these words, "A young man of uncommon qualifications and extraordinary abilities; let him be assigned as secretary of the Board."[4]

He continued in this post until the invasion of Kentucky under the command of General Braxton Bragg. He served as Assistant Medical Inspector of the army and in this capacity was involved in the battle and capture of Mumford and in the Battle of Perryville. He was personally responsible for the removal and treatment of the hundreds of wounded and is said to have operated for over twenty-four hours.

After the Battle of Perryville he was reassigned as clerk in the office of the Medical Director of the Army of Tennessee in Chattanooga. He was offered, but refused, the position as Medical Director. At this time he was only twenty-four years of age. He was appointed as Judge Advocate of the General Court Martial of the Army of Tennessee in 1863. He was with the army of General Joseph Johnston in the attempted relief of the besieged army of General Pemberton at Vicksburg and retreated with Johnston's army.

He married Miss Minerva Patrick on July 4, 1863, the day following the surrender of Vicksburg. He was assigned as a surgeon with the Army of Tennessee as it retreated toward Atlanta from Chattanooga under Johnston and established and served in several hospitals along the route of retreat. He was detached from the defeated army and transferred to Mississippi and finally surrendered at Lauderdale Springs.

After the war Dr. Daniel and his family moved to Galveston in 1866 and set up a practice. His wife became ill and died in 1867; an infant daughter died a short time later. He served the populace of Galveston faithfully during the severe yellow fever epidemic of 1867.

Dr. Daniel was appointed as Professor of Anatomy in the Texas Medical College[5] during the 1867-68 term. He was also appointed as Professor of Surgery but declined the appointment for unknown reasons. He became ill and resigned his appointment and moved to New Orleans and entered into business. He married Miss Fannie R. Smith, a relation of General Sam J. Gholson, a United States Senator. Four children were born to this union and three, Marie, Fannie and Gertrude survived to adulthood.

Dr. Daniel moved to Lake Village and served there through the yellow fever epidemic of 1878. He kept accurate records and made a detailed report to the U.S. Congress. As a result, he was appointed Sanitary Inspector by the National Board of Health in 1879. He was placed in charge of the National Quarantine organization south of Vicksburg in 1879.[6] F.E. Daniel opened a practice and worked there from 1878 to 1881 but, because of recurring illness, he again moved to Texas. He established the family in Sherman and tried to practice there. Again, bad health and a business failure caused him to move, this time to Fort Worth. Dr. Daniel's second wife died in February 1884; he had lost his only son the year before.

Frustrated by his inability to practice because of constant health problems and by the desperate financial straits he found himself in, he decided to involve himself in medical publishing. He associated himself with Dr. W.B. Brooks of Fort Worth and they began publishing the *Texas Courier-Record of Medicine* on a financial shoestring.[7] The journal proved to be an immediate success and attracted the attention of the State Medical Association, which passed a resolution stating in part, "It is hailed as a medical organ of a high degree of merit, a fit representative and exponent of rational medicine . . . whose teachings based on an acceptance of a profound reverence for the National Code of Ethics, advocate a higher code of morals, a higher standard of education and unity, harmony and in concord in professional ranks."[8]

After one year Dr. Daniel, for unknown reasons, sold the *Courier-Journal,* moved to Austin, and founded *Daniel's Texas Medical Journal* which was an immediate success. There is no doubt that Daniel's principal contribution to the Texas medical profession came through his editorial efforts. Daniel's editorial in the first issue was a flowery, philosophical treatise, full of optimism. He was enthusiastic for the future of medicine.[9]

Medical publications in Texas followed three general lines depending on the originator and his successors. In 1884, the date of the founding of Daniel's editing activities, there was only one other publication, the *Southern Homeopathic Pellet* which was replaced by the *Southern Journal of Homeopathy* in 1884.[10]

Daniel's Texas Medical Journal was commonly called the "Redback" and became widely read. This publication continued until 1893 when Dr. Daniel changed its name to *The Texas Medical Journal*. Daniel apparently made this change in hopes of gaining statewide acceptance and probably with hope that it would become the official organ of the Texas State Medical Association. At this time he was the secretary of the association. However, in 1905 the *Texas State Journal of Medicine* was founded by the Texas State Medical Association. This was the year that Daniel was president and he was very much opposed to the new journal. He did not rale against it, but he objected vigorously and wrote an editorial in his own journal entitled "Rash Action of the House of Delegates."[11]

Dr. J.C. Chase was the secretary that year and had been appointed as one of a committee of two to recommend whether the association should publish a journal. Dr. Chase became editor, and he and Dr. Daniel began a long, angry exchange that lasted for several years. Daniel continued to publish editorials attacking the management and policies of the *Texas State Journal of Medicine* and Dr. Chase. Even at Dr. Chase's retirement as secretary, Daniel was very ungracious.[12]

Daniel's The Texas Medical Journal, however, continued after his death in 1914 with his third wife Josephine as its editor until 1919, when the name was changed to *Practical Medicine and Surgery*. This publication continued another five years until Mrs. Daniel merged it with the *Texas Medical Insurance and Health Conservation* which, until 1917, had been the *Texas Medical News*. It was first founded in 1892 as the *Texas Sanitarian* until the name change in 1885. The *Texas Medical News* was principal competition of the *Texas State Medical Journal*. They were similar in size and content. The two journals coexisted on a friendly basis but with frequent and spirited exchanges.

DANIEL'S TEXAS MEDICAL JOURNAL.

ESTABLISHED JULY, 1885.

PUBLISHED MONTHLY. — SUBSCRIPTION $2.00 A YEAR.

Vol. VIII.   AUSTIN, JUNE, 1893.   No. 12.

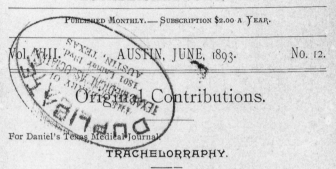

Original Contributions.

For Daniel's Texas Medical Journal.

TRACHELORRAPHY.

G. J. STARNES, M. D., SAN ANTONIO, TEXAS.

[Read before the Lone Star Medical Association, at Galveston, Texas.]

THE subject under consideration has been a topic of so many
discussions and furnished a thesis for so many writers
within the last decade, that I feel myself wholly incompetent to
interest you with a paper. However, I shall endeavor to present
the treatment and the principal features of the operation, together with a few cases operated upon by myself, thereby hoping
to have you, in the words of Munde, "see the string on which
my beads are strung."

We mean by trachelorraphy a suture, a term used to describe
the operation for the repair of the lacerated cervix, better known
in this country as "Emmet's operation." Dr. Emmet, of New
York, first conceived the idea in 1862, and later, in 1868, read a
paper in support of his views before the New York County Medical Society. I shall set forth, first, the treatment preparatory
to an operation, and also, the treatment of the conservative,
which sometimes relieves the existing symptoms and often pro-
motes a cure. The classes of lacerations are generally three:
unilateral, bi-lateral and stellate or star shaped, either of which
may be diagnosed by the touch.

The initiatory treatment for a recent laceration should be: vagi-

A page from *Daniel's Texas Medical Journal.*

VOL. XXI.   NOVEMBER, 1903.   No. 5.

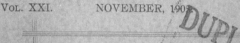

TEXAS

Medical Journal.

Subscription, $1.00 a Year, in Advance.
Single Copies, 10 Cents.

PUBLISHED AT AUSTIN, TEXAS, BY
F. E. DANIEL, M. D.,
PROPRIETOR.

PRINTED BY THE VON BOECKMANN-JONES CO.

Entered at the Postoffice at Austin, Texas, as Second-class Mail Matter.

TWENTY-FIRST YEAR.

Cover from the last issue of *Daniel's Texas Medical Journal* in 1893.

EDITORIAL DEPARTMENT.

F. E. DANIEL, M. D., Editor.

S. E. HUDSON, M. D., Managing Editor.

A. J. SMITH. M. D., Galveston, Associate Editor.

EDITORIAL STAFF:

PROF. J. E. THOMPSON, M. D., Texas Medical College, Galveston; Surgery.
PROF. WM. KEILLER, M. D., Texas Medical College, Galveston; Obstetrics and
  Gynecology.
PROF. DAVID CERNA, M. D., Texas Medical College, Galveston; Therapeutics.
PROF. A. J. SMITH, M, D., Texas Medical College, Galveston; Medicine.
DR. ISADORE DYER, Tulane University; Dermatology.
DR. R. H. L. BIBB, Saltillo, Mexico; Foreign Correspondent.
DR. ROBT. MORRIS, Charity Hospital, N. O.; Clinical Reports.

——o——

The JOURNAL is the official organ of the Austin District Medical Society, the West
Texas District Medical Society and the Galveston County Medical Society.

CHRYSALIS AND BUTTERFLY.

Salutatory.

SHALE, BRETHREN! This number of DANIEL'S TEXAS MEDI-
CAL JOURNAL completes Vol. 8. It rounds out and finishes
the *eighth year* of its sunny existence,—for its career has
been like a summer day, unclouded by trouble—unhindered
by any misfortune. It has flourished, thank you, like
the fabled and famous green bay-tree; prospered and
grown like a well fed and healthy infant; grown and
grown, till, in fact,—it has gotten too big for its breeches,
(figuratively speaking and in a Pickwickian sense). Up, up,
up, higher and higher has it climbed the ladder of success till
it has left all competitors, and is, itself, in the vernacular of the
day, *away out of sight*. (How is that for high?) So, this JUNE
number is a *memorial* number; it commemorates at once, the
birthday, and the *demise* of DANIEL'S TEXAS MEDICAL JOURNAL.
Nay, start not; not dead,—nor sleepeth, not by a large majority.
I... simply changed form,—cast off its too small trousers,
... to, speak, and with *July* will don the long
...wn man!

Editorial Page from the last issue of *Daniel's Texas Medical Journal* in
1893, announcing the change of name to the *Texas Medical Journal*.

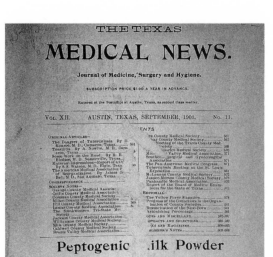

Left: The front cover of the *Texas Medical News*, the principal competition for Daniel's own journal. Bottom: The front cover of F.E. Daniel's book, *Recollections of a Rebel Surgeon*.

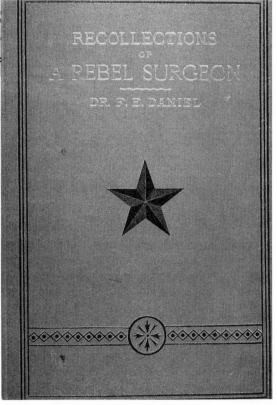

As with all publications there were a few problems. There is a letter to the editor of the *Texas Medical Journal* by a doctor who had been billed after paying for the subscription which demanded that his one dollar be returned and his subscription canceled.[13]

The editorial offices of the *Texas Medical Journal* were at 622 Congress Avenue in Austin. Dr. Daniel and his family resided at 200 West Seventh Street with a telephone number of 1026.

There were a number of other medical publications that existed at various times during the life span of F.E. Daniel. They included: *The Texas Health Journal, The Texas Medical Practitioner, Southwestern Medical Record, The Texas Medical Gazette, Texas Clinics, Southern Medical Review, Dallas Medical Journal, South Texas Medical Record,* and *Medical Annals of Southwest Texas.* None of these had the circulation of the *Texas Medical Journal* or the *Texas Medical News.*[14]

In 1886 upon the death of Dr. Burt, who was the secretary of the Medical Association, Daniel was appointed to fill this office until the next meeting in April 1887. At that meeting he was elected secretary for a period of five years. He also served on the Publishing Committee of the State Medical Association. His duties included the editing and printing of the *Annual Transactions* which was a hardback book.

He became the American Secretary of the Section on Dermatology of the 9th International Medical Conference and was also named as a delegate of the Texas Medical Association to the American Medical Association.

Dr. Daniel served as a member of the Committee on Medical Legislation of the State Association and in this capacity wrote a bill for the regulation for the practice of medicine which was adapted by the Association at their meeting in 1884. It was printed in the *Transactions* and a thousand copies were printed in pamphlet form for general distribution. Dr. George Cupples of San Antonio was made chairman of the Committee and was delegated to present the bill to the state legislature.[15] As has been usual with efforts of organized medicine to influence the legislature, the legislature did not pass the bill and apparently did not seriously consider it. This result offended the association, and they ceased trying to procure any legislation for a number of years. Dr. Daniel was completely disgusted.

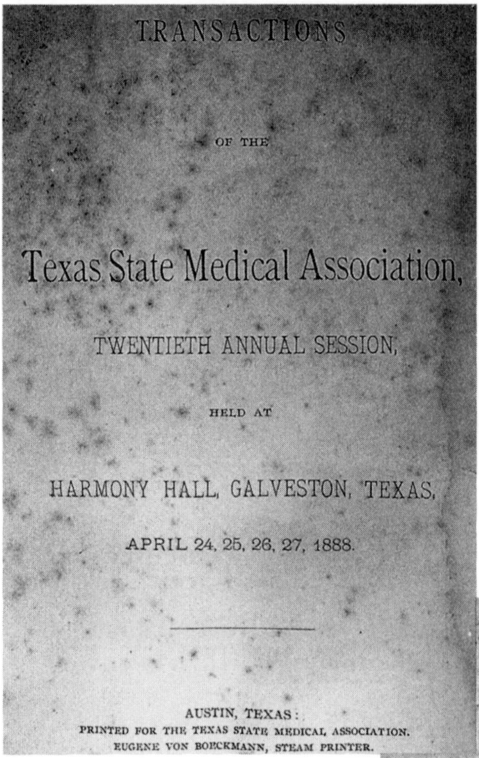

TRANSACTIONS

OF THE

Texas State Medical Association,

TWENTIETH ANNUAL SESSION,

HELD AT

HARMONY HALL, GALVESTON, TEXAS,

APRIL 24, 25, 26, 27, 1888.

AUSTIN, TEXAS:
PRINTED FOR THE TEXAS STATE MEDICAL ASSOCIATION.
EUGENE VON BOECKMANN, STEAM PRINTER.

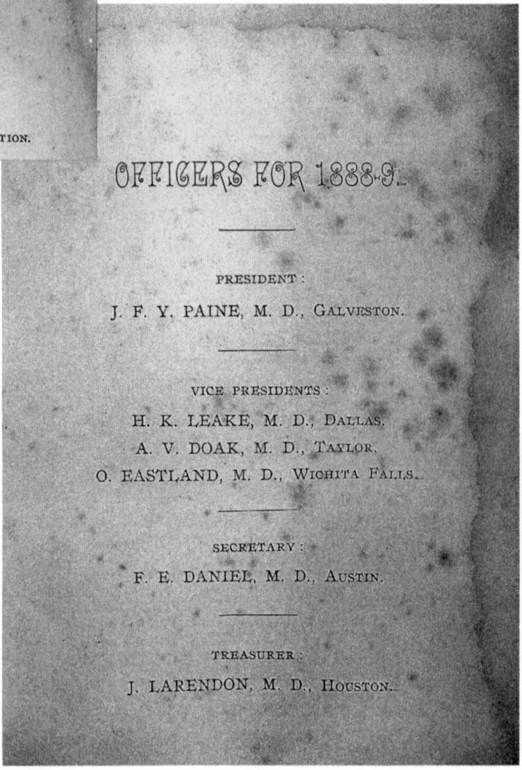

The Transactions of the Texas State Medical Association, showing on the second page (bottom) the name of F.E. Daniel as Secretary.

OFFICERS FOR 1888-9.

PRESIDENT:

J. F. Y. PAINE, M. D., GALVESTON.

VICE PRESIDENTS:

H. K. LEAKE, M. D., DALLAS.
A. V. DOAK, M. D., TAYLOR.
O. EASTLAND, M. D., WICHITA FALLS.

SECRETARY:

F. E. DANIEL, M. D., AUSTIN.

TREASURER:

J. LARENDON, M. D., HOUSTON.

Dr. Daniel's report as Chairman of the Section of Dermatology was accepted and appeared in the *Transactions* in 1886. He also received an invitation to address the Association of American Medical Editors and delivered the address titled "Texas Medicine and State Medicine in Texas" in 1885 in New Orleans. He was elected Secretary of the State Medical Association that year. Dr. Daniel was a member of the Travis County Medical Society and the Austin District Medical Society and was a major force in each of these.

One of his notable speeches presented to the Williamson County Medical Society was on the topic "Necessity of Organizing the Medical Profession."[16]

Daniel was a man of deep convictions and had the courage to express his views and to fight for the principles that he believed in. In 1887 an unfortunate controversy occurred with Dr. Daniel as its focus. Dr. J.R. Briggs of Dallas had received an award from the State Association for the best prize-essay of 1885 and Daniel, apparently acting in a dual role as editor of *Daniel's Texas Medical Journal* and as Secretary of the State Medical Association, either wrote or permitted to be written an editorial which accused the committee that had judged the essays of partiality to Dr. Briggs.[17]

Dr. Briggs presented a three-page accusation against Daniel, charging him with falsely representing his medical journal as the official organ of the association, of appropriating money from the association, and of being a "firebrand," a stirrer up of strife and a fomenter of discord. Probably a major motive for Dr. Briggs' displeasure was his displeasure at not having been elected president of the association.

Dr. Daniel reacted promptly, denying all charges. The Judicial Committee met and cleared Daniel of the charges. Dr. Briggs was also exonerated of the charges that Daniel brought against him. This would seem to be the end of the controversy but it surfaced again in 1891. Dr. Daniel resigned as secretary in 1890 "for the sake of harmony in the ranks and prosperity of the organization." His resignation was accepted but he was appointed to fill the office until the next election. Dr. Briggs who edited the *Health Journal* continued to use it to accuse Daniel of "conduct unbecoming a physician and a gentleman."

The Judicial Committee reopened the case in 1891 and again

absolved Dr. Daniel of all accusations and charges and at the same time recommending the expulsion of Dr. Briggs from the association. Dr. Raines of Mineral Wells moved that the report of the committee not be received. Dr. Daniel rose to the occasion by recounting his services to the association and reminded them of his desire to resign, and he requested that he be allowed to step down. He said that he was actuated "by a sincere desire to secure and preserve peace and harmony."

The association accepted his resignation and again recommended that Dr. Briggs be ejected from the association. Dr. Briggs made several appeals to national bodies but his expulsion was permanent. The Judicial Council reviewed the prolonged confrontation and concluded that the conflict was essentially personal and more than anything a clash of egos, resolving that members keep matters of a personal nature out of the State Association Meetings. Dr. Briggs continued to press his case for several years but finally gave up and his name disappeared from the roster of the Association.

Dr. Daniel published a book in 1899, *Recollections of a Rebel Surgeon*, which is an anecdotal record of Dr. Daniel's experiences in the Civil War.

It is written for the most part in the third person as if Dr. Daniel were interviewing "The Old Doctor," who is actually himself. Some of the stories are humorous, some tragic, and some pathetic and emotional. There are many descriptions of camp life in the Confederate Army. There are several battlefield descriptions and several accounts of surgery for the wounded. One story relates with humor his capture by the Union army and his very brief time as a prisoner of war. The military stories roughly follow the course of the part of the war that Daniel experienced. It is not in very good chronological order. A reader must be knowledgeable of the war and of a number of battles in order to remain oriented to the text. This small book, however, has found a place in Civil War literature, is well-recognized today, and is of considerable monetary value. It was written, or at least published, over thirty years after the conflict, but the writing reveals an excellent memory for the events described.

F.E. Daniel's early life and career up to 1887 were chronicled by L.E. Daniell in *Types of Successful Men* published in Austin in 1887.[18] Dr. Daniel was a man of violent emotions and opinions which often found their way into print in his journal. A humorous example is his recording of an episode at the Mental Hospital where a doctor threw a spittoon at an employee with whom he was angry; Daniel wrote an editorial on the use of the throwing of spittoons as a disciplinary measure.

He carried on a spirited editorial debate with several of his competing medical journals, but for the most part these discussions were on a very professional basis. Despite his quick temper and sharp pen, he was always trying to improve the profession and its care of patients. Daniel became a potent force in the medical affairs of Texas. His reputation and that of his medical journal made him particularly effective in shaping the course of the Texas Medical Association.

The standards of medical practice were not as clear then as they are today. There were three general schools of thought, the allopathic school, the homeopathic group and the eclectic school. These disciplines were not enemies and they often worked together, particularly to weed out charlatans and in setting training standards.

The Texas Medical Association had only ninety-two members in 1885, primarily due to apathy and the inconvenience of communication and travel. However, due to aggressive campaigning by several, including Dr. Daniel, there were 451 names on Dr. Daniel's roster by 1889. The Society was not wealthy; in 1888 it showed a balance on the books of only $28.97.

Surgeon George Cupples, who died April 19, 1895, four days before the annual meeting of the State Medical Association, was one of the founders of the association and its first president. He was with little doubt the most outstanding surgeon in Texas at that time, and Dr. Daniel published a "panegyric" on him in the May issue of the *Texas Medical Journal* with the closing statement, "In the bright Empyrean realms far beyond the skies—the abode of Eternal God, may his gentle spirit find its guerdon of rest; and when the archangel shall recount his many benefactions to suffering man, may a crown of glory, too be his, amen."[19]

In 1889 they decided to become incorporated under the laws of the state and a new charter was written by a number of designated trustees and signed by twelve members and by Dr. Daniel, but with the coming of the new century, the Texas Medical Association seemed to be making little progress in membership or in finances. A reorganization of the American Medical Association was accomplished in 1900-1901 making all county societies the organizational unit and all of these making up the State organization and all state organizations making up the AMA.

F.E. Daniel was at the forefront of trying to build up the association. He had been involved in much controversy, and his editorial in 1895 "Shall We Abolish the State Medical Association?" helped to convince some of the majority of doctors who were not members to join.[20] He said "We are working upon a wrong plan and our efforts are as futile as pouring water through a sieve." He suggested a campaign to enlist every doctor in the state in the association and that all of the local societies should become active in the state association by sending delegates to the state meeting.

Dr. Daniel was also enthusiastically interested in the problems of the mentally ill. He gave a speech titled "A Plea for Reform in Criminal Jurisprudence." He recommended restrictions upon marriage of the "mentally unfit."[21] He, along with Gideon Lincecum, recommended castration in all "natural criminals and the criminally insane," thus "closing the bloody gates of Hell and limit the opportunity to inflict their progeny on the next generation."

Dr. Daniel was married for the third time on June 3, 1903, to Josephine Draper. There were no children from the marriage. Mrs. Daniel began to assist in the publishing of *The Texas Medical Journal* and, as her husband's health began to fail, took over the entire responsibility for publishing the journal. She continued in this role after his death as previously noted. After the merger with *Texas Medical Insurance and Health Conservation* in 1925, she continued as editor of the new *Practical Medicine and Surgery*. Mrs. Daniel finally sold the journal to Dr. George L. Servoss in 1929, ending the existence of the journal founded by F.E. Daniel. Mrs. Daniel was recognized for her career in medical publishing in the Texas Women's Hall of Fame in 1917.

Dr. F.E. Daniel was elected President of the Texas State Medical Association in 1904 to serve in 1905. He was introduced at the meeting in Galveston by Dr. Frank Paschal of San Antonio, who was the retiring president. His presidential address, a lengthy discourse entitled "Sentiment and Science," was a philosophical comparison of the facts and theories of science and their opposition to what he called sentiment but which is a synonym for religious belief and a belief in God and miracles.[22]

He accepted the theories of Darwin and Huxley and insisted that they were scientific fact not theory. He portrayed a mechanical view of life and believed all phenomenon, physiological processes and psychological behavior to be a matter of logic and chemistry that could be rationally explained.

He reviewed much of the scientific discoveries and achievement up to his time. He admits near the end of the address,

> But Sentiment still adheres to tradition and superstition. It is the popular and prevailing belief taught from thousands of pulpits and the altars of prayer in the households of millions of intelligent, earnest, good people. It is so firmly fixed and rooted in the human heart that science cannot shake it. The arrows and missiles from the quiver of science glance harmless from the battlements as from the walls of adamant; for back of all the 'energy' and 'physical laws'; back of all the phenomenon of human life and of the universe there is something intangible, inscrutable, infinite and incomprehensible that cannot be revealed by microscope or scalpel nor weighed or estimated. We must fall back on Sentiment and Faith and call that something the First Great Cause and bow in humility and reverence before the universal manifestation of His might, majesty and Power! Let it be false or true. Let it be knowledge or belief, fact or fancy, faith or fable, it is pleasant to think that there are angels that guard us, and at death waft on spirit wings the souls of the pure in heart to that land of promise of which our mothers told us. It is consoling and sustaining to believe and hope that our dear loved ones departed are there, and that we shall meet them. Who knows?

These excerpts do not give full credit to a very scholarly and intellectual address. This speech, better than anything, gives us a glimpse into his mind and shows him to be familiar with the classics and with history.

Portrait of Dr. Daniel's third wife, Josephine Draper Daniel, who carried on his publishing work after his death.

Portrait of Dr. Ferdinand Eugene Daniel, taken at the time of his election to the presidency of the Texas State Medical Association in 1905.

L.E. Daniell, his biographer, gives us from his personal knowledge and contact the following description of Dr. Daniel.

He is a man of genial and courteous disposition and is characterized by uniform politeness to all. Is excitable at times, but is incapable of cherishing malice. His conversation, like his writings, is vivacious, sometimes sparkling. The accompanying portrait would lead one to believe that he is sour and taciturn, whereas he is genial, companionable and of nearly uniform 'good humor.' His leading traits are affection for children and love of God's creatures, especially the flowers; and he has great compassion for the dumb brutes. Moreover, he has been called a born optimist, looking on the bright side always and whatever happens, believes that 'all things are for the best.' He leads a quiet life, devoting his time to the conduct of the Journal, attending to his duties as Secretary of the State Medical Association, and in the training of his three children. Is a staunch Episcopalian, having been brought up in that faith and confirmed by Bishop Gregg in March 1866, at Galveston; all of his children have been brought up in the faith."[23]

Dr. Daniel made an address of welcome to the American Medical-Psychological Association meeting in San Antonio in April 1905. It is full of beautiful rhetoric but also had a basic theme of urging the association to study and investigate the causes of insanity and the reason for its recent increase in incidences. He reiterated his opinion that some way should be found to prevent the propagation of mental illness by preventing pregnancy in the victims.

After his term as president of the State Medical Association he continued to campaign for those things he believed in and to serve on committees. His health began to fail, he gave up most of his activities, and he died at his home on May 14, 1914. Dr. Daniel is buried in Oakwood Cemetery in Austin.

Dr. Ferdinand Eugene Daniel served the Confederate Army both as an enlisted soldier in combat and as a talented medical officer. He was the leading figure in medical journalism from 1885 until his death. In the position of Secretary and President of the Texas Medical Association, he had enormous influence in the shaping and maturing of this association. He was at times controversial, but always striving for improvement in the standards and practice of medicine. His pen left an indelible impression on Texas medicine.

The marble tombstone of Dr. F.E. Daniel in the Oakwood Cemetary in Austin, Texas.

ENDNOTES

1. L.E. Daniell. *Types of Successful Men of Texas* (Austin: Eugene Von Boekman, 1890), 393.

2. *Confederate Military History*, Extended edition, vol. XV (Texas)(Wilmington, N.C.: Broadfoot, 1989), 365-66; M. Yeary (ed.). *Reminiscences of the Boys in Gray* (Morningside, 1985), 172.

3. Daniell, op. cit., 393.

4. Ibid., 394.

5. Ibid., 395.

6. Ibid.

7. Ibid.; J.M. Coleman. "Medical Journalism in Texas." *Texas State Journal of Texas* 51 (1955), 486-88.

8. P.I. Nixon. *A History of the Texas Medical Association* (Austin: University of Texas Press, 1953), 112.

9. F.E. Daniel. *Daniel's Texas Medical Journal* 1 (Austin, 1953), 1.

10. Coleman, op. cit., 486.

11. Ibid.

12. Nixon, op. cit., 248.

13. Daniel, op. cit., 2.

14. Coleman, op. cit., 487.

15. Daniell, op. cit., 396.

16. Ibid.

17. Nixon, op. cit., 135, 163; Daniell, op. cit., 37.

18. Daniell, op.cit., 37

19. Nixon, op. cit., 191.

20. Ibid., 185.

21. Ibid., 195.

22. F.E. Daniel. "Sentiment and Science." *Texas State Medical Journal* (May-June 1895).

23. Daniell, op. cit., 398.

BIOGRAPHICAL SKETCH OF AUTHOR

(See page 59)

GREENSVILLE DOWELL, M.D.
1822-1881
by
Joseph P. McNeill, M.D.

★ TODAY, AS TEXAS ENJOYS NO SMALL measure of the limelight on surgical leadership both nationally and internationally, we should not fail to recognize and pay homage to our vast heritage in this field that began soon after Texas gained its independence from Mexico in 1836. We can be proud of our contemporary surgeons whose names I am hesitant to mention for fear of leaving out some whose contributions, although great, have failed to be popularized in the news. Nevertheless, we have many Texas surgeons who hold high places in the leading medical centers and national organizations of these United States, but most of our early heroes of Texas surgery were educated elsewhere and migrated to this state to teach and practice their art. World recognition first came to Texas surgeons in a report made to the Texas Medical Association in 1886, based on an extensive state-wide survey of all the practicing surgeons at that time by Dr. George Cupples, "probably the most outstanding surgeon in Texas at the time he lived." In this report Dr. Cupples concluded, "The surgeons of Texas, country doctors though they be, though no long string of academic honors illustrate their names, are second to those of no country in the variety, the boldness and the success of their operations, in practical skill, in fertility of resources, and in that self-reliance founded on knowledge, without which no man can be a successful surgeon."[1]

The worldwide response to this report was reported in the *Texas Medical Journal* shortly thereafter.

The Committee (Dr. Cupples, Chairman) has received

letters of warm commendation from the most distin-
guished medical men of Europe and America.
Amongst the lights who have complimented the
work, we may be pardoned for mentioning Bowditch,
Gregory, Lawson Tait, S.W. Gross, Senn, Battey,
Richardson, Barker, Bodenhamer, Pepper, Amhurst,
Packard, Sinclair, T.G. Thomas, W.L. Lee and others.
This great compliment the endorsement of the whole
profession of America and part of Europe, should stir
the pride, and stimulate the zeal of surgeons.[2]

This early recognition of Texas surgeons was not a happen-
stance but rather the result of the groundwork laid up by earlier
Texas surgeons who established an academic atmosphere in the
state founded on scholarship, integrity, boldness, and communication with other surgical centers of the world. An in-depth
study of this state's early history of medicine and surgery reveals
that Dr. Greensville Dowell played a major role in establishing
this heritage that we today privileged to enjoy.

Dr. Dowell was born in Albemarle County, Virginia, September 1, 1882, the same year Louis Pasteur was born in France.
He was the son of James and Frances (Dalton) Dowell. In
addition to the regular curriculum taught in the local schools,
his early education included the study of classical and modern
languages. In 1837 the family moved to Tennessee, and in 1844
Dowell began his medical education, studying under his brother,
Dr. Alep Dowell, in Raleigh, Tennessee. He taught school for
two years prior to this "three miles from Raleigh, between the
Wolf and Lucchatchie rivers."[3]

He attended medical lectures at the University of Louisville
and received his doctor of medicine degree in 1846 from Jefferson Medical College, in Philadelphia, then he practiced medicine
in Como, Panola County, Mississippi, and in Memphis, Tennessee, from 1846 to 1852. In 1852 he came to Texas where he set
up practice in Gonzales County and "in September 1853, I
settled at Sandy Point, Brazoria County, forty-five miles west of
Galveston."[4]

During the Civil War Dr. Dowell served in the Confederate
Army.

The origin of this rare likeness of Dr. Greensville Dowell is unknown. Courtesy of the Library of the Texas Medical Association, Austin, Texas.

In June 1863, I was sent to Galveston to take charge of the Negro hospital, and that summer we had a general epidemic of dengue, and I had it in September. In 1864 I was placed in charge of Cook's regiment of heavy artillery, in addition to my duties at the Negro hospital. Nothing unusual occurred, and the health of the troops was excellent until about the middle of August, when yellow fever broke out from a blockade runner.[5]

The doctors couldn't agree on a positive diagnosis of this disease. Some believed it to be malaria, and others pronounced it yellow fever. Dr. Dowell said the disease was marked by so many peculiarities, so different from our malarial fever with which I was familiar, having practiced for seventeen years in two of the most malarial districts in the United States, Mississippi, and Brazos bottoms, in full practice, besides living in a doctor's shop at Raleigh and Germantown, Tennessee for nine years, making pills and waiting on patients for all the doctors of each place. So I claimed to know as much of malarial fevers as anybody, having had many attacks of almost every variety myself. We said of this disease it was not malarial fever, and if it were not yellow fever, we knew it was different from anything we ever saw.[6]

Some of the doctors signed statements that there were no cases of yellow fever in Galveston, but three days later they retracted their statements and signed cards saying there was an epidemic. By the first of September there were five or six cases of black vomit, and Dr. Dowell declared it to be yellow fever.

There was great alarm and many soldiers were talking of deserting. It was then they threatened to court martial me, and I believe they would have done so, but for Dr. W.R. Smith and Lieut. Col. Manley, of my regiment, who had had the fever; he seconded my move to quarantine all the forts where the heavy artillery troops were stationed, and a strict quarantine was kept up until after several severe frosts, which entirely protected all the troops, even at Fort Scurry, only two hundred yards from the city hospital.[7]

Greensville Dowell

A copy of Dr. Dowell's signature taken from an old Galveston Medical Journal in the Library of the Medical Branch of the University of Texas, Galveston.

When the Civil War ended in 1865, Dr. Dowell made his home in Galveston until his death in 1881. The medical department of Soule University, the Galveston Medical College, was opened in November 1865, and the first course of lectures was in session for six months. The college was reorganized in 1886, and Dr. Dowell was named professor of anatomy and later appointed professor of surgery.

Dr. Dowell, whom Dr. Albert O. Singleton has described as "a stormy petrel but courageous and progressive," did not get along with other members of the staff. In 1873, "dissensions arose, and Dowell, being regarded as the Jonah, was petitioned to resign, which failing, the faculty members resigned in a body, leaving the professor of surgery alone in his glory."[8] He was the chairman of all the departments until Soule University moved to Louisiana and its medical department was closed.

Dr. Dowell was one of a group of Galveston doctors who foresaw the termination of the medical school; therefore, in order to continue medical education in Texas, they organized a corporation and received a charter from the state of Texas on March 29, 1873, to form the Texas Medical College and Hospital. The charter stipulated that a board of trustees should be appointed, and Dr. Dowell was named to this board. The trustees appointed a Board of Examiners to give oral and written examinations on a competitive basis for professorships in the new school. They advertised in three daily newspapers for sixty days seeking the best qualified applicants to take these examinations for the various professorships.

Seven professors were chosen, some of them members of the previous faculty. "Dr. Ashbel Smith, examiner of surgery, stated that in all fairness, Dr. Dowell had won the professorship of surgery and that he would hold that position even though the faculty of the earlier school had resigned in protest to his autocratic rule."[9] This position he held until his death on June 9, 1881, at the age of fifty-nine years, in the same year that the Texas Medical College was closed to make way for the establishment of the Medical Branch of the University of Texas authorized by the State of Texas.

Dr. Dowell was married in June 1849 to Sarah Zelina White, the daughter of John H. White of Como, Mississippi. She was also the "half-sister of George W. Littlefield of Austin, regent and benefactor of The University of Texas."[10] They had two sons and one daughter. After the death of his first wife he married Mrs. Laura Baker Hutchison of Galveston in 1868. "On the night of the wedding the boys resolved to give them a charivari, but the doctor considered the mock serenade an insult. He grabbed a club and rushed out to disperse the crowd and in the melee sustained a severe fracture of the right arm." The disability was of considerable embarrassment to him on his wedding night.

The six-foot tall doctor has been described as an autocratic intense man, and he had very strong opinions as to the care and treatment of his patients.

> No nurse should be put in charge of a case that will not follow the directions of the doctor or doctors in attendance. This is a great curse in this city, many taking upon themselves to change their medicines as well as openly violate the doctor's instructions; *such should always be discharged----the doctor or the nurse should be discharged at once.*
>
> I have never in all my life had so much trouble in getting my directions carried out. Many of my prescriptions were thrown away by the nurses; one of them was smart enough to say, when a doctor came in, she always left. Where my directions were followed fully, I scarcely lost a case . . . .
>
> I was several times refused permission to see my patients by a lady nurse, because I gave calomel and water. May God forgive her, for she knew not what she was doing.[11]

Dr. Dowell's first important contribution to surgical literature was recorded in the *Medical Record* published in August 1866. In this article he gave a detailed report on the application of subcutaneous silver-wire sutures with a curved, three-inch needle with the eye in its center, of his own design, in which he closed the fascial defect of the inguinal region in these hernias. During his lifetime Dr. Dowell published some twenty-three scientific articles and treatises, a prodigious number for a physician of his time.

The two most important and those which include the major portion of his contributions are separate treatises on hernia and yellow fever. The treatise on hernia, published in book form in 1876, is entitled *"Treatise on Hernia: a New Process for its Radical Cure and Original Contribution to Operative Surgery, and New Surgical Instruments* by Greensville Dowell, M.D., Professor of Surgery in Texas Medical College, Late Professor of Surgery in Galveston Medical College, Formerly Professor of Anatomy in Galveston Medical College, Surgeon to the Medical College Hospital, Member of the American Medical Association, Member of the Texas Medical Association, Member of the Galveston Medical Society, Honorary Member of the Boston Gynecological Society, Etc., Etc., Etc."[12] This was published in Philadelphia by the D.G. Brinton Company and registered by the Surgeon General's office library with the number 80055.

In this exhaustive work, a student of the history of hernia repair is given a wealth of information of all that was known about the subject up to and including Dr. Dowell's time. In it he discusses the classification, signs, symptoms, embryology, etiology, anatomy, epidemiology, morbidity, mortality, and finally the method of radical cure of this malady which during his time was responsible for 1 percent of all the male deaths throughout the United States.

Conservative by nature he operated only when all conservative measures at his disposal were exhausted. The treatise included fourteen engravings of various trusses designed to contain many types of hernia with an explanation of their application. Concerning the use of a truss he wrote, "Before applying any truss the part over which the pad fits should be well bathed with alum and whisky, cologne, water, sugar of lead water, bay rum, or solution of tannin, to prevent chafing and tenderness . . ." And finally he gives a detailed description of his method of radical cure of hernia with the use of the subcutaneous silver-wire sutures to obliterate the fascial defect in such cases. A detailed description of Dr. Dowell's method is as follows.

> The only instruments used in the author's method are a double spear-pointed, semicircular needle, with an eye in each point, silver wire, a piece of cork, soft

TREATISE ON HERNIA:

WITH

A NEW PROCESS FOR ITS RADICAL CURE,

AND

ORIGINAL CONTRIBUTIONS TO OPERATIVE SURGERY,

AND

NEW SURGICAL INSTRUMENTS.

BY GREENSVILLE DOWELL, M.D.,

PROFESSOR OF SURGERY IN TEXAS MEDICAL COLLEGE; LATE PROFESSOR OF SURGERY IN GALVESTON MEDICAL COLLEGE; FORMERLY PROFESSOR OF ANATOMY IN GALVESTON MEDICAL COLLEGE; SURGEON TO THE MEDICAL COLLEGE HOSPITAL; MEMBER OF AMERICAN MEDICAL ASSOCIATION; MEMBER OF TEXAS STATE MEDICAL ASSOCIATION; MEMBER OF GALVESTON MEDICAL SOCIETY; HONORARY MEMBER OF BOSTON GYNÆCOLOGICAL SOCIETY, ETC., ETC.; ETC.

PHILADELPHIA:
D. G. BRINTON, 115 SOUTH SEVENTH STREET.
1876.

Title page of Dowell's *Treatise on Hernia.*

Illustration showing different hernias and Dr. Dowell's method of crushing the spur of double barrel ileostomy with a special clamp of his design.

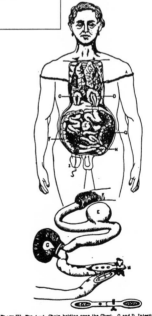

PLATE III—FIG. 1.—A. Chain holding open the Chest. C. and D. Intestine in Diaphragmatic Hernia. E. Appendiformial Hernia. F. Intussusception. G. Intestinal Hernia. H. Artificial Anus. I. Cæcum.

wood, or a roll of adhesive plaster. The operation is performed by the following method: the parts being well shaven, if in the inguinal region, or in any site where there are hairs, three lines are then drawn, with a small brush and tincture of iodine, parallel to the direction of the hernial orifice, centre line immediately over the internal orifice, and passing down to the external orifice, if the hernia be oblique-inguinal; in other varieties immediately over the greatest enlargement of the tumor. The needle is then taken hold of by the left hand at its unthreaded end, then the right hand, with the thumb and forefinger, pulls up the skin and superficial fascia as high as it can be done, to the right of the middle line, letting the middle line be just below the point of the thumb. The threaded end is then pushed through the fold held below the point of the thumb and index finger. The fold is then let loose, and the threaded end taken by its point with the thumb and fingers of the right hand; it is then pulled on until the unthreaded end comes just under the outside line of right side of operator and left side of patient. The index finger of the left hand is made to invaginate the integuments as far as possible, and the finger pushed to the right, under the left tendon of patient, feeling well the wall. The right hand then raises the needle so as to have its point directly over the point of the finger and a little to the outside of it. The needle is then pushed directly down through the tendon into the peritoneal cavity; at this stage the point of the index finger of the left hand is raised to the right side of the patient and held under the tendons; the needle is then moved about, to see if it be loose, and turned in its curve, so as to carry the curved portion of its point under the invaginated integuments, etc., to about one-quarter of an inch of the right tendon; the end is then brought out on the outside line of the patient's right side; this is done by pressing down on the threaded end held by the surgeon's right hand. The index finger of the left hand is then taken out and the threaded end let go, and the unthreaded

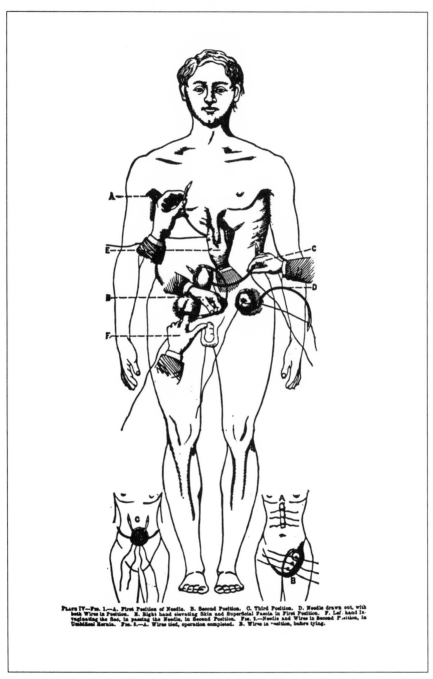

PLATE IV—FIG. 1.—A. First Position of Needle. B. Second Position. C. Third Position. D. Needle drawn out, with both Wires in Position. E. Right hand elevating Skin and Superficial Fascia in First Position. F. Left hand Invaginating the Sac, in passing the Needle, in Second Position. FIG. 2.—Needle and Wires in Second Position, in Umbilical Hernia. FIG. 3.—A. Wires tied, operation completed. B. Wires in position, before tying.

Illustration showing Dr. Dowell's method of hernia repair.

end is then held by the thumb and index finger of the right hand. It is now gently pulled on until the threaded end comes above the tendon. The point threaded is then reversed, and keeping well down on the tendon is finally pushed out at the first puncture and pulled entirely out, leaving the two ends of the ligature close together in the same puncture. We have thus put a ligature entirely around the two sides of the rupture, with a sufficient portion of the tendon and muscle to give the thread sufficient surface to act on. And now, by pulling on the two ends, the rupture is closed internally, by the *replacing of its natural support,* and then the ends are tied around a roll of adhesive plaster, a piece of cork or soft wood. If one ligature does not close the opening so you cannot push the joint of your finger under the wire, another wire is put in in the same way; before tying the first, you may, and must, put in enough to completely close the rupture, and they should not be more than a quarter or half an inch apart. The operation can be performed from either side, but it is best, in inguinal hernias, to start the needle from the side opposite to the ilio-pubic ligament. This enables you to push down the needle by the side of the ligament, but if you start on the side in the second position of the needle, you may go under the ilio-pubic ligament.

An interesting case report was recorded in his treatise as follows.

Before I got any case to operate on with my needle, or an opportunity to insert the cuts in my journal (*Galveston Medical Journal*), my office was burned, and my needles and electrotypes were lost. But I had prepared an article on hernia for my journal, and published it in the November and December numbers of 1866, from which I have taken most of the above report, and which may be consulted for further particulars. I sent again to New York for my needle. . .

Another interesting case report is recorded as follows,

John Foster, aged about thirty-two, German sailor, was admitted into the Galveston Medical College Hospital, then under my charge, for a wound of the scalp, resulting in traumatic erysipelas. He recovered from this, and finding him suffering from a very large scrotal hernia of the right side, we proposed to cure him, and explaining the nature of the operation to him, he consented. He had been operated on in Calcutta, by what I supposed was either Gerdy's or Wurtzer's method; and he said it had done him a great deal of good, as before that it came half down his thighs, and could not be kept up with a truss. The hernia was as large or larger than the two fists together. He was not well prepared, being dissipated, and was drunk when first brought into the hospital. But being anxious to be operated on, and impatient to leave the hospital, we operated on him February 18, 1872. The bowels being moved in the morning, chloroform being given Profs. Rankin, Goodwin, and the medical class of 1871 and 1872, were present—four ligatures were put in and tied over a soft piece of wood wrapped with a roller bandage. Patient vomited much from the chloroform, and had hiccough in the first twenty-four hours. We moved his bowels with castor oil, to see if there was any intestinal obstruction; the bowels were freely moved, but the hiccough and vomiting continued; pain around the umbilicus, with tenderness over the stomach, but little in the line of the ligatures. The hernial sac became distended to its full size and form, hot and tense, some heat of skin, and pulse one-hundred and twenty. Blister over stomach, and morphine continued, with solutions of lead and laudanum. Scrotum very tense on the fifth and sixth days, oedematous, and crackling with gas. Exploring needle used on the sixth day; serum and blood came out. The part was freely lanced, and the bowels moved on the seventh day, and the ligatures taken out after the action on the bowels. The line of the ligatures perfectly tight; no fluid could pass into the peritoneum. Fever continued; testicles and scrotum poulticed, and morphine internally; continued to vomit what he drank, but no stercoraceous matter. Would get up in the night and empty his own chamber mug; pain and swelling in sac continued to increase, and finally, there being perceptible fluctuation, an abscess was lanced, which discharged about half a pint of sanious pus, but with no fecal odor. The poultices were continued, and another abscess was finally lanced, discharging a large amount of pus, as before. After this he continued to improve rapidly, his vomiting ceased, and his appetite returned. He got drunk twice and fell eight feet down a ladder, without the hernia returning.

Dr. Dowell noted the following points that should be given attention in performing this operation.

A.The bowels should always be moved three hours before the operation.

B.The body should always be in a horizontal position, with the hips above the head, and legs slightly flexed on the thighs.

C. Hernia should be carefully reduced.

D. Patient should be thoroughly anaesthetized with ether or chloroform; I prefer chloroform.

E. Needle should be started from the ventral or median side, in all cases of inguinal hernia. Wires should be pulled in with waxed thread, as in vesicovaginal fistula.

F.Wires should not be left in longer than the eighth day, and a support used afterward, either by truss or bandage, and patient kept in bed ten days, at least, after the wires are taken out, and not allowed to get up without an abdominal support. One patient, Thomas Nelson, 16 years of age, remained in bed only one night, and on the eighth day, before the wires were taken out, was at the railroad depot, walking around as if nothing happened. Children never complain, and all have been cured.

G.From a quarter to half an inch of the sides of
the orifice should always be included in the wire.

H.Bowels should always be moved before the
wires are taken out, with enemas of water and soap
(soapsuds), or water and castor oil.

In Dr. Dowell's closing remarks concerning his method of
radical cure of hernias he stated that he believed "there will never
be a better method invented than the author's; but of this we are
not sure, as we have seen, in our day, so many improvements
made on what was once thought perfect."

He was well informed on all surgical literature both here and
abroad and from which he quoted frequently giving proper
credit to all new innovations. He believed, "To advance in any
science, one should be familiar with all that others have done
and attempted to do. Failures are as valuable as successes and
anything that carries plausibility should be noted." He also
discusses other methods of radical cure of hernia, including
excision of the sac, ligation of the sac, exposing the sac and
applying irritant, excision of sac and scrotum (this method only
mentioned to be discarded as barbaric).

STATISTICAL RESULTS.

OPERATORS.	NO. OF CASES.	CURES.	FAILURES.
Dowell........................	68	60	8
Wilkerson.........	12	7	5
Bacon........................	1	1	
Trueheart....................	9	6	3
Powell	2	2	
Rankin......................	1	1	
Worthington..............	1	1	
Neeson......	1	1	
Worthington & Bibb.....	1	1	
Totals......	96	80	16

Statistical results of Dowell's hernia repair. These data were used in his
report to the American Medical Association 1876.

He also mentioned Belmas method in which the sac was exposed and the neck covered with goldbeaters skin. Various methods of plugging and invagination were described only to be discarded because of the high incidence of failure. His modification of Wurtzer's method in which a specially designed clamp was used to hold the reduced hernial contents in place while subcutaneous sutures were applied was described. He stated he had only used this procedure on cadavers. He further described a method of sac ligature, scarification of the sac neck, acupuncture and injection of the sac with iodine with the admonition that peritonitis would ensue in the event the iodine escaped into the abdominal cavity.

Dr. Gross's method ("Principles and Practices of Surgery, 1872"), which consisted of cutting down on the parts, freshening the edges of descent, and approximation were condemned because of the high incidence of recurrence. He credited Dr. Wood of Cincinnati with a method of subcutaneous suture with braid, of the fascial defect in the inguinal region, a method not unlike his own. He then commented that some oblique hernias could be cured with a truss, but the direct hernias could never be successfully treated in this manner.

Irreducible and strangulated hernias were of particular concern to Dr. Dowell, and he discussed at length its conservative and radical treatment but said, "delay is dangerous and the surgeon who does not act promptly is responsible for the patient's life." He described both internal and external methods of cutting the strictured area without opening the sac. On irreducible hernias, he wrote,

> Use gentle, steady taxis; if unsuccessful, etherize (the patient) and repeat taxis and warm water enema. Chloroform a second time (and) if this fails, resort to surgery without letting (the patient) come out from the influence of chloroform, performing the herniotomy with a longitudinal incision along the course of the hernia. . . .open sac and examine contents, if ruptured, gangerous bowel encountered, remove the dead bowel and make an artificial anus, suturing the normal bowel to the skin. Then cut the stricture, and if the bowel is viable, return it to the abdominal cavity,

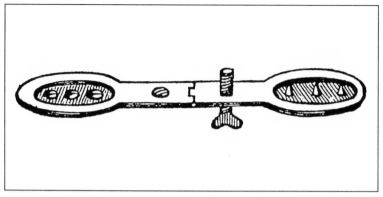

Drawing of a clamp used by Dr. Dowell to crush spur of double barrel
ileostomy.

if the bowel viability is doubtful leave it outside, dress
the wound and reassess in three or four days to determine if it can be put back in.

Concerning irreducible umbilical hernias he wrote, "This I
cannot believe as I have never seen a case in either hospital or
private practice, and I am now old enough to be an authority on
such a subject."

He described a method of treatment of the incarcerated
diaphragmatic hernia in which the strictured area was incised
transabdominally, the hernial contents examined and resected if
gangrenous with an end-to-end anastomosis; there is not, however, any recorded evidence that he ever performed this procedure. He described a new instrument of his invention for crushing the septum of an artificial anus by crushing the spur of the
double-barreled ileostomy. He concluded the treatise on hernia
by giving his total experience including a table of all cases
operated on and their results up to the date, September 12,
1876.[13]

In the same year he presented a paper to the American
Medical Association on the radical cure of hernia and listing
ninety-six operations and eighty cures.[14]

Although practicing in Galveston throughout the Civil War,
he most surely had friends or relatives who were killed or
wounded in this holocaust, but he only mentioned his difficulty
in communication with, and securing instruments from his

colleagues in the occupied South.

In 1860 he was in correspondence with a Dr. Middleton of Charleston, S.C., concerning the experiences the two of them were having with the radical cure of hernia. Shortly thereafter he wrote, "The Civil War came on and Dr. Middleton's manuscripts were burned up. The blockade was established and I could not get any more instruments made, and we did not have another instrument maker in the South; so I did nothing until 1866."[15]

Even as today, skullduggery among surgeons was occasionally seen in the early days of Texas surgery. A certain Dr. C.H. Wilkerson who was a student, resident and preceptor, was named many times in his treatise as the assisting doctor in his operative procedures. In 1872, after Dr. Wilkerson had established himself in private practice in Galveston, Dr. Dowell wrote,

> Dr. C.H. Wilkerson operated on a French boy about twelve years old assisted by Dr. Calloway and myself. I directed him how to hold the needle and every step of the operation, he using my needles loaned him for the purpose. Dr. Wilkerson published this case in the *Galveston Medical Journal* (my own journal) without mentioning my direction. He, using my needle, and carried out my entire method as though it were an original operation of his own only claiming I gave the chloroform, claiming all the credit for himself. This was put in while I was absent from the city which made it much worse, showing so little gratitude, and complacency to his former preceptor. I thus speak of the case, as it was republished in several journals and no mention made of its being my process and method, Dr. C.H. Wilkerson claiming all the credit himself. It is due him, to say that his apology was that it was universally known to be my operation that he did not think of it; but before I submitted the manuscript to the printers, I put in a note stating that it was my process and method that was used. He or the printer took this out but the printer denied it. Ingratitude has no bounds and if I cannot rely on my own (pupils) to establish my precedence in this operation, who can I rely on?[16]

But each sinner has his day of retribution as Dr. Dowell wrote later, "Dr. Wilkerson told me that the hernia in his patient had returned from his lifting and hauling sand,"[17] about the first of April 1872.

The first portion of the second section of his treatise on hernia entitled "Original Contributions to Operative Surgery"[18] deals with the problem of urinary calculi. He believed the cause to be the ingestion of limestone water, some form of dyspepsia or de-arrangement in the organs of assimilation. He described the operations for removal of bladder stones pointing out the advantages and disadvantages of each, he himself preferring the lateral operation through the perineum in which the membromous urethra and prostate were incised to gain access to the bladder cavity. He described in detail his technique using a variety of lithotomy knives, some of his own design. He noted that the mortality of his own experience was one percent and the causes of death from this procedure were "shock, chloroform intoxication, hemorrhage, cellulitis, peritonitis, cystitis, prostatitis, pyleitis, urinary extravasation." He noted that urinary calculi was a rare occurrence in Texas owing in part, no doubt, to the general use of cistern water. He complained that suitable instruments could not be obtained as it was during the war when the blockade was in effect. He described one case of an obstructing urethral stone removed by the use of a hair pin. He next considered the problem of urethral stricture, listing the causes as inflammation caused by cantharides, turpentine, gin, etc., the passage of calculi, injury from bougies, bruises, contusions, and specifics such as gonorrhea, syphilis, and gleet. Conservative treatment consisted of urethral dilatation and when this was unsuccessful he resorted to internal urethrotomy and in extreme cases, external urethrotomy. He described in detail his technique and instruments used to perform these procedures. Success in the treatment of these difficult urethral strictures was attributed to his use of a self-retaining urethral catheter of his own design. Of this he said, "After all cases of urethrotomy, internal or external, I use my new retention catheter, keeping it in place until the patient develops free flow of urine. With my present experience I would consider myself criminal if I did not use the catheter in all cases."

"My success in treating strictures requiring external and internal incision is greater than any statistics published and I

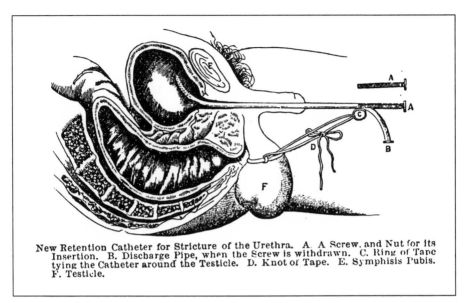

New Retention Catheter for Stricture of the Urethra. A. A Screw, and Nut for its Insertion. B. Discharge Pipe, when the Screw is withdrawn. C. Ring of Tape tying the Catheter around the Testicle. D. Knot of Tape. E. Symphisis Pubis. F. Testicle.

Dowell felt that this self retaining catheter anchored to the scrotum was the most important feature of his method of treatment of urethral stricture.

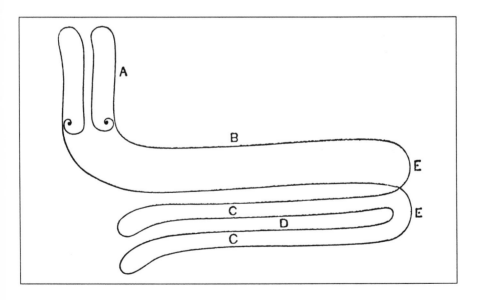

Improved wire speculum for vagina and anus.

attribute it alone to the use of the catheter, and the mode of its retention."[19] The advantage of this mode of retention of his urethral catheter was not only cleanliness of the patient and minimal urethral irritation, but that its mobility prevented puncture of the bladder and did not produce pain in the event of an erection.

On the treatment of urethral stricture he quoted frequently from the works of contemporary surgeons; Dr. Gouley, Sir Henry Thompson, Professor Van Buren, Dr. Markoe and Professor S.D. Gross. His indications and techniques for both internal and external urethrotomy he discusses together with a careful description of post-operative care and his long-time results. After describing the difficulty he had in treating a long standing fistula-in-ano which later proved to be a carcinoma he wrote,

> I was anxious to get full view of the ulcer and one day returning to my office I saw a piece of No. 6 wire, and it at once struck me, that I could bend this wire as to accomplish my object. I did bend it in nearly the shape as shown in the illustration. This gave me a full view of the entire ulcer and I diagnosed it colloid cancer, and putting my patient under chloroform, I applied to the entire surface (with sponge mop) an eschartic.
>
> Having had such good success with this speculum in the anus, we had two sizes larger made for the vagina, which we find, for ordinary use, better than any speculum we have ever used. In a few cases, we have found the vaginal walls disposed to fall between the tines of wire, but this has been remedied by wrapping it with thread or gum elastic cord, or by double bending the wire.

He lists the advantages of the speculum, not the least important of which is that

> it costs two dollars, and can be had for even less, while Sims' costs seven, Bozeman's twelve, Knott's eighteen, Bivalve, German silver, five.
>
> Messrs. George Tiermann & Co., 67 Chatham Street, New York, made these improved instruments

of three sizes. Two for the vagina and one for the rectum. All of my instruments can be had of this firm.[20]

In the treatment of varicose veins he employed subcutaneous ligation with a special four-inch cutting needle with an eye on each end. "I apply this method to cure varicocele and I always ligate in varicose ulcers before attempting any other treatment. . . . It is next to impossible to cure an old (varicose) ulcer without rest and I have been unable to cure varicose ulcers without ligating the veins or putting on elastic stockings."[21]

In this treatise he also gave a lengthy dissertation on diagnosis and treatment of dislocations of the joints of the upper extremity.

> In studying arrow wounds, I found there was not in any surgery I could find a good and efficient arrow extractor. Surgeon Bill's was believed to be the best, but it was to my eyes impracticable and unscientific. So, with a few hours of thought I produced one. It is from six to eight inches long, or a little longer than an ordinary bullet forceps, and the blades are made flat and cross each other, so as to be only of the same width of the full opening of its claws.
>
> This, though lately brought out, will prove a valuable instrument to the United States Surgeon, especially at this time, as it is a very difficult operation to remove arrow heads, frequently requiring a deep incision. One-third of the inhabitants of the globe use arrows, and every surgeon on our western prairies should have one of these instruments in his case.

The last few pages of the "Treatise on Hernia" is devoted to the case histories of two difficult but successful surgical procedures which his vanity and pride compelled him to report although they had no bearing on the remainder of this treatise. The first report described the removal of a huge tumor of the lower jaw which required excision of the middle one-half of the mandible during which an estimated three pints of blood was lost.

The second report described the removal of a three and

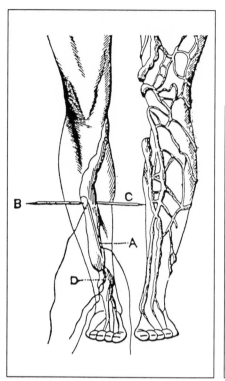

Jacob Yancy, Osteo-fibroid Tumor, removed
12th of April, 1876.

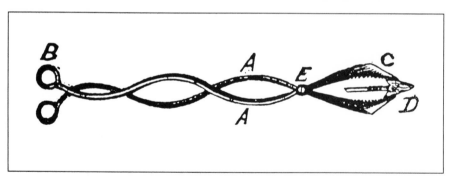

Top left: Dr. Dowell's method of subcutaneous ligation of varicose veins.
Top right: This tumor, "as large as a child's head," was successfully
removed by Dr. Dowell.
Bottom: Arrow extractor.

one-half pound fibroid tumor from the thigh with an estimated blood loss of only three ounces. Both patients recovered completely in three weeks despite suppuration of both wounds. Dr. Dowell commented, "These two cases had been examined by several surgeons who pronounced them incapable of removal, assuming that if it was attempted, immediate death from hemorrhage would likely be the result."[22]

In January 1863, while practicing in Brazoria county, Texas, he published in the *American Journal of Medical Science* an article entitled "On Trismus Nascientum"[23] which from the description of signs and symptoms of the disease must surely have been what we know today as tetani neotorum. He listed the following causes of the disease.

> 1.Improper management of the umbilical cord causing congestion in the umbilical vein which in turn spreads to the liver.
> 2.Displacement of the occipital bone in parturition.
> 3.Retention of the meconium and want of proper cleansing of the skin when the child is first dressed, and
> 4.Lastly, it may be caused by any disease that will produce tetanus in old persons.

In 1879 he reported in the *Virginia Medical Monthly* a new method of operating on hemorrhoids utilizing his curved cutting needle with an eye at the point to ligate them and excise the hemorrhoidal masses. He noted that two patients on whom he performed this procedure subsequently developed cataracts and suggested that cataracts might be a complication of hemorrhoid surgery.[24]

His lengthy and comprehensive treatise on yellow fever was published in 1876[25] and its description is best given by Dr. Dowell himself in his preface and introduction. The character of the man is vividly appreciated in these words.

> This work was undertaken, with the sole object of furnishing to the profession a rational and more definite mode of diagnosis of yellow fever, from the other diseases treated of in it, and to give, as the author

YELLOW FEVER

AND

MALARIAL DISEASES

EMBRACING A HISTORY

OF THE

EPIDEMICS OF YELLOW FEVER IN TEXAS;

NEW VIEWS ON ITS DIAGNOSIS, TREATMENT, PROPAGATION AND CONTROL;

DESCRIPTIONS OF

DENGUE, MALARIAL FEVERS, JAUNDICE, THE SPLEEN AND ITS DISEASES, AND
DIARRHŒA HEMORRHAGICA; WITH PRACTICAL REMARKS ON
THEIR SUCCESSFUL TREATMENT, ETC.

BY GREENSVILLE DOWELL, M.D.,

PROFESSOR OF SURGERY IN TEXAS MEDICAL COLLEGE; LATE PROFESSOR OF SURGERY IN GAL-
VESTON MEDICAL COLLEGE; FORMERLY PROFESSOR OF ANATOMY IN GALVESTON MEDICAL
COLLEGE; SURGEON TO THE MEDICAL COLLEGE HOSPITAL; MEMBER OF AMERICAN
MEDICAL ASSOCIATION; MEMBER OF TEXAS STATE MEDICAL ASSOCIATION;
MEMBER OF GALVESTON MEDICAL SOCIETY; HONORARY MEMBER
OF BOSTON GYNÆCOLOGICAL SOCIETY, ETC., ETC.

PHILADELPHIA:
MEDICAL PUBLICATION OFFICE, 115 SOUTH SEVENTH STREET.
1876.

Title page from Dowell's *Treatise on Yellow Fever.*

believes, a more successful plan of treating that disease.
Much that had been prepared for the illustration of the
subject of yellow fever has been crowded out by the
insertion of matter relating to other diseases, which
the author thought would make the main subject
plainer, and the book more valuable to the general and
professional reader. It is also designed to assist boards
of health and health officers, in diagnosing infectious
diseases from those that are not infectious, and to be
to the practitioner a guide in the critical point of
diagnosis; and especially to warn nurses from assuming too much authority, by telling them what they
should do and what they should not do. To the patient
it points out the danger of violating the doctor's
instructions. The author assumes that yellow fever can
be treated successfully, and that the great fear of the
disease will be removed by following implicitly the
doctor's directions. He warns persons exposed to the
disease against all false hopes from the use of supposed
prophylactics, and relying on quarantines, instead of
putting their houses in order to ward off or mitigate
the effects of the disease.

To the critics, we have to say: We have tried to be
as accurate as possible, and to relate facts as they are,
however conflicting they may be. Many points in
reference to yellow fever are still unsettled, and the
author has given the why and wherefore of his belief
on every point. When discussing one of these questions on a special occasion, his confreres wished a
resolution introduced to ascertain on which side the
gentleman was (meaning the author). The prompt
reply was 'on the side of truth.' I never resort to special
pleading to prove a theory. I relate facts, regardless of
all theory. The seeming want of system must be ex-
cused, on the grounds of many of the articles having
been published before, and to have changed them
would have militated against their truthfulness. There
are some discrepancies in dates and numbers, which
occurred by oversight, as the reports were made at
different periods of the epidemics, and by different

authors, one giving his opinion and dates, and another
a different one; but the table of places, elevation, and
mortality, will correct most of these.

Where I have differed from my friends, I have
done it alone in the interest of humanity and science,
and in no spirit of criticism.

In his introduction he states,

In compiling this little work, I have had in view the
false impressions I had obtained from our textbooks
and the compilations now in publications, which I
propose to correct from my personal experience,
which is now equal if not superior to anyone living in
the United States, as I have treated over two thousand
cases in hospitals and private practice; and I will refer
only to those publications which have corresponded
with my experience, to wit: the writings in the *New
Orleans Medical Journal*, by Morton Dowler and others, upon its symptoms and treatment; the post-mortems made by Bennet Dowler in the Charity Hospital,
Louisiana; Dr. Hertado, of Spain, in Spanish, published in 1822 (the latter, I believe, is the best history, and
most correct one on diagnosis I have read up to this
day, and corresponds exactly with my own experience); Report of Surgeon General Blair, of the West
Indies, during the great epidemic of 1851, '52, '53, and
'54, made to the British Admiralty, giving a number
of cases treated in the British Navy; number of deaths,
and observations on the urine; the pulse, and many
post-mortems; showing *that there are no permanent or
universal pathological lesions* in yellow fever, and
which Bennet Dowler has proved to be true in his
investigations. I also wish to correct the error that the
adjective yellow attached to its name has produced,
making many believe that all patients turn yellow
before and after death, which is not true, as not more
than one in six becomes yellow; and of those who die
of black vomit, not more than one in three turns
yellow before or after death. I think the Latin names

febris typhus icterodes and febris cum nigro vometo, much better, as more die of black vomit than any other condition. I also wish to show that the yellowness of the skin is not due to bile, but to the haematin of the blood exuded through the capillaries and into intercellular spaces, having more the appearance of yellowness from a contused wound, turning (as such wounds usually do when fatal or about to slough) livid, and even blue-black. When the contusion ends in resolution or when yellow fever ends in convalescence, the yellowness gets brighter, until the skin gets perfectly clear. I wish to show that dengue is much like a mild case of yellow fever, but the fever lasts longer, and is much higher than yellow fever; but it never kills, treat it as you will; while yellow fever is very fatal, treat as you may. Both are epidemics in the Southern States, but the range of dengue seems to be more limited than yellow fever. They do sometimes occur together, but are distinct diseases, and do not have the relation one to the other that intermittents have to remittents, as one never runs into the other. Both are fevers sui generis. Neither occurs outside of settled districts; never found in our worst malarial districts that are sparsely settled, and never occur where intermittents and remittents are most common. Cold below freezing stops both, while intermittents continue indefinitely. No one ever has a second attack of either, so far as my observation goes, and I have had an opportunity to see as much of these diseases as anyone I know; besides, I have lived thirty years in the Mississippi and Brazos bottoms, practicing in Panola county, Mississippi; Memphis, Tennessee; and Columbia, Brazoria county, Texas; and ten years in public and private hospitals, where all these diseases were common. Hence, I feel confident in speaking and writing as I do. No one is competent to write on yellow fever who has not seen several epidemics and at least, several hundred cases. The disease is so protean in its types, and changes so with epidemical influences, that it is congestive one year, asthenic and inflammatory in another, requiring different treatment; and different determinations are to be met, as one year the stomach will be most affected, in another the brain, and another the kidneys. But every epidemic having more or less of these peculiar types requires care and skill in the physician to meet them. Hence, no routine practice can be followed with uniform success, and every case must be treated according to its symptoms and the tendencies of its determination, and to meet these I have reported so many cases, with symptoms and special treatment of each case, giving prescriptions and results.

I have thought best to give an outline of what I wish to establish, before bringing forward the proof; hence, I have given, in a few pages, what I consider now established, in its history, pathology, and treatment, and then I have given my proofs. The book will be of interest to the non-professional as well as professional readers. The chromos will gave a good idea of the color of the skin, in the worst cases as well as the mildest; but the color of the skin is like the pathological lesions, no two exactly alike. The subject of quarantine I have treated fully, believing that much can be done sanitary measures on shipboard and on land; but exclusion by quarantine I consider impossible.

Also included in this treatise is a detailed chart of yellow fever in the United States giving the elevations above sea level of localities where yellow fever had appeared since 1668.[25] For the preparation of this chart and other studies he was cited as being one of the "most acute medical geographers and meteorologists of early Texas," by S.W. Geiser in his article on "Men of Science in Texas from 1820 to 1880."[26]

Some historians[27] have given him credit for suggesting that the mosquito was the offending vector in the transmission of yellow fever. Actually, Dr. Carlos Finley made the prediction some five years later in 1881. Dr. Dowell's implication of the mosquito was very tenuous as illustrated in the following paragraph.

Hence there must be some cause, specific and sui generis, that produces it. This cause I have assumed is animalcular or fungotic (microscopic), and partakes of the nature of the grasshopper of Egypt and the western prairies, or the smut in cereals; but these are too small to be observed with any instruments we now have, and have so far eluded demonstration; but if we compare the effects of cold and heat on gnats and mosquitoes, it will not be difficult to believe it is of the same nature, as it is controlled by the same natural laws. That it is animalcular and not vegetable is also demonstrated by its occurring in towns and cities, where there is much dead animal matter, and not in the country, where vegetable matter is abundant.[28]

Yellow fever was a most dreaded disease in the early history of the United States. In the city of Galveston alone, there were twelve epidemics between the years of 1839 to 1873 during which over four thousand people died from the disease. The worst epidemic in 1866 claimed the lives of 1,150 victims. He volunteered and gave freely of his services to several communities stricken with yellow fever and received a gold medal from the citizens of Vicksburg, Mississippi during their epidemic of 1878. Dr. W.L. Coleman of Calvert, Texas, wrote of his invaluable aid during the epidemic of 1873.

By the following Sunday, October 19, we were in deplorable condition. I had relapsed badly. Dr. Field was dead and Dr. Gilson dying. There were over a hundred sick with the fever; and they were dying six or eight a day. On Monday a delegation of physicians from Houston and Galveston arrived with nurses, rolled up their sleeves and went to work in earnest. I fell into the hands of that old veteran yellow fever physician, Greensville Dowell, of Galveston, and thanks to a kind Providence and skill, I and my children, six cases in all, recovered without the loss of one. I shall ever hold him in grateful remembrance of his untiring attentions, and for the words of cheer which were ever ready to fall from his lips. May Heaven bless him in his declining years.[29]

VOL. 111. OCTOBER, NOVEMBER & DECEMBER. NOS. 10, 11, 12.

THE

GALVESTON

MEDICAL JOURNAL;

A MONTHLY RECORD OF MEDICAL SCIENCE.

FIVE DOLLARS PER ANNUM

Greensville Dowell, M. D., Editor.

PROFESSOR OF SURGERY IN GALVESTON MEDICAL COLLEGE.

GALVESTON:

OFFICE MEDICAL JOURNAL

1868.

Title page from the *Galveston Medical Journal.*

Galveston Medical College advertisement in the *Galveston Medical Journal.*

For five years from 1866 to 1871 Dr. Dowell established, wrote for, edited, and published the monthly *Galveston Medical Journal*, the first medical periodical of Texas. The price was $5 per year. This journal, widely circulated in the state, contributed greatly to the dissemination of medical knowledge.

A somewhat more mellowed and human nature of Dr. Dowell can be gleaned from his welcoming address to members of the Texas Medical Association when they met in Galveston in 1877. This address could have served as a model for any chamber of commerce for years to come. In it he said,

Mr. President and Gentlemen of the State Medical Association: It becomes my pleasing duty to welcome you to Galveston, and in the name of the medical profession and citizens of this city, we welcome you back; and hope that your stay may be pleasant and profitable to you; we have prepared a programme so you may divide your time between business and pleasure. As Galvestonians, we are proud of our city, which is now in its forty-first year, and has 40,000 (estimated) inhabitants. It is situated on a beautiful island, between gulf and bay; and from the top of our new Tremont Hotel you can see all over our city, and view ships sailing many miles out at sea. We have a beach of thirty miles, that, on the wettest, dryest, or windiest day can be ridden or driven over without mud or dust. We have three railroads running out of the city to all parts of the United States, and ships sailing to all parts of the world. We have wealthy and enterprising merchants and bankers; many very able and distinguished lawyers; wise and prudent physicians; able and devout ministers; large and beautiful churches, and what is better, large and intelligent congregations. Of newspapers, I believe we have three or four—the best in the state, if not equal to any in the United States. The health of our city is equal to any in the world, and still improving. Twelve years ago we had thirty-six physicians and 13,000 inhabitants; now we have not so many physicians, and 40,000 inhabitants, and it is our daily remark we have not so much to do as then. Our city has been drained and low places filled up, and the city kept so clean we have had no epidemic of yellow fever for ten years, and when it has prevailed in our country towns, the citizens have fled here for protection. We have no chills or fevers, as in many other parts of the South, and no endemic disease on our island. I have thus hastily spoken of what we are, but let us see what we will be. It is no stretch of the imagination to say the state of Texas will hold and support 40,000,000 people and not be as thickly inhabited as France or Belgium. That Galveston will be as large as New York is now, and railroads will carry coffee and sugar from here to Alaska by our projected railroads, almost on a straight line, and bring gold and silver from those distant regions. We will have others going to the City of Mexico and the Pacific Ocean. We certainly have a bright future before us.

What shall we say to you as physicians? It was with little pride we heard, at the various associations we attended last summer, our State eulogized for her efforts to establish a State Board of Health; a law regulating the practice of medicine, and the establishing of a Medical College where the professors are elected by competitive system; asylums for the insane, the blind and deaf; for these we are equal with the oldest of the States, yet we need schools for feeble-minded children, asylums for the care and cure of inebriates, which will depend on the Association to assist in organizing and putting into operation.

To consume no more time, we hope we may have a harmonious session, and be the means of doing much towards the advancing of our noble and honorable profession. We again bid you welcome.[30]

Throughout the later years of his life, Dr. Dowell suffered from recurrent bouts of biliary colic complicated with jaundice. These experiences he vividly records in his treatise on yellow fever as follows.

I became gradually yellow in December 1870, but was

able to be up and about. I had had, for two years previous, fever and several severe attacks of bilious cholic, relieving myself by taking chloroform in teaspoon doses, or by inhalation, with quinine and calomel to break the fever. While under the influence of jaundice, I was called to see a surgical case at Houston, and after I had operated on the case, feeling much fatigued, I rode out to the fair grounds and was caught in a slight sprinkle of rain. On my return I felt chilly and had a hard ague that night; vomited all night; was very sick; left my patient (though I had high fever and was still sick at my stomach) and went home on the cars. My fever cooled in seven or eight days; was partially delirious. Prof. Rankin, who attended me, said I had haematuria for two days. I got better and continued my lectures in the college, but my skin continued yellow. I was up and down until the last of April, when I had another high fever, with pain in my gall-bladder and neuralgia in my head, which was dreadful. I took chloroform almost continually, to relieve the pain. At last I dreamed it was my teeth, and sent for a dentist and had seven taken out. I began to improve, and as soon as I could sit up, I started to Philadelphia and attended the American Medical Association meetings. Staid in Philadelphia two months; took prescriptions from everyone that would prescribe for me.

I went to New York on the 4th of July, and staid there a month. One day I had a hard shaking ague, shaking even the bed at Metropolitan Hotel. I took calomel and quinine, twelve grains, in six pills, one every two hours, for two days, and was up again and about, and could walk around, but no change in my urine or skin, both were still very yellow. I returned to Philadelphia, was always constipated, and took seidlitz powders, citrate of magnesia, Kissingen water, and many other things, but all did no good. My landlady at Philadelphia said she would cure me. She had some pills that cured her son when he came home from the army in Virginia. He was as bad as I was, and

many doctors had worked with him and not cured
him. She gave me three of Bragg's pills. I took one dose
before I left Philadelphia, and another in Washington,
D.C., where I stopped. These purged me and I had the
diarrhea for two whole years afterward. At times I
would take a pound of chloroform in a night, to stop
the pain in my liver and to check the diarrhea. The
chloroform always relieved me, and I would be able
to go out and walk around. I stopped one week at my
brother's, in Albemarle county, Virginia, and when I
left I rode twelve miles on horseback to Charlottesville
to take the cars for home. That night I had a chill and
was very sick. I did not stop, but got a sleeping car at
Lynchburg, to Montgomery, Alabama. They wanted
several times to put me off, but I would not let them,
until finally they changed the cars in Montgomery.
Then I had to take a regular car, and that day I had
another chill, and was forced to lay down on the floor
of the car until my fever left. I took quinine, rested a
day, and finally arrived home at Galveston, as yellow
as I left. As soon as I got home I commenced to blister
over my liver and stomach, putting one on after another, as they healed up, until I got so sore I could not
bear them. I could walk around all the time when I did
not have the fever. I had a good appetite all the time,
and could eat anything. It did not affect my stomach,
but my stools were white, like milk, and much too
frequent. The blisters helped me. Finally I started up
to Dallas county, stopping at Houston a week. While
there I had cramp colic. My friend, Dr. Hudspeth,
roomed with me. I took a bottle of chloroform that
night, and he was alarmed, and thought I would kill
myself; the next day I went up to Mexia, and stayed
with Dr. Rankin. He gave me some pills, but the water
was limestone and affected my bowels so, I was afraid
to remain there, but I got better and went to Corsicana,
and stayed with Dr. Watkins. He persuaded me to quit
medicines altogether, and I took his advice. I went on
to Dallas. There my diarrhea was so bad I got a bottle
of gin and took it, but it did me no good, so I got on

the stage and went to Bonham, where I rode around
with Dr. Dorset and considerably improved; from
there I went to McKinney and to Lebanon, where I
stayed for nearly two weeks, with Dr. Shelburn; one
night I had a severe attack of colic and took a bottle of
chloroform. From there I went to Sherman and
Denison, then in the woods, and over into the Indian
nation, where I ate smoked beef (jerked beef), and
turnip greens; these stopped my diarrhea. There was a
spring on the road from Sherman to Denison that was
chalybeate, and when I partook of it I felt better. I
stayed up there until the 28th of November, the
thermometer being down to 19°. I went home very
much improved, and commenced my course of lectures. In six weeks I was as bad as ever, and had another
dreadful attack, being as yellow as before. I was carried
to Austin, nearly dead, but the day after I got there I
was able to walk, and my jaundice had nearly left me.
I stayed in Austin two months, and returned well, as
I thought.

Returned to Austin in April, remained until some
time in June; returned and had fine health that summer
and winter, with the exception of my spell at Calvert,
while I was attending yellow fever. My wife had
dengue while I was at Calvert, but I did not have it this
year, as I had had it in 1863. Next spring I was still
subject to spells of diarrhea. I remained better and
worse until March 1874, when I had a diarrhea, and
neuralgia, from toothache. I took a dose of morphia
and went to bed with fever; with a terrible pain in my
head. I had been having toothache before I took the
diarrhea, but paid no attention to it. I had such severe
pain in my head that I called for chloroform and took
it for seven days; every time I waked up my head
would ache, and I would take the chloroform; all the
doctors that my wife sent for failed to relieve me. At
last she put a large blister over my stomach, six by six,
and when it drew it brought me to my senses, for I had
not recollected anything for six days, and had taken
and wasted eight pounds of chloroform. When I came

to I told the doctors I had had a chill and the neuralgia
passed from my liver to my head, and if they would
give me quinine and calomel I would get well; they did
give me the old prescription, twelve and twelve grains,
in six pills, one every two hours. That evening Dr.
Bibb and J.T. & W. Brady carried me to Houston, to
Mr. Brady's; when I got there I was able to walk, but
very yellow. My finger and toe nails were soft, from
the chloroform, and I could belch it up. I took a warm
bath, which helped me very much. That night the
neuralgia returned, and instead of giving me chloroform, they gave me brandy, which made me furious,
and my sufferings worse, until they were compelled to
give me chloroform. I told Dr. Bibb it started in my
teeth, as it did before I went to Philadelphia, and one
night I dreamed it was my teeth and sent and had seven
pulled out, and I got better; so the next morning I had
all my upper teeth taken out, but one root was broken
off. It pained me so that after dinner I went to Dr.
Fielding's and had it taken out. My neuralgia did not
return, and we went to Dallas that night, on the cars.
I lay all night with my head in the window, and the
cool breeze kept me from fever.

At Dallas I thought I would go out to the wash-
room and bathe my head, but was pushed down by a
ruffian and came near going into spasms. However, I
got to the hotel, and took some brandy, fell asleep and
continued to improve. My gums were very sore, and
the yellowness of my skin continued for nearly a
month. While suffering from my gums I began to
smoke tobacco, and have used it ever since, but never
before in any way. I was always temperate, never
drank liquors, unless for medicine, and was never
drunk. I went from Dallas to Denison, and stayed at
both places two months, and completely recovered. I
went home and stayed six weeks; had a slight fever and
became afraid I would be taken down again. I went to
Austin, stayed there a week, but the water, being
limestone, started my bowels, so I went from there to
Lampasas Sulphur Springs, where I stayed two weeks,

but the water was limestone, and though I would not
drink, it, even the coffee I drank made me have diarrhea. I was sent for to go up to San Saba county, and
from there I rode around in McCulloch, Llano, and
Mason counties, among the raids of the wild Indians.
I improved all the time, but on my return I was taken
very sick at Mr. Moses', where I had stopped all night,
and my colic returned, but I stopped it with brandy,
and rode to Liberty Hill, where I stayed a week and
improved. I stopped a week in Austin, reaching
Galveston about the 10th of November. From this
time on I had no more symptoms of jaundice, but
every change of weather would give me diarrhea,
which I found I could check with peach brandy, and I
would get well without anything else, or without
turning yellow. I had no more spells until April 1,
1876, but was able to practice and had become very
fat, weighing 196 pounds.

In April, I went to Marshall, to attend the meeting
of the State Medical Association, and while in Marshall
I became badly constipated. They used mostly well
water and spring water which was chalybeate; this, no
doubt, caused my bowels to become constipated. After
the Association adjourned, I went out with Dr. Orman Knox to Jonesville. He studied medicine with my
brother before I did, and I had not seen him in thirty
years; while there, I went out with him every day. It
being a malarial district, and there having been heavy
rains, my constipation got worse. I took some salts and
other remedies, but they did me no good. I was compelled to go to Marshall, and went there feeling very
bad; while there, I was taken very bad with fever,
became delirious, took some chloroform and other
medicines Dr. Thomas prescribed for me, and my
fever broke. I went away on the second morning to
Jonesville, and went out with Dr. Knox, to see one of
our patients; had to use a great deal of chloroform; it
made me very sick, and when we got back to the
doctor's I had fever; I told him to make me up some
calomel and blue mass pills, and while he was fixing it,

I took some chloroform on my handkerchief and fell asleep. I did not recollect anything until Sunday (this was Tuesday evening); when I woke up I was vomiting terribly, my head ached to bursting, and I begged the nurse to let me have some chloroform. They had refused to give it to me, and I had become conscious but I begged so hard, the nurse left me to beg some for me, but while he was gone, I opened the window, jumped out, and ran as if for my life, to a puddle of water in the field, and laid down in it, I was so hot. They brought me back, but as soon as I was in bed I became unconscious, and did not recollect anything until the next Wednesday. When I became again conscious, and vomiting terribly, I was yellow, almost livid. They would not give me any more chloroform. and I continued to suffer; I would get so hot, I thought I would die; I belched up the chloroform for a week; my finger and toe nails became soft, as before; my mouth and throat very sore; the water brash was terrible; saliva poured from me. I believe chloroform produced it, as I had it every time after I had used it to excess. I had taken (Dr. Knox says) five pounds, and that he gave it to me until it would not produce sleep. He said I talked to him perfectly rational, and said I would die if he did not give it to me; called him cruel and unkind; knowing my reputation and general good habits, he humored me until he sent for my wife, who knew its effects on me; when I was so bad in Galveston, she said I prescribed for patients I did not recollect ever seeing; and Dr. Knox says I prescribed for a patient that I had completely forgotten until he came to see me after I had gotten well. The chloroform produced the effect of mania-a-potu on me, for I could see and imagine anything; saw plainly my first wife; saw Dr. Knox's father, and many other strange things, and although I was awake all night, I could see them at any time during the night. After I quit vomiting the water brash was terrible on me, yet I had a good appetite, and recovered from my jaundice in a few days. My finger and toe nails became soft, as they had done on

1. PLACE OF DEATH		2 USUAL RESIDENCE (Where deceased lived. If institution: residence before admission).
a. COUNTY Galveston		a. STATE Texas b. COUNTY Galveston

b. CITY (If outside corporate limits, write RURAL and give precinct no.) OR TOWN Galveston	c. LENGTH OF STAY (in this place)	c. CITY (If outside corporate limits, write RURAL and give precinct no.) OR TOWN Galveston

d. FULL NAME OF HOSPITAL OR INSTITUTION (If not in hospital or institution, give street address or location)		d. STREET ADDRESS (If rural, give location)

3. NAME OF DECEASED (Type or Print)	a. (First) GREENSVILLE	b. (Middle)	c. (Last) DOWELL	4. DATE OF DEATH June 9, 1881

5. SEX Male	6. COLOR OR RACE White	7. MARRIED, NEVER MARRIED, WIDOWED, DIVORCED (Specify)	8. DATE OF BIRTH	9. AGE YEARS 59	MONTHS	DAYS	IF UNDER 24 HRS. Hours	Min.

10a. USUAL OCCUPATION (Give kind of work done during most of working life, even if retired)	10b. KIND OF BUSINESS OR INDUSTRY	11. BIRTHPLACE (State or foreign country) Virginia

12. FATHER'S NAME	BIRTHPLACE	13. MOTHER'S MAIDEN NAME	BIRTHPLACE

14. WAS DECEASED EVER IN U.S. ARMED FORCES? (Yes, no, or unknown) (If yes, give war or dates of service)	15. SOCIAL SECURITY NO.	16. INFORMANT'S SIGNATURE

17. CAUSE OF DEATH Enter only one cause per line for (a), (b), and (c)		MEDICAL CERTIFICATION		INTERVAL BETWEEN ONSET AND DEATH
	I. DISEASE OR CONDITION DIRECTLY LEADING TO DEATH*(a)	Chloroform *this is a lie* Poisoning		
*This does not mean the mode of dying, such as heart failure, asthenia, etc. It means the disease, injury, or complication which caused death.	ANTECEDENT CAUSES Morbid conditions, if any, giving rise to the above cause (a) stating the underlying cause last.	DUE TO (b)		
		DUE TO (c)		
	II. OTHER SIGNIFICANT CONDITIONS Conditions contributing to the death but not related to the disease or condition causing death.			

18a. DATE OF OPERATION	18b. MAJOR FINDINGS OF OPERATION		19. AUTOPSY? YES ☐ NO ☐

20a. ACCIDENT SUICIDE HOMICIDE (Specify)	20b. PLACE OF INJURY (e.g., in or about home, farm, factory, street, office bldg., etc.)	20c. (CITY, TOWN, OR PRECINCT NO.)	(COUNTY)	(STATE)
20d. TIME OF INJURY (Month) (Day) (Year)	(Hour)	20e. INJURY OCCURRED WHILE AT ☐ NOT WHILE WORK ☐ AT WORK ☐	20f. HOW DID INJURY OCCUR?	

21. I hereby certify that I attended the deceased from _____, 19___, to _____, 19___, that I last saw the deceased alive on _____, 19___, and that death occurred at _____ m., from the causes and on the date stated above.

22a. SIGNATURE C.H. Wilkinson & A. Wilson M.D.	(Degree or title)	22b. ADDRESS	22c. DATE SIGNED

23a. BURIAL, CREMATION, REMOVAL (Specify)	23b. DATE	23c. NAME OF CEMETERY OR CREMATORY

23d. LOCATION (City, town, or county)	(State)	24. FUNERAL DIRECTOR'S SIGNATURE

25a. REGISTRAR'S FILE NO.	25b. DATE REC'D BY LOCAL REGISTRAR June, 1881	25c. REGISTRAR'S SIGNATURE

State of Texas
City of Galveston

I hereby certify that the above is a true and correct copy of the certificate as recorded in the City Health Department of Galveston, Texas.

Issued
NOV 15 1973

Registrar of Vital Statistics

Copy of Dr. Dowell's death certificate prepared from the original record in the city Health Department of Galveston. Note the stated cause of death was "Chloroformpoisoning," but "this is a lie" is penciled in the same space, probably by a friend or member of the family. Note also the certificate is co-signed by his friend, Dr. C.H. Wilkerson, who attempted to take credit for Dowell's hernia operation.

the former occasions. I was dreadfully blistered, and even after I got up and rode around, I had to go to bed for a week, as the blistered surfaces threatened to mortify. They are still sore, and itch and burn, but they no doubt saved my life each time. Nothing I took did me any good but blisters. Chloroform always eased me, and I believe, until the last spell, it did me good, and allowed the gall-stones to pass off, and I would get easy. Mercury always made me more yellow; seemed to excite the liver to action and the secretions could not pass off, except through the kidneys, and skin. But I was compelled to take it to break my fever, as quinine alone made me worse and increased my fever.

In these three attacks I took everything that was ever recommended for jaundice. Blisters cured me, or always did me good. Sulphuric ether is said to dissolve gall-stones, but it was always so sickening to me I did not give it a fair trial. I have not tried the choleate of soda. I hope all is true that is said of it.

I will remark, before closing, I always administer chloroform on a towel or pocket handkerchief, and never allow it nearer than half an inch to an inch from the mouth or nose, and in the horizontal position. I have never had a fatal result. I once took some internally, pouring it into a tumbler by moonlight, which came near killing me. I was unconscious from 11 p.m. to 7 a.m.[31]

Dr. Dowell's death certificate is recorded in Galveston City Hall. It is signed by C.H. Wilkerson, the same Dr. Wilkerson who attempted to take credit for his hernia operation. The cause of death is listed "Chloroform Poisoning," but "this is a lie" is penciled in in bold but faded script. This notation was probably made by some member of the family who resented that his death was due to either suicide or drug abuse. The fact that he had for several years before his death suffered from biliary colic and jaundice, which by his own admission was treated by chloroform inhalation, would lead one to believe that he probably died from natural causes.

Dr. Dowell's untimely death came on June 9, 1881. His

obituary was carried in five scientific journals[32] besides being printed in the June 10 issue of the *Galveston News* which reads as follows.

> Dr. Greensville Dowell, an old and honored citizen, and one of the most prominent physicians in Galveston, died at St. Mary's Infirmary yesterday afternoon. Though a long sufferer from a malignant malady and periodically stricken down, Dr. Dowell was considered very vigorous for a man of his years, and his last confinement was only of a few days duration. The announcement of his death will be a surprise to many of his friends.
>
> Dr. Dowell entered the Confederate service from Galveston and served with distinction during the war as a surgeon, and since then has occupied a high position in this city both as an instructor and practitioner of medicine and surgery. He was the author of several medical works and was widely known throughout the state.
>
> A few days ago he was taken seriously ill and was removed from his boarding house to St. Mary's Infirmary by request of the surgeon of this institution who has been a pupil of his and who desired to gave him the best possible attention.
>
> Dr. Dowell leaves a wife and a large number of descendants to mourn his loss. His funeral will take place at 10 o'clock this morning from the Masonic Hall.[33]

Lest those of us who are privileged to practice our art here in this great state of Texas forget, it is right and meet for us to occasionally review the life of Dr. Greensville Dowell, the first processor of surgery in our state who established and maintained an academic atmosphere based on scholarship, intellectual curiosity, ingenuity, boldness, and communication with other surgical centers of the world. All surgeons will forever be indebted to this truly fabulous physician in earlier Texas.

ENDNOTES

1. George Cupples. From the report of the Special Committee on Surgery of the Texas Medical Association, 1886.

2. Albert O. Singleton. Address of the President. "The Surgeon in the Romantic Story of Texas." *Annals of Surgery* vol. III, no. 5 (May 1940).

3. Greensville Dowell. *Yellow Fever and Malarial Diseases, Embracing a History of the Epidemics of Yellow Fever in Texas; New Views on its Diagnosis, Treatment, Propagation and Control* (Philadelphia: Medical publications office, 1876)

4. Ibid.

5. Ibid.

6. Ibid.

7. Ibid.

8. Singleton. Address of the President, op. cit.

9. J.F.Y. Paine. Opening Address, University Medical XI. (October 1906).

10. Ibid.

11. Dowell, *Yellow Fever*, op. cit.

12. Greensville Dowell. *A Treatise on Hernia; with a New Process for its Radical Cure, and Original Contributions to Operative Surgery, and New Surgical Instruments* (Philadelphia: D.G. Brinton, 1876), 205; Greensville Dowell. "Subcutaneous Suture for the Radical Cure of Hernia. *Medical Record* 1 (August 1, 1866), 265-66.

13. Ibid.

14. Greensville Dowell. Radical Cure for Hernia." *Transactions of the Texas State Medical Association* 6 (1874), 113-15.

15. Dowell, *Treatise on Hernia*, op. cit.

16. Ibid.

17. Ibid.

18. Ibid.

19. Greensville Dowell. "Report of a Case of Stricture of Urethra, with Critical Remarks upon its Treatment by External Urethrotomy." *Proceedings of the Texas State Medical Association* 3 (1871), 41-45.

20. A New Wire Speculum for the Anus and Vagina. *Proceedings of the Texas State Medical Association* 3:45-46, 1871. With illus.

21. Dowell, *Treatise on Hernia*, op. cit.

22. Ibid.

23. Greensville Dowell. "On Trismus Nascentium." *American Journal of the Medical Sciences* 45 (January 1863), 51-56.

24. Greensville Dowell. "Hemorrhoids and New Mode of Operating; with a Report of Two Cases of Cataract Following the Removal of Hemorrhoids by Ligature." *Virginia Medical Monthly* 6 (1879/80), 542-46.

25. Dowell, *Yellow Fever*, op. cit.

26. S.W. Geiser. "Men of Science, 1820-1880." *Field and Laboratory* 26 (1958), 123.

27. James Carroll. "Yellow Fever—Popular Lectures." *Texas State Journal of Medicine* 1 (August 1905), 69-76; Pat Ireland Nixon. "Surgery: A Cultural Factor in Early Texas." *Texas State Journal of Medicine* vol. 53 (March 1957); Singleton, Address of the President, op. cit.

28. Dowell, *Yellow Fever in Texas*, op. cit.

29. Ibid.

30. Ibid.; Greensville Dowell. Address of Welcome, 9th Annual Session, Texas State Medical Association. *Transactions of the Texas State Medical Association* 9 (1877), 2-3.

31. Dowell, *Yellow Fever*, op. cit.

32. *Medical and Surgical Reporter* 44 (June 18, 1881), 700; *Medical Record* 19 (June 18, 1881), 700; *Southern Practitioner* 4 (August 1882), 265; *Texas Medical and Surgical Record* 1 (July 1881), 303-304; *Transactions of the American Medical Association* 33 (1882), 546-49.

33. *Galveston Daily News* (June 10, 1881).

OTHER WORKS BY GREENSVILLE DOWELL

Original Contributions to Surgery, with Inventions of Instruments, and New Operative Procedures (N.p., n.d.) A thesis, read before the medical examiners of the Texas Medical College for the professorship of surgery.

Dislocations of the Humerus at the Shoulder Joint. *Medical and Surgical Reporter* 35 (August 12, 1876), 123-25.

Dislocations of the Humerus at the Shoulder Joint (Scapulo-humeral). Dagas' Diagnostic Signs. Report of Three Cases of Medio-glenoid, Subclavicular Variety, Reduced by a New Method and Process. *Transactions of the Texas State Medical Association* 8 (1876), 143-47. Line drawings.

Fibro-cystic Tumor of Ovary; Ovariotomy; Recovery; Remarks. *Virginia Medical Monthly* 6 (1879), 132-38.

Filaria Sanguinis Hominis. *Galveston Medical Journal* 1 (1880), 13.

History of Yellow Fever and Dengue in Texas. *Transactions of the American Medical Association* 27 (1876), 487-89.

Lithotomy: Report of Cases. *Transactions of the Texas State Medical Association* 7 (1875), 198-202.

Medical Topography of Galveston. *Galveston Medical Journal* 1 (1876), 123-29.

New Processes and New Instruments in Minor Surgery; Incisions and Needles. *Virginia Medical Monthly* 7 (1880/1881), 768-70.

Report of Four Cases of Hernia Treated by the "Subcutaneous Silver Wire Suture" Method Inverted. *Medical Times* 6 (July 22, 1876), 509-10.

Report on Hernia. *Transactions of the Texas State Medical Association* 7 (1875), 206-208.

Rupia - Accompanied by Gout. *Proceedings of the Texas State Medical Association* 2 (1870), 33-37.

Some Suggestion in Reference to Yellow Fever. *Medical and Surgical Reporter* 41 (August 16, 1879), 133-34.

Texas Yellow Fever and Dengue Epidemic of 1873. *Transactions of the Texas State Medical Association* 6 (1874), 156-66. Replication by E. Palmer, 166-68.

Galveston Medical Journal, vol. 1-5 (1866-1871), n.s.v.1. vol. 1-3 (January-March 1880).

OTHER WORKS ABOUT GREENSVILLE DOWELL

Atkinson, W.B. *Physicians and Surgeons of the U.S.* (Philadelphia: 1878), 199.

Dictionary of American Biography, vol. 5, 412-13.

Field and Laboratory 26 (July-October 1958), 123.

Handbook of Texas, vol. 1, 517.

Kelly, H.A. and Burrage, W.L. *American Medical Biographies* (Baltimore: 1920), 327.

Red, Mrs. George Plunkett. *The Medicine Man in Texas* (Houston, Texas: c1930), 117-18, 209-11.

BIOGRAPHICAL SKETCH OF AUTHOR

JOSEPH P. MCNEIL, M.D. was born in Clarksville, Virginia in 1912. He received his medical education at the University of Texas Medical Branch in Galveston, graduating in 1942. He served a medical internship in the U.S. Army while serving his country from 1943 to 1946, rising to the rank of major.

He returned to Texas to serve a surgical residency at the Medical Branch from 1946 to 1950. From 1950 to 1955 he served as Clinical Instructor of Surgery at Southwestern Medical School in Dallas. From 1952 to 1968 he was Director of Surgical Education at Gaston Episcopal Hospital and served as Chief of Surgery there from 1976 to 1980.

He was a member of the Dallas County Medical Society, the Texas Medical Association, the American Medical Association, the American College of Surgeons, the Texas Surgical Society, the Southwestern Surgical Congress, the Singleton Surgical Society, the Western Surgical Association and the Southern Surgical Club.

Dr. McNeil was also a member of Alpha Omega Alpha and St. Luke's Episcopal Church. He was the author of a number of surgical papers and was intensely interested in medical and surgical history.

Dr. McNeil sustained a myocardial infarction and died suddenly while apparently recovering October 6, 1982, at the age of sixty-six years.

ACKNOWLEDGMENTS:

To Dr. Robert S. Sparkman for providing me the opportunity to study this interesting early Texas surgeon.

To my wife, Christine, for her help in the research.

To Mrs. Barbara Kelso, librarian at the Medical Branch of The University of Texas in Galveston, for her help in securing references.

To The University of Texas Southwestern Medical School Library for help in preparing the bibliography.

To Mrs. Kris Reagan, my secretary, for typing and proofreading.

JAMES FENTRESS, M.D.
1802-1872
by
R. Maurice Hood, M.D.

★DR. JAMES FENTRESS WAS A LEADING figure in the settling and development of the areas of Caldwell and Bastrop Counties in the years 1836 to 1872. Today he is largely unknown except to a handful of Central Texans.

He was born in Montgomery County, Tennessee, on May 9, 1802.[1] Little is known of his childhood and early life although the Fentress family was large and contained at least two physicians and two lawyers, one of whom became a county judge. The Fentress family in later years was regarded as one of the prominent families of Tennessee.

James enrolled in the University of Kentucky Medical School and was graduated in about 1830. While residing in Montgomery County, he became involved with another prominent family, the Hardemans. Thomas B. Hardeman had helped to organize Hardeman County and was prominent in establishing the Masonic Lodge in Bolivar, Tennessee. Fentress was appointed as one of the county commissioners of Hardeman County. He also joined the Masonic Lodge. He undoubtedly met his future wife there, Mary Ophelia Hardeman, the daughter of Thomas J. Hardeman and his wife Mary Ophelia Polk Hardeman, who was a relation of President James K. Polk.

Dr. Fentress migrated to Texas in 1832 for health reasons. About twenty-five members of the Hardeman family also moved to Texas at about this time.[2] He first settled in Matagorda County and shortly afterward joined the Texas Army under General Sam Houston, serving in Captain Deaf Smith's spy company. At the Battle of San Jacinto he participated in the burning of Vince's Bridge. He also saw Santa Anna during the battle. One inconsistency in the records indicates that Fentress was assigned to Burlesons' company of volunteers.

Dr. Fentress migrated to the Cedar Creek community in Bastrop in 1836 and set up a medical practice. He married Mary Ophelia on June 18, 1840. Shortly afterward the family moved to the area of Prairie Lea on the San Marcos River and joined several of the Hardeman family who had also moved from Matagorda County. This group of settlers became known as the San Marcos Colony.

Fentress built a home, calling it "Rinconada" and using it as home, office and hospital, a common practice at that time. A letter from one of the family states that the only photograph ever made of James Fentress is known to have been destroyed. His granddaughter describes him as a Scotsman with a medium-thin face and short, pointed goatee. His eyes were small and set close together. She stated that his eyes gave an intellectual gleam and clarity that was notable.[3]

Shortly after the Texas Revolution, one Vincente Cordova, a resident of Nacogdoches who was a Mexican sympathizer, was commissioned by the Mexican government to stir up local Indian tribes. The object was to attack and harass the settlers and hopefully get them to leave. It was discovered that an attack was planned, and General Burleson organized a volunteer force to deal with Cordova's force. The enemy force was found on Mill Creek about six miles east of Seguin and a battle began. Fentress, an expert marksman, persuaded one of Cordova's deserters to identify him. He then took careful aim and fired, seriously wounding Cordova by fracturing his arm. This injury terminated the battle; Cordova and his force fled toward Mexico.[4]

The activity that brought Dr. Fentress the most recognition was his participation in the Battle of Plum Creek. In August of 1840, a large number of Comanche Indians from West Texas invaded Central Texas without warning. They swept southward past Gonzales and attacked Victoria and Linnville and many intervening farms and homes. A number of people were killed and storehouses and homes looted and burned. Some captives were also taken. Central Texans were alerted and hastily formed a force to intercept the returning Indians. Many of the Comanches were drunk and carrying and wearing some of their loot, including women's clothes and parasols.[5]

The rapidly accumulated force of Texans were under the overall command of General Felix Huston. General Edward Burleson, who had fought at San Jacinto and who was later to be elected as Vice President of the Republic of Texas, was in command of the Prairie Lea contingent. He had also been a delegate to the Convention of 1833. He commanded a group of Texans including Monroe Hardeman and James Fentress.

There were a number of men in the volunteer force who were either already famous or soon to be.[6] Matthew Caldwell was an early settler in DeWitt's Colony, a delegate to the convention at Washington-on-the-Brazos, and a signer of the Declaration of Independence. He was an active soldier in the war for independence and in a number of Indian battles. Benjamin McCullough was renowned as a soldier in the Army of the Republic of Texas, Indian fighter and Texas Ranger, and was later to become a general in the Confederate Army and be killed at the Battle of Pea Ridge on March 7, 1862. Henry McCulloch, brother of Ben, was also a participant and also became a Confederate general. One of the most notable Plum Creek participants was Jack Hays, who acquired a reputation as an Indian fighter and later became a commander of a company of Texas Rangers. He also commanded the First Regiment, Texas Mounted Volunteers in the War with Mexico.

The Indians were ambushed along Plum Creek southeast of the present location of present-day Lockhart, and a large number were killed with no loss to the outnumbered Texans. This decisive battle marked the end of the major excursions of the Comanches and was the last major Indian battle in Texas.

During the battle, Dr. Fentress recaptured one of the Indian captives. This woman had an arrow lodged in her chest and Fentress, with the help of Dr. Brown, removed the arrow without complication.[7] As far as the writer has been able to discover, this is the only account of an operation performed by James Fentress although there were many.

Dr. Fentress practiced in Prairie Lea for about twenty-five years. His home/office/hospital, Rinconada, served many people in Central Texas over the years. He was a participant in the organization of Caldwell County in 1848.[8] He and his wife had one son, Thomas Hardeman Fentress, who enlisted in the Confederate Army in Sibley's Brigade just as it departed on its ill-fated expedition to conquer New Mexico for the South. One source states that he was wounded at the Battle of Glorieta Pass and subsequently died in Albuquerque. Another account states that he died of pneumonia. He was said to have died in the arms of Joe Sayers, a future governor of Texas.[9]

James Fentress was a man of many talents.[10] He played the violin, or fiddle as it was commonly called, for many of the dances and social activities in both the Bastrop and Prairie Lea areas. He was also recognized as a dancer of considerable ability. Many of the social affairs lasted until daylight with the fiddlers' having played all night. He also kept a number of fine horses which he loved to race.

Dr. Fentress was active in the Masonic Order and became a charter member of Lodge 114 in Prairie Lea in 1852. When Caldwell County was organized by an act of the legislature in 1848, James Fentress was listed along with nineteen other families.[11] He was also one of four men who organized the Methodist church in Prairie Lea in 1853.

There is no record of James Fentress' participating in the Civil War. The granddaughter of Elizabeth Polk Hardeman, however, records a fateful incident in 1868. During the reconstruction era, Federal troops which were made up of freed slaves under white officers occupied the area of Prairie Lea. One morning a young white male had some difficulty with the soldiers and was injured. He went to Rinconda to seek help from Dr. Fentress. The soldiers pursued the injured man and demanded that Fentress surrender him. The demand was refused and the soldiers departed at dusk and promised to return the following morning. The men in the house barricaded it as best they could. The women filled every available container with water in case the house was set afire. The women, armed with a Derringer pistol, then took refuge in the upstairs rooms. One of the black house servants guarded the stairway armed with a double-bladed axe.

After several hours of drinking, the Federal soldiers marched to the house with burning pine knots for light and singing the tune of John Brown's Body. They rushed the house only to meet the fire from Dr. Fentress' two horse pistols. The attack was repelled and eleven soldiers lay dead in front of the house.[12] The

The State of Texas memorialized the life of James Fentress with a marker on which the wording is still legible.

The broken tombstone of Mary Fentress, who is buried beside her husband.

The grave of James Fentress in the Masonic Section of the Prairie Lea Cemetery. The memorial marker placed by the State of Texas is beside the original, vandalized grave stone.

attack was not resumed, but Fentress realized what the result of this incident would be, fled to Mexico, and did not return until martial law was terminated. The women dispersed to other homes in the area to be hidden. Dr. Fentress returned to Prairie Lea in 1870 and lived there until his death on July 7, 1872. The cause of death is unknown. He was buried in the Masonic Section of the Prairie Lea Cemetery and was survived by his wife, who lived until July 13, 1888, and is buried beside her husband.

The State of Texas recognized the life of James Fentress by erecting a marble monument beside his broken tombstone, which had been inscribed,

Dr. James Fentress
Participated in the Battle of Plum Creek
Born in Tennessee May 9, 1802
Died July 7, 1872

The rifle used by Dr. Fentress at the battles of San Jacinto, Plum Creek and against Cordova, was given by the family to the Alamo Collection of Historic Relics and resides there.[13]

Nothing survives of his home although the Hardeman home

The city limit sign of the town of Fentress, named for its first doctor, James Fentress. It is about two miles from the site of the Fentress home, which at that time was in Prairie Lea.

still exists. The town of Fentress, six miles west of Prairie Lea, was named after Dr. Fentress in the 1890s after it grew up around the Smith Gin Company mill.[14]

The name of James Fentress shines only dimly through the obscuring clouds of time. Only a few people still recognize his name, but it is recorded in the historical libraries of Lockhart, Bastrop and Luling. He was a man of honor, a physician, a religious man, and a fiery patriot of his adopted state who served as a soldier of the Republic of Texas, and a respected citizen of Central Texas.

ENDNOTES

1. Francis W. Wilson. "Dr. James Fentress." *Plum Creek Almanac* 13 (1995), 119.

2. Francis W. Wilson. *The Hardeman Impact on Early Texas History* (Luling, Texas: Wilson), 8.

3. Elizabeth Polk Hardeman Thompson. Undated letter, Mary Whittington Library for the Geneological and Historical Society of Caldwell County, Luling, Texas.

4. Wilson, *Hardeman, op. cit.;* Wilson, "Fentress," op. cit.

5. Wilson, *Hardeman,* op. cit.; Donaly E. Brice. *The Great Comanche Raid* (Austin: Eakin Press, 1987), 11, 67, 69.

6. Zama Withers (ed). *Historical Caldwell County Where Roots Intertwine* (Dallas: Taylor Publishing Co., 1984), 4, 7.

7. Wilson, "Fentress," op. cit.

8. Withers, op. cit., 7.

9. Katherine Thompson Rich. Letter undated, Mary Whitington Library for the Genealogical and Historical Society of Caldwell County, Luling, Texas.

10. Ibid.

11. Withers, op. cit.

12. Rich, op. cit.

13. *The San Antonio Express* (January 1937).

14. Withers, op. cit.

BIOGRAPHICAL SKETCH OF AUTHOR

(see page 59)

Dr. Ford as a young man while in practice in San Augustine, Texas.
Courtesy The Center for American History, University of Texas at Austin.

John Salmon (RIP) Ford, M.D.
1815-1897
by
R. Maurice Hood, M.D.

★JOHN SALMON FORD IS AMONG the most colorful and dramatic figures in early Texas history. He served his adopted state in many capacities over a period of fifty years and proved successful in the varied roles he assumed. In recent years he has not received the attention that his life warrants. His medical career has been mentioned but generally downplayed in the accounts of his life.

He was born in the Greenville District of South Carolina on May 26, 1815. His parents derived from ancestry in Virginia; his great-great-grandparents left Virginia prior to the Revolutionary War. His grandfather, John Ford, a major in the war, returned home to practice law but became ill with a lung infection and died at the age of forty-five. His son William assumed control of the family fortunes. The family migrated westward and located in Lincoln County, Tennessee. William Ford proved to be an able man and accumulated about two hundred acres of land.[1]

There were several children born to William and Harriet Ford, but a girl, Elizabeth, and John Salmon were the only survivors to adult life.[2] John Salmon Ford was born May 26, 1815, while the family was still in South Carolina. An oft-quoted statement from his Memoirs stated that he "had the capacity to get into fights with the boys, to fall in love with the girls, and to stake a hand in the deviltry set on foot by his playmates. The old ladies of his neighborhood looked upon him as a kind of prodigy and predicted he would be killed for his general 'cussedness' before reaching the age of maturity, or hung for some infernal mischief he might commit."[3]

John Ford died, leaving several children. His son, William, was born in 1785. He was an honest man; always candid in his expressions of opinion, and fearless of consequences. He married Harriet Salmon by whom he had children, all of whom died in early life, except Elizabeth, and John Salmon Ford. The latter was born in Greenville District, South Carolina, May 26, 1815. William Ford emigrated to Lincoln county, Tenn., in 1817. He went to Texas after annexation, where he died in Travis county in 1867, aged eighty-two years.

John S. Ford, at an early period of existence, exhibited some marked and rather positive traits of character. He possessed the capacity to get into fights with the boys, to fall in love with the girls, and to take a hand in the deviltry set on foot by his playmates. The old ladies of his neighborhood looked upon him as a sort of prodigy, and predicted he would be killed for his general "cussedness" before reaching the age of maturity, or hanged for some infernal mischief he might commit. In 1834, while reading medicine under Dr. James G. Barksdale of Shelbyville, Bedford County, Tennessee, he volunteered to wait upon his friend, Wilkins Blanton, who had contracted smallpox, in a virulent form. He was eventually sent outside of town to a small house. One of the attendants, an old darkey, died of the disease. Blanton recovered. The young pill-pedler got his name in the newspapers.

The war of Texas independence commenced in the fall of 1835. The capture of San Antonio gave to the Texians a fame for gallantry, and caused many men in the U.S.

Page from Dr. Ford's Memoirs discussing childhood problems and which also mentions his apprenticeship under Dr. James G. Barksdale of Shelbyville, Bedford County, Tennessee. Courtesy The Center For American History, University of Texas at Austin.

His education took place in the one-room, log-cabin schools common to the time in rural Tennessee. He was an apt student with an inquisitive mind and rapidly exceeded the educational facilities of the curriculum. He was an avid reader and gained a good knowledge of literature. He was also a student of the Bible.[4] His later writings demonstrated a command of the English language and of literature.

Ford was not content with the relative inactivity of his rural setting and desired more of an intellectual pursuit. He decided to become a doctor and began to study medicine under the aegis of Dr. James G. Barksdale of Shelbyville at the age of nineteen in 1834. This was a common means of medical education at the time, particularly in frontier or rural situations. Licensing was rarely required at that time. His medical education probably lasted two years before he and his mentor decided that he was a qualified physician.

He began the practice of medicine and soon attracted the attention of the community when a friend, William Blanton, contracted smallpox. The disease was recognized and the presence of a single case was sufficient to produce panic. The victim was isolated and Ford, apparently immune, stayed with and ministered to his friend and to two slaves who also developed the disease. Their confinement was in a cabin outside the town. All of the victims survived and the young doctor became immediately well known and respected for his courageous act.[5]

Dr. Ford at about this time (1834-35) married Mary Davis. Little is known about the woman or the marriage, but the union was broken by divorce in 1836. There were two children, a son and a daughter, who apparently stayed with their father.[6]

Events in Texas in 1835 and 1836 affected the lives of many Tennesseans who became sympathetic to the Texians who were trying to become independent from Mexico. Many of the Texas residents had come from Tennessee and had families there. The Mexican president, Antonio Lopez de Santa Anna, had issued a number of regulations which were unpopular, and his punitive actions had resulted in an armed skirmish on October 2, 1835. The news of events in Texas roused the ire and concern of their families in their home state. Their concern and anger resulted in the formation of several contingents of volunteers who went to Texas to assist in the resistance to Santa Anna and the fight for independence.[7]

Dr. John Ford was determined to raise a force from Shelbyville to go to Texas. The news of the Declaration of Independence and the battles of Goliad and the Alamo raised tempers
to a fever pitch. Ford prepared an ardent address, to motivate
his neighbors, which was subsequently printed and distributed.
Ford hoped to be chosen as captain of the Shelbyville troops;
however, with the later news of the battle of San Jacinto, Ford
resigned and briefly resumed his practice.[8]

Ford by this time had an overwhelming desire to go to Texas
and proceeded to close his practice and strike out for the land of
opportunity. The war for independence was over and Texas was
now a Republic. He left his daughter with his parents and began
his journey, sailing down the Mississippi and then up the Red
River. The route to Texas after debarking from the ship on the
Red River is not recorded; however, they probably left the river
at Natchitoches and traveled southward to the Sabine River
where they crossed on either the Patterson ferry or the Gaines
ferry from there to the area of San Augustine.

Ford, having used most of his meager funds, was nevertheless
able to purchase an old wagon to carry him and his belongings
across the border into Texas. There was a sign of the side of the
wagon, "John Salmon Ford, Doctor." Once in San Augustine,
he set up his medical practice at the age of twenty-one. His
practice flourished and he became well respected. His fees as
listed in his medical journal were moderately high for the times
but still less than those of well established physicians. One page
lists a charge of twenty-five dollars for delivery of a baby. Like
many rural doctors of the time he mixed and dispensed the
medicines which he administered.

He was patient and did not press his patients for payment.
He took time to listen to and counsel his patients. He became
recognized as a good physician, and his practice grew and began
to include many of the more affluent citizens.

There are no records of surgical procedures in his journal
but there were undoubtedly many. One is known, that of his
removal of a piece of bone from the brain of a child.[9] Ford also
participated in the care of plague victims of an epidemic that
followed Santa Anna's incursion into the San Augustine area.
His journal contains seventy-six entries 1844, indicating that he

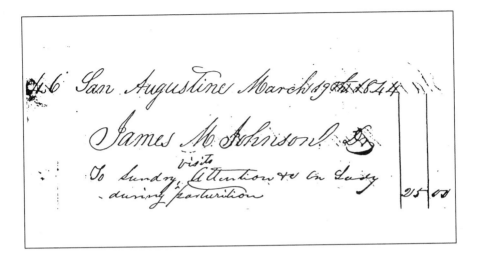

Entry from Dr. Ford's Medical Journal of attendance of Mrs. James M.
Johnson on March 19, 1944. Courtesy of The Center for American
History, University of Texas at Austin.

was engaged in the full-time practice of medicine from 1836 to
1844.

In the summer of 1838, Vicente Cordova, a resident of the
Nacogdoches area loyal to Santa Anna, began encouraging
Cherokee Indians to attack the Texas homesteads and communities. John Ford joined a San Augustine volunteer force under
Captain H.W. Augustine and dispersed the Indians. He then
resumed his practice, but this was just the first of many inter-
ruptions of his professional life to engage in military activities.

Dr. Ford was a man of many and varied talents whose
interests began to widen early. He was appointed as a deputy to
the Shelby County Surveyor, Richard Hooper, and spent several
months surveying the area where the city of Marshall is now
located.[10] He became active in many community activities including teaching a boy's class at the Union Sunday School and
became a part of a group of actors in forming the "Thespian
Corps." In this connection he wrote two plays, "The Stranger
in Texas" and "The Loafer's Courtship," both of which were
produced successfully.[11]

In 1839 the Cherokee Indians became a serious problem.
There were regular raids and atrocities perpetrated on the popu-

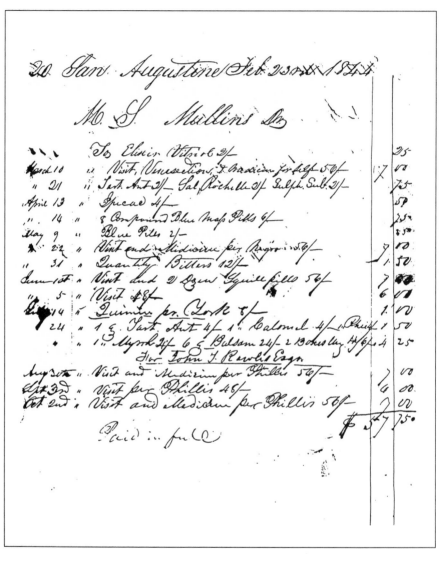

Entry from Medical Journal recording office visits, treatments prescribed, and charges for Mr. M.G. Mullins.

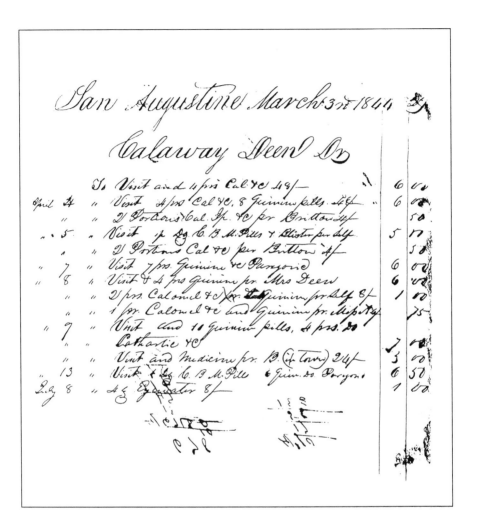

Medical Journal entry for patient Calaway Deen showing visits and treatments.

lace which prompted President Lamar to declare that the Indians had no legal rights to lands. Despite negotiations it was necessary to send a military force to Chief Bowles' village, where the chief and many of his warriors were killed. Ford accompanied the volunteers but his involvement was not reported.

Apparently dissatisfied with his medical practice, Ford became interested in politics and ran for representative to the Texas House to represent San Augustine. He lost the election to H.W. Augustine and Sam Houston,[12] then spent the winter (1840-41) in surveying. With the advent of spring, however, political fever again developed; he again sought election to the House but polled the least votes of any candidate. This episode ended his political aspirations for several years.

Dr. Ford began to study law and in 1841 or 1842 was licensed to practice law,[13] but there is no record that he ever practiced. He apparently had resumed his medical practice full time from 1841 to 1844. His medical journal has a separate page for each family, listing the service performed, medicines given and fees. His usual fee for an office visit and medicine was three dollars. Most medicines were fifty cents to one dollar regardless of the drug used.

A review of his journal shows some of the drugs he prescribed, including ipecac, blue mass pills, guille pills, quinine, balsum, calomel, camphor, and laxatives. This list, typical of the day, reflects the lack of specific medications and the reliance on symptomatic treatment. The exception was quinine which was effective in treating malaria and was the first, disease-specific drug in medical history. There is also an account of venesection or "cupping," the removal of blood from the patient, a widely used method of treatment detrimental to the patient.

After 1844, references to medical practice are infrequent and his medical efforts were largely terminated after the death of his second wife, Louisa Lewis Ford, whom he had married October 26, 1845. When she became ill Ford personally cared for her until her death. He made a third and successful attempt to be elected to the House of Representatives in 1844. After the election he traveled to Washington-on-the-Brazos to take his seat. He was made chairman of the Committee on Retrenchment and served on the committees of Indian Affairs, Education, Finance, and a special committee to examine the Report of the Commissioner

of the General Land Office. Ford had become a personal friend
of Sam Houston and aligned himself with the minority which
supported Houston.

Ford was the representative who introduced the resolution
to accept the offer of the United States to accept Texas into the
Union. This bill was introduced on June 16, 1845, and passed
both houses on June 23. Austin had become the capitol and the
center of political activity. After his marriage in October 1845
the family moved to Austin. Dr. Ford decided to take up the
publishing business and purchased the *Texas National Register*.
He was a democrat and changed the name of the publication to
the *Texas Democrat*. His paper became a success and he became
a highly respected and influential personality. He was at the
forefront of the affairs of business and of state politics. He stood
high in the estimation of Texas politicians.

At this point, his wife of only nine months became ill, died
on August 5, 1846, and was buried in Oakwood Cemetery in
Austin.[14] The grief-stricken Ford gave up his newspaper and,
apparently seeking escape, went to San Antonio and joined a
company of Texas Rangers who were just becoming involved in
the War with Mexico. The Rangers had been discharged by
Zachary Taylor but were recruited again when Colonel Samuel
Curtis called on the state for assistance. In response, Colonel
John C. (Jack) Hays recruited a force of volunteers. John Ford
answered the summons and joined the Ranger force in Captain
Samuel Highsmith's Company of Texas Mounted Volunteers.
Thus the doctor, the lawyer, the surveyor and the editor became
a Texas Ranger, the activity for which he was to achieve the
greatest fame and recognition.[15]

The Ranger force under Hays proceeded to Mexico with the
initial mission of protecting the army's supply lines, but their
principal duty was to pursue groups of guerilla raiders. They
became very proficient at this activity. Ford was named adjutant
to Jack Hays and in this capacity earned his sobriquet "R.I.P."
It was his duty to write letters to the families of deceased Rangers
and he adapted the practice of ending each letter with these
initials to stand for "Rest in peace." For the rest of his life he was
Rip Ford or Old Rip.

Probably to get into combat, he was instrumental in forming
a "Spy Company" composed of fifty picked Rangers, the very

best available. Ford was elected their captain, the highest compliment that the men could pay him and demonstrating that he had their full confidence. This select company set out to discover guerilla groups *before* their raids took place rather than after the damage had been done.

A short time later the Texas Ranger force joined the main body of American troops and advanced toward Mexico City. They were repeatedly attacked by partisan groups which the Rangers consistently dealt with effectively. In Mexico City, Hays was personally involved in the negotiations which removed Santa Anna from power.

There is little doubt that the Rangers were the most effective unit in the American army and were so recognized. Hay's Rangers came to be feared by the hostile populace of Mexico City. There were two or three incidents where Rangers were injured and one killed; Ranger's retaliation was swift and vicious. Upon the death of a Ranger, Adam Alsens Roberts' company rode into the area and the next morning there were eighty bodies of Mexicans by count.[16] General Scott was outraged and demanded disciplinary action but Colonel Hays faced him down and there was no punishment for any Ranger.

As the Rangers rode homeward, John Ford, for reasons known only to him, decided to resign his commission and leave the Rangers and was mustered out May 14, 1848. He was officially recognized for his courage and service. Upon his return to Austin, Ford temporarily resumed control of the *Texas Democrat* but soon sold it to its previous owner. Whether he resumed any medical practice is not known.

With the occurrence of the California gold rush, enthusiasm for establishing a road from Central Texas to El Paso surfaced. John Ford was easily persuaded to lead the expedition in coordination with Robert S. Neighbors. The trek began early in 1849, their route carrying them through Comanche territory although no major incidents occurred. This trip was entirely successful and the road was the route of choice for a number of years until the railroad appeared. This trail was known as the Ford-Neighbors Trail. A by-product was the organization of several counties along the route.[17]

John Ford's return and stay in Austin was not prolonged. There were almost continual Comanche raids with pleas coming from many people in the valley begging for help. General George M. Brook, commanding only a small force, asked the governor for Ranger assistance. Three companies were formed with John Ford's being elected captain of one of them with an official commission. The other two companies were led by John H. Grumbles and Henry Smock.[18]

The Rangers marched to Corpus Christi and began patrolling the border as far as Laredo. There was much marching but very little fighting initially. According to Hughes it was this company that gave Ford the Sobriquet of "Old Rip" which was attached to him for the rest of his life.[19] Others state that this occurred earlier when Ford was the adjutant for Jack Hays.

Ford insistence on military discipline and drill was not cheerfully accepted by the generally undisciplined Rangers who were used to more independence. The first skirmish was along the Nueces which resulted in no fatalities to the Rangers but in the wounding and subsequent death of "Old Higgins," Ford's favorite mount. There were several skirmishes and two Rangers were killed.

Several other battles were fought between small detachments of Ford's Rangers and small bands of Indians. Ford became involved in a revolution led by Jose Maria Carbajal and there was severe fighting around Matamoros. Ford received a wound to the head which resulted in a concussion temporarily disabling him. Ford received considerable criticism for becoming involved in this affair.

In December 1851 Senator Edward Burleson died and Ford ran in a special election and won a seat in the Texas Senate. By 1852 the border conflicts with Ford's involvement were over and he was back in Austin. He purchased the *South-Western American* which proved to be a successful venture and further increased his popularity. A volunteer infantry company was formed named the Texas Guards, the members of which elected Ford as their captain. Ford's short term as a senator was marked by his efforts to incorporate Austin and create an ad valorem tax system and establish a liquor tax.[20] These efforts were successful. Ford's popularity was such that he was elected mayor in 1854.

Ford, in addition to the office of mayor, undertook to be the town marshal. He gave up the *South-Western American* and began to publish the *Texas State Times* which soon became a permanent weekly publication. He carried on a lively dialogue with the *State Gazette* which wasted no love on Ford. He left the Democratic Party during this time and supported the new Know Nothing Party, a short-lived coalition of Whigs and native-born Americans. Ford finally abandoned this party and returned to the Democratic fold.

In 1857 Ford was called upon to head a military expedition to Northwest Texas, later termed the Canadian River Campaign. The Comanche raids to exposed areas had become worse and the army forces had been pulled back out of the area. Ford recruited as many men as possible seeking old Rangers with whom he had fought. Among his officers was Ed Burleson, Billy Pitts and Henry McCulloch. Officers already in the field were Lieutenant J.H. Tankersley and Lieutenant Allison Nelson. General Twiggs denied the company a supply of Colt revolvers, their favorite weapons, but almost all had at least one and many two revolvers. All had muzzle loading rifles.

Ford asked Indian Agent Ross to raise and lead an Indian contingent of one-hundred men to augment his force. The company traveled northwestwards to a point where Hubbard Creek joined the Clear Fork of the Brazos River about twenty miles from the site of present-day Breckenridge. They made camp and named it Camp Runnels. He was awaiting McCulloch's Rangers, who failed to appear. The time was spent in training and drill.

On April 22, 1858, the contingent of 102 Rangers marched northward and on the 26th was joined by 113 Indians of several nations under Agent Ross. The Comanches were elusive but a camp was finally discovered. This encampment was Tenewa Lodge of Chief Iron Jacket with about 350 warriors. Ford and his total force attacked at once and the battle raged for about six hours until Ford's men and their mounts were exhausted. One Ranger was killed and seventy-six Comanches were killed and most of their horses captured. Iron Jacket was among the dead.[21]

A larger Comanche force from the Nokoni Lodge came to the aid of their comrades and Ford asked the Indian contingent to attack. After a stand-off battle the Rangers advanced, but the Comanches retreated and Ford's effort to entrap the Indians was unsuccessful. The Rangers were worn out, their horses jaded, and their food supply was exhausted. Ford decided to terminate the campaign and the force returned to Camp Runnels.

There was another abortive campaign northward in the area of the South Leon River and Mercer Creek but little was accomplished and considerable controversy stirred up. Ford mustered out his men and returned to Austin and the political arena until the next call came. His last service as a Ranger came in November 1859. There were increasing tensions along the border particularly in the Brownsville area. The conflict between English Law and Hispanic Law was not resolvable. The Mexicans felt that they were being discriminated against by the American court system; they were consistently losing their land to the Americans.

One Mexican, Juan Nepomuceno Cortina, a member of a wealthy, respected family, began to be a problem. He raised a group of followers and began to harass the Brownsville area. He had an ongoing feud with the city marshal of Brownsville. On September 28, 1859, Cortina attacked Brownsville and several Americans were killed and anarchy reigned. The citizens were terrorized and pleaded with the army and the governor for help. Cortina, now a prominent figure with many followers, seemed to be a real military threat. The first effort at rescue came from a group of Rangers under W.G. Tobin. These men were far below the usual level of Ranger quality and were labeled by Fehrenbach as "street sweepings." Major S.P. Heintzelman arrived on the scene with 165 soldiers and led his force and Tobin's against Cortina. Tobin's Rangers refused to fight but Ford's soldiers drove Cortina from the field.[22]

Governor Runnels was falsely informed that the entire South Texas area was under attack and that Corpus Christi had been invaded and burned. He immediately sent John Ford to the scene. Ford left Austin with only eight men but recruited more on his way to the valley and arrived with fifty-three effective fighting men.

Ford and Heintzelman immediately launched a campaign against Cortina who had retreated to Rio Grande City. They assailed Cortina's camp head-on, and Cortina's 300-man army ran away after sixty of them were killed. Cortina lost most of his arms and supplies and fled into Mexico. The Mexican government either could not or would not control the rebel. Ford and thirty-five of his Rangers crossed the river and attacked

Cortina again. One Ranger and thirty Mexicans were killed. Ford returned across the river but crossed again the next day with forty-seven Rangers. Cortina had now accumulated a force of eight hundred men. Ford wisely did not attack this force and went back into Texas. Six weeks later Ford reentered Mexico and went to La Mesa where he had been told that Cortina and his army were. On this occasion George Stoneman and his cavalry attacked with Ford but only a minor skirmish resulted. Rip Ford, unimpressed with the results is said to have told Stoneman, "Captain, we have played Old Scratch----whipped the Guardia National, wounded a woman and killed a mule."[23]

Colonel Robert E. Lee arrived on the scene and told the Mexicans to control Cortina or there would be war. This firm diplomacy was heeded and the border warfare ceased for the moment. The Cortina affair made John Ford a Texas hero particularly among the young.[24]

Ford returned to Austin and resumed his normal duties. It is of interest that Major Heintzelman and Captain George Stoneman both attained fame in the Union in the Army of the Potomac. Robert E. Lee became the South's leading general and commanded the famed Army of Northern Virginia.

The Civil War fever engulfed Texas almost immediately following the election of Abraham Lincoln in 1860. Sam Houston was convinced that secession was wrong and as governor would have no part in it. This stand essentially ended his career and left him an old and disappointed man. There were many strident voices demanding secession, John S. Ford's among them.[25] A secession convention was convened in Austin at the end of January 18, 1861. A vote was taken on the motion to secede on February 1, 1861 and the vote was 174 for and 7 against. The proposal was submitted for a popular vote and the result was 46,129 for and 14,697 against.

There was wild enthusiasm for the Confederacy as the war began. Recruiting, drill and arming of companies from every community was the activity of the day. Some Texas troops were assigned to the Army of Northern Virginia and became the major part of Hood's Texas Brigade which won eternal fame in Lee's Army. Other regiments joined the Army of Tennessee and fought as hard but winning few laurels.

Ford was appointed a colonel of State Cavalry[26] and sent to the Rio Grande where he was first able to negotiate a surrender of Fort Brown and its supplies from George Stoneman and Captain Hill. It was anticipated that this would require force but this was avoided. Colonel Ford was assigned as commanding officer of conscripts.[27]

Ford and his men patrolled the border area and the area near Brownsville where invasion was likely to occur. The Mexican raids were suppressed for several months. Because of political opposition Ford was denied a commission in the Confederate Army. He was to remain as superintendent of conscripts and administered his duties without partiality and in fairness. Ford resigned on November 1, 1861, and returned to Austin with his third wife, Addie Smith whom he had married May 31, 1861, and who was about half his age. A new daughter was a prompt arrival.

A concentrated effort by many Texas politicians to obtain a commission for Ford was made. This failed; for reasons unknown, General Bee had become a bitter enemy of Ford and was the principal force against his receiving a commission. Ford was able to make friends with General John Magruder in San Antonio who had been placed as Commander of the District of Texas, New Mexico and Arizona after Lee had removed him from command after the Seven Days Battle near Richmond, Virginia. Magruder was unable to secure a commission for Ford from Jefferson Davis, but he did reappoint him as superintendent of conscripts in March 1862 and, despite his lack of a commission, Ford was addressed as colonel and treated in every way as an officer.

Federal troops occupied the lower Rio Grande Valley and the local residents demanded assistance. Ford tried to persuade Magruder to let him lead a force to the valley. Confederate Major A.G. Dickinson was able to convince the general of the necessity of agreeing to Ford's request, and Ford was ordered to proceed. He was to command all troops south and west of San Antonio. This included a Ranger Battalion and Baird's Fourth Arizona Cavalry Regiment in addition to as many companies as Ford could muster. Other units included Nolen's unit from Corpus Christi and Captain A. J. Ware's Battalion from the area of San Patricio. Considerable time was spent by Ford in organization, and this delay brought considerable criticism from his political enemies. The force left San Antonio on March 17 led by John Ford who, for the first time, had a commission in his pocket. Not having an official Confederate commission, Ford named his unit Calvary of the West.[28]

Ford's military unit marched to Laredo then began a slow movement toward Brownsville. He encountered elements of the Union Army near Las Rucias and a general battle developed which resulted in a complete rout of the Union forces of about one-hundred men. There were twenty killed and thirty-six taken captive. Ford's losses sustained three dead and four wounded out of a force of about 250 engaged. Ford's forces continued to increase until he had about fifteen hundred men. They set on the 100-mile march to Brownsville. Union forces were encountered as they arrived at Brownsville and for several days the two groups engaged in sporadic firing but no battle developed. On July 30, reconnaissance revealed that the Union Army forces had abandoned their positions and concentrated at Brazos Santiago. The Union forces then attacked Ford and were defeated and fled to Brazos Island. Ford reported Union losses of 550 and his losses of a few killed and wounded and three missing.[29]

For four months both groups were idle as it seemed apparent that the war was lost for the Confederacy. Colonel Theodore H. Barrett decided against orders to attack Ford's forces at Palmito. Ford gathered forces and met Barrett and completely defeated him. The Union losses were high. The 34th Indiana Regiment lost 220 out of 300 men, there were 111 prisoners.[30] A few days after the battle Ford received word of the final defeat and surrender of the Confederate armies which had occurred before the Palmito Battle. Therefore, Ford had the honor of participating in the last battle of the war. Colonel Ford was designated as one of the officers to arrange paroles for the Confederate soldiers and was himself paroled on July 18, 1865.

Ford was involved in one last effort against Mexican raiders then settled in Brownsville. He served on three newspapers the last being the *Sentinel*. He served as the foreman of the federal grand jury in Brownsville, as a cattle inspector for Cameron County and as Mayor of Brownsville.

A new crisis developed in Austin as the Radical Republicans led by Governor E.J. Davis attempted to hold onto their power. There was a bitter disagreement over the constitutionality of the

Photo of John S. Ford in Confederate uniform as a colonel. Courtesy of Lawrence T. Jones, III, private library.

Photo of John S. Ford as an older man near the time of his retirement. Courtesy The Center For American History, University of Texas at Austin

gubernatorial election of 1873. The election was an overwhelming defeat of the Republicans by the newly reconstituted Democratic Party. Despite the defeat Davis was determined to stay in power. Denied federal troops, he called out a mixed detachment of state troops to enforce his desires. The new governor, Coke, appointed Henry McCulloch and the Travis rifles to oust Davis. McColloch became ill and Coke appointed W.P. Hardeman and Rip Ford, who was on his way to Austin leading a large contingent of angry Texans, to take over.[31] On January 16 there was a dangerous confrontation which seemed to be headed for an all-out battle. Ford got the attention of the crowd and forcefully addressed them and persuaded them to let the forces designated by the governor handle the matter. The dangerous confrontation was defused and Davis, recognizing the futility of his position, disappeared from the scene. This episode was certainly one of the most important things that Ford ever accomplished. Hardeman stated that twenty thousand lives had been saved by Ford's action.

In the summer of 1879 a crisis had developed in Austin in

the administration of the state's Deaf and Dumb Institution. Henry McCulloch had been the superintendent, gross mis-management became apparent, and he was forced to resign. Governor O.M. Roberts appointed Ford to the position on September 1. He held this position until December 31, 1883, and did a superlative job in managing and improving the institution. Illness forced his resignation.[32]

During Dr. Ford's last years he occupied himself in writing his memoirs, a very voluminous series of hand-written manuscript which he did not publish. They reside in the History Center at the University of Texas. The memoirs represent a most excellent history of early Texas. Given the fact that there is bias, the writing is one of the most important documents of early Texas. The memoirs were published in 1963 by Stephen B. Oates, who edited them and titled them "Rip Ford's Texas." Much of the biographical material of this and all other studies of John Ford have come from his memoirs and his medical journal.

Dr. Ford was vitally interested in history and was instrumental in the establishment of the Texas Historical Association. On its founding day, March 2, 1897, he and Mrs. Aspen Jones, Guy M. Bryan, John H. Reagan, Governor O.M. Roberts and others were made honorary life members. Just a month before his death he published an article in the quarterly titled "Fight on the Frio." On October 1, 1897, Dr. Ford suffered a stroke and died on November 3, 1897.[33]

Dr. John Salmon Ford is without doubt one of the most colorful figures in Texas history. No one served so long (1836-1883) in public service as he did. No one served in as many roles as he occupied, including physician, surveyor, Texas Ranger, State Representative, Senator, Indian fighter, publisher, trail blazer, Civil War officer, mayor of Austin and Brownsville and finally superintendent of The Deaf and Dumb Institution. He was a very real, fearless hero by any standard. He was the last of the old Rangers to die. Today's Texans should be grateful for his years of service and contributions to their state.

ENDNOTES

1. M.L. Moore. "John S. 'RIP' Ford." *Ten More Texans in Gray*, W. Curtis Nunn (ed.) (Hillsboro: Hill Jr. College Press, 1980).

2. John S. Ford. Memoirs. The Center For American History, University of Texas at Austin.

3. W.J. Hughes. *Rebellious Ranger, Rip Ford and the Old Southwest* (Norman: University of Oklahoma Press, 1964), 8.

4. Ibid., 4.

5. Ibid., 5.

6. Ibid., citing Ford Hamilton de Cordova Ford's grandson in September 1958.

7. Ibid.

8. Ibid., 6; Moore, op. cit., 2.

9. Moore, op. cit.

10. Hughes, op cit., 7.

11. Ibid., 7.

12. Ibid., 9.

13. Ibid., 10.

14. Ibid., 20.

15. Ibid.

16. Ibid., 40.

17. T.R. Fehrenbach. *Lone Star, A History of Texas and Texans* (New York: MacMillan, 1968), 492.

18. Hughes, op. cit., 75.

19. Ibid., 79.

20. Ibid., 108.

21. Ibid., 144.

22. Fehrenbach, op cit., 515.

23. Ibid., 519.

24. Hughes, op. cit., 178.

25. Ibid., 191.

26. Ibid., 192.

27. Fehrenbach, op. cit., 376.

28. Ibid., 377.

29. Ford, op. cit., VI: 1142.

30. Fehrenbach, op. cit., 391.

31. Ibid., 433.

32. Hughes, op. cit., 264.

33. Moore, op. cit., 15.

BIOGRAPHICAL SKETCH OF AUTHOR

(see page 59)

Portrait of Dr. Berthold Hadra made at about the time he was on the
faculty of the Texas Medical College at Galveston.

Berthold Ernest Hadra, M.D.
1842-1903
by
A.O. Singleton, Jr., M.D.

★IN A REPORT OF THE COMMITTEE on Surgery of the Texas Medical Association in 1886, George Cupples summarized the early period of Texas Surgery, "The Surgeons of Texas----country doctors though they be and with no long string of academic honors illustrating their names, are second to those of no country in the variety, the boldness and success of their operations, in practical skill, in fertility of resources and in that self reliance founded in knowledge without which no man can be a successful surgeon."[1] In regard to Berthold Hadra, a member of this group, this was probably an understatement. He has been described as an unhappy, humorless, frustrated man, a medical wanderer, a financial failure, a man ahead of his time, but as one looks deeper into this record, a different evaluation might well be in order.

He was born on November 8, 1842, in Brieg, Silesia, then part of Germany. We don't know what influenced him to seek a medical career. His father was a chief forester for the government. After finishing school in Brieg, he studied at the universities of Breslau and Berlin, acquiring the qualifications necessary to practice medicine and surgery. As an assistant surgeon in the Prussian Army, he served his country during the Seven Weeks War between Austria and Germany in 1866. Following this, he married Auguste Beyer. In 1869 he and his wife emigrated to the United States. He had prepared for this new venture by serving as a ship's doctor on a ship sailing between Bremen and New York so he could practice speaking English. Their son Frederick was born on the voyage. Berthold Hadra was twenty-four years old at the time.

Following in the wave of Germans migrating to Texas, the Hadras settled in Houston. Many German communities were being organized, particularly in the San Antonio area which still to this day reflects its Teutonic influences. Although many such emigrants fled Europe to avoid military service, Hadra was not of their number; when the Franco-Prussian War occurred, he tried to return to his old regiment in the German Army. Before permission could be obtained, the war was over. His patriotism was further reflected by naming his second child, born at this time, "Sedana" in honor of the German victory at Sedan.

Two years after arriving in Houston, Dr. B.E. Hadra moved his office to Austin, Texas, in 1872 and a year later had established a private infirmary, according to the *Daily Journal*. An advertisement in *Daniel's Texas Medical Journal* announces the opening of "Private Infirmary for Female Diseases on December 15, 1885 by Dr. B.E. Hadra."[2] We don't know what caused the move from Houston, but Austin with its beautiful hilly scenery along the Colorado River surrounded by Germanic settlements must have offered more attractions than the flat, humid Houston terrain, and probably resembled the old country that he had left. He must have integrated well into the community because in 1874 he was a delegate to the German Citizens convention. At the same time his scientific interests were evident as he demonstrated the existence of trichinella spiralis in meat in the butcher shops of Austin. In the following year he acquired a partner, Dr. Robert Miller, of Bastrop, a community about thirty miles from Austin. The same year a third child, Ernest, was born. This child's mother died when he was seven years old.

Several years later, Dr. Hadra married Ida Weisselberg, the daughter of a friend and colleague. Within a year a son James Marion was born, followed a year later in 1878 by a daughter named Ida after her mother who died at the delivery. Now, one hundred years later, it is hard to realize how many mothers as well as children were lost during childbirth. Victoria would have never been Empress of Great Britain if her first cousin Charlotte and baby had not died during childbirth.

Hadra's third and last marriage was to his second wife's sister, Emma Weisselberg. They had no children but Emma, the aunt-stepmother, was highly praised "as the dearest mother to all of us that anyone could be" according to her stepdaughter Ida.[3]

Hadra was admired and respected by his Austin colleagues and was chosen in 1878 as a delegate to the American Medical Association from the Texas State Medical Association. This same year he moved to San Antonio, entering into partnership with Dr A.E. Carothers in the practice of medicine and surgery. He was also associated with the health department and is frequently mentioned in the proceedings of various medical meetings. He was very productive in preparing, presenting and publishing on a variety of medical topics. In 1883 he was appointed to the Board of Regents of the University of Texas where he was associated with the great Ashbel Smith. He was one of the pallbearers at Smith's funeral in 1886.

In 1885 the Hadra family moved back to Austin. He remained a prolific writer including non-medical articles and fiction in the form of short stories and writing. His fiction was never published. His reputation as a diagnostician and surgeon increased both locally and internationally. Patients came to him from many countries and he made excursions into Mexico to perform surgery.

Hadra's professional high point came in 1888 when his book *Lesions of the Vagina and Pelvic Floor* was published and he was made Professor of the Science and Art of Surgery at the Texas Medical College in Galveston.[4]

The book was well received by his contemporaries. His understanding of the pelvic diaphragm and the repair of cystocele and rectocele was masterful. Later reviewers of his work also found it impressive. In *One Hundred Years of Gynecology* James V. Ricci credited Hadra as being the first to recognize the relation of the pelvic diaphragm to rectocele and cystocele and to devise a proper operation to correct these conditions. R.A. Leonard, in his 1944 *History of Gynecology* reported that Hadra and Sanger in Germany and later Walkins in America did pioneer work in the field of plastic surgery of the anterior vaginal wall. The work of Hadra was the beginning of modern operations for prolapse according to Howard Taylor (1941).[5]

Hadra's appointment to the professorship of the Science and Arts of Surgery of the Texas Medical College in 1888 resulted in a move to Galveston where he had four productive years, but in 1891 when the private school was replaced by the Medical Branch of the University of Texas, Dr. James Thompson of

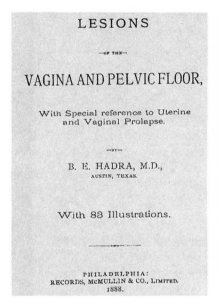

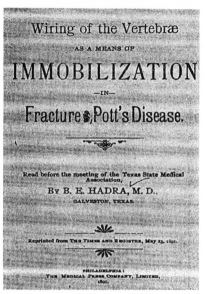

The title page of Dr. Harda's book on lesions of the vagina and pelvic floor, published in 1888.

The title page of a presentation by Dr. Hadra on wiring of the vertebrae to immobilize the spine in patients with Pott's disease.

England responding to an advertisement in Lancet, replaced Dr. Hadra. Why Dr. Hadra was not retained was not known, but this was a great disappointment to him. In 1891 Hadra made another important contribution in advocating wiring of vertebrae as a means of immobilization in Pott's disease.[6]

Among the number of Hadra's distinguished surgeon friends was Dr. J. Marion Sims, the renowned gynecologist of New York after whom Hadra's third son was named. The great surgical pioneer, Dr. Nicholas Senn of Chicago, often came to Texas to discuss surgical problems with Hadra, although the fact that Senn was a great duck hunter probably also encouraged his visits. At least he wasn't seeking a tax deduction for a hunting trip since income taxes were not a problem at that time. In a presidential address before the Texas Surgical Society, my father related a story about one such visit told him by Dr. A.C. Scott, one of the founders of the Scott and White Clinic. Dr. Hadra had published a report of performing nine Kraske operations for cancer of the rectum and Dr. Senn wanted to discuss this paper.

Dr. Scott was present during the two-hour presentation of these cases. Dr. Hadra exhibited the pathological specimens, each of which was removed from the fruit jar in which it had been carefully preserved. There was much discussion between the two surgeons only part of which was intelligible to Scott since much of it was in German, but he could tell that Dr. Senn was deeply interested and highly pleased with Dr. Hadra's description of his work. As they were saying goodby, Scott without thought of embarrassing anyone curiously asked Dr. Hadra how many patients who had received the benefit of this operation had recovered, to which he replied "They all died----They all died."[7]

Hadra returned to San Antonio in 1891 where he regained most of his old practice and also became chief surgeon of the Southern Pacific Railroad. In 1899 he was elected Vice President of the Texas Medical Association. In the same year he suffered a severe concussion when a runaway horse caused him to be thrown from his buggy. He had a stroke about a year later and recovered slowly.

He was brought to Waco by Dr. Harrington to be head surgeon in a clinic being founded in that city, but shortly after in 1900 he was lured to Dallas to be the Professor of Clinical Surgery in the Medical Department of the new University of Dallas which was being organized. One of the things that influenced Dr. Hadra to move was the thought that teaching would be less of a strain than practice to one with his infirmities. In the same year he was elected President of the Texas Medical Association at the first session held in the Twentieth Century.

On July 12, 1903, at 10:00 p.m., Dr. Berthold Ernest Hadra was found dead, seated in his office, by his son James. He was sixty years old. He was buried in Austin, survived by his wife and five children. The eldest son, Frederick, who had served as a major in the Medical Corps of the United States, died in Hawaii on December 25, 1917. His third and last wife died in 1940. His daughter Ida, Mrs. P.C. Vines of Dallas, was the only surviving child in 1960.[8]

Perhaps we can gain a better picture of Hadra from some of his writings. I have tried to use his language as far as possible. In 1889, as chairman of the section on Gynecology of the State Medical Association of Texas, he discussed the extent to which abdominal surgery should be performed by the general practi-

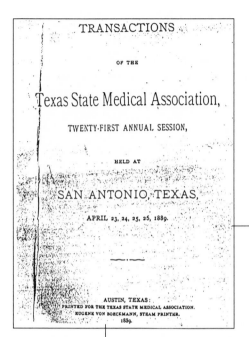

TRANSACTIONS

OF THE

Texas State Medical Association,

TWENTY-FIRST ANNUAL SESSION,

HELD AT

SAN ANTONIO, TEXAS,

APRIL 23, 24, 25, 26, 1889.

AUSTIN, TEXAS:
PRINTED FOR THE TEXAS STATE MEDICAL ASSOCIATION.
EUGENE VON BOECKMANN, STEAM PRINTER.
1889.

Hadra's address as chairman of the Section on Gynecology at the 21st Session of the Texas State Medical Association

SECTION ON GYNECOLOGY.

ABDOMINAL SURGERY—ADDRESS BY CHAIRMAN.

B. E. HADRA, M. D., GALVESTON, TEXAS.

By an agreement with the Chairman of the Section on Surgery, my remarks are to be directed to abdominal practice, as much as it forms a common field between gynecological and general surgery. Understanding that my address should not consist of a mere enumeration of the additions, made during the last year, but that it rather should bring before this body some general points or principles, I choose to ventilate the question, how far abdominal surgery should be in the grasp of the general practitioner, and how he could best acquire the necessary aptitude.

Abdominal operations are yet viewed as something distinct, a specialty, as for instance, ophthalmology; still, if we consider that a great number of the most important structures and organs: liver, gall bladder, stomach, intestines, spleen, ureters, ovaries, tubes, uterus, bladder, descendent aorta, and so on, have frequently to be approached by the knife, I can with difficulty conceive why aggression on half of the body should be left out of the list of the general surgeon. It can certainly only be attributed to the novelty of the procedure that such a division is made, and, perhaps, also, to the natural timidity to enter the internal body. But after the fact is once established that the open-

tioner, and how such an individual could best acquire the necessary aptitude to perform the same.

According to the author, "Whoever lays claim to the title of surgeon ought to be prepared to perform a laparotomy as readily as an amputation." He included caesarian section as a procedure the country practitioner should be able to perform successfully. After his opening remarks, which would seem to encourage the general practitioner to perform more abdominal surgery, Hadra then described the limitation of success by the less skilled and uninformed doctors, and the advantages of better training and experience in one who is to perform surgery. He would increase the period of training in medical school and suggested more post-graduate training, and refresher courses. "It makes little difference whether a young man prepares himself under the title of a student, a post-graduate or an assistant, be sure he must spend a proportionate time to become proficient." While the less-well-trained doctor may be forced to perform emergency surgery for which he should prepare himself as well as possible, he should refer elective work to more experienced hands. We are cautioned against the young doctor who sets up as a specialist without the proper background. Hadra concludes,

> If fate should not favor you with abdominal cases, do not forget that new fields for surgery and fascinating operations have been opened, which will, if successfully performed not less cite the admiration of the community. But even if you do not have the chance to open a skull or a belly, console yourself with the thought that you may nevertheless become a rich man, a great doctor, and an honored member of the profession.[9]

In 1898 Hadra in his chairman's report to the section on surgery of the State Medical Association of Texas reviewed changes which had taken place during the year between surgery and medical practice. More surgery was being performed with the exception of brain surgery where the mood had become more conservative.

In the treatment of lung disease, surgery had made striking progress, especially by French surgeons in the treatment of

TRANSACTIONS

OF THE

Texas State Medical Association

THIRTIETH ANNUAL SESSION,

HELD AT

HOUSTON, TEXAS.

APRIL 26TH, 27TH, 28TH AND 29TH, 1898.

AUSTIN, TEXAS:
THE EUGENE VON BOECKMANN PUBLISHING COMPANY.
1898

The address of Dr. Hadra to the Section on Surgery, presented at the 30th annual session of the Texas State Medical Association.

SECTION ON SURGERY.

THE PRESENT POSITION OF SURGERY IN ITS RELATION TO MEDICINE.

REPORT OF CHAIRMAN.

B. E. HADRA, M. D.,

SAN ANTONIO, TEXAS.

In briefly surveying the changes which have taken place during the last year and the period just preceding it, with special reference to the interchange between surgery and practice, I may state that the encroachment of the former into the realms of the latter has steadily progressed with only one exception, and that is in brain surgery. Here the much too active inclination of the surgeon has somewhat receded on account of the warnings of the most experienced authorities, who have clearly shown that under existing conditions of diagnosis many of the deeper seated or of the more extensive new growths will either not be found or not be made approachable by the knife. This field of cutting treatment must therefore be greatly narrowed. The same appertains to surgery for epilepsy unless the localization is perfect or visible traumatism is responsible. On the other hand, abscess following otitis has become better defined as to locality and accessibility, and will, I trust, soon become one of the best worked out and most successful surgical acts when early undertaken.

In the treatment of lung diseases further conquests have been made by surgery, at least attempts in this direction have been pushed more vigorously, especially by French surgeons, as for the treatment of abscesses, gangrene, foreign bodies, etc., by direct intervention. The diagnosis of pulmonary malignant

abscesses, gangrene and foreign bodies. The diagnosis of pulmonary malignant growths had improved. The pleura and heart
growths had improved. The pleura and heart were more actively
attacked than formerly. Drainage of the pericardium had not yet
become a procedure free from objections. Abdominal surgery
including the kidneys, pancreas and liver had increased together
with stomach and intestines. Hadra, quoting Billroth, made the
frightening statement that "All medicine has to become surgical." He concluded with more rational remarks, "the old idea
that the same disease should be reviewed differently by the
surgeon as compared with the general practitioner, should be
discarded. There is one way to approach a disease and that is
through and from every standpoint."[10]

In his annual message in 1901 as President of the State
Medical Association of Texas, Dr. Hadra urged the reorganization of the State Medical Association so as to divide the scientific
and administrative sections of the meeting; the first open to all
practitioners; the later to elected representatives of the various
county societies. He was in favor of a national department of
health.

He wanted more financial support from county and district
societies. He voiced opposition to the passage of a law to regulate
the practice of medicine in the state, one of his main reasons
being "the acknowledgment of the disciples of sham science as
our equals." Another criticism was that "the law was the most
generous invitation to the rankest and most insolent medical
abortions to our state." He then suggested that a committee
should be formed to study the matter and to come up with a
proper regulation to regulate medical practice in the state. Most
of this was obviously stimulated by the appointment of unquali-
fied individuals to medical appointments in Texas. He recommended a reduction in dues from five to three dollars and the
abolition of initiation fees. He also ruled that papers would be
read by title only if their author was not present to read them.[11]

In his Presidential Address given at the same session, Dr.
Hadra opened with,

> Expecting perhaps to be listened to by parents who
> have to select an occupation for their son or perhaps
> by a young lady who has good reason to weigh the

TRANSACTIONS

OF THE

STATE MEDICAL ASSOCIATION OF TEXAS

THIRTY-THIRD ANNUAL SESSION

HELD AT

GALVESTON, TEXAS,

April 23rd, 24th, 25th and 26th, 1901.

AUSTIN
VON BOECKMANN SON
D

Title page of Dr. Hadra's presidential
address to the Texas State Medical
Association at its 33rd annual session.

THE REPORT OF THE COMMITTEE ON THE TREASURER'S ANNUAL REPORT.

To B. E. Hadra, M. D., President Texas State Medical Association.

DEAR SIR: We, your committee appointed to examine the annual report
of Treasurer, beg leave to report that after a careful examination of the
statements, vouchers and receipts, we find same correct, we ask the adoption of same.

J. D. OSBORN,
TAYLOR HUDSON,
C. M. ALEXANDER.

Dr. Taylor Hudson was asked to take the chair by the President.

PRESIDENT'S ANNUAL MESSAGE.

The President then read his annual message and recommenda-
tions, as follows:

GENTLEMEN: The necessity of co-operative and organized efforts and the
improvement of the social and economic conditions of the profession is too
urgent and obvious to allow a continuation of the old dignified let-go policy.
The steadily increasing complexity of the machinery of modern society
demands a frequent adaptation of its parts to each other and to the whole.
There is nothing wrong and nothing egotistic in an active struggle for that
purpose as long as the methods and objects remain legitimate and benefit
society generally.

The most comprising action has, as a matter of course, to emanate from
the national organization. In fact it is hard to understand how one hundred and fifty thousand educated and influential citizens could have waited
so long in patience without undertaking any decisive steps toward improving their own conditions. Let me mention one of many objects which now
and then looms up in daily literature as an almost visionary aim; it is the
creation of a national department of health with its own secretary, which
certainly ought to be earnestly pursued.

The greatest obstacle to desirable efficiency of the national organization, I think, consists in the mixing up of the purely scientific with the
purely administrative or political purposes. While the first requires the
most liberal and the least restricted forms, the latter demand a well disci-
plinized and methodical handling by strictly fixed methods. The two
ought, therefore, to be separated, and if the same body attends to both, the
time and manner must be distinct. From such consideration we must hail
with great satisfaction the plan inaugurated by the American Medical Association to create a separate delegate body of about one hundred and fifty

pros and cons of the different callings of young men, I chose for my subject a discussion of the social standings of the physician compared with that of the members of other so called learned professions.

He attempted to carry out the task by comparing the learned physician scientist and the practicing physician, pointing out that they often overlap. "Although the medical genius is as essential to progress, he is less often recognized as compared to great soldiers, politicians, etc" or, as Hadra says,

> history will not give them all seats in the same row. With the deepest humiliation must I state that even the most moderate expectations of the doctor will be disappointed. There is no science to whose disciples so little glory is accorded by people and by general history. [German construction constantly appears in his English writings.]

He probably overstates the case when he says "Not one doctor has become a historical figure." He then reports a number of polls and lists of "intellectual eminence" which would tend to conform this, but this was before doctors started employing press agents.

> The medical scientist, like the student of many other branches of science, has a very poor prospect to acquire public fame. Although Asiatic cholera may be known only as a queer reminiscence found in the story book of civilized nations, you will not suppose that the good discoverer's name will hold its place of glory, perpetually. His name will have long vanished from the people's almanac while Robin Hood will still be a celebrated figure in song and play. The love for possessions is more forcible with the masses than the fear of disease or even death. I am afraid that the physician's work in our country is viewed too much as a mercenary pursuit which the world does not feel like honoring with triumphal arches.

John H. Divckx in his recent article in the *Pharos* on Dr. John Arbuthnot, the physician to royalty and the creator of "John Bull," repeats the same theme, "when doctors play significant roles in history as they sometimes do, it is usually not by practicing medicine."[12]

Hadra felt that the newness of our country, and the lack of government help for institutions and schools, were factors that had to be overcome before more scientists, including doctors of medicine, reached the halls of fame. He compared the practicing physician with members of other learned professions such as preachers, teachers and philosophers, druggists, engineers, architects and electricians. He felt that "fixation" in their positions eliminates this group, and he came up with doctors and lawyers as the rivals in the leadership of social affairs of a secular nature. The lawyer in the United States seemed to be the winner. Hadra's theory was that the lawyer, by mental training or experience, tends to act more logically than the physician. Comparing his European upbringing with the American system, he felt "that we are less rigid in our training, and one is in a better position to enter any field that he chooses. In contrast to the logically trained mind of the lawyer, medical art is the art of probabilities." He concluded,

> The medical man is surely the most human and humane of all professional men; he never wavers to even kill his own goose that lays the golden egg, when common welfare so demands. You see him daily teach you how to prevent disease, although he lives on its very existence.
>
> [The physician] may be better loved by the community, loved by more people than the lawyer, thought more of as a man, and a citizen: still he will have to stand back when he comes to the load of public honors of the street and the political arena. And thus, I will close my tedious discourse, hoping that you will think of the doctor, if not better than before, at least not worse.

Not a very encouraging recruitment speech.[13]

Hadra's second and last work entitled *The Public and the*

Doctor by a Regular Physician[14] was privately published in 1902 and perhaps gives us a better picture of the author than would an autobiography. We now see Dr. Hadra as a real human being, not just a list of titles. It was written for the laity in an attempt to inform the general public as to medical affairs. Hadra felt that they were poorly informed and he hoped to improve the relationship between the physician and the masses. Present information was obviously inadequate as shown by the increase in quackery. "It is written by a regular physician and is offered to such persons as are amenable to reason. The fanatic or stupid will be as little affected by it as by anything else beyond his grasp." The book was written to be presented by physicians to their patients and other persons to better inform them in these matters and in the fore page was "Presented Compliments of Dr. _____," where the donor's name could be written. "We are sure that good fellowship and confidence will be enhanced by it" wrote Dr. Hadra.

In the first chapter, which is an attack on medical cults, a distinction is made between the allopathic or regular physician who practices according to scientific principles and the many cults such as the

> homeopathic, eclectic, osteopathic, Christian Science, physiopathics and other pathics who are taken by the public as scientific rivals but are in reality, vagaries of fantastic minds or schemes for making money. These are based on dogma while scientific medicine is changeable and based on evidence.

He saved his most severe criticism for Christian Science which he considered the most dangerous since it is coupled with religion and deprives the sufferer of assistance and treatment. In chapter two he points out that not every regular doctor should be recommended. "He should not be a fanatic, politician, hard-drinker, dude, or lack common sense." He made allowance for a second class of practitioners who fulfill the needs of poorer or less attractive communities. He felt that the belief that practitioners are at their best when drunk was a fabrication. He concludes this chapter with the suggestion that a physician should be studious and keep abreast with the progress and development of science. "However, all our well-meant advices may be of no avail." The individual may select a doctor because "he drives a conspicuously fine horse or wears a stove pipe hat or has a finely shaped foot or blows the trombone well."

In his next chapter he attacked "specialists" (to be distinguished between the true specialist), "quacks and others who use gadgets and advertisers, and patent medicines." The following chapter explains how medicine is taught and discusses certain scientific principle, medical problems, and preventive medicine. He wistfully recalled that the Chinese doctor is paid only when the patient is well, "surely there must be some compensation to the doctor for the loss of trade which necessarily follows the prevention of disease."

In chapter five the relationships between the physician and the patient are discussed. He divides doctors into the family physician, the true specialist and the "occasionally consulted." He advises how to chose a doctor if you are new in a community. "Try to find out if your candidate is a gentleman." This can be confirmed "from your lady neighbors who, as a rule, know every mean or criminal thing about every man, or women in town." He mentions the value of medical organizations in picking a physician although he mentions that "many weak brothers are members. Do not believe that medical societies are formed as business schemes for robbing the people." He supports the general practitioner, but warns the general specialist who pretends to know everything that he may be a phony or a fool. He then addresses himself to the patient's conduct toward the physician and many pet grievances come to light.

> If the doctor makes a mistake, no unnecessary resentment should be shown. It is bad policy—Do not sulk; nothing is more disturbing to the necessary freedom of the doctor's mind and the patient will suffer in consequence. Be polite to the doctor as one cultured person to another. To call out in the doctor's presence 'Jim, get another doctor' or similar remarks, will not be exactly proper." Other admonitions are "Be considerate of the doctor, he is very sensitive. Stick to your family physician. Do not send unnecessarily at night and at once. Do not gossip about doctors.

He discusses how to change doctors by a gentlemanly explanation on the part of a patron to his physician. He also mentions that all monetary obligations should be taken care of before the separation.

Dr. William O. Wilkes of Waco did not think Hadra ever told a joke or indulged in frivolous conversation,[15] but Mrs. Josephine Hadra felt he had a keen sense of humor, and a quality wit which made him sought after as an after-dinner speaker, though this was not flourishing in his final years.[16]

The supposedly humorless Dr. Hadra relates a funny story in his final book after warning the reader not to call the doctor out at night "A doctor was called by a very unpromising looking man to go and see a child at a great distance. The man candidly stated that he had nothing to reward the doctor with, and that he had come at night in order that the doctor should not lose any of his precious time during the day." Hadra concludes, "If there were justice in the world the fee for a night call should equal the pay for a day's work so that the doctor would lose nothing by resting the following day." The picture of the family doctor's keeping an endless vigil by the patient's side was not very pleasing to Dr. Hadra, who felt that "it doesn't do justice to the patient or the physician." He also believed that the "doctor shouldn't serve as nurse, house maid, washerwoman, or servant girl."

We are warned that we shouldn't gossip about the doctor's mistakes. "Do not go with a shotgun after him, you may get into trouble." He seemed to be quite concerned about gossips because we are repeatedly warned against such persons.

He was very much against abortions and would break with the patient rather than perform one. "The doctor will be able to stand the punishment of your spiteful glances; he is used to all kinds of cuts and slights." The repetition of such remarks makes one feel that Dr. Hadra must have been a very sensitive and often hurt individual. He criticized the humble patients who become rich and drop their physicians who were not "sell" enough for them. "One must not scare the children with the doctor."

He points out the perils of taking advice from other persons rather than their doctor. He illustrates this with a story of a boy who went to the drug store to have a prescription filled for a sick sister. The lad was asked who his doctor was, "oh none yet;

Mother found a prescription on the street and she thought she would first try that."

He complains about delinquent doctor bills. "Only a small portion of the people are in the habit of paying their doctor as promptly as they pay their milkman." He mentions many so-called prominent people who he calls "dead-beats."

He scorned the idea that most physicians are wealthy, citing that "the average physician's income in the United States does not reach more than $700 or $800 a year, about the same as a street car driver or dry-goods clerk who do not have to worry over making out bills and making collections." He confesses that a few doctors in the large cities may make fifty to one hundred thousand dollars a year, "The complaints of the rich that they are charged too much must take into account that the poor pay nothing." Office visits at this time were two dollars. He believed in charging for telephone consultations, more for night calls. House calls were three dollars and long trips one dollar per mile.

Malpractice was not omitted. "The main difficulty will always be to prove the fault to be with the doctor and most verdicts go with the doctor though some suits are greatly justified." This was in the good old days.

His final remarks are reserved for the ladies. He cautioned female patients not to take up the doctor's time with gossip or too detailed an account of their case, "An invitation to rid the doctor's office of these friends without wounding their feelings would make a fortune." He resents the patient "subscription and ticket fiend who mulcts the doctor for a dollar when he does not know where his office rent is to come from." He also resents the social "consultation" when patients want to talk shop. His best example of this is the "woman sitting next to her family doctor at a concert, during the performance of a Beethoven Symphony who pesters him the whole time with a description of her baby's summer complaint."[17]

Dr. Hadra has been presented in the past as a man ahead of his time, too superior for his contemporaries, a financial failure who wandered over Texas looking for success which he did not find. My impression was that he had a very successful life. Migrating to a new land, he gained recognition and respect from his colleagues who awarded him high honors. He was a productive author whose excellent contributions were well accepted in his own lifetime. The fact that he moved his residence about the state may indicate courage and a desire always to improve his opportunities, or the successful individual who is never satisfied. Perhaps he was also one of those persons who enjoy change and new contacts and experiences. A lack of sense of humor has been suggested but this has been denied by his family and perhaps by his writing. *The Public and the Doctor* will bring chuckles from any reader whether intentional or not. His writing indicated a concern for money, His daughter has indicated "He was a great surgeon but such a bad business man that he never made any money at all."[18] He never refused to treat anyone and many large fees that he collected were applied to helping other persons. Though at times financially embarrassed, he never succumbed to any wrong doing. To quote from his book *The Public and the Doctor,*

> A good and able doctor may in adverse circumstances have a hard time to be justly appreciated, and many unfortunates who have had to wait too long for that event, have gone wrong from sheer desperation; but as a rule the deserving will be patient, manly, and honorable endeavor, reach the goal, and need not indulge in uncouth practices.

A photograph of the tomb of Dr. Berthold Hadra in the Oakwood Cemetery in Austin, Texas. His wife is entombed in an identical crypt on his left.

So he didn't become rich. But he preserved the unselfish reputation one associates with saints.

He did experience heartbreaks in the death of two wives, but he always found excellent replacements and had a devoted and happy family. He was disappointed at not being appointed professor of science at the University of Texas Medical Branch at Galveston, but he was rewarded with an appointment of professor of surgery at the new school in Dallas and died peacefully while at work, still a prominent figure in American Medicine.

Dr. Hadra was buried in Oakwood Cemetery in Austin, Texas.

ENDNOTES

1. George Cupples. Report of the Committee on Surgery of The Texas State Medical Association. *Texas State Medical Journal* 1 (1885-86), 472.

2. G.W.N. Eggers. "Berthold Earnest Hadra (1842-1903), A Biography." *Clinical Orthopedics* 21 (1961), 32-39.

3. Ibid.

4. B.E. Hadra. *Lesions of the Vagina and Pelvic Floor*, Philadelphia Records (McMullin and Company, 1888).

5. P.I. Nixon. *A History of the Texas Medical Association* (Austin: University of Texas Press, 1953), 57, 80, 96, 110, 154, 167, 211, 212, 220, 221, 224, 225, 240.

6. B.E. Hadra. "Wiring of the Vertebrae as a means of Immobilization in Fracture and Pott's Disease." *The Times and Register* (May 23, 1931), 1-8.

7. A.O. Singleton. "The Surgeon in the Romantic History of Texas." *Ann. Surg* 3 (1940), 685; "An Account of the Early History of Surgery in Texas," Presidential Address before The Texas Surgical Society, October 1932.

8. Eggers, op. cit.

9. B.E. Hadra. "Abdominal Surgery." Address by Chairman. *Transactions of the Texas State Medical Association* 21(1889), 199-206.

10. B.E. Hadra. "The Present Position of Surgery in its Relationship to Medicine." Report of Chairman. *Transactions of the Texas State Medical Association* 30 (1898), 167-71.

11. B.E.Hadra. President's Annual Message. *Transactions of The Texas State Medical Association* 33 (1901), 21-24.

12. John H. Divckx. "Dr. John Arbuthnot." *Pharos* (Summer 1979).

13. B.H. Hadra, B.E. Annual Address. *Transactions of the Texas State Medical Association* 33 (1901), 61-80.

14. N.O. Wilkes. *History of The Waco Medical Association with Reminiscences and Irrelevant Comments* (Waco: 1931), 251-53.

15. B.E. Hadra. *The Public and the Doctor, Dallas, Texas.* (J. M. Coville, The Franklin Press, 1902).

16. Eggers, op. cit.

17. Hadra, *Public and the Doctor*, op. cit.

18. Eggers, op. cit.

BIOGRAPHICAL SKETCH OF AUTHOR

ALBERT O. SINGLETON, JR., M.D. died suddenly on July 3, 1980, while on vacation in Colorado. His death was unexpected and a great shock to his family and to his many friends and colleagues throughout the country.

Dr. Singleton was born in Galveston, Texas, on August 3, 1915, the oldest of two sons of Dr. and Mrs. Albert O. Singleton, Sr. His father was a nationally known surgeon and was Professor of Surgery and Chairman of the Department of Surgery at the University of Texas Medical Branch in Galveston from 1927 to 1947.

Dr. Singleton, Jr., was graduated in 1932 from Ball High School in Galveston, Texas, then attended the University of Texas from which he received a B.A. degree in 1935. He received his M.D. degree from the University of Texas Medical Branch in Galveston in 1939. He had an outstanding academic record in medical school and was elected to Alpha Omega Alpha Honor Medical Society. After graduation from medical school, he had an internship at the University of Pennsylvania from 1939 until 1941, following which he had residency training in Surgery at the University of Michigan in Ann Arbor, Michigan, from 1941 until 1942. In 1942 he entered the Medical Corps of the U.S. Army, from which he was discharged with the rank of major in 1946. After his army service, he returned to the University of Michigan as an instructor in general surgery, and completed his training in surgery in 1947.

On July 1, 1947, Dr. Singleton returned home to Galveston and was appointed Assistant Professor of Surgery at the University of Texas Medical Branch and became Associate Professor in 1953. He spent the remainder of his surgical career at the University of Texas Medical Branch in Galveston and was an active member of the full-time teaching staff at the time of his death. During his tenure at the University of Texas Medical Branch, Dr. Singleton was very active in surgical research, clinical surgery, and teaching, and contributed more than one-hundred papers to the surgical literature.

In addition to regular contributions to the surgical literature, Dr. Singleton was active in the affairs of the many professional organizations of which he was a member. He was a member of the Galveston County Medical Society, the Texas Medical Association, the American Medical Association, the American College of Surgeons, the Southern Surgical Association, Southwestern Surgical Congress, the Southern Medical Association, the Western Surgical Association, Texas Surgical Society of which he was president in 1974, the Frederick A. Coller Surgical Society, and the Singleton Surgical Society of which he was past-president.

In July 1942 Dr. Singleton was married to Joan Anderson of Ann Arbor, Michigan, and they had three children, Albert O. Singleton, III, M.D., Gail Anderson Singleton Welply, and Elizabeth Anderson Singleton, all of whom survived him. He is also survived by his wife and his brother, Edward B. Singleton, M.D.

Dr. Singleton was a fine gentleman and a respected surgeon and teacher. He will be remembered with affection and honor by his family, his friends, his students, and his patients.

—ED. B. ROWE, M.D.

Portrait of Dr. Ferdinand Ludwig Herff.
Courtesy Dr. August Herff, Jr.

Ferdinand Ludwig Herff, M.D.
1820-1912

Eminent physician and surgeon
Courageous and idealistic pioneer
Distinguished organizer and citizen
Courtly gentleman - even in a hovel

by

Vernie A. Stembridge, M.D.,
with acknowledgement to Dr. August F. Herff, Jr.

★FERDINAND LUDWIG VON HERFF was born to Baron Christian Samuel von Herff and Eleanora Freiin von Meusbach in Darmstadt, Germany, on November 29, 1820, and died in San Antonio, Texas, on May 18, 1912. He was the oldest of the seven von Herff children.[1]

Ferdinand's family background is unequivocally traceable back to 1559 with roots extending back to the thirteenth century. His ancestors had the family name "Herve" and, as French Huguenots, endured religious persecution and sought asylum from the implacable inquisition. Forced to flee from France to the area now known as Belgium, the family of professed Protestants prospered somewhat but overall gained little. Continuing to be targets of religious harassment, in about 1550 they again were forced to relocate, to the Rhenish Provinces of Germany. With this move to the Duchy of Hesse-Darmstadt along the Rhine River, the family modified its name to Herff to reflect a more Teutonic attitude. Here six generations of the Herff lineage consistently assumed positions of increasing responsibility and leadership with such titles as Tax High Commissioner, Senator, and Burgermeister (St. Goar). On August 1, 1814, the knighting

of Herff's grandfather in recognition of excellent judicial services, bestowed nobility on the family, permitting the title of
"von" and authorizing a crest.

Ferdinand's father, a well-recognized writer on jurisprudence and Chief Justice of the Hessen Supreme Court, instilled
the importance of education, culture, and contacts. Upon completing the Giessen Gymnasium, young Herff had a most fortunate opportunity. His uncle Dr. Von Rehfuss, a well-known
diplomat and distinguished author, was President of the University of Bonn. Ferdinand enjoyed the privilege of living in the
President's home. With enthusiasm for learning, dedicated dili-
gence and terrific endurance, young Herff pursued the pure
sciences and languages, studying German, French, English, Latin
and Greek.

As was the custom of the day, many notables on their
journeys spent restful time in academic environs. Thus, Herff
was able to interact with many nobles: Prince Albert, the Duke
of Coburg who later became the beloved consort of the renowned Queen Victoria, Prince Albert's brother who later
succeeded to the title Duke of Coburg, the Czarina of Russia,
Crown Prince Frederick of Prussia and later Emperor of Germany, and many others. Among the notable scientists Herff met
were Johannes Mueller and Alexander von Humboldt, the distinguished naturalist, explorer and botanist. Although many
years his senior, Humboldt took great fancy to young Herff and
showed him many kindnesses, including the use of the microscope.

Added to this milieu, young Ferdinand became an active
member of the "Student Korps," an exclusive fraternity bound
by a rigid code of honor. Their camaraderie generally included
active discussions of political matters of the day accompanied by
beer drinking which often concluded with loud singing; on one
occasion Herff's boisterousness caused him to be jailed. On a
dare, Ferdinand swam the Rhine for a distance of twenty miles.
While membership guaranteed social position, participants conducted themselves with medieval methods of defending their
honor. Challenges, depending upon the gravity of the offense to
one's honor, might end in duels with pistols or sabers. Credited
with as many as twenty-three duels, most of them with flat
bladed swords (schlagers) but at least one with cavalry sabers and

one with pistols, Herff carried to his grave numerous upper body scars of his youth.

With a sense of culture and refinement and a thirst for human associations, Herff struggled over his future. The study of pure sciences was foremost in his mind, especially botany due to the influence of Humboldt and the Prince of Wied; however, he realized these were not practical lifetime vocations and directed his studies into medicine with the early ambition to be a professor of surgery. Enrolling in medicine at the University of Berlin, Herff had an intellectual and personal presence which facilitated his studies with the notable medical faculty of the day: Johannes Peter Mueller (physiology), Matthias Jacob Schleiden (pathology), and Johann Friedrich Dieffenbach and Karl Ferdinand von Graefe (surgery and ophthalmology). This forward-looking faculty inculcated many modern concepts about understanding and treatment of disease. Not the least of these new concepts involved microscopy and ophthalmology. His continuing friendship with Humboldt and the Prince of Wied reflected favorably upon Herff's personality and mental capacities.

Existing law required that a student take his final two years of medical education and final examinations at his home university; for Herff this was the University of Giessen. Herff completed his formal studies in November 1842 with a public defense of his required thesis. The published thesis, "Die Gynakologie des Franz v. Piemont" consisting of eighty-eight pages with 133 references, dealt with fifteenth-century Italian gynecology. The Doctor of Medicine degree was awarded in March 1843.

After graduation, Herff sat for the "Physicate" examination, which admitted him to medical service under the State, and was appointed a surgeon in the Hessian Army. As a 23-year-old Prussian military surgeon, Herff went about his duties with boundless energy, courage and an indomitable spirit. He developed an unusual knack for plastic surgery in correcting facial deformities, using flaps from the forehead to create noses and ears. He reported these results in his first scientific article appearing in the 1844 *Heidelberg Annals*. Additional recognition came from his successful drainage of a tuberculous abscess (an unaccepted practice) which he reported in 1846 in *Rhenish Archives*. This accomplishment later brought him a medical defeat when the Duke's hairdresser suffered from a tuberculous abscess. On royal command, the Duke summoned Herff, sending his carriage and four to bring Herff to the castle in grand style. Much difficulty was encountered during the procedure and the patient died, whereupon a humiliated Herff was summarily dumped out the back entrance in the dead of night to find his own way home. Herff's article, however, did provide for a future meeting with the famed Rudolf Virchow.

He achieved recognition as a superlative physician and surgeon and became well established among his peers. War mutilations brought eye injuries that permitted Herff to use his knowledge acquired from von Graefe. He became noted for the rapidity of his surgery, which was a truly welcome asset for frequent amputations; he was able to perform such feats in less than three minutes. This period of surgery (1842-1847) was used for testing the advent and use of anesthetics, ether and nitrous oxide. Although practicing prior to the understanding of the germ theory, Herff maintained a fastidious approach to surgery, religiously using plenty of soap and water as well as clean, short-sleeved shirts and an easily cleaned rubberized apron.

Europe was in political turmoil during this time. Stimulated by the success of liberal movements in France and Italy, similar political movements now surfaced in Germany. The industrial revolution created unrest, particularly among the middle class, and, in the attempt to balance supply and demand, a new doctrine of socialism became prominent. In active foment, those in this social and intellectual atmosphere sought relief from governance by nobility and its police state, desiring to replace it with an idealistic movement which centered on brotherly love and good will. Many organized groups began to seek relief by moving to America. The German emigration was not unique, witness Shaker communities, Amana colonies, and Brook farms.

In Germany, Herff and other university-educated men became inoculated and possessed of this idea. Having its origin in 1842, a group of dispossessed German noblemen formed "Mainzer Verein" or "Adelsverein," The Society for the Protection of German Emigrants, which offered the German middle class and peasants an alternative to the harsh conditions that prevailed in the newly industrialized Germany. This group ultimately founded colonies in Wisconsin, Iowa and Texas, with New

Braunfels being the initial community in Texas. Reports back to Germany from these establishments were frank, offering pro-and-con views of immigration, particularly about Texas. It is interesting that Ferdinand Roemer, a famous German scientist who visited Texas 1845-1847 and reported extensively on its geology, animal and plant life, cautioned against German settlements along the Llano River in the region of Castell and Leiningen, the exact future location of Herff's Bettina.[2]

Herff was taken with the emigration concepts and, being a natural leader, began to form an alliance composed mostly of educated professionals and artisans from almost every stand of life. Some were from the best families of Darmstadt and included Herff's schoolmate from Giessen, Gustav Schleicher. With the formation of "Die Vierziger," composed of forty like-minded individuals, Herff was prepared when organizers Hermann Spiess and Prince Karl Solms-Braunfels approached with the offer to donate lands in Texas, part of the Fisher-Miller Grant which later proved to be a white elephant, but the land required settling promptly. Cautiously, Herff took a leave of absence from the army determined to establish a Texas colony. This bold decision meant severing ties to the mother country, as well as with his sweetheart Mathilde who was opposed to the venture.

In January and February 1847, contracts were signed with the U.S. Government and with Count Castell, respectively, to colonize the land along the Llano River at its junction with Elm Creek. Having generated $12,000 in currency and promises of supplies, co-signed by Count Castell representing the Adelsverein, the group prepared to depart. The "ultimate" group consisted of thirty-three members, having dwindled from the original forty. To facilitate the arrangements in Texas, Herff and Spiess preceded the group, traveling via the newly instituted Trans-Atlantic steamer with its recently devised screw propeller, embarking from Hamburg and landing in New York. In an oral interview in 1890 Herff recalled the journey.

> I landed in New York in . . . 1846 [sic]. The railroad south only reached as far as Wheeling, Va [sic], from whence we staged it to New Orleans and thence to Galveston and Indianola by water. We arrived at this place at the end of April 1847. I was one of the earlier

arrivals of our Society to which I belonged, the bulk
of my associates came over in August 1847.

Herff met the group on their arrival in Galveston and
secured passage for all via a schooner to Indianola, where needed
supplies would be obtained and from where a direct road connected with the interior of Texas and the Southwest.

After struggling across the country via New Braunfels and
Fredericksburg, they arrived at the junction of Elm Creek with
the Llano River, the beautiful, crystal clear "Silvery Llano" in
September 1847. Here they established a community of the
Icarian type as proposed by Etienne Babet, and called it Bettina
in honor of Goethe's celebrated friend, Bettina von Arnim, a
leading German intellectual of her day.[3] Laggards developed
from the beginning. In spite of all the advantages the society gave
them by furnishing provisions and implements, the courageous
pioneers had to contend with all the difficulties incident to
clearing of the wilderness; however, they were completely de-
void of the necessary practical knowledge. Initially enthusiastic,
the settlers faced the stern reality of living, including plowing
and manual labor that were unanticipated chores. Dissension
developed among the heterogeneous group when shelter construction and agricultural duties were not performed. After all,
these people were artisans and professionals each wanting to do
his own thing without a sense of organization or the willingness
to accept any system of community discipline. Added to this
confusion was the anticipated, but unrealized, threat of Indians.
While attempting to overcome some of the insurmountable
difficulties, the colony became impoverished. Within a year the
community of Bettina failed, bankrupt financially as well as in
spirit.

Despite Herff's best efforts to turn around the community's
misfortunes, his own perception was not one of failure and he
became convinced that Texas would be his permanent home. A
variety of experiences led to this conclusion. He had come as a
colonizer, yet despite organizational mistakes, he was certain
about the potential of the land and of the opportunity for its
development. He understood clearly the pros and cons of com-
munal life but was more deeply impressed with the need for
discipline and leadership.

While Herff came primarily as a colonizer rather than as a physician, he did pioneer in bringing to Texas the best in medicine and surgery. He had brought many items: instruments, microscope, and supplies including ether, all of which helped him bridge the areas of ignorance in medical science in primitive Texas. In addition, his facility with languages enabled him to develop an ease of communication with both the Apache and Comanche Indians. An anecdote provides a clue to his medical abilities; approached by an Indian chief to remedy his failing eyesight, Herff diagnosed the problem as advanced bilateral cataracts. Having brought specialty surgical instruments, he set about to remove the opacified lenses. He decided to use cistern water rather than the heavily laden mineral ground water. With his fine hand lens and 160x microscope, he found the cistern water infested with numerous small moving bodies, "animalcules," which he removed by boiling. Artificial light from a lantern or fire would pose a great danger in the use of ether needed for anesthesia, so he reasoned that the operation should occur out-of-doors on a clear day, cloud free, windless, dust and insect free. With utmost cleanliness, he extracted the cataracts while bystanders waved off flies with palm branches. The chief's eyesight was restored and, being immensely satisfied, he promised to return with a gift for Herff. Six months later, suddenly and with apology for the delay, the Indian Chief appeared with the gift of a Mexican servant girl. The Indian vanished as quickly as he had appeared. The girl, who later married Hermann Spiess, one of the German pioneers and a friend of Herff's, was put to work in the galley of the community. Herff's many successes as a doctor brought him notoriety, and he learned much from the Indians as to how they treated injuries and handled outbreaks of disease such as smallpox.

In Herff's possession were letters of introduction from Humboldt to facilitate his dream of exploring the Rocky Mountains and California, but this was not to be. In 1848 the urge to return home to Germany overcame his wanderlust; nevertheless, Herff was deeply imbued with the desire to ultimately call Texas home. Despite his overall rugged experience, he retained the courtly manners for which he would become noted.

Within a week after his return to Darmstadt, he married Mathilde Kingel-Hofer of a noble Giessen family which included

Baron Wilhelm von Hoffman, the celebrated chemist who discovered aniline dyes and who was to visit the Herffs many years later in San Antonio. Mathilde was a gifted pianist with a remarkable soprano voice in stark contrast to the completely unmusical Herff. Mathilde became his strong, vital, accomplished helpmate.

Political turmoil persisted in his native land, and because he had taken a leave of absence from the army, he was soon pressed into obligatory medical service. The need for his services was great and a welcome solution to the ebb in his finances. Herff became an eyewitness to several major battles, which focused his duties on the treatment of battle casualties. Surgical cleanliness continued to be his hallmark, as he maintained everything in a tidy state.

In 1847 Semmelweis published his seminal work on puerperal sepsis' being transmitted by soiled hands, instruments and garments, and it was at this time that Herff added chlorinated lime solution, or in some instances iodinated compounds, to his surgical regimen of hand washing and skin preparation. The overall military infection rate in the community of surgeons was high, yet Herff's infection rate remained low even though the "germ theory" was still about thirty years away. Alleviation of pain on the battlefield was a serious problem. Oral administration of opiates and laudanum was possible, but the drugs weren't generally available on the battlefield. Hypodermic injection of opiates had been introduced, but the technique was not in use for combat. The lack of drugs created major problems, and consequently soldiers and surgeons alike welcomed the rapidity of Herff's surgery. Despite all of these difficulties, he remained determined to return to Texas when his commission expired.

With expiration of his army commission, Herff's plans began to crystallize. He had tasted the fruits of personal freedom and knew firsthand of the need for discipline. With marriage, courage and a financial golden nest egg, *das goldene Ei*, he planned the departure for Texas with expected thoroughness. The permanence of the move was evidenced by the inclusion not only of his surgical instruments but also of Mathilde's clavier and her carefully packed wedding dress.

Why Texas when Wisconsin and Iowa were other popular German immigrant sites? Convinced of the "wholesomeness of the climate," the cheapness of the land, the availability of basic necessities of life, and the great ease with which the necessities were obtained, Texas was his first choice. Herff's original plan was to form another immigrant group and to this end he carefully and thoughtfully scripted "the plan," a detailed treatise of sixty-seven pages entitled "The Regulated Emigration of the German Proletariat with Special Reference to Texas—Being Also a Guide for German Emigration,"[4] written in 1848 but not published until after their departure in 1850. General interest in his venture to transplant underprivileged Germans waned for several reasons and was never implemented. The Adelsverein supported the concept but scandals and mishaps hampered its efforts. Prince Karl of Solms-Braunfels became involved in land swindles and questionable land titles. Baron Ottfield Hans Von Muesebach, Herff's cousin whom he had never met, had replaced Prince Karl. When approached by Herff, even Humboldt took a hands-off position. Likely of greater importance, many peasants expressed no desire to be managed or directed by German aristocrats. Thus, Herff's well-intentioned plan faded away. Though his utopian view was never realized, Herff took his own family to Texas.

The Herffs sailed from Germany landing at Galveston in December 1849. The pampered aristocratic wife was rudely awakened by the abrupt change to a pioneer life and quickly became disillusioned by being jerked about during the long ox-cart journey. They settled in New Braunfels and upon becoming citizens dropped the nobility designation "von." To Mathilde's own amazement she readily formed scores of long lasting friendships, but New Braunfels was not a thriving place for Herff to practice medicine. By April 1850, he had decided that his future should be in San Antonio, a more prosperous, more populous, more cultured and more cosmopolitan place, and an entirely appropriate place to raise their family. So they moved.

Despite San Antonio's outward appearance as an old Mexican town of one-story, flat-roofed adobe or stone houses on unpaved, dusty, narrow streets and plazas, it was the principal trading point between Mexico, Santa Fe, El Paso, New Orleans and points north. Living conditions were decidedly primitive. Indians often attacked caravans carrying merchandise. The previous year the town had been ravaged when a cholera epidemic at its height took the lives of fifteen to twenty people each day. Herff encountered medical quackery and lax legal control in San Antonio, but he joined Dr. George Cupples in strictly abiding by and believing in ethical behavior for both business and professional dealings; the formation of The American Medical Association and its adoption of a Code of Ethics in 1847 had a positive influence nationwide and even in Texas.

Herff's early patients were primarily the indigent, which went along with his dedicated spirit of humanitarianism. He had arrived in San Antonio with only ten cents in his pocket, which he purportedly gave away to a half-starved blind beggar, but that same evening he relieved a man in great suffering who gratefully awarded him five dollars. He frequently bartered for payment as his disappointment continued over the dearth of paying patients. Further, it was difficult for him to raise fees for those who could pay and not be in conflict with other physicians in the community. Mathilde was eager but disenchanted, especially with the crudity of the frontier, and had frequent bouts of nostalgia. Nevertheless, she again rapidly formed friendships and took in voice and piano students to supplement their meager income. It was difficult to break into society, to establish a practice of medicine, and to rear a family, but with heads held high they forged forward with success.

Indians formed much of Herff's early patient base. He spoke their language but they were considered less than human according to the prejudices of the time. Comanches, Kickapoos and Lipans had no inherent fear of the surgeon's knife, but Indian successes did little to foster his practice. Much of Herff's surgery took place under primitive conditions, outdoors or in barren rooms. Despite the circumstance, Herff always proceeded with knowledgeable deliberation and rapidity of actions. His continued fastidious operative technique with excellent surgical results was cause for justifiable pride.[5]

In 1854 a single case put Herff's name on the tongue of all San Antonio. A popular Texas Ranger was to undergo a perineal lithotomy to remove two large bladder stones. Veramendi House was the operating theatre, in full view of an eager crowd grouped around open windows and doors. It was Herff's first use of chloroform. When the Ranger began to snore loudly,

Herff became anxious and finished the operation without further anesthetic. Among the audience was Ranger "Big Foot" Wallace, who later praised Herff saying, "He removed a stone as big as my fist, he pulled and pulled, and the man got well." Herff described two stones, one the size of a turkey's egg and the other the size of a hen's egg but bound together. The operation was a success and the patient had a prompt uneventful recovery. Thereafter, Herff's reputation quickly spread and convinced many doubters that surgery in Texas could be safe and effective.[6]

The Ranger story made him famous overnight. Although his practice grew at an astonishing rate and their finances became healthier, Mathilde continued providing piano and voice lessons. The couple retained their practical values that had been their strength in less affluent times. Domestic and professional duties always came first. Herff was somewhat careless about finances, and his wife fortunately developed a pecuniary thriftiness. Their children were instilled with various cultural assets and were taught German, Spanish and French.

There were no hospitals, and operations were performed with only occasional professional assistance. Procedures were often accomplished with instruments at hand, in full public view and in the most meager of surroundings. Farmhouses and streets under the shade of trees became operating theatres for his truly prodigious feats, yet they were conducted under as scrupulous conditions as possible. In 1855 he served as City Physician for San Antonio with the munificent salary of ten dollars a month.

A broad spectrum of patients presented themselves. Trauma, abdominal and pelvic maladies, cataracts and other eye conditions, as well as plastic surgery became common procedures. He became notorious for his ability to treat arrow wounds, consequently inflicted patients sought him out, including James H. Cook who rode horseback 130 miles to have an embedded arrow in his calf successfully removed.[7] Herff's first hysterectomy was successfully performed in 1856 and is thought to be the first in Texas, and perhaps in the country. Despite the increase in paying patients, indigents remained a significant part of his practice throughout his career. His clearly defined task was to "heal the sick." Poets, statesmen, drunkards, white, red or black, he treated them all equally.

The economic survival of the environs of San Antonio was
not tied to slavery as it was elsewhere in Texas. In fact most of
San Antonio's population was uneducated and nomadic and thus
lethargic concerning the Civil War. Of the educated group,
about one-third were of German origin and found difficulty with
the position of the Confederacy. Mostly they maintained an
attitude of neutrality, or *pretended* to endorse the Confederate
position. The majority was passively or actively opposed to the
Southern cause; some fled to Mexico. Resistance was tantamount
to treason, and ruffians roamed the countryside creating havoc
in the name of the Confederacy. Herff's basic allegiance was to
medicine. Previously he had been a contract surgeon with the
U.S. Army, but in the early days of the Civil War he briefly
became a brigade surgeon for the Confederate Army; in recognition of his services Herff received a chair from Robert E. Lee
which is now on exhibit in the New Braunfels Museum. Because
of his known sympathy with the Union cause, Herff received
warnings and threats but continued with his medical practice.

With hopes and dreams of the Confederacy crumbling and
with Herff's being considered an outsider, he took the opportunity for a family pilgrimage to Germany. His return to Germany
was not indicative of any patriotic deficiency but rather the
idealistic belief in the dignity of man which had prompted him
into the field of medicine in the first place. This change of venue
provided his six sons with a new educational experience, European study and travel. Learning the Teutonic methods in a
German-English school, they acquired practical knowledge with
emphasis on discipline, the anathema of inefficiency, the observation of corporal punishment, and a rigorous curriculum.

In 1865 with their financial nest egg vanishing, Herff became
a contract surgeon with the Prussian Army, receiving a handsome salary. The brief Prussian War left a large number of
mutilated victims who benefited from Herff's valuable expertise.
During the nearly two years spent in Germany, they renewed
friendships. Herff never aired his political views in an offensive
manner, although they had changed from his earlier days in
Germany. He came to the grudging realization that one's future
was inexorably becoming one's past. The family returned home
to Texas in December 1867.

The period of Reconstruction brought political chaos; medically it was a time of hardships including epidemics of cholera and diphtheria. But it was also a time that saw Herff's practice continuing to flourish. He soon became known as one of San Antonio's safest, most effective and well-respected physicians. Among his patients were the President of Mexico, three state governors, several noted ministers, top generals, and some of the wealthiest people in the country. Yet surgical feats continued to be performed under primitive conditions, such as the removal of elephantiasis of the labia while the patient lay on a cot under a chinaberry tree. A patient who had been disemboweled during a fight in a livery stable, with dung and straw mixed among the protruding intestines, amazingly recovered after thirty minutes of Herff's intensive washing, cleansing and suturing.

The lack of satisfactory operating space was clearly evident. The public had deep superstitions about hospitals, officials were disinterested, and quackery was rampant as were curious home remedies of unusual nature such as cockroach tea, rattlesnake necklaces, etc. Despite the public's reluctance, even open fear, of hospitals, Herff aggressively sought private funds for the establishment of a hospital. Recalling the adage, "When things *seem* totally hopeless, they *can* improve," the Santa Rosa Hospital was fully established in 1869.[8]

Herff continued to exhibit his wisdom through self-reliance and a medical sixth sense. He had the uncanny ability to travel great distances by horse and buggy to see a large number of patients. He had the faculty to arrive at a correct diagnosis quickly and the courage to take action. He has genuine claim to many medical "firsts" in Texas: first cataract operation (and perhaps in the U.S.), 1847; first perineal lithotomy, 1854; first trephine for Jacksonian epilepsy (and perhaps in the U.S.), *circa* 1853; first hysterectomy (and perhaps in the U.S.), 1856; first diagnosis of uncinariasis, 1864; inadvertent but successful appendectomy, 1878; first gastrostomy, 1879.[9] Many anecdotes exist concerning his practice.

> The gastrostomy case deserves elaboration. A young girl, Susie Lumley, had swallowed lye resulting in a stricture of the esophagus. Efforts to dilate the stricture were fruitless, and so Herff performed a gastrostomy. The girl's nutritional recovery was marginal at

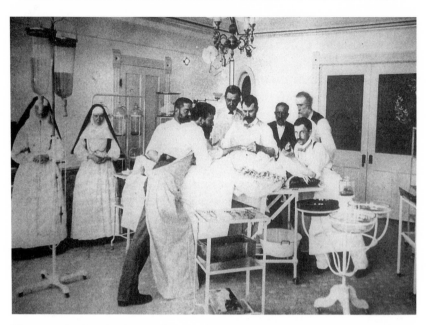

Photograph taken in the Herff Operating Room Suite, Santa Rosa Hospital, *circa* 1880, with Dr. Herff, standing second from right, overseeing the Herff surgical team. Courtesy Sister Francesca, Incarnate Word University, and Mrs. Mary Ann Delmer.

first, then Herff added her saliva (mastication) to the regime and the nutritional result was miraculous. The case was presented at a medical meeting in New Orleans. The favorable result attracted the attention of the notorious Philadelphia surgeon Dr. Samuel D. Gross, who wrote Herff a commendation and requested permission to incorporate the case in the new edition of his book.

Herff was presented with a patient whose eye was swollen, red, and had vision loss. Further, eyesight was beginning to fail in the opposite eye as well. Predicting sympathetic ophthalmia, Herff advised extirpation of the initially involved eye so as to save the remaining good eye. Such was performed and sight was retained.

A newly arrived surgeon told of a case that he never got to perform. He was proud of the prospect of

Prominently involved in educational programs at Santa Rosa Hospital, this photograph shows Herff front and center with the first class of graduates in 1903. Courtesy Bexar County Medical Society and Mrs. Mary Ann Delmer.

operating on a boy with a hydrocele. During the buggy ride on their way to Santa Rosa Hospital, the mother insisted that they stop off for a curbside consultation with Herff. Whereupon Herff quickly removed a lance from his pocket, made a swift incision decompressing the cyst and said, 'There, that's all!' The lady asked how much she owed Herff, he replied one dollar, and the newly arrived surgeon lost a case.

Once a husband rushed into the room while Herff was operating on his wife's breast and threatened to shoot Herff if she died. Herff lay down his surgical knife and said, 'if you want your wife to die, shoot now!'

At age eighty-four, Herff successfully performed an emergency operation for an ectopic pregnancy in a country kitchen using hastily assembled utensils with spoons as retractors. This involved a family member, 'Aunt Lizzie'.

Herff developed an unusual technique concerning arrow removal, using duck billed forceps to encompass the arrowhead prior to removal.

When a doctor appeared on the San Antonio scene sporting a high hat and Prince Albert coat, believing he was doing the proper thing, the new doctor was quickly disillusioned when Herff drew him aside and told him to put on some suitable clothes befitting the time and place, or else run the risk of 'acute' lead poisoning.

In the brush on what is now Sixth Street, Herff removed a huge ovarian cyst.

Herff had been called to see 'the lady of the house' who was having 'pelvic problems.' Upon arrival a woman met Herff at the door and Herff, despite protestations, wasted no time in performing a pelvic examination. Upon completing the task, Herff was informed that 'the lady of the house' was located in a rear bedroom.

One occasion found Herff attending a servant girl complaining of severe abdominal pain. During the visit, she delivered a baby. The girl's explanation was that she must have gotten it from the bathtub. Herff accepted her explanation with compassion.

Herff had laboriously cleansed and dutifully closed a disembowelment resulting from a razor. The patient's wife came upon the scene and in a fit of hysteria flung herself across the patient, whose recently sutured wound promptly broke open. Herff, thinking the situation was hopeless, covered the wound with only a bandage. The patient fully recovered.

Once when robbery was attempted, Herff scared off his assailant by leveling obstetrical forceps at him.

Many, many other anecdotes could be told, as referenced materials expound such stories. His last operation was in 1908 at the age of eighty-seven.

Medical responsibilities not directly involving patients did not escape Herff's notice or involvement. On November 15, 1853, he met with a handful of earnest, progressive physicians to hold the first annual session of the State Medical Society which had been formally organized the proceeding January. Much later, in 1909, Bliem described the meeting.

> Imagine the scene: a frontier village of 3,000 souls; the vast trackless wilderness of mesquite brush stretching out in every direction; and in the lair of wild beasts and the hunting grounds of more savage Indians. Here in a country separated by at least 500 miles in any direction, a medical meeting was being conducted by the distinguished Dr. George Cupples from famous Universities Edinburgh and Paris, and by the equally well recognized Dr. Herff from The Universities of Bonn, Berlin and Giessen.

Thus, it was that, side by side, Cupples and Herff set many medical practice standards. They gave tone and direction to the medical profession through their active participation in the establishment and continued involvement in organized medicine.[10] Both were absorbed in the following activities: examiners for the Texas State Board of Medical Examiners; in 1853 organizers and among the thirty-five charter members of Bexar County Medical Society and also the Texas Medical Association (elected to honorary membership in 1903); charter member of West Texas Medical Association in 1876, and being elected Life Member in 1892. Both will forever serve as an inspiration to their successors. Herff was active in publishing medical journals and helped establish the West Texas Medical and Surgical Record which, although short lived, was a credit to medical journalism.

Herff addressed the 1878 and 1889 meetings of the Texas Medical Association and in the latter address compared the medical progress made since the previous meeting. Herff stated,

> it is true we cannot boast of great medical discoveries or meteor-like theories advanced by members of this

> Association. But let us have all the advantages which
> our more fortunate brethren in the older States pos-
> sess; Let us have hospitals, libraries, laboratories, mu-
> seums, and it will not be long before we may enter the
> arena and win the prize in Texas. . . .Texas is inferior
> to none in scientific zeal, and superior to many in
> brotherly feeling existing between its members.

Herff was a keen medical observer and is credited with early
detection of enteric parasites, and the first to recognize hookworm in Texas. Dr. Allen J. Smith in the first published report
on indigenous hookworm in Texas appearing in the *Texas Medical Journal* in 1894 acknowledges Herff's personal observation
thirty years before in 1864. The TMA Committee on Surgery
in 1886 collected and analyzed major surgeries in Texas.[11] A total
of 1,875 cases from about the state were assembled, and the two
leading surgeons were Cupples with 221 major operations and
Herff with 214. Nearly one fourth of all major operations in
Texas were performed by these two accomplished San Antonio
surgeons! Herff never lost interest in the advances of medicine.

Because many of his patients were poverty stricken, it took
him two to three times as many patients to earn even a small
profit. On occasion, Herff's performances were often flamboyant and somewhat daring. It was a challenge for other surgeons
to live up to his high standards and strong sense of responsibility.
He could be both intimidating and inspiring. There was a certain
"bravado" in his makeup, but he always kept his surgical skills
honed to the highest level.

During the summer months Herff commonly retreated to
his residence in Boerne. During a stay in 1886, Herff sustained
serious injuries when he was thrown from his buggy. Recovery
was slow and the comminuted fracture of left arm never completely healed. Temporarily, he decided not to see patients, a
decision which made medical news.[12] Herff took to donning a
cape to mask the partially functional limb, producing a dramatic
and even more distinguished appearance.

Two testimonial stories are offered concerning esteem and
respect for Herff, the first reflecting a *patient's* viewpoint and the
second from his *colleagues*.

Patient: In 1886 Geronimo, the famous Apache Indian Chief, while imprisoned at Fort Sam Houston requested a visit from Herff. They conversed in Apache and together recalled many medical stories in which Herff had been involved with Indians, including a squaw's cataract removal many years previously.

Colleagues: In 1891 when the University of Texas was establishing the medical school in Galveston, there was a concerted statewide movement, led by Dr. Trueheart of Houston, to have Herff appointed as its first Chairman of Surgery. Despite this testimony, Herff declined to have his name submitted.

Herff was a civic-minded, well-read and highly cultured man with varied interests outside medicine. With clarity of mind and genuine interest in affairs of the world, he readily engaged in philosophical discussions but let others freely express themselves and permitted them their convictions. His background had instilled an infinite compassion for those less fortunate than himself. A family history of religious persecution made him more tolerant, and his memories of political repression made him liberal in his outlook. Years of hardship and deprivation followed by success made him neither greedy nor cautious with his wealth nor vain nor proud. He had respect for the self-made man and empathy for the downtrodden.[13]

Maintaining his cultural interests, Herff was often involved in societal and business affairs of the community.[14] He was an active member of the Hessian Association of Physicians and Surgeons, the Darmstadt Society of Natural History and San Antonio's prestigious Casino Club. In addition he was a director of the San Antonio National Bank, was affiliated with the San Antonio Loan and Trust Company, and was identified with the La Costa Ice Company, the first to manufacture artificial ice in the U.S. In every quarter, he enjoyed universal esteem and respect and was held as a widely popular citizen.[15]

In 1886, there was a push in San Antonio to have Herff become politically involved by running as a Republican for the Bexar County Congressional seat. He declined with the following reasoning.

I am too old (66 years) to undertake the hardships of
a canvass and the altogether new and unaccustomed
duties of such a position; my English is so bad, I could
never make a public speech without creating merri-
ment; a Republican wouldn't have a chance to win in
Texas; moreover, I am a socialist (not in the sense the
word is used sometimes now by the enemies of social
reform, who put the miserable anarchist with social-
ists) and would express my opinion regarding labor
and capital publicly that would lose me the few votes
I might get on account of my being a Republican.

His love of the land led him to become a major landowner
near Boerne. Purportedly his ranch holdings were greater than
ten-thousand acres, including parts of present-day Camp Bullis
and Camp Stanley which were on occasion leased to the U.S.
Army. Their Boerne Ranch for many years was a haven for the
extended Herff family during the summer months. In 1881
family and friends erected a stone obelisk on the beloved property. This twelve-foot structure was placed on Malakopf Mountain overlooking Boerne. After seventy years of exposure and
vandalism, Drs. John B. and Ferdinand P. Herff in 1952 had the
obelisk completely rebuilt with limestone blocks. Later, the
Herffs granted land to Boerne for a City Park and for the high
school. Through the years the original Herff land has been
bequeathed to Herff's progeny, and today the land about Mount
Malakopf and the obelisk remains in family hands with the
gatepost sign reading "Herff Ranch-1852."[16]
      A remarkable Boerne ranch story takes place in 1888 when
the Lipan Indians were on one of their final rampages. There was
considerable commotion in the Boerne area which could be
heard from the Herff ranch as many nearby houses, ranches and
farms were raided. However, the Herff property was spared. The
next day at their gatepost the Herffs found a lone Indian arrow
with a white feather!
      Ferdinand and Mathilde were absolutely devoted to one
another. Throughout their lives they were as one. Both had great
longevity and were physically large individuals, Herff being
about six feet tall and weighing over two-hundred pounds. In
San Antonio they lived in the same unpretentious house they

built in 1855 at 308 East Houston Street, site of the current Nix Professional Building. The house bordered the San Antonio River, which provided Herff the opportunity for frequent swimming. This dwelling was not only their home but was used to see patients. Upon his wife's death in 1910, Herff was totally devastated and it is widely thought that his grief led to his own demise.

The Herffs had seven sons, one of whom died accidentally in infancy. All adult sons became professionals in the fields of architecture, law, banking and medicine, and in each instance they became successful and highly respected. Concerning medicine, informal records of the Texas Medical Association indicate the great likelihood that Ferdinand Herff's medical legacy to Texas includes the largest number of physicians from a single progenitor. Two sons became physicians: Johann (John) and Adolph. Three grandsons entered medicine: John Bennet, Ferdinand Peter, and August Herff, to be followed by a fourth generation, August Herff, Jr. There have been direct physician descendants not bearing the name Herff: William M. Wolf, Jr. and Bill Kennon, fourth and fifth generations respectively. Three doctors married into the Herff family tree: Dr. W.M. Wolf, Dr. Charles S. Venable and Dr. William Kennon.[17]

Herff looked forward to a practice associated with his sons. Unfortunately in 1882, shortly after entering into an affiliated practice, his eldest son Johann-John succumbed to fatal perityphlitis (acute appendicitis) in helpless circumstances (Dr. Reginald Fitz' sentinel treatise clarifying the role of acute appendicitis did not appear until 1886). Following this misfortune, Herff developed and truly enjoyed the close medical collaboration with his other son Adolph and with his eldest grandson John B. son of Johann-John.

In November 1908 on the occasion of his eighty-ninth birthday, Dr. Herff was honored to have in attendance his brother and sister from Germany, the Baroness Neufville, age eighty-five, and His Excellency Lieutenant General August von Herff, age seventy-nine.

Herff died at home with his family at his side on May 18, 1912 at the patriarchal age of ninety-one years and six months. Death was due to "old age" weakened by the effect of lingering "la grippe."[18] There was an outpouring of appreciation for this

great man. The obituary published by the Bexar County Medical
Society states,

He was truly in all respects a remarkable man, a
brilliant star amid the galaxy of Texas medical profession. His zeal and interest in his profession never
waned, and he has left an example worth imitation by
every physician. He came to us already a distinguished
man. Distinguished in birth, in ability and in achievement. How he maintained and advanced that distinction none know better than his colleagues. Original in
his profession, brilliant, forceful and progressive, yet
he was always ethical, liberal, and even charitable to
the members of the profession. As a man he was
modest, as a friend he was true, and as a citizen he was
pure. As a christian, he would have said in all humility,
'Write me as one who loves his fellow man.'[19]

Numerous other obituaries carried highly salutary comments.[20] Posterity biographies appear in *The Handbook of Texas*
and *The New Handbook of Texas*.[21] Herff's estate, valued in excess
of $1.1 million, was divided equally among his remaining sons
and his eldest grandson.[22] Mrs. S.C. Red concludes her biography of Herff with,

Although he died rich in worldly goods, owner of a
vast estate, every dollar of it was clean, and he was
richer by far in the mental treasures with which his
wonderful mind was filled and in the friends who
mourned his death.

Herff shunned both encomium, that which brought him
enthusiastic praise, and opprobrium, that which would bring
disgrace to others; however, there were four acknowledgements
that he treasured.

In 1882, he received an Honorary Medical Degree
from Saint Louis University Medical College of Physicians and Surgeons.

In 1883, he was honored by a Jubilee Degree from the University of Giessen upon the fiftieth anniversary of his graduation.

As proof that a prophet is 'not always without honor in his own country,' a notable event occurred on May 1, 1905. At that time there was unveiled in the Carnegie Public Library and presented to the City of San Antonio, a beautiful bronze bust of Dr. Herff. This loving tribute was made possible by the contributions of hundreds of devoted and admiring friends. The work of art was designed and executed by Pompeo Coppini, a popular artisan of the day, and had previously been displayed in the Texas State building at the St. Louis and Philadelphia expositions in 1904.[23]

On December 9, 1909 Dr. M.J. Bleim delivered an address before the Bexar County Medical Society, a truly panegyrical occasion honoring Herff. This most eloquent recitation extolled the many facets of Herff's life and has found its way into numerous publications.[24]

Some of Herff's adages include:

"Nothing proves the truth like time."
"Professional satisfaction is its own reward."
"True aristocracy is actually the best democracy."
"No one can be more cruel to a proletarian
than another proletarian."

The inscription on the Herff Obelisk, located on Malakopf Mountain, Kendall County, reads,

Upon this site one spring morning in 1881 a group of admirers assembled to honor Dr. and Mrs. Ferdinand Herff. Many prominent San Antonians were present, and the venerated couple accepted their warm praise with utmost modesty. The gathering was jubilant when the surprise of the day was revealed. Heaps of

Recent photograph of obelisk atop Malakopf Mountain, Kendall County.

Bronze bust of Dr. Herff on display in the Texana Section of the San Antonio Public Library. Commissioned by innumerable friends, created by Pompeo Coppini, the exquisite bust was unveiled in 1905.

Left: Herff headstone.
Bottom: Herff burial plot in San Antonio City Cemetery Number 1. Note Tower of the Americas in background rising above the treetops.

stones had been stockpiled upon the mountain top and now, according to plan, volunteers went energetically to work, building them into a mortar-free obelisk a dozen feet tall. Between the rising tiers eager ladies cached mementos—rings, bracelets, gold coins, earrings and gloves. Long before sundown the task was finished and an address was delivered dedicatory to the doctor and his wife. As the tired, but still enthusiastic celebrators descended into the valley, they could see their handiwork pointing confidently toward the sky, illuminated by the flickering light of a huge bonfire. The pillar stood until 1951 after having successfully resisted tornadoes, lightning, ice, and rampant Comanches. Then it suddenly collapsed, probably because of the depredations of vandals or treasure hunters. This more permanent replacement of the original structure is dedicated to the memory of Doctor and Mrs. Ferdinand Herff. Mrs. Herff, the loyal companion of years; and Doctor Herff, the Pioneer, Botanist, Scientist, Linguist, and Surgeon.

Erected by Doctors J.B. Herff and F.P. Herff
Legend by Doctor F.P. Herff
June 1, 1953

The Texas Historical Commission Historical Marker erected in 1982 reads,

Dr. Ferdinand Ludwig von Herff
(Nov. 29, 1820 May 18, 1912)

The son of a prominent German family and a veteran of the Prussian Army, physician Ferdinand Ludwig von Herff first came to Texas in 1847. By 1860s he had set up practice in San Antonio, where he was an active civic leader. His medical innovations made him a prominent physician in the Southwest. Dr. Herff and his wife Mathilde (1823-1910) owned a ranch at this site and, through their interest in the area, led in the development of Boerne. Local residents honored their many contributions with a monument here on Malakopf Mountain, a site favored by the Herffs.

ENDNOTES

1. The following six reference materials have served as major sources for the personal and professional history of Dr. Herff, and for many of the anecdotes and quotations used in this biography:

Henry B. Dielmann. "Dr. Ferdinand Herff—Pioneer Physician and Surgeon." *The Southwestern Quarterly* LVII (1954), 265-84.

Ferdinand Peter Herff. *The Doctors Herff—A Three Generation Memoir*, Laura L. Barber (ed.) Vol. I (San Antonio: Trinity University Press, 1973), 1-130.

Kurt Lekish. "Dr. Ferdinand von Herff—Idealistic Pioneer and Distinguished Texas Physician." *Texas Medicine* 82 (1986), 48-52.

P.I. Nixon. *A Century of Medicine in San Antonio* (Lancaster, Pennsylvania: Lancaster Press, Inc., 1936), 141-44, 170-83, portrait opp pg 176.

George Plunkett Red. *The Medicine Man in Texas* (Houston: Standard Printing and Lithographing, 1930), 129-34.

Clarence R. Wharton. "Texas Under Many Flags." *American Historical Society*, Vol. 4 (1930), 25-27.

2. Ferdinand Roemer. *Roemer's Texas 1845-1847*, Oswald Mueller (trans.)(Austin: Eakin Press, 1995), 284-87; Ferdinand Herff, Oral Interview, May 19, 1890, Vertical Files, Texana-Genealogy Section, San Antonio Public Library.

3. Ferdinand Herff, *The Doctors Herff*, op. cit.; S.W. Geiser. *Naturalists of the Frontier* (Dallas: Southern Methodist University Press, 1948), 142-44; *A History of Kendall County—Rivers, Ranches, Railroads, Recreation 1836-1986* (Boerne, Texas: Kendall County Historical Commission for Sesquicentennial, 1986), 117-20; P.I. Nixon. "Ferdinand Herff." *Handbook of Texas* vol. 1 (Austin: Texas State Historical Association, 1952), 801.

4. Ferdinand von Herff. *The Regulated Emigration of the German Proletariat with Special Reference to Texas, 1850*, Arthur L. Finck, Jr. (trans.)(San Antonio: Trinity University Press, 1978.)

5. Herff, *The Doctors Herff*, op. cit.; Lekish, op. cit.; Nixon, "Herff," op. cit.

6. Wharton, op. cit.; Red, op. cit., Herff, *The Doctors Herff*, op. cit.; Lekish, op. cit.; Nixon, "Herff," op. cit.

7. James H. Cook. *Fifty Years on the Old Frontier: As Cowboy, Hunter, Guide, Scout and Ranchman* (Oklahoma City: University of Oklahoma Press, 1957), 64.

8. Herff, *The Doctors Herff*, op. cit.; Nixon, *Century of Medicine*, op. cit., Lekish, op. cit., Geiser, op. cit.

9. Wharton, op. cit.; Red, op. cit.; Herff, *The Doctors Herff*, op. cit.; Nixon, "Herff," op. cit.

10. Nixon, *Century of Medicine*, op. cit.; M.J. Bleim. "Dr. Ferdinand Herff—Medical Pioneer of Texas," presented originally as an address before Bexar County Medical Society in 1909, as published in *Southern Medicine* (1947), 41-47; P.I. Nixon. *A History of the Texas Medical Association 1853-1953* (Austin: University of Texas Press, 1953).

11. George Cupples. Report of Special Committee on Collection of Surgical Cases, Transactions Texas State Medical Association, 1886.

12. "Accident to Ferdinand Herff." *Daniels Medical Journal* vol. 2 (1886), 38.

13. Diehlman, op. cit.; Nixon, "Herff," op. cit.

14. R.L. Biesele. *The History of the German Settlements in Texas 1831-1861* (Austin: Von Boeckmann-Jones Co., 1930), 155; Frederick Chabot. *With the Makers of San Antonio* (San Antonio: Artes-Graficas, 1937), 386-87; Mary A. Maverick. *Memoirs* arranged by Mary Maverick and her son George Madison Maverick, edited by Rena Maverick Green (San Antonio, 1921), 117.

15. Herff, *The Doctors Herff*, op. cit.; UT Institute of Texan Cultures, "The Texians and the Texans, The German Texans." Booklet (San Antonio: UT Institute of Texan Cultures, 1970); Garland A. Perry. *Historic Images of Boerne* (Boerne: Perry Enterprises, 1982), 103-109, 165, 245, 289-97.

16. Herff, *The Doctors Herff*, op. cit.; *A History of Kendall County*, op. cit.; Juanita Herff Chipman, Personal Communications, 1997 & 1998.

17. Ibid.

18. Ferdinand Herff. Obituary, *San Antonio Light* (May 18, 1912).

19. Ferdinand Herff. Obituary. *The Bulletin*. Bexar County Medical Society, vol. 2 (1912/13), 21-22.

20. Ferdinand Herff. Obituary. *Texas Medical Journal*, vol. 27 (1912), 473-76; Ferdinand Herff. Obituary. *Texas State Journal of Medicine*, vol. 8 (1912), 104-105

21. Nixon, "Herff," op. cit.; Vernie A. Stembridge. "Ferdinand Herff." *The New Handbook of Texas*, vol. 3 (Austin: Texas State Historical Association, 1996), 570.

22. Ferdinand Herff. Report of Last Will and Testament. *San Antonio Light* (April 21, 1913).

23. Red, op. cit.; "Dr. Herff—Distinguished Physician Honored" (with illustration). *Texas State Journal of Medicine*, vol. 1 (1905), 27.

24. Bleim, op. cit.

OTHER PUBLICATIONS BY FERDINAND HERFF

The Regulated Emigration of the German Proletariat with Special Reference to Texas, translated by Arthur L. Finck, Jr., originally published in German by Franz Warrentrapps verlag Publishing Company, Frankfort a/M, 1850 (San Antonio: Trinity University Press, 1978).

"Die Gynakologie des Franz v. Piemont, Giessen." Thesis, 88 pages (G. F. Heyer, 1843).

"Gastrostomy in the case of an oeophageal stricture." *St. Louis Courier of Medicine*, vol.ii (1879), 589-91.

"Gastrostomy performed to establish a permanent fistula in stricture of the esophagus." *New Orleans Medical and Surgical Journal*, vol. VIII (1880), 16-24.

"Chloroform versus Ether." *Texas Courier-Record of Medicine* 8 (November 1890), 69.

"Further remarks upon parasites." *Texas State Medical Association* 27 (1895), 349-53.

"Report of parasitic entozoa, encountered in general practice in Texas for more than forty years." *Texas State Medical Association* 26 (1894), 412-16.

BIOGRAPHICAL SKETCH OF AUTHOR

VERNIE A. STEMBRIDGE, M.D., currently holds positions as Ashbel Smith Professor and Emeritus Chairman of Pathology at the University of Texas Southwestern Medical Center at Dallas.

Reared in El Paso, he obtained the baccalaureate from Texas College of Mines (now UTEP) and the Medical Degree from the University of Texas Medical Branch, Galveston. Following a rotating internship at Marine Hospital, Norfolk, he returned to Galveston to receive residency training in anatomic and clinical pathology. He remained at UTMB on the faculty, rising from Assistant to Associate Professor.

For three years (1956-59) he served in the US Air Force at the Armed Forces Institute of Pathology where he established the Section on Aviation (later Aero-Space) Pathology, for which he received the Legion of Merit.

Returning to Texas, he accepted the position as the first fulltime director of surgical pathology at Southwestern Medical School-Parkland Memorial Hospital, Dallas, and was elevated to full professor in 1961. He was director of the Tumor Clinic at Parkland from 1960-1976.

He served as chairman of the pathology department at Southwestern, as director of pathology laboratories at Parkland from 1966-1988, and subsequently was appointed Interim Dean Allied Health School-Southwestern from 1988-1991. Although formally retired in 1993, he remains active in departmental and institutional affairs.

His contributions to medical literature have involved mainly cardiovascular disease, cancer, environmental and immunopathology. During his career he has been president of the Dallas County Medical Society, The Texas Society of Pathologists, the American Board of Pathology, the American Society of Clinical Pathologists, the Association of Pathology Chairmen, and the American Registry of Pathology. He has been the recipient of numerous distinguished service awards including being designated Outstanding Alumnus from UTEP and UTMB.

Doctor Stembridge has an abiding interest in history, especially medical history, and is a Life Member of the Texas State Historical Association.

Anson Jones, M.D., was the last President of the Republic of Texas.
From the frontispiece engraving in Anson Jones, *Memoranda and
Official Correspondence Relating to the Republic of Texas, Its History and
Annexation* New York: D. Appleton & Co., 1859.

Anson Jones, M.D.
1798-1858
by
Martin L. Dalton, M.D.

★ IN THE SHADOW OF OUR STATE Capitol stands the Lorenzo de Zavala State Archives Building. In the portico of this building stand two larger-than-life bronze statues. One is of General Sam Houston, best known of all Texans, and the other is of Anson Jones, M.D., Physician and Surgeon. When one first sees these statues, curiosity is aroused as to the identity of Dr. Anson Jones. What places him in such a prestigious position adjacent to General Houston?

The legend on the base of the statue lists his rather imposing accomplishments, including "Veteran of San Jacinto, Congressman of the Republic of Texas, Minister to the United States, Founder of the Medical Association of Texas, and the last President of the Republic of Texas." Because he was the last of the four presidents of the Republic of Texas, David Burnet, Sam Houston, Mirabeau B. Lamar, and Anson Jones, the author's interest and determination to learn more about this early Texas physician was aroused.

Anson Jones was born January 20, 1798,[1] near Great Barrington in the Berkshire Mountains of western Massachusetts, known also as the birthplace of the poet William Cullen Bryant. Great Barrington is famous as the site of the first open resistance to British rule in America on August 19, 1774. His parents, Solomon and Sarah Strong Jones, were of English ancestry; his father was a tenant farmer. His early education took place in a rural school taught by his sister Sarah. Despite the handicaps of poverty and physical weakness, he decided to study medicine and, in 1817, moved to Litchfield, Connecticut, as an apprentice

Jefferson Medical College. When Anson Jones was graduated from the school, classes were held in the Tivioli Theater. Courtesy Scott Memorial Library, Thomas Jefferson University, Philadelphia.

under Dr. Daniel Sheldon. He completed his apprenticeship under Dr. Amos C. Hull of Utica, New York and received his handwritten diploma on August 7, 1821.[2]

After several early practice failures in New York, he moved to Philadelphia. After six months of limited success, he closed his office and spent two years practicing in Caracas, Venezuela. He lived frugally, enjoyed modest success in Venezuela, and returned to Philadelphia in 1826. Because of a feeling of medical inferiority to his physician-colleagues, he enrolled at the then relatively new Jefferson Medical College. At that time, classes were being held at the old Tivioli Theatre.[3] He was a classmate of Dr. Samuel D. Gross and received his diploma in March 1827.

Once again failure pursued him, and in 1832 he moved to New Orleans. A business swindle and personal illness pressured him to leave there in 1833; having become acquainted with Captain Jeremiah Brown, whose ship, the *Sabine*, was sailing for

Brazoria, Texas, he elected to go along. On October 20, 1833, he arrived in Brazoria, much in debt and with only seventeen dollars in his pockets. He found Texas much in turmoil due to increasing problems with Mexico. According to his biographer, Herbert Gambrell, Dr. Jones was one of the first, if not the first, physician with formal medical training to arrive in Texas.[4] Brazoria had been founded in 1829 and was a commercial center and a rapidly growing community. He became a friend of William Barret Travis and was able quickly to establish a successful medical practice.

Relations with Mexico deteriorated rapidly and Texans, meeting at Washington-on-the-Brazos in March 1836, declared their independence from Mexico. David Burnet was elected interim president and the Constitution was adopted March 16, 1836, ten days after the fall of the Alamo. On this same day, Anson Jones enlisted as a private in the Texas Infantry. Under General Houston, he participated in a series of retreats eastward from the Colorado River. Determined to fight, he reluctantly consented to take the post of surgeon to the Second Regiment. On April 18, 1836, General Houston learned that Santa Anna was at the San Jacinto River, less than one day's march away. Ironically, this information was obtained from a captured Mexican courier who was carrying the saddlebags of William Barret Travis, who had been killed at the Alamo. Orders were given to prepare for attack and Anson Jones made a quick decision. He turned his patients over to his assistants and quickly joined his fellow soldiers. On April 20, 1836, a field hospital was set up at the home of Vice President Lorenzo de Zavala, as this was the only building in the area. Here Anson Jones, along with Surgeon General Alexander Ewing and Dr. Nicholas Labadie, prepared for the treatment of the wounded.

At noon on April 21, 1836, General Houston gave his order, "Fight and be damned!" The story of the Battle of San Jacinto is well known. Following his participation in the battle as an infantryman, Dr. Jones laid aside his rifle and then assisted in the care of twenty-three wounded Texans, including General Houston who had suffered a gunshot wound of the left leg.

After this great Texas victory, Anson Jones was made Assistant Surgeon General. He completed his military duties and returned to Brazoria in mid-summer of 1836 and resumed the practice of medicine. He maintained a keen interest in politics and announced his candidacy for the Second Texas Congress and was subsequently elected in 1837. Largely due to his efforts, the charter of the corrupt Texas Railroad, Navigation, and Banking Company was repealed. He was directly responsible for the regulation of the practice of the healing arts in the Republic of Texas. On December 18, 1837, Congress appointed a board of eleven "medical gentlemen" to regulate the practice of medicine. He urged the creation of a Medical Society of the Republic of Texas and is credited as being the founder of the Medical Association of the State of Texas. He also helped to found the Philosophical Society of Texas and served as its first Vice President. He founded the Masonic Grand Lodge of Texas and was its first Most Worshipful Grand Master.

In 1838 he was appointed Minister to the United States by President Houston and became quite familiar with politics at the international level; from this experience he began to plan for the annexation of Texas. Unfortunately, disagreements with President Lamar prompted his recall. Meanwhile, his longtime friend, William Wharton of Brazoria, died, and Anson Jones was appointed to the Senate. In 1840 he married Mary Smith McCrory of Austin.[5] Sam Houston, who assumed his second term as president in 1841, appointed Anson Jones Secretary of State, and in this position his fame and importance increased and he became even more familiar with international politics. At the urging of General Houston, he was a candidate for the presidency and was elected President of the Republic of Texas on September 2, 1844. In Texas he had advanced from penniless immigrant to president in a little over ten years.

At this time, the issue of annexation of Texas was at a crucial juncture in the United States. Texas became the central issue of the 1844 United States presidential campaign, with James K. Polk for annexation and Henry Clay against. Ironically, George M. Dallas was the vice-presidential nominee. England and France stood ready to guarantee the independence of Texas, regardless of the outcome of this election. Polk was elected and annexation of Texas was assured.

On March 3, 1845, shortly before leaving office, President John Tyler urged prompt annexation of Texas. However, President Anson Jones had signed an agreement with the British and

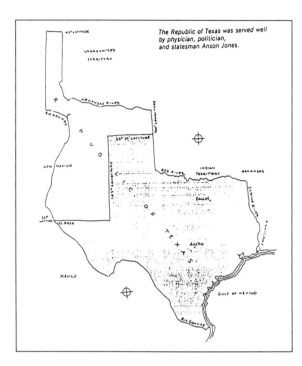

The Republic of Texas was served well by physician, politician, and statesman Anson Jones.

Left: Map of the Republic of Texas *circa* 1836. Bottom: Campaign flag of James K. Polk and his Vice presidential candidate, George M. Dallas in the presidential elelction campaign of 1844. The Annexation of Texas was the central issue of the race.

French foreign ministers to delay action on annexation for ninety days, while they endeavored to obtain an acknowledgment of Texas independence from Mexico. Throughout the Republic of Texas, citizens held mass meetings denouncing Jones for his inaction. Hoping to wait until his emissary from Mexico returned, Jones continued to delay annexation to the increasing displeasure of Texans. It should be noted that he was sincerely trying to obtain the best possible political future for the Republic of Texas and that, as a result of these negotiations, Anson Jones was responsible for Texas' entering the Union with all of its public lands intact.

Ultimately, the Annexation Convention was called by Dr. Jones and on July 4, 1845, the Ordinance of Annexation was passed by a vote of fifty-five to one. A constitution proposed for the future State of Texas was adopted August 28, 1845. The United States Congress approved the Texas Constitution, and President Polk signed the Act on December 29, 1845, making Texas officially a state. A special election was held and J.P. Henderson was elected governor, much to the chagrin of President Jones. In a public ceremony at noon on February 19, 1846, in Austin, the Republic of Texas became the State of Texas. In his speech, Dr. Jones said,

> The great measure of annexation so earnestly desired by the people of Texas is happily consummated. The lone star of Texas, which ten years hence arose amid clouds over fields of carnage, has passed on and become fixed forever in that glorious constellation which all free men and lovers of freedom in the world must reverence and adore, the American Union. The final act in this great drama is now performed. The Republic of Texas is no more.[6]

A bitter Anson Jones returned to Washington-on-the-Brazos and to his farm, named "Barrington," for his birthplace. In its current state of restoration at Washington-on-the Brazos State Park near Brenham, Texas, it is now called the "White House of the Republic of Texas."[7] One room of Barrington was a schoolroom where his sister Mary tutored Sam, Charles, Sarah and Cromwell Anson. He reportedly had a library of over one thousand books. He gained wide respect in the area as a doctor, farmer, and former famous public servant. He completed his Republic of Texas history and memoirs, *Memoranda and Official Correspondence*, requiring approximately ten years. He continued to wait for a new political call that never came. Anson Jones finally came to the realization that few Texans understood his role as the "Architect of Annexation." In 1849 an unfortunate fall from a horse permanently rendered his left arm useless and constantly painful. He sought medical advice, including his old classmate, Dr. Samuel Gross, in Louisville, all to no avail.

In 1851 he was suggested as a candidate for the vice presidency of the United States, but this never materialized. In December 1856, W.B. Stout of Clarksville sought to nominate him from the floor of the Texas Legislature as a candidate for the United States Senate.[8] Anson Jones, full of excitement, went to Austin for a full week before the legislature convened and renewed his old political acquaintances. However, when the votes were counted, he had not received even a single vote.

He became progressively depressed, sold his farm, and prepared to move to Galveston. On a preliminary trip to Galveston, he stopped over at the Old Capitol Hotel in Houston, which had formerly been the Capitol of Texas where he had enjoyed great fame and popularity. For four days, he brooded there and became progressively despondent. On the morning of January 9, 1858, he was found in his room with a bullet through his head.[9] He was buried at Glenwood Cemetery in Houston. His tombstone lists his major accomplishments and concludes with this last retort, "To them the sand to thee the marble." Suicide was fairly common among early Texans. Four of the fifty-nine signers of the Texas Declaration of Independence, including its author George Childress, ended their lives by their own hand after experiencing personal reverses.

Dr. Anson Jones, soldier and Assistant Surgeon General of the Republic of Texas, patriot, diplomat, Texas congressman, author of the bill creating the Texas Board of Medical Examiners and founder of the Medical Association of Texas, and the last President of the Republic of Texas, certainly deserves an eminent position in the annals of the history of Texas medicine. As an early Texas physician and surgeon, he set a standard of excellence which has seldom been equaled.

Anson Jones died in Houston at the Capitol Hotel, the site of the first capitol of
the Republic of Texas. Courtesy of the Houston Public Library.

ENDNOTES

1. Herbert Gambrell. *Anson Jones, The Last President of Texas* (Austin: The
University of Texas Press, second edition 1964), 3.

2. Chester V. Kielman. Personal Communication. Barker Texas History
Center, Austin, July 1978.

3. Robert T. Lentz, Archivist. Personal Communication. Thomas Jefferson University, Scott Memorial Library, Philadelphia, October 1978.

4. Herbert Gambrell. Personal Communication. Department of History,
Southern Methodist University, Dallas, (Emeritus), May 1978.

5. Walter G. Stuck. "Dr. Anson Jones, Last Texas President." *The Southern
Surgeon*, vol. 10 (August 1941), 606.

6. Ernest Wallace and David Vigness. *Documents of Texas History* (Austin:
Steck Co., 1963).

7. Douglas R. Schoppe, Park Superintendent, Washington-on-the-Brazos
State Historical Park. Personal Communication, April 1978.

8. T.W. Clarke. "Anson Jones: Doctor and Diplomat." *New York State
Journal of Medicine*, vol. 50 (1950), 65.

9. Dorothy Glasser, Head Librarian, Texas and Local History Department,
Houston Public Library, Houston, Texas. Personal Communication, August
1978.

BIOGRAPHICAL SKETCH OF AUTHOR

MARTIN L. DALTON, M.D., FACS was born in Columbus, Georgia, and educated in the Eufaula, Alabama, public schools, then at Auburn University and the University of Alabama in Birmingham School of Medicine. After a rotating internship at Caraway Methodist Medical Center in Birmingham, he received his general surgery and cardiothoracic surgical training at the University of Mississippi Medical Center in Jackson, under the tutelage of James D. Hardy, M.D. His residency training was followed by a two-year fellowship at the Walter Reed Army Institute of Research prior to joining the faculty of the University of Texas Southwestern Medical School with Watts R. Webb, M.D., and Robert R. Shaw, M.D. In 1966 Dr. Dalton moved to Lubbock, Texas. When the faculty of the new medical school at Texas Tech University was selected in 1968, he was made Chairman of the Division of Thoracic Surgery. In 1983 Dr. Dalton returned to the Department of Surgery at the University of Mississippi Medical Center where he worked closely with James D. Hardy until his retirement in 1988 and, thereafter, with Robert S. Rhodes, M.D.

From 1988 to 1990 he was Chief of Surgery at the Jackson, Mississippi, VA Medical Center. In October 1990 Dr. Dalton joined the surgery faculty at Mercer University School of Medicine and became Program Director in May 1991 and Chairman of the Mercer University School of Medicine Department of Surgery on July 1, 1991. Through his efforts, the general surgery residency received full accreditation on February 6, 1992. At present, Dr. Dalton continues as Program Director of the General Surgery Residency at the Medical Center of Central Georgia and Professor and Chairman of the Department of Surgery of Mercer University School of Medicine. He is a consultant to the Carl Vinson VA Medical Center in Dublin, Georgia, and currently serves as the Secretary of the Georgia Chapter of the American College of Surgeons.

Dr. Dalton and his wife Alice have two grown daughters, Lucy and Jenny, who live in Atlanta, Georgia.

Portrait of Dr. Nicholas D. Labadie. ca. late 1850s.
Courtesy Lawrence Jones.

Nicholas D. Labadie, M.D.
1802-1867
by

William F. Hood, BSed, M.S., and R. Maurice Hood, M.D.

★ AS AN EARLY SETTLER IN TEXAS, Nicholas Labadie pursued a relatively unknown but distinguished career in the colonists' struggle for freedom with Mexico. Following the establishment of the Republic, he was active and played a significant role in the early history of the City of Galveston.

The son of Antoine Louis Labadie, a fur trader, and Charlotte Berthe *nee* Raume, Nicholas Labadie was born in Windsor, Canada West, on December 5, 1802. Labadie's mother was the daughter of Pierre and Charlotte Chapaton and the widow of Lieutenant Louis Raume of the British army. Both sides of his family were of French descent; his father's relatives are traced back to Francois Labadie, born in the Diocese of Xanites in 1644, who had migrated to Canada as a young man. Some of his descendants returned to France, including the immediate ancestors of Nicholas; however, the name has been known in Canada since the mid-seventeenth century. The Labadie family has furnished many voyagers and soldiers to the Northwest service. According to an old record published in Detroit, Michigan, Antoine Louis and Pierre Descomptes Labadie, Nicholas' grandfather, "served on the western frontier at an early date, and subsequently, in company with several members of their family, moved to Detroit, after retiring from military service, where they spent the remainder of their lives."[1]

Nicholas' father, Antoine, was married three times and was the father of twenty-three children of which Nicholas was the

youngest. Antoine was seventy-two at the time of Nicholas'
birth and died when Nicholas was five years old.[2] Nicholas
Labadie was reared on the frontier in Canada West and received relatively few educational advantages during his youth.
However his family, devout Catholics, saw that he was well
educated in all religious observances and his duties to his
fellow-man.[3]

Even though the War of 1812 occurred during Labadie's
youth and there was an international border which separated the
Windsor area from Detroit, the French-Canadian communities
moved about freely, retaining the independence of movement
and travel that characterized the fur-trade lifestyle of many of
the families of that time. For reasons not known, young Labadie
was not destined to live the life of his contemporaries. He
decided to travel south into the United States.[4]

At about the age of twenty-one he left Canada for the United
States, traveling to Missouri. It appears from old letters written
by him that he studied for the priesthood from 1824 to 1828 at
St Mary's of the Barrens, a Lazarist college founded in Perry
County, Missouri, in 1820. He studied with John Timon and
Jean Marie Odin, two priests who were leaders in the Catholic
Church in Texas.[5] This was probably his first formal education.
As a result of this religious training and his association with the
fathers, his childhood impressions of piety were probably deep-
ened and strengthened.[6]

For whatever reason or reasons, Labadie opted not to enter
the priesthood, and in about 1828-29 went to St. Louis. He began
to read medicine as an apprentice to Dr. Samuel Merry, a
graduate of the University of Pennsylvania.[7] He defrayed his
expenses by clerking in a local store. As far as his medical
education is concerned, what he learned or how he was taught
is not known. In the 1820s most medical education was casual
at best. There was only one medical school in Canada, the newly
opened Montreal Medical Institution which became McGill
Medical College in 1827. However, apprenticeship remained the
most popular and affordable route into the profession.[8]

A single constant throughout Labadie's life was his interest
in business. He was a good businessman and, if his assets late in
life are any judge, he was a success. In fact, the contacts he made
in St. Louis, including fur traders and adventurers, induced him

to try his fortunes further south down the river. The next we hear of him is in 1830 at Fort Jessup, Louisiana. He conducted his first medical practice here, receiving "calls" while he clerked in a store at the post. He was still unsettled as to where he wanted to finally locate but was considering different business and farming enterprises as revealed in a letter to one of his nephews, a resident of New Orleans.[9]

It was during his short stay at Fort Jessup that he learned something about Texas. His first trip to Texas had a commercial interest and background. He rode west and arrived in Nacogdoches on Christmas Day in 1830 and, writing years later about this trip and subsequent trips to San Felipe and Brazoria, noted that travel was his "only business at the time."[10] Upon arrival in Nacogdoches, he delivered his letters of introduction to Colonel Piedras, the Commandante, and received the good will of the government. A few days later he set out for Austin's colony. One of his letters of reference and introduction, sent to Stephen F. Austin by a former employer, details Labadie's search for a career and location by saying that he was a "young Gentleman, who visits your Country with a view of locating himself somewhere, in your District or Country, Either in the profession of medicine or in the Mercantile pursuits."[11] In reality Labadie never did choose between the two; he remained a medical practitioner with a flair for and involvement in business pursuits for the rest of his life. Arriving at San Felipe, he met Colonel Samuel M. Williams and, wanting to see the country, traveled with him to Brazoria.

One month later Labadie was in New Orleans in the company of Captain Henry Austin and others he had met. He was convinced by these gentlemen that he should return to Texas. This he did after obtaining a large supply of medicines. He sailed in the small schooner *Martha*, commanded by Captain James Spillman, and landed at Anahuac on the north bank of the Trinity River on March 2, 1831.[12] He was at once employed by Colonel Juan Davis Bradburn as a surgeon of the local Mexican garrison of about three-hundred men. Colonel Bradburn also gave Labadie a town lot on which to build his home and office.[13] Following his business instincts, Labadie also opened a store in partnership with a Mr. Wilson. His medical practice around the garrison and with the local citizenry, combined with his interest in the store, soon began to bring him good returns.[14]

Shortly after his arrival and settlement at Anahuac, Labadie met and married Miss Mary Norment, a Mississippi lady and a sister of one Thomas Norment who was a volunteer in the patriot cause and participated in the Battle of San Jacinto.[15]

The community of Anahuac had only existed for ten years and Labadie arrived just in time to become heavily involved in what became known as the Anahuac Disturbances. The colonists were unable to secure title to their land from the government and believed themselves to be unfairly taxed by the customs office. At the same time, Bradburn impressed their slaves for labor details without compensation.[16] Labadie was among those who confronted Bradburn and eventually forced the departure of the entire Mexican garrison. As a result, it may be implied that Nicholas Labadie was a pioneer in the creation of Texas independence.[17]

He was not involved in the uniformly successful campaign of 1835, but the excitement of some of the volunteers who had seen action in San Antonio that autumn stirred Labadie and his neighbors to action. Following a meeting in Liberty County in February 1836, about seventy men decided to volunteer for the Texas Army. On March 11, 1836, they set out with full equipment for San Felipe. Their initial enthusiasm was dampened somewhat by the news that the Alamo had fallen.[18]

This group of men became part of Captain William M. Logan's company of the 2nd Regiment of Texas Volunteers. These volunteers were not a trained military unit, merely a group of men traveling towards the Texas Army and Sam Houston. Unavoidably, medical problems arose on the march which Dr. Labadie handled in the manner of the times and, by his own evidence, did so effectively.

> During our march from the Trinity to the Colorado, I had frequent calls to relieve the common complaints among our men occasioned by exposure, such as cramps, colics, and diarrhoea, and I therefore found the stock of medicines with which I had filled my saddlebags, very useful. At times it was with much difficulty I could keep up with the company, as I had often to remain behind, till I could relieve those at-

tacks, and then had to travel in the night. . . . Yet not
a single death occurred in our company.[19]

His company reported to General Houston at Beason's
Ferry on the Colorado River on March 20, 1836. After joining
the main army, the first military action of this company was to
retreat. However, Labadie was absent from the main army,
scouting with a company of volunteers under Captain Karnes.
The army retreated to the Brazos Swamp, an area with many
medical disadvantages related to the necessity of drinking swamp
water, according to Dr. Labadie.[20] Rejoining the encamped
army at Groces Ferry, Dr. Labadie was appointed Surgeon of
the 1st Regiment of Regulars by General Houston on April 6.
This promotion gave him charge of the medicine chest which
had been hauled on an ox cart on the retreat.[21]

Labadie relates how the surgeon's mess prepared breakfast
with a very inefficient commissariat the day before the battle at
San Jacinto. A pot of questionable swamp water was put on to
boil, with a handful of "half-pounded" coffee. One of the surgeons managed to procure a dozen eggs which were added to the
coffee. An alarm sounded and the meal was quickly consumed
with each man's drinking a bit of the boiling coffee as best he
could and most devouring an egg or two. When Labadie noted
that "when the eggs were found to contain chickens, I surrendered my share to others, who finding them well cooked swal-
lowed them quickly. . . ."[22]

Prior to the battle, an effort was made to reorganize the army
and its attendant medical staff. Dr. Ewing was named surgeon-
general and he in turn named Labadie as surgeon to the First
Regiment of Regulars. When the Battle of San Jacinto took place
on April 21, 1836, the surgeon-general had ordered no specific
assignments for the various medical officers, who then decided
"that it was best to follow the line, and fight with our arms as
circumstances might direct." During the battle, Dr. Labadie
fought as a volunteer in Captain Logan's company on the left
wing of the army which was commanded by General Sidney
Sherman. On at least one occasion, Labadie found himself working a cannon in the action against the Mexicans. Here is Labadie's
account, as seen from the point of view of a combatant physician.

... the writer with four others find themselves within twenty yards of some of the enemy's cavalry, thinking the while, it was [our force]. As they wheeled to retreat, we saw our shots tell on them effectively. We reload, and run some twenty yards to fire, and this was repeated some four or five times, when we found ourselves in the midst of the enemy's baggage, from which they were running for life. A young man by my side received a ball in his hip, which caused him to fall against me . . . . Having pursued the enemy into the woods, we found many had thrown themselves into the bayou, having only their heads above water. It was here that one or two women were killed by some one aiming at their heads, probably mistaking them for men, and two or three others taken prisoners.[23]

After the battle the realization of a doctor's duties set in; the wounded needed medical care. A total of nineteen Texans required medical care. At General Houston's request, Dr. Labadie attended some of the at least 280 wounded Mexicans. He had refused to do this when asked by Dr. Ewing, Dr. Anson Jones and Colonel Hockley. The wounded Mexicans had gone three days without medical aid when General Houston, sending for Dr. Labadie said, "Everyone points out you as the only surgeon willing to perform your duty. I want you to take care of the wounded prisoners. Go to them; don't let them suffer." To this Dr. Labadie replied, "I have attended on the garrison at Anahuac eleven months, day and night, for which I have never received one cent through the rascality of Bradburn, and I have resolved never to attend on that nation again, unless my pay is secured to me." General Houston promised to pay Dr. Labadie $300 but, to quote Labadie, "I faithfully discharged that duty, but have never yet received the first cent of the promised compensation."[24] For whatever reason, Dr. Labadie left no details of any of the medical treatments given in relation to the battle.

During this time, Dr. Labadie was not healthy himself, suffering from rheumatic pain that he blamed on sleeping on the wet, cold ground during the march to join the army. This was apparently forgotten during the excitement of the battle, but afterward he was not well at all. "The stooping position I was compelled to assume to dress the wounded as they lay upon the floor, caused my pains to be still more acute."[25]

While treating the wounds of the Mexican prisoners, Dr. Labadie was asked to speak to a prisoner whom the guards could not understand. Labadie's Spanish was good and he soon found that the prisoner in question was Santa Anna. It was Labadie's privilege to introduce the defeated Santa Anna to Sam Houston, who was having his own wound treated at the time. A number of years later, Dr. Labadie related this experience to the press.

> While I was engaged in attending the wounded Mexi-
> can prisoners, A Mr. Sylvester rode up to the prison
> square with a prisoner who refused to enter. I was
> called upon to interpret, as neither the sentinel nor Mr.
> Sylvester could speak Spanish. He replied: 'I want to
> see General Houston. Is he in camp?' 'Yes,' I replied.
> 'Mr Sylvester take this man to yonder oak tree where
> General Houston lies.' As they departed the prisoner
> whose wounds I was dressing, a Mexican Lieutenant,
> whispered to me: 'Est il Presidente' (He is the presi-
> dent). I at once folded my instruments and followed
> after them and met Colonel Hockley calling me to
> come quickly as I was wanted. I found General Hous-
> ton lying on his back on the ground under the oak
> tree. He was wounded and on his left the prisoner was
> sitting on a chest. He politely returned my salute and
> I said to him in Spanish, pointing: 'This is General
> Houston, do you want anything of him?' He replied:
> 'Tell General Houston that General Santa Anna stands
> before him a prisoner.' Houston hearing this inter-
> preted, appeared much surprised, and turning on his
> left side, said: 'General Santa Anna, in what condition
> do you surrender yourself?' 'A prisoner of war,' said
> he, and continued 'while I was in the camino royal-the
> public highways-I met two of your soldiers to whom
> I surrendered myself a prisoner of war.'
>
> 'Well,' said General Houston, 'tell General Santa
> Anna that so long as he shall remain in the boundaries
> I shall allot him, I will be responsible for his life.'
>
> Upon hearing this, Santa Anna's countenance

brightened. He said: 'Tell General Houston that I am
tired of blood and war and have seen enough of this
country to know that the two people cannot live
under the same laws and I am willing to treat with him
as to the boundaries of the two countries.' In reply,
General Houston said: 'Tell him I cannot treat with
him, but the cabinet that is in Galveston will make a
treaty with him. . . .' Here the pressing against us
interfered with the conversation and the guard had to
force them back. Colonel Hockley appearing with a
young Zavalla to serve as interpreter, I returned to my
wounded, who had been taken across the bayou to the
Zavalla place, which was thereafter used as a hospital.[26]

Years later, Sam Houston claimed not to remember ever
meeting Dr. Labadie.[27] The source of his remark was a speech
in which he devoted almost all of his effort to attacking a
reminiscence about San Jacinto written by Labadie and defending his own patriotism and military skills. The main criticism,
one expressed by many others as well, was that Houston had to
be coerced into fighting at San Jacinto, that he wanted to halt
the troops in the middle of the fighting, and that he had come
unfairly to have a major share of the credit and glory for winning
the battle.[28] The following is an example of this kind of claim
from the account of April 21 by Labadie, "Every man was eager
for it [battle], but all feared another disappointment, as the
commander still showed no disposition whatever to lead the men
out.[29]
   Conditions at the "hospital" were pitiful. So limited were
the supplies, especially bandages for dressing wounds, that Dr.
Labadie searched the pile of plunder picked from the battlefield.
He found sheets, beeswax, and tallow. The tallow was used in
making a soothing salve. While this was happening, some soldiers accidentally discharged a Mexican pistol. The ball grazed
the chin of Colonel Handy, who fell but was not severely
wounded. However, the burning wad from the pistol fell into
some cartridges which ignited, setting fire to everything. Labadie
put the fire out with water from the bayou. Later he was
presented with a bill for fifteen dollars by the government for

the sheets used in making bandages.[30] To compound the bad conditions at the Zavalla place, food was very scarce and it was common that the surgeons went many hours without food. They took care of the wounded who often were lying on "pallets" with just a candle for light.

After the battle, under orders from Secretary of War Thomas J. Rusk, Dr. Labadie started for Galveston with some prisoners. With permission he was allowed to visit his family at Anahuac. The times and events had dealt harshly with the inhabitants of the area. Upon his arrival, Labadie found one of his houses burned and the other pillaged. Dysentery, measles and whooping cough had swept through the group of about three-hundred families.[31] One of his two children had died and his remaining child and his wife, like so many others, were without basic necessities. At reports of the approach of the Mexican Army, the people of the Anahuac area had fled for safety but were stopped by flooded rivers and forced to camp on wet, swampy ground. Food was eventually obtained from Galveston, but by that time even Dr. Labadie's health was permanently damaged. "Deprived of all wholesome food, my pains again returned worse than ever, and for one week, I was deprived of all consciousness, and, on recovering, I found my hearing had departed-I was deaf."[32] Nicholas Labadie was thirty-four at the time and never did regain his hearing. This condition had to be a trial for anyone, but more so for a doctor. However, this did not prevent him from the practice of his profession.

In the winter of 1837 Dr. Labadie moved to Galveston. Before this, when and for how long is not known, he had lived on Lake Charlotte in what is now Chambers County where he owned land. Galveston was not a very hospitable place at the time of his arrival. Most of the population of the island was living in tents. He was one of the first residents of the city and one of the first to engage in business as he opened a drug store on the corner of Twenty-second and Market streets. Here he had his office and practiced medicine and dispensed drugs.[33]

A majority of the people were without proper housing and Dr. Labadie was soon busy; 1839 brought the first of nine recorded epidemics of yellow fever or, as Labadie referred to it, "vomito."[34] In addition to the added work as a physician, it also brought personal grief as his twenty-four-year-old wife died in the epidemic. This left him with three young daughters, Sarah, Charlotte and Mary Cecelia ranging in age from five months to six years. In spite of this loss, Labadie made Galveston his home and was to spend the remainder of his life there. He managed to give the needed attention to his own family and, at the same time, be everywhere among the sick. He did this not only during the epidemic of 1839 but in every other epidemic until his death.

While he was primarily occupied with his professional efforts, he stayed heavily involved in business and community opportunities. By this time he was held in high esteem. In fact, enterprises which would improve Galveston would often receive his backing and assistance. He established a line of sailing vessels between Galveston and Pensacola, Florida, by which he furnished a significant amount of lumber which went into many of the early structures in the city. In addition, he built a wharf at the foot of 27th Street, which bore his name into the twentieth century. He took the initiative in establishing the first Catholic church in Galveston, St. Mary's Cathedral on Center Street.[35] On December 9, 1840, Labadie married Mrs. Agnes Rivera, a daughter of John and Jennet Harkness. This marriage produced one son, Joseph. His marriage to Agnes Rivera was the first consecrated in this church. His second marriage ended in 1843 when Agnes died during a subsequent yellow fever epidemic. His third marriage was to Julia Seymour of Guilford, Connecticut who survived him and died in 1888.[36]

Labadie's wholesale and retail store was first opened in 1838 in his name, but by the 1860s it was Labadie and Barstow after his son-in-law had joined the business.[37] The store offered drugs, dye stuffs, paints, window glass, "fancy articles," stationary, medical books, Catholic books and Bibles, seeds, cypress and pine lumber and shingles, bricks and other building materials.[38]

Politically, it appears that Labadie remained a Texan first and an American second. He strongly supported the South in the Civil War and is reported to have attempted to join the army, but he was rejected due to physical problems and age.[39] However, he did serve on a medical examining board to the First Brigade of Texas state troops in 1863.

Not long after the Civil War, Nicholas Labadie completed his life's work. In February 1867 he became ill with what was diagnosed as typhoid fever. After approximately six weeks he

Portrait of Dr. Nicholas D. Labadie. ca. 1865, taken in Brownsville,
Texas by photographer Louis dePlanque.
Courtesy The Center for American History.

died in Galveston on March 13, 1867. He was buried in the Catholic Cemetery, Galveston. He was sixty-four years old, a dedicated doctor with an excellent reputation, a success in business, and children and grandchildren to mourn his passing and carry on the family name.

Concerning Labadie's medical life, it can be said that he and other doctors of his era struggled with ignorance no less doggedly than physicians of today. His failings may reflect a general lack of knowledge more often than stupidity or brutality. However, the treatments of the nineteenth century make practitioners such as Labadie appear brutal by current standards. The primary forms of treatment were bleeding, puking, and purging. These and other methods must be viewed within the context of the historical era rather than that of the twentieth century. The ancient Greek theory of the four humors was still a part of the medical practitioner's knowledge and understanding in the early part of the nineteenth century. According to this theory, sickness or disease was an indication of an imbalance in the quantities of the humors: blood, phlegm, yellow and black bile. It was theory that if one of the humors was in excess, this excess must be removed as quickly as possible. This was known as depletive treatment or theory. It is now known to be wrong, but it was not irrational. It was based on a rational but incorrect theory.[40]

Based upon what little is known about Labadie's practice, we can deduce that he was a practical and sensible man. While the medical profession knew little of the true nature of epidemics such as cholera and yellow fever, Labadie's advice was based on common sense. In discussing cholera, a disease that devastated Texas in the 1830s, he advised burying the stools and not permitting them to remain in the sickroom, "so as to destroy the poison from the stools," even though he did not have any modern knowledge of sanitation.[41]

Labadie's efforts to understand epidemics is chronicled by looking at yellow fever, a disease he had to contend with throughout his lifetime. His puzzlement on how to prevent the disease was shared by his peers. However, he was able to truthfully examine the facts. One mystery was why quarantine seemed ineffective.[42] Following is an excerpt from Labadie's notes written near the end of life's experience with the disease.

Our city fathers did once pass a quarantine law, and built a hospital on Mosquite Island, now Fort Point. By day and by night they had men and drays cleaning yards, alleys, &c...never was a town more clean and nice. Whilst we were comforting ourselves in our happiness and certainty in our supposed security, and no steamship to arrive, as they had left for the north to be repaired, and no arrivals from N. Orleans or any other port, a servant, German girl, in the employ of Mr. J. Berlocher, living on the Strand, was taken sick and died with black vomit (the virulent form of yellow fever) before anyone was aware of her real disease She being a stranger had not been out of the house for weeks, and only about four months at this place from Germany. About that time many were taken sick; so it went on increasing.[43]

In his time, the reputation of Nicholas Labadie was one of a compassionate and sensible physician even though he was poorly trained. He was highly and widely acclaimed at the time of his death. The *Galveston News* stated, "Galveston never lost a better citizen; not the poor, or those suffering and in want, a better friend. . . . To those in destitute circumstances, his services and his medicines have been freely given without money and without price."[44]

ENDNOTES

1. *History of Texas* together with a *Biographical History of the Cities of Houston and Galveston*, 338-39.

2. H.F. Howell and C. Denissen. *Genealogy of the French Families of the Detroit River Basin, 1701-1911*, vol 1 (Ann Arbor: Edwards Brothers Inc., 1976), 576-77.

3. *History of Texas*, op. cit., 339.

4. Charles G. Roland. "A Canadian Pioneer in Texas: Dr. Nicholas Labadie, 1802-1867." *Texas Medicine* , Heritage Series, vol. 82 (July 1986), 51.

5. "Nicholas Descomptes Labadie." *The New Handbook of Texas*, vol. 2 (Austin: Texas State Historical Association), 1178.

6. *History of Texas*, op. cit., 339.

7. Manuscript Biography of Labadie, Philip Crosby Tucker Papers, item 77-0003, ff 1-14. Galveston, Rosenberg Library.

8. C.G. Roland, op. cit., 51.

9. *History of Texas*, op. cit., 339.

10. N.D. Labadie. "Narrative of the Anahuac, or Opening Campaign of the Texas Revolution." *Texas Almanac* (1859), 30.

11. D.R. Hopkins to Col Stephen F. Austin, Dec 20, 1830, in E.C. Barker, E.C. *Annual Report of the American Historical Association for the Year 1922. The Austin Papers* vol. 2 (Washington: U.S. Government Printing Office, 1928), 565.

12. N.D.Labadie, op. cit., 30.

13. "Labadie," *The New Handbook of Texas*, op. cit., 1179.

14. *History of Texas*, op. cit., 339.

15. Ibid., 340.

16. M.H. Krieger. "Anahuac Disturbances," in *Handbook of Texas*, vol. 1 (1952), 43; "The Disturbances at Anahuac in 1832," in *Quarterly of the Texas State Historical Association* 6 (1903), 265-99.

17. C.G. Roland, op. cit., 51.

18. C.G. Roland. "War Amputations in Upper Canada." *Archivaria* 10 (1980),73-84.

19. N.D. Labadie. "San Jacinto Campaign." *Texas Almanac* (1859), 42-43.

20. C.G. Roland. "A Canadian Pioneer in Texas: Dr. Nicholas Labadie, 1802-1867." *Texas Medicine*, Heritage Series, vol. 82 (July 1986), 52.

21. E.C. Red (Mrs. George Plunkett). *The Medicine Man in Texas* (Houston: Standard Printing and Lithographing Co., 1930), 52-53.

22. *The Galveston News* (Thursday, March 14, 1867), 2.

23. N.D. Labadie, op. cit., 45.

24. Red, *The Medicine Man*, op. cit., 53-54.

25. N.D. Labadie, op. cit., 56.

26. Red, *The Medicine Man*, op. cit., 53.

27. "Sam Houston Campaign of 1836, and its Termination in the Battle of San Jacinto." *Texas Almanac* (1860), 18-35. On page 18, Houston refers to Labadie, saying "the individual is unknown."

28. C.G. Roland, op. cit., 53.

29. N.D. Labadie, op. cit., 53.

30. Red, *The Medicine Man*, op. cit., 55.

31. C.G. Roland, op. cit., 53.

32. N.D. Labadie, op. cit., 63.

33. *History of Texas*, op. cit., 341.

34. K. Davis. "Year of Crucifixion: Galveston, Texas." *Texana* 8 (1970), 140-53. See page 143.

35. C.G. Roland, op. cit., 55.

36. An undated manuscript sketch of Labadie's life, presumably written by his son Joseph. Galveston, Rosenberg Library, Ebenezer Barstow Papers, item 82-0003, ff 18; R.B. Blake. "Nicholas Descomptes Labadie." *The Handbook of Texas*, vol. 3 (1952), 953.

37. *The Galveston News* (March 15, 1867), advertisement on page 1.

38. C.G. Roland, op cit., 55.

39. Undated manuscript biography, op. cit., 11-12.

40. C.G. Roland, op cit., 54-55.

41. Nicholas Descomps Labadie Papers, Dr, Labadie's Cholera Remedy. Galveston, Rosenberg Library, item 22-0021; C.G. Roland, op cit., 54.

42. C.G. Roland, op. cit., 54.

43. "Cases of yellow fever treated by N.D. Labadie in the epidemic of 1864." *Galveston Medical Journal* 2 (1867), 847-61. See 856-57.

44. *The Galveston News* (Thursday, March 14, 1867), 2.

BIOGRAPHICAL SKETCHES OF AUTHORS

WILLIAM F. HOOD, BSed, M.S., the son of R. Maurice Hood, M.D., was graduated with a Bachelor of Science in Education in 1971 and received a Master of Science degree in 1977 from Abilene Christian University. He taught Life Science in the Leander Independent School District from 1977 to 1980. He was then employed by the Texas Department of Water Resources/Texas Water Development Board where he performed environmental surveys and drafted environmental assessments relating to the federal and state Construction Grants Program. He was then transferred to the State Department of Highways and Public Transportation, Automation Division, in 1985 as a technical writer. In 1987 he was transferred to the Environmental Affairs division as Staff Wildlife Biologist and permit specialist in the Natural Resources Management Section. He has prepared or assisted in the development of two environmental curricula for the department's Design School and has prepared a curriculum in conjunction with the U.S. Army Corps of Engineers and the Environmental Protection Agency for department-wide presentation of the Section 404 program.

William Hood serves as an instructor in the department's ongoing Design School, the Maintenance Supervisors Workshops, as well as in periodic departmental wetland and Section 404 training sessions. He is an invited speaker at several of the department's annual Transportation Conferences, the International Association of Right-of-Way Engineers' annual meetings, the fourth National Conference on Transportation Solutions (TRB), and the Association of General Contractors' Annual Administrative Conference.

For biographical sketch of R. MAURICE HOOD, see page 59

Portrait of Gideon Lincecum

Gideon Lincecum, M.D.
1793-1874
by
Howard R. Dudgeon, Jr., M.D.

★ THE NAME OF GIDEON LINCECUM is hardly a household word in Texas, even in the homes of Texas doctors, yet this man influenced the early practice of medicine in Texas to a considerable degree. He was, for those days of the nineteenth century, an expert in the diverse fields of botany, entomology, farming, archeology, and the Choctaw language. In fact, he was very fluent in Choctaw and knew and wrote much of the history of this people in their own language. He was familiar with the plants used by their medicine men and incorporated many of them into his practice of "botanic medicine." Fortunately he was a prolific letter writer all of his life and expressed his opinions—not always correct ones—on many subjects.

He was born in Georgia, moved to Texas, and lived in Washington County at Long Point near Brenham for many years. An unreconstructed rebel after the Civil War and unwilling to live under Yankee rule during the days of Reconstruction, he moved with one of his daughters and her children to Tuxpan, Mexico. Here he lived and farmed for several years, but in the last year of his life he returned to Washington County to die and be buried on Texas soil.

The United States was a small, struggling nation of thirteen states when Gideon Lincecum was born April 22, 1793, in a tiny frontier settlement in Warren County, Georgia. His ancestors were a mixture of English, Scotch, Dutch and French. He was very fond of his maternal grandmother, Miriam Bowie, aunt of the celebrated James Bowie, inventor of the lethal Bowie knife and one of the heroes of the Alamo.

His father, Hezekiah Lincecum, born in or about 1770, was a strong, hard drinking man who constantly moved his family westward with the ever-expanding frontier. Hezekiah's mother was Sally Hickman, whom Gideon described as "able to outrun anybody, was healthy, energetic, ingenious, industrious, frugal, but entirely illiterate."[1]

Gideon's grandfather, also named Gideon, moved from North Carolina to Warren County, Georgia, where he served as a captain of a ranger company and was killed during the War for Independence in a battle with the Muskogee Indians, who were allies of the British. His widow, Miriam Bowie Lincecum, moved with her six children to South Carolina. After the war she returned to her looted and burned home in Georgia. Aided by her neighbors and two surviving slaves, this strong and determined woman rebuilt her home and re-established her farm.

Miriam, with her three daughters and only remaining son Hezekiah, slowly rebuilt their lives and fortunes. The other two sons had been shot by the British shortly after the battle of Cowpens. Hezekiah grew into a giant of a man who consumed large amounts of whiskey and engaged frequently in fights. He was briefly converted and joined the Baptist Church but quickly backslid and resumed his riotous ways. He married Sally Hickman and she remained steadfast to him, uncomplainingly sharing his turbulent life. Hezekiah was constantly on the move, always seeking new frontiers and new adventures.

During one of their many moves along the frontier, Hezekiah and his driver became drunk and fell off the wagon carrying his family, and in the ensuing runaway by the horses his mother Miriam received a severe neck wound from which she bled profusely. Gideon describes the wound as being "a gash three inches long and exposing the blue trunk of the great neck veins." He put pressure on the wound and later pulled the edges of the laceration together. This, his first attempt at emergency treatment, probably saved his grandmother's life. He stated that this experience inclined him toward the practice of medicine.

Gideon was the first of ten children. At the age of fourteen, he attended school for the first and only time of his life. He received only five months of schooling in the primitive and transient schools on the Georgia frontier. At the end of five months he could read, write, and do arithmetic to the double root of three. His teacher gave his class many poems to memorize; at the age of sixty, Gideon still remembered many and could still recite them word for word. From the foundation of this scanty schooling, he built onto his education for the rest of his life by constant reading and study. He became an avid reader, and his mind and personality were forever changed by exposure to the works of Erasmus Darwin, grandfather of Charles Darwin. The study of this book pointed him forever toward the fields of science.

As a result of quarrels with his father, Gideon left home. He served for a short time in the American army in the War of 1812. He may have done some fighting, but most of his duties were concerned with military first aid and other services to the sick and wounded. Today he would be called a medical corpsman. After the war he married Sally Bryan and returned to his father's farm. Sally's brother, Joseph, later married Gideon's sister, Mary.

In spite of only five months of schooling, Gideon agreed to teach in one of the Georgia country schools. He describes his pupils as children who had "been borne and raised where I found them, among the cows and the drunken cow-drivers and they were positively the coarsest specimens of humanity I have ever seen. At playtime their conduct was indescribable and intolerable; the married men being the ring leaders in the devilment." Many country schools of that day enrolled as many grown men and women as students as it did children, not the best environment in which to learn.

By March 1818, Hezekiah and his children, with their families and slaves, had moved to Tuscaloosa, Alabama, which was at that time a small log cabin village. While here Gideon "practiced medicine" in the office of a Dr. Isbell. No record of any surgery done by Gideon can be found. He probably mixed drugs prescribed by Dr. Isbell. Perhaps no surgery was attempted because this was in the days before anesthesia. Gideon did occasionally bleed some of his patients. He also cut planks, operated a billiard table, and did other odd jobs. Obviously his medical practice was neither large nor lucrative. In November 1818, Gideon and his father moved again, this time to the banks of the Tombigbee River near the present location of Columbus, Mississippi. Here Hezekiah was at last content and lived on this land until his death in 1840.

During his early years, Gideon lived near the Muskogee Indians. Many of his playmates and later friends were of this tribe. From them he learned much Indian lore and how to use the bow and arrow and the more lethal blowgun. He became an expert marksman with these weapons. A good blowgun and good, strong, healthy lungs could hurl one of the arrows or darts about seventy-five yards, far enough and powerful enough to kill a man. Later in life he lived with and traded with the Choctaw, Chickasaw and Cherokee Indians. A number of these tribes lived on or near the Tombigbee River in Mississippi. It was during this time that he learned to speak fluent Choctaw, and it was also during this time that he developed his interest and his knowledge in the animals, insects, plants, and the flowers of the forest and plains.

His knowledge of Indian herbal medicine came from an Indian medicine man of great reputation who lived in the Choctaw Nation. For six weeks Gideon was alone in the woods with this man studying plants and their medicinal uses. He wrote all of his notes in Choctaw. The plants that he learned about here are the ones he used in his medical practice in later life.

As Columbus grew in size so did Gideon grow with it into numerous activities. He became a legal chief justice and also chairman of a school commission, organized a county court and appointed its officers, surveyed and leased town lots, organized a Masonic lodge and became its first Worshipful Master. He had become a jack-of-all-trades and master of few.

Gideon formed a partnership with John Pitchlyn, Jr. and opened a trading store in the Indian Nations. However, this ended in disaster when the store was robbed and Pitchlyn was murdered. This left Gideon heavily in debt. Additionally, Gideon was disabled for three years with an unexplained illness, perhaps tuberculosis, although this is never made clear in any of his letters or notes.

In 1834 some of the people of Columbus became interested in the possibility of migrating to Texas. Lincecum was appointed as physician for the committee to go to Texas and to report on the living conditions there. They were to leave on November 20, but Gideon was the only one of the ten committee members who appeared at the appointed place. If necessary, he was determined to go alone. He managed to raise a traveling purse of

$1,050 from his medical practice. Finally five other men decided to go along with him.

On January 9, 1835, Gideon departed for Texas with $1,050 in his pocket and his five traveling companions. They arrived in Spanish Texas in February where they found an abundance of game and wild geese. There were also large herds of wild horses. Gideon, an expert marksman, kept the party well supplied with venison which they ate with honey taken from a "bee tree." After exploring as far as the modern site of Bastrop, his companions decided that they had seen enough of Texas and were ready to go home. Gideon decided to stay and explore further to the southwest. He ventured into the area of San Marcos and to the south of San Antonio.

While in Southwest Texas, Gideon was held captive by a tribe of Plains Indians. No harm came to him because he could speak Choctaw to them. He made friends with the tribe's medicine man, because, as Gideon said, "I was also a medicine man." He left the Indians on good terms and traveled east until he reached the home of his friend Barnham and visited for three weeks. He then went to San Felipe to examine and treat Gail Borden who had been ill for a long time. While at San Felipe he joined with a group of volunteers being raised by Moseley Baker to meet the invading Mexican Army. Lincecum was to be appointed surgeon to the forces that would defend Texas west of the Brazos River. However, after three days, remembering his wife and ten small children in Mississippi, he decided to return home. At Alexandria, Louisiana, he encountered a cholera epidemic which was decimating the local population. Fortunately he escaped contracting cholera and arrived home on August 5, 1835, after an absence of seven months.

Shortly after returning from Texas, Gideon resumed the practice of medicine. He had had no formal training, but this was not uncommon in the profession in those days. A man who had great influence on the direction of his life was Dr. Henry Branham of Etonton. As was the practice in those days, Lincecum "read medicine" under Dr. Branham, cleaned his office, washed his instruments, and drove him on his calls to his patients. The chief medical text that he studied was *Zoonamia* by Erasmus Darwin.

Gideon borrowed one hundred dollars after his return from

Texas, bought a stock of drugs and set up shop. He studied the plants and methods used by the local Indians and incorporated some of them into his practice. He became convinced that the current allopathic system of medicine harmed more patients than it cured. It was the practice of allopathic doctors to purge most patients with large doses of calomel and jalap—ten grains of each. The patients were also bled often and extensively, a carryover from the teaching of Dr. Benjamin Rush, a famous doctor of the eighteenth century in Philadelphia. Gideon became convinced that bleeding was detrimental and stopped the practice. He was converted to the virtues of "botanic medicine" after reading a book by Samuel Thompson, a New Hampshire blacksmith, published in 1833 and entitled *A New Guide to Health or The Botanic Family Physician*. This unusual system of medicine was based on the use of a "cure all" consisting of lobelia, cayenne, No. 6 and steam baths.[2]

Lobelia is an obsolete drug that was used formerly as an expectorant and emetic. Another name for it is Indian Tobacco. Cayenne was a very hot red pepper. What was in No. 6 is today unknown. The hot steam bath is self-explanatory although its benefits were less apparent. Gideon served as the doctor for a large and wealthy plantation with many slaves. He used the "botanic method" and was favorably impressed with the results of his ministrations. No doubt it was less heroic treatment than the popular bleeding and purging method, but it probably caused less damage to the patients. He continued this method of medical practice, utilizing various other Indian herbal remedies, for the rest of his professional life. Apparently he attempted no surgery at this time other than the dressing of wounds.

Gideon prospered and later opened a hospital near his home. He practiced for seven years and recorded a total of $51,000 in fees in addition to his cash collections. In September 1847 he decided to go to Texas, quickly closed his office, and left for "the promised land" in March 1848.

He had thirteen children, all born in Mississippi. Four of his children had died before the move to Texas. Most of the family, along with twenty slaves, traveled by ship to Galveston and then by wagon to Houston. Here Lycurgus Lincecum, the oldest son who had come to Texas overland with his own wagon train, joined them. From Houston they traveled by horseback and wagon to Long Point in Washington County. They arrived on April 22, 1848, which was Gideon's fifty-fifth birthday. In November 1848 Gideon bought 1,828 acres, part of the original grant to Stephen F. Austin, from Moses Austin Bryan for $1,371 in gold. It was fine, fertile black land, and all the farm work was done by his twenty slaves. Long Point was eleven miles from Brenham. In nearby Independence, Baylor University had its beginning. Sam Houston lived here for awhile and was converted when Rufus Burleson, second president of Baylor University, had the honor of immersing him in nearby Rock Creek. So in this famous and historic area, Gideon Lincecum began a new chapter in his life on his plantation "Mount Olympus." Washington County had a population of about four thousand people at this time, of whom over half were slaves. The county had more of the feeling and character of the Old South than of the New West.

Shortly after arriving in Long Point, he circulated printed announcements stating that he and his sons would engage in the practice of botanic medicine. However, he found many things to occupy his time besides medical practice. By the beginning of the Civil War he had stopped practicing completely. During the Civil War, when most of the younger doctors were serving in the army, Gideon resumed his practice to some extent. He treated his neighbors, his slaves, and all soldiers, including some escaping Yankees who came by his home.

After the Civil War he had to resume his practice in order to support his family. He was issued a license to practice medicine in Washington County by the U.S. Army. During all this time he carried on a running battle with the allopathic doctors of the Galveston County and Houston City medical societies. They considered him to be a quack, and he considered them to be quacks. The conflict was never resolved. Gideon once gave an opinion of the practice of medicine in his day and time, "I practiced medicine for forty years. It's a humbug and does more harm to humanity than all of the wars." Nevertheless, he continued to practice to the end of his life.

Lincecum educated all his children, both male and female, to be doctors. He trained all of them in the botanic method of medicine, and all of his sons practiced medicine at one time or other. Lucullus Lincecum practiced medicine all of his life and during the Civil War took care of the families of soldiers. He had two sons who became doctors. One son, Addison, was graduated from a Texas medical school in 1903, was elected vice-president of the Texas Medical Association in 1912, and later served as mayor of El Campo, Texas.

Gideon's favorite child was Sarah Matilda, who was always called Sally. She, of course, had been trained by her father to be a doctor, but there is no record that she ever practiced medicine. He taught her to play the violin and piano and she shared his interest in botany. On December 19, 1865, she married William P. Doran, who became a well-known newspaper writer. Gideon's children and grandchildren numbered sixty-seven. A perfectionist, he was never quite pleased with their accomplishments.

From 1850 to 1859 Gideon devoted much time and thought to ways to improve the human race. He arrived at the conclusion that sexual behavior was the cause of the evils of the entire world. He felt that his theory should be applied to the large criminal class in Texas and proposed to legalize castration as a substitute for capital punishment. He claimed that castration would serve as a very strong deterrent to crime and as a check to the propagation of the criminal types. He wrote hundreds of letters and published a statement on the subject, mailing 676 copies to lawmakers, newspapers, scientists, doctors, and many others. Gideon claimed that he once castrated "a degraded, drunken sot" who was having delirium tremors and that the man later became a model citizen and thanked him for the operation.

The Lincecum Memorial was presented to the Texas Legislature in 1855. Dr. Ashbel Smith, legislator from Harris County, made the motion that it be referred to the Judiciary Committee, where it quietly died. In 1856 it was introduced again and, after much hilarious laughter, was referred to the Committee on Stock and Stock Raising. Again it died in the committee room. Gideon always referred to his memorial as his "sin-destroying and soul-purifying proposition."[3]

Gideon was probably an agnostic most of his life—certainly all of his adult life. He was constantly in conflict with the local ministers. He frequently wrote to his nephew John Lincecum of Bear Creek, Louisiana, whom he often feared was in danger of "getting religion." He once listed for John those individuals whom he would prune (castrate). Among those listed were deceivers, liars, drunkards and praying superstitionists, but his first choice would be the ministers. Needless to say, he and the ministers did not get along very well.

Regardless of how we view the punishment of castration today, during and after the Civil War it was frequently and illegally applied. Some Texas citizens regretted that the legislature had not passed the proposed Lincecum Law. It is obvious that in the bitter battle between organized religion and science Gideon was definitely not on the side of the angels.

Despite his views on religion, Gideon made lifelong friendships with a number of the religious and educational leaders of Texas. Two of the better known were A.W. Ruter, a Methodist leader of Rutersville College, and Judge R.E.B. Baylor for whom Baylor University was named. He valued Judge Baylor's fiddle playing but not his preaching.

He became upset when his nephew John Lincecum joined the church because his father, Grant, was dying. Gideon's favorite daughter, Mrs. Sally L. Doran, waited until after her father's death to join St. Peter's Episcopal Church in Brenham. There is no record that Gideon ever joined any church. He described his ethical creed as follows, "The whole desire of my heart has always been and still is that I may in all my different stations in life, steer clear of any wrong to or in any way give offense to my fellow creatures."

Washington County was a rich farming county and produced much cotton. During the year 1859 Gideon was very busy with his many and varied interests. Apparently he, with many others, did not notice the ominous clouds of the approaching Civil War. He did not raise cotton; his main crops were corn, sugar cane, and grapes.

The year 1859 was a period of accelerated mental activity for Lincecum. His routine was to check his meteorological instruments each morning. He made his rounds barefooted, for he never wore shoes in warm weather or in the mornings during the winter. He was regarded as a handsome man, six feet tall with straight black hair, piercing steel blue eyes under heavy black brows, and weighing about 195 pounds. He also studied the animals, insects, trees, and plants of the area wherever he resided.

Gideon became interested in phrenology and devoted considerable time to its study. Frequently he went to Houston or Galveston, part by stage and part by the Washington County

railroad, to hear lectures on phrenology. He could travel to
Galveston in twelve hours, a very swift trip for the time. In
August 1859 he bought a microscope purchased in New York
for $27.50 to aid him in the study of the animalcule in the water
and other fluids.

There had been a drought in Washington County for several
years and some of the farmers were planning to move. However,
Gideon had been studying drought cycles in the county, as
indicated by tree rings for the previous 141 years. He was able
to convince many of his discouraged neighbors that the drought
would not be permanent. The extent of his knowledge in many
different fields was truly amazing. He also studied the banks of
Yegua Creek and found evidence of lush tropical plants which
had grown there many eons before.

The year 1860 started in a bad way, with the drought in its
seventh year in Washington County. For lack of water, the
Lincecum herd of cattle, four hundred in number, was driven to
Dripping Springs in Hays County and remained there until the
end of the Civil War. Gideon bought an eight-horsepower engine
for $850 and began to drill a well in an attempt to get much needed
water. After drilling to a depth of two hundred feet at a cost of
$1,600 and finding no water, the project was abandoned.

In the latter part of 1860 the people of Washington County
began to worry about a Negro insurrection incited by northern
fanatics. They were people who prowled about the country
preaching, selling maps, mending clothes, etc. According to
Gideon, five or six towns in the upper counties of Texas were
almost completely destroyed by fires set by these agitators.
Following these fires, thirty to forty black men and ten to twelve
white, some of them preachers, were hung or shot by the local
population.

Soon other distractions occurred. Gideon was in favor of
Texas' again becoming a republic and taking no part in the
looming war. Sam Houston, Governor of Texas, was trying to
persuade Texans to remain in the Union. On March 2, 1861, the
People's Convention adopted an ordinance uniting Texas with
the Confederacy. They unseated Governor Houston when he
refused to take the oath of support to the Confederacy. All of
these actions upset Gideon very much; he still refused to believe
that there would be a war.

However, when the conflict did come, Gideon threw himself wholeheartedly into the war effort. He regretted very much that it had not come a generation earlier so that he would have been young enough to go. He never doubted that the South would be victorious. The blockade did not bother him very much, even when the government appropriated all of his woolen blankets. He devised a machine to spin the long Spanish moss from East Texas trees and used it for his bedding.

After two years of war, the Lincecums, their children, grandchildren and slaves—about a hundred in number—were desperately short of cloth for clothes. Gideon did not fold his arms and do nothing. He made his own spinning wheel and carding machine and shared its production with his less-inventive neighbors. He also learned how to make dyes from the various plants and trees. As one can see, Gideon was a very determined and resourceful man.

As the war progressed there was more and more loss in the value of money and less money with which to pay war taxes. Most of the horses were taken for army use and very few returned after the war was ended. Nevertheless, the hospitable Lincecums usually had a house full of guests. Soldiers on furlough, passing travelers and old friends crowded the house at all hours of the day and night. His goods and food supply decreased daily, but he continued to feed the hungry soldiers and treat the sick ones. On rare occasions a stray Yankee appeared and he, too, was fed and housed. Since he was short of gunpowder, Gideon resorted to his favorite hunting weapon, the bow and arrow, to increase the family food supply. He was very expert with this weapon.

The Civil War ended on April 9, 1865, but word of peace was slow to reach Texas. The last battle of the war was fought May 12 at Palmito Ranch, twelve miles east of Brownsville, and was won by the Texas forces under the command of Dr. "RIP" Ford.

At the end of the war, 50 percent of the population of Washington County was black. Some of the farmers employed free Negro labor or rented land to them, but Gideon and his sons prepared and farmed their own land. Through necessity he returned to the practice of medicine, going into the woods to obtain the plants he needed to concoct his own remedies. Following the war, things went fairly well until the beginning of

1866 when the shadow of Reconstruction began to darken the Texas horizon.

Gideon was a collector all of his life. He took two annual camping trips in Texas each year when time would permit. On these expeditions he would dig for the bones of vanished animals and men. Before he read the works of Darwin, he had instinctively embraced the theory of evolution to his own satisfaction. He once wrote, "all of our dry land animals and plants have over the ages crept from beneath the ocean waves to the dry land." He studied animals, insects, plants, the geology of the region and anything else that attracted him. He was an expert on the native grasses of Texas. He corresponded with many of the well-known Northern scientists, some of whom visited him at Long Point. He also kept a record of Washington County weather for the Smithsonian Institute. For many years Gideon provided the *Galveston News* with a monthly summary of the local weather. At the end of the Civil War he was able to furnish the state geologist with a five-year survey and summary of Washington County weather.[4] Immediately after the Civil War, Dr. James Webb Throckmorton was Governor of Texas; he and Gideon knew one another and shared some correspondence. Throckmorton's appointment of Gideon's friend Samuel B. Buckley to be state geologist pleased Gideon very much, and he sent many local rock specimens to Buckley for his examination and study. During the summer of 1867, Governor Throckmorton was removed from office and with him went Lincecum's friend, Buckley. It was at this time that in one of his letters on mineral wealth in Texas Gideon predicted that the state had almost boundless wealth in coal and petroleum. This was over three decades before the Spindletop well was brought in near Beaumont, and four to five decades before the discovery of the great East Texas oil fields. Gideon Lincecum was indeed a very remarkable man.

After the Civil War, when he had time, he would go to a small building he had built about forty feet from his main house where he would study the various insects that abounded in Washington County. He watched a dirtdauber sting into paralysis his "pet" tarantula and gave the species the name "tarantula killer." Today the dirtdauber is referred to as "the tarantula hawk." He kept bees in his little house, and a swarm of them would follow him when he went into the forest. He wrote extensively on the habits and building practices of his bees.

In his little red cedar house Gideon patiently hatched cotton worms (boll weevils) in order to study their habits and to find the best method of destroying them. He warned his neighbors many times that they must destroy the cotton worm because it could destroy cotton farming in Washington County. His neighbors paid him no heed, and much of their crop was ruined. Gideon studied and wrote about the Texas agricultural ants and told how they built cities, farmed, had slaves, milked their cow-like aphids, and waged war. At first, most scientists did not believe him, but time proved him to be correct.

In December 1860 Gideon read Charles Darwin's *The Origin of Species* and highly approved of the theory. He corresponded for several years with Darwin, expounding his theories on the Texas ants. In April 1861 Darwin read Lincecum's letters on the Texas ants to the Linnaean Society of London, and in 1862 they were published in the journal of the Society.[5] In 1868 just before he moved to Mexico, he was unanimously elected a corresponding member of the Philadelphia Academy of Natural Sciences, an honor not passed out indiscriminately, especially to an unknown doctor in post-Civil War Texas. Founded in 1787, this was the oldest and most learned academy of its kind in the United States.

On February 2, 1867, Sally, Gideon's wife of fifty-three years, died. He was lonely and despondent for the rest of his life. He often recalled their wedding-day reception at his father Hezekiah's house. The many guests consumed a beef, a goat, a sheep, three hogs, two turkeys, a fat goose, a chicken, a duck, many pies and cakes, eighteen gallons of peach brandy, and six dozen bottles of wine. A lively fight followed the wedding.

Gideon remained a lost soul after the death of his wife. For the first time in his seventy-four years he felt alone, even though all of his children, except one, lived nearby. The year before the death of his wife he had given his children 170 acres, retaining for himself only his house and 350 acres; he now turned the house over to his youngest son Lysander and his wife Millie. He kept the use of his little red-cedar house and sold half of his remaining land. He used the money to pay for the construction of a large wagon, which he called an "ambulance," equipped with a bed in which Gideon slept, a writing desk, and a large tent of his own construction. There was also ample space in the wagon for scientific and camping equipment. It was pulled by a team of strong grass-raised horses.

Thus equipped, he set out with three companions on an extensive tour to the west of Brenham. They were well armed, as they were going into Indian country. They went to Austin, Lampasas, Belton, Cameron, Marble Falls on the Colorado River, New Braunfels, and finally to San Antonio. The expedition lasted three months and covered twenty-eight counties. Gideon studied the soil and the grasses and even located deposits of coal and iron. He wrote a report and sent it to the governor, Dr. James W. Throckmorton.

In August 1867 Gideon and his daughter contracted yellow fever during one of his exploring expeditions in his "ambulance." This was a bad year for yellow fever in Texas and many people died of it. He treated himself and others with lobelia and quinine. He finally recovered after a long illness. It was at about this time that he began to consider moving to the Tuxpan River area of Mexico. He was becoming more and more irked by Yankee "Reconstruction" and its effects on life and business in Texas.

A friend, John Henry Brown, wrote to him from Mexico urging him to come to Tuxpan, telling him that it abounded in medicinal herbs, roots, and gums. Many other unhappy Confederates had already gone to this area of Mexico. Gideon planned to go overland in his "ambulance" but later decided to go by ship. He even urged former Governor Throckmorton to join them, but Throckmorton refused. Gideon's children could not understand his desire to go to a new country at the age of seventy-six, and, they resolutely opposed his going. To his delight, however, his daughter, a widow with seven children, decided to go with him to Tuxpan. On June 9, 1868, they sailed from Galveston aboard the schooner *San Carlos*. Seven days later they arrived at the mouth of the Tuxpan River.

Tuxpan, midway between Tampico and Veracruz, was Gideon's heaven and his paradise on earth. He gloried in the hard work he had to do to develop his land but fretted constantly because none of his other children would join him at his new home. He cleared his land with an axe and machete and later built a sugar mill and produced large amounts of sugar. All of this done by a man almost seventy-seven years old. In all he cleared about twenty acres. During his first years in Tuxpan he continued his contributions to the Smithsonian Institute sending snakes, marsupial rats, vampire bats, boneless frogs, insects, and over one thousand butterflies. In 1871 about forty-two American families lived in the Tuxpan valley and there was much visiting and partying among these lonesome Confederates.

Dr. George Bradford, a twenty-four-year-old doctor from Galveston, came to Tuxpan and quickly fell in love with Gideon's granddaughter, Attilia Campbell. They were soon married and Gideon turned the supervision of farm activities over to George. Gideon was now able to devote more time to his scientific activities, including limited study and excavation of two ancient Indian cities, Tabuco and Tomilco. Later he explored several pyramids southeast of Papantla. From his knowledge of Indian history Gideon deduced that the pyramids had something to do with the worship of the sun, and he referred to them in his letters as "Temples of the Sun." Here was a man with only a few years of formal education exploring ancient cities and making remarkably accurate deductions about the people who had lived there. At about the same time Heinrich Schliemann (1822-1890), the father of modern archeology, was digging up Troy (1873). It was he who later discovered the gold of Mycenae. Gideon's work antedated by about thirty years the discoveries of the great English archeologist Sir Arthur Evans (1851-1941), who excavated the ruins of Knossos on Crete and re-discovered the glories of the Minoans.[6]

In October 1872 Sam Houston Jr. landed in Tuxpan, broke, unknown and alone. Gideon invited him into his home and he stayed there until he obtained a job on a farm for eighteen dollars a month. Sam turned out to be a heavy drinker and finally returned to Texas where he later married Miss Lucy Anderson of Georgetown, Texas.

Gradually many of Lincecum's friends returned to the United States. Early in 1873 there was a severe outbreak of smallpox in Tuxpan and no vaccine was available. The Mexican people died at the rate of one or two a day. Gideon unsuccessfully tried to obtain material for vaccination of the unprotected.

Suddenly, and without explanation, he returned to Texas. Nowhere did his many letters give any clue as to the reason for his return. Perhaps he was just homesick. He visited his children and then settled down in his home at Long Point. It may be that

Tombstone in Texas State
Cemetery

DR. GIDEON LINCECUM

A VETERAN OF THE WAR OF 1812
INTERNATIONALLY FAMOUS BOTANIST
FRIEND OF DARWIN
BORN IN GEORGIA
APRIL 22, 1793
DIED AT LONG POINT
WASHINGTON COUNTY, TEXAS
NOVEMBER 28, 1873

Erected by the State of Texas
1936

he planned to return to Tuxpan, but his health slowly deteriorated and he postponed his return.

When Gideon was seventeen years old he had worked in an Indian trading post in Eatonton, Georgia, for a kind old man named Ichabod Thompson. Thompson had brought from Savannah, Georgia, a black English violin and gave it to Gideon as a Christmas present. On receiving the present in 1810, Gideon stepped outside, barefooted and in his nightgown, put the violin to his shoulder, and played a popular tune of the day called "Killiecrankie," based on an old Scotch ballad written by Robert Burns. This became a tradition, and every Christmas morning he would arise at dawn and barefooted and in his nightgown he would step outside and play the tune three times. Gideon carried his violin with him on all his moves and travels and enjoyed playing it for his own pleasure and for the pleasure of others. He considered the violin the greatest and most beloved present that he had ever received. December 25, 1873, was the last Christmas that he played "Killiecrankie."

In the spring of 1874 his health slowly began to decline and he took to his bed with a weakness of both legs. His mind remained clear to the end and he died November 28, 1874. He was buried next to his wife in the Mount Zion Cemetery near his home in Washington County as he had requested. His old black violin shared his grave. In 1936, the year of the Texas Centennial, his body and his old violin were removed to the State Cemetery in Austin and placed in a grave in Row One of the Austin Plot in the row that is dominated by the grave of Stephen F. Austin.

We, today, would not consider Gideon Lincecum to be a doctor of medicine and I am sure that legally he could not practice now. When the University of Texas Medical School opened in Galveston in the Fall of 1891, it was estimated that only 20 percent of the doctors practicing in Texas had had at least one year of formal medical education.[7] In fact, until the Medical Practice Act was passed in Texas in 1907, a doctor did not have to be a graduate of a medical school to practice medicine in Texas. My father wrote in his notes concerning the medical school in Galveston that about one-fourth of his class (1899) attended medical school for only four or five months and then withdrew to begin the practice of medicine.

Gideon seldom, if ever, purged or bled his patients, a very common practice of his time which caused much morbidity and some deaths. He was a man who did many things well and had many sound and well-reasoned ideas, often far ahead of his time. If he had lived in the Middle Ages in Italy or France instead of in the wilds of pre- and post-Civil War Texas, he would have been thought of and called a Renaissance Man.

ENDNOTES

1. Lois Wood Burkhalter. *Gideon Lincecum 1793-1874; A Biography.* (Austin and London: University of Texas Press, 1965).

2. P.I. Nixon, M.D. *A History of the Texas Medical Association 1853-1953* (Austin: University of Texas Press, 1953).

3. P.I. Nixon, *The Medical Story of Early Texas* (San Antonio: M.B. Lupe Memorial Fund, 1946), 16-17, 376-84; P.I. Nixon. "A Pioneer Texas Emasculator" 36 (May 1940), 34-38.

4. S.A. Geiser. *Naturalists of the Frontier*, (Dallas: SMU Press, 1948), 274.

5. *Agricultural Ants of Texas.* Journal of the Linnaean Society, Zoology, vol. VI (1862), 79ff.

6. *The University of Texas Medical Branch at Galveston, A Seventy-Five Year History*; by the Faculty and Staff (Austin and London: University of Texas Press, 1967).

7. H.R. Dudgeon, Sr., M.D. *My Recollections of the Medical Department of the University of Texas at Galveston, 1896-1913.* Transcribed by Howard R. Dudgeon, Jr., M.D., Unpublished.

BIOGRAPHICAL SKETCH OF AUTHOR

HOWARD R. DUDGEON, JR., M.D., was born in Galveston June 18, 1911. His father was Adjunct Professor of Surgery (1903-1913) until the family moved to Waco in 1913. Dr. Dudgeon attended the University of Texas at Austin from 1928-29, Baylor University in Waco from 1929-31, and the University of Texas Medical School in Galveston 1931-35. He did an internship and residency at Providence Hospital in Waco from 1935-38.

In World War II, Dr. Dudgeon served in the Army Medical Corp from November 6, 1940, to January 29, 1946. He served overseas in the Southwest Pacific Theater for three long, bloody years under McArthur from May 1942 to January 1945. He then served in New Zealand, Australia, New Guinea and the Dutch East Indies. He has held the following medical appointments:

Chief of Staff and Chief of Surgery at both Hillcrest and Providence Hospitals, Waco, Texas

President, McLennan County Medical Society - 1957

President, Texas Medical Association 1967-68

President, Texas Surgical Society - 1974

President, 12th Medical District - 1953

President, Third District of American College of Surgeons.

Member, Credentials Committee of the American College of Surgeons for Texas 1950-75

Member, House of Delegates of the Texas Medical Association from 1952 to date

F.A.C.S. received in 1942 while in Australia

Fellow, Texas Surgical Society - 1947

Team Doctor for Waco High Tigers - 1960-81

Dr. Dudgeon has held the following political Positions:

Member, Waco School Board, 1946-58

President, Waco School Board, 1956-58

Waco City Council 1966-70

Mayor, City of Waco, 1969-70

King, Waco Cotton Palace, 1983

Dr. Dudgeon, retired and living in Waco, Texas, is the author of thirty-three articles published in medical journals.

Frank Paschal in middle age. Courtesy of the University of Texas
Health Science Center at the Rare Book Division of the
San Antonio Library.

Frank Paschal, M.D.
1849-1925
by
Arthur S. McFee, M.D.

★ALONG WITH BOSTON, San Francisco and New Orleans, San Antonio is regarded today as one of the four most unique cities in the United States. Probably the most characteristic is New Orleans, spreading along the banks of the Mississippi River and having a distinct flavor compounded of Acadian, French, Spanish and Negro cultures. Boston is the quintessentially reserved New England city. San Francisco is a great metropolis, developing as the result of the energy and exuberance of the American west. Of the four, one of the most vibrant is San Antonio. After more than three centuries, it makes no excuses. It is a hybrid derived from early Spanish and Canary Island colonists, local Indians, the proximity of Mexico, and solid later arrivals from a variety of European countries. It started almost by accident, developed as an outpost of empire, and began a steady metropolitan growth in the mid-nineteenth century. Frank Paschal was to play a prominent role in the development of San Antonio as the city it has become today, a role which far transcended the practice of medicine and surgery; it represents only one man's contribution. It is also the story of the efforts of many others who formed this unique community.

A brief history of this city provides some appreciation of the arena in which Frank Paschal, who grew with the city, was to be effective. It is a fascinating narrative, including activity, disaster, a capacity for growth, and a wonderful diversity in a growing community to which this talented surgeon devoted the latter half of his life. Among the four unique cities, San Antonio is *prima inter pares*. Too far north of Mexico to be a truly Spanish colonial city, too far east to be characteristically southwestern, not on the direct path to anywhere and thus isolated, and certainly not a border town, it has nevertheless become one of the most visited and largest cities in the United States. Its location and diverse heritage are the reasons for its attractiveness and vibrancy. Sound public health and professional medical decisions, at the right time in its development, helped to insure its success.

In 1691 a group of Spaniards traveling east with the colonial governor, Don Domingo de Teran, stopped at the headwaters of the San Antonio River. Father Damian Massenet, a member of the party, was called upon to christen the location; he named the site "San Antonio de Padua" because the camp was made on his day, June 13. Indians had used the campsite, known to them as "Yanaguana," for more than a thousand years.

Spain, conscious of the value of her colonial holdings in Mexico and well aware of French exploration, had developed an ambitious and ingenious policy of guarding the colonies. Without sufficient colonists, the government proposed to use Native Americans as defenders of Spanish holdings. Indians would be educated in mission communities and would function as farmers and Christians, presidios would be established to protect missions, and colonists would be recruited after towns had been established. Set up in Madrid, the system could not possibly have taken into account the vast spaces involved nor the complexity of dealing with both hostile and peaceful tribes. That it was conceived at all is a remarkable piece of imaginative government thinking. San Antonio was to become a major outpost in this empire.

In 1718 Father Antonio Olivarez arrived at the site of San Antonio de Padua, which he had previously scouted as being a place where water supply would support a strong community. On May 1 of that year he established a mission, San Antonio de Valero, substituting the name of the Spanish viceroy, the Marquis de Valero, for Padua. A few days later the new Spanish governor, Martin de Alarcón, arrived to establish a presidio which he named San Antonio de Bejar (Bexar) in honor of the viceroy's brother, the Duque de Bejar, a recently killed Spanish hero. Two years later another mission, the second of five to be formed, was established. The missions were supported by Spanish priests from colleges at Queretaró and Zacatecas in Mexico. Fully fifty years was to pass before Father Junipero Serra would start north from the same colleges to establish the famous mission trail and the growth of grapes in California.

The missions were not completely successful in that many Indian tribes remained hostile and unconverted. Many tribes did, however, find a home and protection in the system, which reached its effective peak in Texas between 1730 and 1775. In this period thousands of Indians learned Christianity, farming, livestock husbandry, and developed elaborate irrigation systems. Disease brought by settlers from Europe was one of the more effective contributors to the collapse of the system towards the end of the eighteenth century. In March of 1731 a group of colonists arrived, recruited from the Canary Islands. The senior male members of this group were granted the title of Hidalgo, in consequence of their not having arrived at the colony of their initial expectation. This group, along with the existing presidio, formed the Spanish colonial nucleus in South Texas.

As might be expected in a developing border town, life was not always peaceful. Skirmishes existed between the inhabitants and the priests over water rights and Indian labor; the garrison was poorly paid and charged heavily by avaricious suppliers; all were involved in conflicts with the hostile Indians, and local in-fighting among Spanish officials themselves was not unknown. Much has been faithfully recorded and, in spite of it all, civilian government progressed. Set at the several levels of pueblo (the smallest unit), villa (an intermediate level), and ciudad (a full city), government did become organized. In time the Villa of San Fernando de Bejar was named for the heir to the Spanish throne. On May 8, 1744, the first stone of the present church now known as the Alamo was laid and blessed. By 1749 the tower of the Church of San Fernando, on the main plaza of the city, dominated the skyline. Behind the church lay the Plaza de las Armas, or the military plaza, as it does today. Both mission and presidio had moved nearly a mile eastward from the original location of San Antonio de Padua. They remained on the San Antonio River. Pueblos, the Presidio of San Antonio de Bejar, the Mission of San Antonio de Valero and the surrounding villas would amalgamate as the city of San Antonio. By 1749 a metropolitan core existed some three decades after its first colonization.

The nineteenth century brought much activity to San Antonio. Revolution had developed in France, in America, and to a degree in England. It is not surprising that such activity appeared in Spanish colonial America. American adventurers with Mexican allies sought to "liberate" Texas from Mexico and were crushed by royal forces in 1813. Nevertheless, the Spanish colonial government did not receive much support from home, and in 1820, in the dying years of Spanish influence, the governor agreed to allow Moses Austin to bring three hundred families into Texas to act as a buffer between San Antonio and hostile Comanche Indians to the north.

In 1821 Mexico rid itself of Spanish rule, and the new government ratified the agreement with Moses Austin. A flow of colonists soon was seen in eastern central Texas; shortly they were to outnumber the Hispanic population. San Antonio now experienced change. No longer a provincial capital after Texas had been merged with the Mexican state of Coahuila, where Saltillo was the capital, San Antonio lost status and became isolated as much from political affairs in Mexico City as from those in the developing United States to the north. In general, however, Texas residents north of the Rio Grande were content with the status quo and with the Mexican constitution as established in 1824.

In 1833 Antonio Lopez de Santa Anna, elected as President of Mexico, seized dictatorial powers and abolished the constitution of 1824. His demands on residents in the north were resisted and an army sent by him to quell opposition was defeated at Gonzales, Texas, in October 1835. Santa Anna's brother-in-law, Martin Perfecto de Cos, at the head of this army, then engaged in skirmishes around the city and retreated into and fortified San Antonio. A two-month siege ensued, finally resulting in a guerrilla conquest of the city and the surrender of General Cos in December 1835. Most felt this episode ended Texan union with Mexico, and a small garrison was left in San Antonio after the militants disbanded. In 1836, approximately two months later, Santa Anna himself led a rapid attack on San Antonio with five thousand troops. His aim was to kill or remove all rebellious Texans and firmly settle Texas within the boundary of Mexico. On March 2, 1836, the Texas Declaration of Independence was signed, establishing a constitution and a government for the

Republic of Texas. On March 6, 1836, Santa Anna broke through the walls of the Alamo after a thirteen-day siege and slaughtered all 181 defenders. Six weeks later he himself was decisively defeated by General Sam Houston at the Battle of San Jacinto and forced to recognize Texas' independence as a price for his release. The newly found Republic of Texas was to last until 1845.

The establishment of the Texas Republic did not mean immediate peace or prosperity for San Antonio. The city remained isolated, although at a strategic location for a variety of trade routes. A gathering of Comanche Indian chiefs in 1840, at which white captives were to have been returned to the city, became a massacre when it was realized that only one young girl was brought with the chiefs as a returning prisoner. Indian raids were coupled with concern about further invasion from Mexico, and indeed in 1842 the town was twice occupied for brief periods by Mexican armies. After the second invasion, the army took a number of prominent San Antonians back to prison in Mexico. Not surprisingly, this threat of constant attack, actual invasion, and a succession of different governments brought San Antonio to a low point. In 1842 its population had dropped to eight hundred from a peak of four thousand a decade earlier, a true nadir.

In 1845 Texas became the twenty-sixth state to join the union. One more battle with Mexico would ensue, fought far from San Antonio. In 1849, the year of Frank Paschal's birth, a young Rutherford B. Hayes described San Antonio as an "old, ruined Spanish town". His comments were not prophetic; in the next decade, the population increased tenfold, fueled by emigration from Germany, England, France, Italy, Denmark, and a variety of other European countries as well as from the northern United States. The culture was mixed and became distinctly unique to the city. The army established San Antonio as a strategic military center, thus affording protection from Indian raids. The threat of Mexican retaliation receded. In spite of its location miles from the coast and from the border, it was situated in the center of south Texas. While at first the city developed as a ranching center, trade routes opened and it could not help developing into the vibrant community known today.

Frank Paschal was born into a family of achievers. From the

outset he was one of a group in which individuals "did" things when others demurred or quailed. The accomplishments, often taken for granted, are impressive. His grandfather, George Paschal, served in the American Revolutionary Army in his teens until 1781, when Cornwallis was defeated at Yorktown where young Paschal was present. At this point in his life, when he was fifteen years old, he had acquired an awesome reputation for probity. In 1802 he married Agnes Brewer, a young lady of exceptional religion and industry. She was also given to some patriotic fervor, favoring revolutionary war heroes. In January 1810, Franklin LaFayette Warren Green Paschal was born; Agnes had a definite reason for the selection of each of these names. This young man would be Frank Paschal's father.

In 1824 Agnes Paschal survived a particularly severe "malignant" intermittent fever. It is noted that she may have been the first in Georgia to do so. That experience, with her known industry, religion, good sense and community responsibility, rather rapidly led to her becoming the "physician in fact" for her neighbors in a wide area. With time and observation, she became conversant with anatomy and finally involved in surgery itself. A family anecdote recalls her performing an emergency surgical procedure in a home after three physicians had left, having given the patient up as unsalvageable. Since one of the doctors left his instruments with the patient, Mrs. Paschal, when she arrived, could perform the lifesaving procedure and did so. She was not specifically trained in either medicine or surgery. She was, however, able to recognize need and to address it. Accomplishment of such a nature cannot in general be passed on as an inherited trait, but the capacity for learning, industry, and responsibility can be and frequently is familial. This rather formidable person, Frank Paschal's grandmother, must have been a constant example.

Franklin LaFayette, Paschal's father, came to Texas in 1836 shortly after the fall of the Alamo in March. He was a member of a group of rather irregular individuals, all of whom came from Georgia, all of whom had land claims in the state, and all of whom apparently had relatively little else to do. Over the next few months he served in several different brigades and acquired a wound in a scouting expedition near Leon Springs. His brother, Augustus, came to Texas to take him back to Georgia to recover. After Texas' independence was established, however, young Franklin returned permanently to San Antonio. Some years later, he met a Miss Francis Roach, a young lady of Scottish descent, and married her on May 30, 1844. Family notes indicate that this marriage was the first marriage between native-born Americans to take place in San Antonio. It certainly is the first such recorded in marriage records. In time Franklin Paschal was to prosper, becoming the first Sheriff of Bexar County, an alderman in the city, and a merchant.

Frank Paschal, the subject of this study, was born on October 22, 1849, one of five children, three boys and two girls. He is said to have been one of the first four American citizens to be born in San Antonio. Until he was eleven he was educated locally in the first public school established in San Antonio; in 1860 his family moved to Monterey where his studies continued both in English and in Spanish. Relatively little speculation is needed to visualize an energetic young man in his early teens developing in a foreign country adjacent to his own. He was into everything. Frank Paschal came to love Mexico, became fluent both in English and Spanish, and was well aware of cultures on both sides of the Rio Grande.

In 1866, having missed the Civil War completely, his family returned to San Antonio. Young Frank started working at Drydens, a local drugstore. Necessarily, this task brought him into contact with illness and remedies. He realized his ultimate goal would be healing. Two years later in 1868 he started reading medicine informally with Dr. George Cupples, then one of the major medical figures in South Texas. Dr. Cupples, in addition to being a respected practitioner with a wide constituency, had been an organizer of the Texas Medical Association in 1853 and had served as its first president. He was an accomplished and effective physician and surgeon who acquired a brilliant and responsive pupil in Frank Paschal. As a student Paschal was privileged to witness many "firsts" introduced by Dr. Cupples into Texas: major operations, complex amputations, and anesthesia with the vast array of surgical procedures which it allowed. Professionally, socially and philosophically the two years spent as an apprentice with Dr. Cupples were valuable indeed.

In 1870 Frank Paschal traveled east to acquire a medical education. A variety of twists of fate led him to the Louisville

Medical College, although that school may not have been his
original destination when he left home. He was a dedicated and
scholarly student, in addition to having enough energy to work
his way through school to provide his own support. The combination of work and study——many long hours and many nights
up until three or four a.m.——allowed him to be graduated with
honors in 1873. He received four of nine faculty votes for this
rating and won three of the six available prizes for outstanding
work in Principles and Practice of Medicine, Materia Medica,
and Therapeutics and Surgery. He won a competitive internship
of one year in the Louisville Hospital in 1874 and returned to
San Antonio with a silk hat, which he had bought as an intern,
and much energy. The trip home included his arrival in Austin
with five cents in his pocket, which allowed the purchase of five
cookies to be consumed between Austin and San Antonio.

Two family accounts exist concerning the next several
months. In one it is said that, six months after his return, neither
the silk hat nor a new office nor a new doctor's carriage had
produced much medical business. Thus, as he was well acquainted with Mexico, he decided to travel there since there were
no doctors and the opportunities appeared much more plentiful.
Indeed, he is said to have responded to a recruiting effort to come
to that country to provide medical help. A second version is that,
after six months in San Antonio of little or no work, he went
south with a group to offer requested medical help in an emergency. He then went to Chihuahua, a major northern Mexican
mining center, fell in love with the place and its surroundings,
and elected to stay. It was to be home until 1892. It is likely that
a good part of each story is true. Chihuahua was medically
underserved and, in the 1870s, was a vigorous growing center. It
is in lovely country.

His journey to Mexico was memorable from many points
of view. From San Antonio to Presidio, the trip required more
than five weeks and was interrupted at that border town by an
epidemic of small pox. Informed that there was no medical help
within one hundred miles, the young man volunteered his
services and began a labor that would extend to almost four
months. It was an informative, firsthand experience of dealing
with poverty, squalor, insufficient medical facilities or supplies,
and their effect upon the patients. Death was never very far from

these individuals and competent help was simply not available.

As if to balance the disastrous situation, one anecdote relates the capacity of individuals to maintain some equanimity. At that time, the death of a Mexican child was regarded as the union of an angel with God. It was a time for rejoicing; a cheerful wake with music, dancing and possibly fireworks was in order. During one such episode, a second child's corpse was brought in and laid beside the one who was being celebrated. Music and activity ceased at once until the musicians who had been engaged for the first baby received an additional $1.50 for the second. There is in this story, in spite of the obvious statement of greed, a kind of courage and acceptance of the facts of life that must have impressed him.

In Mexico, Paschal underwent and passed an examination given in Spanish by the Mexican Board of Medical Examiners. He was the second foreign individual to do so and became licensed to practice anywhere within the country. He was very successful in practice, becoming the personal physician for the American ambassador, for the governor of the state of Chihuahua, and for many other prominent individuals. Ultimately, he took a position as the Chief Surgeon for the Mexican Central Railway. In 1881 he organized the medical department of this venture and served as its chief until 1892. Practice in Chihuahua, which he came to love, flourished and he became a citizen of some substance, owning interests in mines, a flourmill and other ventures. These properties were confiscated along with all other American holdings during the administration of Porfirio Diaz. There is, however, a very nice story that, in one church in northern Mexico, a pair of silver bells exists engraved with the names of Dr. and Mrs. Frank Paschal as a commemoration of their service to the people of this area.

In 1878 Frank Paschal returned to San Antonio to wed Miss Ladie Napier. The couple returned to Chihuahua and made their home there until 1892. All five Paschal children were born in Mexico, and his own personal ties with this country remained strong. Dr. Hugh Hampton Young, in his autobiography, relates a charming story which took place in 1898 or 1899.

I had been away from Baltimore about eight months.
I was heavily in debt, but I felt that I should not return

to my practice until I had been free from fever for a month. It was imperative that I find some way to make money. I had heard a lot about the rich little mining city of Chihuahua in northern Mexico from Dr. Frank Pascal of San Antonio, who had once lived there while chief physician to the Mexican Central Railroad. He had mentioned the fact that there were no qualified surgeons in this town. I wrote to Dr. Pascal and proposed that he and I go to Chihuahua and divide equally the money we made. He replied that he needed a vacation and would be glad to accompany me.

This sojourn, which netted the two surgeons $5,000 in twelve days, ended abruptly when the very impressive uncle of a charming young Mexican girl to whom Dr. Young had been very courteous was said to be desirous that he express his real intentions.

Since in Chihuahua he was an almost unique commodity, Paschal's surgical practice both before and after his wedding was demanding. It was not well organized. While it provided a variety of fascinating anecdotes, it would be incomprehensible to the practitioner of today. The range of operations was unlimited, especially if one were adept and one of only a very few practitioners in a region. Any and every anatomic area was treated. Paschal was accomplished at cataract removal, as recorded in his notes in the 1870s, and numbered the removal of a bladder stone from a well-known Mexican bandit called "The Peacock" as one of his triumphs. In this latter case the patient had sustained a pubic gunshot wound which resulted in hematuria, but no reduced illegal activity. Five years later he was found to have a bladder stone. Prior to any treatment's being initiated, however, the patient was jailed and drafted into the army. From this situation he petitioned Dr. Pascal for help in obtaining a release to have the operation. Needless to say, after his transfer to the hospital the man escaped. Finally, thirteen years after the original injury, Dr. Paschal removed the stone, in the center of which lay the bullet. Dr. Paschal noted, "He made an uneventful recovery; but the knife I cut him with was stolen from amongst my instruments that I left at his home to be cleaned."

More frequently, practice included days which often began at midnight with an emergency and included a variety of patients assembled for treatment before breakfast. The day might require an urgent visit in the country to do an operation in a home and might end with a return in the late afternoon or evening to one or two more difficult situations without much chance for either rest or food. Transport which afforded little protection from the weather—a horse-drawn buggy—was provided by the physician; services were taken to the patient. Seen in the light of current practice with its utilization review, system of major hospitals, centralized support and specialists, the figure of an individual like Dr. Paschal seems a bit like Don Quixote setting out to do battle singly with all the forces of evil. Impressions and knowledge gained in this rather harsh school were to serve him well.

In Mexico he made his initial acquaintance with tuberculosis and wrote touchingly about a young lady whom he was asked to see in the very early stages of the disease, from the point of view of her predictable progress and decline. Experiences like this formed the foundation of much of the work of the latter half of his career as a spokesman for advancing medical practice and public health both in San Antonio and in the state of Texas.

In 1892 his brother George ran for mayor of San Antonio. George enlisted Frank's help in this race, which was granted with the proviso that he would return to San Antonio if George inserted in the mayoral platform a plank for substantial development of good sewer facilities for the city. His insistence, at this early opportunity, appropriately did much to insure that there would be a river in San Antonio along which a river walk could develop. Possibly this item can be listed as the first of his public health accomplishments. As a result of his brother's campaign and request, he returned with his family to San Antonio ultimately to define an area of solid accomplishment in that community for the last three decades of his life.

It is possible to divide Dr. Paschal's professional career in San Antonio into several parts. The impressive fact that emerges is that he was successful in every one of them. There are at least four clear, identifiable areas, all of which overlap and derive primarily from his work as a practicing medical professional. In each defined area, he did as much as would satisfy many another soul as qualifying for a full and productive single career.

To view Dr. Paschal as a practitioner and physician, it is revealing to turn to his grandson, Dr. Walter Walthall, who recounts that nearly all patient physician encounters during the time of his grandfather's practice here were housecalls. The physician rarely spoke with the patient or with the individual calling on the telephone, but went directly to see the individual after contact had been made and he had received the summons. It was an intensely personal and close relationship. He notes that Dr. Paschal was able to determine by the odor encountered in the house if it were safe for his carriageman and whatever grandchild might be with him to come into a home to wait. The characteristic smell of diphtheria (almost unknown today) would alert him to warn those in his own house to be out of the way on his return until he could bathe and send clothes out for disinfecting in the sun. This type of work was the backbone of his practice for more than thirty years. He was highly successful as a practitioner and achieved a state of fiscal independence which allowed him to build several homes, support four years as city physician and to give $10,000 to the Bexar County Medical Society to help provide a permanent home for that group at a time when this sum was princely indeed.

The quality of his practice is attested to by the fact that he was known as "Dr. Ethics" by his colleagues. This title was bestowed at a time when ethics did not mean "Who pays?" but rather "How do you conduct yourself within your profession?" Routinely he was charged by the Bexar County Medical Society with the task of chairing the Committee on Medical Ethics, a precursor of the rather more elaborate, present-day Board of Censors. It fell to him to counsel, to reprimand, to suspend from the Medical Society, or occasionally to expel. Since medical practice then was dependent on active society membership for clinical privileges, the responsibilities assumed were grave. A prominent San Antonio surgeon was found to have agreed to equip an insurance company office in return for receiving all its referrals for on-the-job injuries. The suspension imposed by Dr. Paschal resulted in the surgeon's electing to pursue a year of further study in Europe on "Advances in Surgery."

It is not uncommon that an outstanding individual is elected, almost by acclamation, to speak as the collective conscience of society or of a certain segment of it. It is, however, rare that these

The Physicians and Surgeons Hospital in San Antonio. Frank Paschal
was a major contributing founder.
Courtesy of the Baptist Medical Center, San Antonio.

An ambulance, at the entrance of the Physicians and Surgeons Hospital in
San Antonio in 1903, described as "a modern, thoroughly up-to-date
hospital ambulance with rubber tires, pneumatic swinging bed, and roller
bearing axles. The van is always ready to meet trains or go anywhere for
patients. The cost of this service is $5." Courtesy of the University of Texas
Health Science Center at the Rare Book Division
of the San Antonio Library.

individuals can effectively discipline those around them. A comparison with our present-day system in which the collective standard of a committee is substituted for the type of probity exemplified by Dr. Paschal does not seem an improvement. It does lessen the burden by distributing the onus of discipline to more than one shoulder. Dr. Paschal had no difficulty in assuming this burden, and in this respect there is something to be said for the principle of heredity. Paschal appears to have been a true lineal descendant of his grandfather; such traits were ordained in his very being.

Within the practice of medicine Paschal, with others in San Antonio, was among the principal organizers of the Physician's and Surgeon's Hospital. This hospital was built by a group of business and professional men on a full city block in San Antonio. Initially, it stood amid much lawn and provided hitherto unavailable services. This institution was the precursing nucleus of the San Antonio Baptist Hospital System, in 1998 a conglomerate of at least six active and successful units. Within the Paschal family it is noted that the Paschals built the hospital; the Walthalls, a second generation, bought it and eventually concluded a merger with the nearby M and S Hospital to provide a gift which became the first of the Baptist Hospital System Institutions. The Central Baptist Hospital occupies the original city block----no lawn is apparent now.

A second major area to which Frank Paschal gave much effort was the understanding of medicine, surgery, inflammation, disease in general, and its required treatment. Medical writing of the later nineteenth and early twentieth century is largely descriptive. Clear statements of pathology were relatively new; the work of Pasteur and Welch in Microbiology was still fresh. The concepts of pathophysiology were developing. In an era when papers might be an exhaustive recitation of individual case reports, Paschal's contributions are remarkably fresh and include statements on Appendectomy, Opium and its Alkaloids, Bone and joint operations (with illustrations), Liver abscess draining into the lung, Bladder stones and lithotomy, Malta fever (case report and discussion), Cystic renal degeneration, Caesarean section—too Frequently Done(?), and Education: Relationship to Public Health.

The foregoing list of his contributions is only partial. It

The current Baptist Medical Center which occupies the site of the
original Physicians and Surgeons Hospital. Courtesy of the Baptist
Medical Center, San Antonio, Texas.

spans, in the medical arena of 1998, topics which cover five
clinical specialties and two basic science disciplines. It can be
argued that the explosion of knowledge in the past century has
made specialization inevitable. It can equally be argued, from the
example set by Dr. Paschal, that the focus of an active and
inquiring mind can be exactly what it chooses to be at any one
time. The results of that focused attention can frequently be
cogent and valuable. Frank Paschal was by no means a "Renaissance Man"; he, however, recognized few limits to his interests
in medicine and pursued them well. He formed ideas regarding
disease and its treatment; he spent the time necessary to examine
his theories, and he was willing to write to share views. Dr.
Walthall has stated that he did not attempt to set a fracture or to
treat a joint without reviewing his skeleton. In a similar fashion,
he did not write without reviewing his thoughts and explaining
them unequivocally. In particular, his views on social issues are
direct, uncompromising and correct.

A third segment of Dr. Paschal's medical career in San
Antonio can be gathered under the rubric of Public Health. It
has been investigated in a carefully documented thesis presented
in partial fulfillment of the requirements for a degree of Master

of Arts in History by his grandson, George Hugh Paschal, Jr. The thesis is entitled "The Public Service Aspect of the Medical Career of Dr. Frank Paschal in San Antonio, 1893-1925."

Frank Paschal's first contact with tuberculosis occurred in Mexico and he came to recognize the devastating and relentless progression of the disease. When he returned to San Antonio, he recognized a difficult and increasingly worsening condition— a steadily rising death rate associated with tuberculosis, especially in a population classified as non-resident. In fact, the situation was that, in a time when the only treatment of tuberculosis was rest and fresh air, a large population of infected patients steadily migrated to South Texas for both. Many were without adequate funds and came to live in crowded, poorly kept tenements and rooming houses. The death rate climbed, especially in this group, to appalling figures.

Paschal's efforts were directed widely: an early anti-spitting ordinance which he sponsored; prizes for the best papers written in schools by students on the subject; strict regulations for cleaning hotels and rooming houses where deaths had occurred; proper disposal of waste, and the development of a state sanitarium. The thesis records the trials experienced by Paschal in this nearly twenty-year crusade, which culminated in the establishment of a sanitarium in 1912 at Carlsbad, Texas.

Virtually everything that could be placed in his way was set there in the course of this effort. Indifferent city councils referred his requests to yet more indifferent committees; the newspapers violently disagreed about the infectious nature of the problem; the governor vetoed an initial bill for a sanitarium. All of these difficulties were overcome by persistence, by talking to small groups, by involvement with women's clubs, and by interesting students in the problem. In a time when little was known about this devastating killer, the thrust of Paschal's effort was education and persistence. It succeeded.

In 1898 Alderman Marshal Hicks ran for mayor in San Antonio and urged Dr. Paschal to aid in a program of civic improvement by accepting the post of City Physician. Hicks was duly elected, and for four years (1899-1903) Frank Paschal served in the capacity of City Physician. It was not an easy post. He received $1,200 a year, which could not even approach his practice income. Additionally, he was faced by a new regulation from the City Council reorganizing the Board of Health and establishing terms by which members of this board, appointed by the city, were to serve without pay, excepting in times of epidemic and crisis. Since no one so appointed would serve, Dr. Paschal shared the duties of his post with those of the Board of Health. In this post he was confronted with a variety of problems and very little fell outside his purview. The physical state of the City Hospital required refurbishing and renovation, which he arranged. Small pox occurred as a minor epidemic in 1901 through 1903 and resulted in an action by the San Antonio Board of Education to favor vaccination on a mandatory basis unless the child's actual condition precluded it. Trash disposal, jail and school connections to the city sewer system, removal of stagnant water collections, and the provision of free public water for penniless immigrants from Mexico are only some of the issues he faced during these four years in office. In discussing Dr. Paschal, Dr. F. E. Daniel, the Editor of the *Texas Medical Journal*, in an article entitled "Health Officer" stated that "his shaking up of dried bones was effective in arousing apathetic local administrations and might yet galvanize into action a sluggish governor and legislature".

After 1903 Dr. Paschal was not again to be a paid employee of the city or the state. He did accept a variety of committee posts and chairmanships over the next two decades and continued to speak as an advocate for education and public health. Some of these duties included an appointment from the Texas Medical Association to a committee to secure the legislative establishment of a State Board of Health, an appointment from the Texas Medical Association as Chair of the Committee of State Medicine and Public Hygiene from 1910-1914, and appointments from the San Antonio City Council on committees to control public dust, unsanitary houses, and public health. In 1918, he was appointed by the Texas Committee of the Council of National Defense to the Board of Governors of the Volunteer Medical Service Corps. The list of such appointments is long. Each provided him with an opportunity to air his views in yet another arena.

As one reviews the summary of this service, which continued until he was well into his eighth decade, there appears to be a unifying, constant theme: the absolute obligation of the physician to educate, to warn, to counsel, and to address issues forthrightly as they were individually seen by him. Public health was not a career upon which Frank Paschal embarked; it was a duty waiting to be done and he did it.

The fourth aspect of his professional career was his involvement with organizing medical practitioners and in organized medicine itself. In the last years of the nineteenth and the early ones of the twentieth century, organizations in medicine were not what is perceived in 1998. There were few. They were a primary and necessary means of transmitting information and education to their members. Above all, they were viable organizations allowing widely separated practitioners to exchange problems and risks, and to seek support. Inevitably they came to be custodians of ethical conduct. In time, with growth and much wider communication, many have become what we currently perceive, vestigial or political. As they were originally conceived, they were valuable and vital on a day-to-day basis.

Frank Paschal was deeply involved in organization in medicine and by derivation in the organizations of medicine, which he conceived as necessary and beneficial. Shortly after his return to San Antonio in 1892, he was elected president of the West Texas Medical Society in 1893. By exposing the activity of the New York Medical College in San Antonio, this organization forced state action to close that institution long prior to the promulgation of the Flexner Report. The San Antonio institution was known to graduate its students as full-fledged doctors after six weeks training.

In 1903 Paschal was elected president of a newly reorganized Texas Medical Association. He had been a member of the reorganizing committee, selected the year before, and the presidency was a recognition of this distinguished service. The Texas Medical Association was reorganized under standards recommended by the American Medical Association. Paschal was the first president of the newly reorganized society just as his mentor, Dr. George Cupples, had been the first president of the original organization in 1853, fifty years earlier. His involvement in various committees and appointments with the Texas Medical Association was to be a major feature of his public service in Texas until his death.

In 1914, at a meeting of the Texas State Medical Association in Houston in May, the question of organizing a state surgical society was raised. The parties to that discussion are not known. It is recognized that Dr. James E. Thompson of Galveston was probably the principal mover in this activity. Frank Paschal was one of fifteen surgeons who met at the Tremont Hotel in Galveston in October 1914 to organize what was to become the Texas Surgical Society. Of these individuals, nine would become charter members, including Paschal. This organization is one of the premier state surgical societies in the United States, now in its eighty-fifth year of existence. Its first formal meeting took place in San Antonio on March 6, 1915. Paschal served as president in 1918. The Texas Surgical Society is the principal surgical organization in the state in terms of support from surgeons, education, the setting of standards and cohesiveness. It most closely represents what Paschal would have conceived as the aim and effect of a medical organization.

Perhaps closest to his heart as an organization was the Bexar County Medical Society. His involvement with the society was deep and sincere. After the West Texas Medical Association dissolved (he had been on the Board of Censors for years), the Bexar County Medical Society elected him as Chair of its corresponding board from 1907 through 1911. He sat as Chairman of the Committee on Advertising, Fee Division, Telephone Consultation, Shopping and Practice in 1912. In this capacity he set out a rigid set of ethics rules for those who wished to be members of the society. In 1914 the Bexar County Medical Society adopted the AMA code of ethics, and Dr. Paschal was instrumental during this year for the ejection of one member and for the establishment of rules of conduct for doctors who were practitioners in military service. This service was his last as Chairman of the Board of Censors.

A final and major activity with the society was his leadership in establishing a permanent home for the organization to which he contributed $10,000. The strength of this organization as a county society in Texas is unquestioned and can be laid largely at the feet of its very diligent developers. In 1922 he was elected the first and, at that time, the only life member of the society.

Frank Paschal died on December 20, 1925, in his seventy-sixth year. His life spanned the last half of the most active century known in terms of rapid technological advance and

Dr. Frank Paschal in older age as he appeared on the front page of *Pioneer* in January 1926, in a commemorative issue containing a major eulogy and a variety of other statements upon his death.

encompassed the first quarter of the twentieth century when technology would be consolidated. All of his years were spent in Mexico and in South Texas far from the sites of major advances, yet he was most effective in establishing the benefits of technology in these areas. His life spanned what has been called "The Gilded Age" in American history—a time of unparalleled opulence when huge fortunes were made by those imaginative enough to see opportunity and to use it. In this regard he was clearly a man of his own time, intelligent, resourceful and adept. A deep trait of humanity and respect for life set him very much apart from the highly successful business barons of the era. He was no less intelligent than they, but much more caring.

It is worth some consideration to note that the first half of his life prepared him uniquely for the second. Medical learning in the 1870s, together with one year of internship, provided an individual with little else but credentials and some familiarity with how hospitals were run. A baptism by fire on the way to

Mexico in 1873 acutely showed him the role of the single medical professional in a desperate situation. In Chihuahua, a lovely town but not a medical metropolis, he filled a role that today would be taken by five or six separate practitioners. In those two decades, out of the country in an area less socially conscious than the United States, he had an opportunity to observe, to try to correct, and to conclude. The accomplishments of the thirty-three years in San Antonio grew as naturally from his work in Mexico as twigs from branches and branches from trees.

San Antonio in 1892 had a few more than thirty-eight thousand inhabitants. It would grow to 230,000 in the next four decades, nearly a six-fold increase. In 1890 the city edged out Galveston to become the largest city in the largest state. Frank Paschal lived and practiced in this vibrant, growing community for the last thirty years of his life. He was in a city that was not immune to all of the problems of rapid development. New buildings crowded out old; landmarks were demolished; streets were widened indiscriminately, and colorful old customs set aside or reduced. His voice was a calm, constant call for science in public health, for reason in decision making, and for sane public responsibility. His contributions cannot be considered without some appreciation of the area and time in which they were made. Like so many others of that time, he was able by his native talents to note what needed to be done and to do it selflessly and well.

It has been said of Frank Paschal and his mentor, Dr. George Cupples, that they were similar to Elijah and Elisha of biblical note. It is an apt comparison if one considers only the transfer of responsibility and an authoritative voice. Dr. Cupples was instrumental in helping to bring medicine to San Antonio and South Texas as a true pioneer physician and surgeon. Frank Paschal did much more than accept responsibility for medical care; he became a major public force for good and, as such, was able to influence the development of one of the significant urban areas of the United States in ways that he would never himself have conceived.

Commerce Street in San Antonio in the early 1900s.

Commerce Street in San Antonio in the 1910s. The growth of San Antonio in the early twentieth century occasioned steps such as arbitrary street widening at any cost. Used by permission of L.F. Fisher, *San Antonio Outpost of Empires*, The Maverick Press, San Antonio.

A stand in an open air market in San Antonio purveying Mexican food and chili.

A stand in an open air market in San Antonio purveying fruit. The obligatory growth of the city in the first part of the twentieth century abolished many such colorful features in the city. Used by permission of L.F. Fisher, *San Antonio Outpost of Empires*, The Maverick Press, San Antonio.

BIBLIOGRAPHY

BOOKS, ATTRIBUTED ARTICLES, AND THESES

Frank Paschal. "Treatment of abscess of the liver by drainage." *Richmond & Louisville Medical Journal* xxviii (Louisville 1879), 113-16. *Index Medicus* (1879) Ser. 1, 1:389.

G.H. Paschal, Jr. "The public service aspect of the medical career of Dr. Frank Paschal in San Antonio, 1893-1925." Thesis, Trinity University, San Antonio, Texas, 1956.

Hugh Young. *A Surgeon's Autobiography* (New York: Harcourt-Brace and Company, New York, 1940), 82ff.

"The relation of the medical profession to public health." Thesis. *Texas Medical Journal* xviii (December 1902), 237-39.

"On the governor's veto of the tuberculosis bill." Thesis. *Texas State Journal of Medicine* v (May 1909), 26-28.

UNATTRIBUTED ARTICLES

"Cases of pelvic cellulitis." *Gaillard's Medical Journal* xxviii (New York 1879), 513-18. *Index Medicus* (1880) Ser. 1, 2:37.

"Abdominal pregnancy of ten years' duration; recovery." *American Medical Weekly* xiv (New York 1882), 29. *Index Medicus* (1882) Ser. 1, 4:82.

"Intervention in pregnancy complicated with albuminuria." *Texas Medical Journal* xi (Austin 1895-6), 354-56. *Index Medicus* (1895/1896) Ser. 1, 18:165.

"Civilization and tuberculosis." *Texas Medical Journal* xii (Austin 1896-7), 314-16. *Index Medicus* (1896/1897) Ser. 1, 19:525.

"Internal hemorrhage." *Texas Medical Journal* (Austin 1898-9), 248-54. *Index Medicus* (1898/1899) Ser. 1, 21:552.

"The differential diagnosis between yellow fever, dengue fever, malarial fever, and acute yellow atrophy of the liver." *Texas Medical Journal* xix (Austin 1903-4), 255-56. *Index Medicus* (1904) Ser. 2, 2:104.

"The tuberculosis problem in the state of Texas." *Texas State Journal of Medicine* ii (Fort Worth 1906-8), 205-207. *Index Medicus* (1907) Ser. 2, 5:19.

"Resection of the knee-joint, with report of case." *Texas State Journal of Medicine* ii (Fort Worth 1906-7), 303. *Index Medicus* (1907) Ser. 2, 5:537.

"Intestinal obstructions." *Texas State Journal of Medicine* iv (Fort Worth 1908-9), 98-102. *Index Medicus* (1908) Ser. 2, 6:852.

"Education and its relation to the public health." *Texas State Journal of Medicine* vii (Fort Worth 1911-12), 271-73. *Index Medicus* (1912) Ser. 2, 10:333.

"Local diseases amenable to surgical treatment as a cause of acquired psycho-neuroses." *Texas State Journal of Medicine* ix (Fort Worth 1912-13), 15. *Index Medicus* (1913) Ser. 2, 11:694.

"The necessity for centralization of power for protecting public health." *Texas Medical Journal* xxx (July 1914), 32-33.

"Congenital malformations of the rectum and anus." *Texas State Journal of Medicine* xiv (Fort Worth 1918-19), 220-22. *Index Medicus* (1919) Ser. 2, 17:61.

"Treatment of impassable strictures of urethra by combined suprapubic cysto-tomy and external urethrotomy." *Texas State Journal of Medicine* (February 1922) 17:489-91. *Quarterly Cumulative Index to Current Medical Literature* (1922) 7:552.

"Caesarean sections performed too frequently." *Medical Records and Annals* xvii (San Antonio 1923), 103-107. *Index Medicus* (1923) Ser. 3, 3:819.

"Encysted foreign bodies." *Annals of Surgery* (January 1924) 79:114-17. *Quarterly Cumulative Index to Current Medical Literature* (1924) 9:618.

BIOGRAPHICAL SKETCH OF AUTHOR

ARTHUR S. MCFEE was born in Portland, Maine on 1 May 1932. He was educated in the public schools in Portland, and attended Harvard College and Harvard Medical School. He received graduate surgical education at the University of Minnesota, achieving a Master of Science degree in Biochemistry and a Ph.D. in Surgery. After a two-year stint of duty with the United States Navy in Vietnam and in Charleston, South Carolina, he came to the University of Texas Health Science Center at San Antonio in 1967 as one of the founding members of that institution in the Department of Surgery. He was named a full professor in 1974 and became the Chief of the Division of General Surgery in 1996. His curriculum vitae includes 123 entries, 82 articles accepted in peer journals and a unique experience as consultant to the American Academy of Orthopedic Surgeons for the first five editions of Emergency Care and Transportation of the Sick and Injured. His entire professional life has been spent in the education of surgeons. Probably the two most rewarding experiences of his career have been the privilege of developing two medical institutions from their founding: The United States Navy Hospital Ship Repose recommissioned in 1965, and the University of Health Science Center at San Antonio which opened to accept students and patients in 1969.

Dr. McFee is a member of twenty surgical organizations and has served as the recorder of the Western Surgical Association. He has been vice president, council member and president of the Texas Surgical Society (1996). He is an active member of the American College of Surgeons and a senior member of the American Surgical and Southern Surgical Associations.

1940 drawing by Henry Anthony DeYoung of Amos Pollard, M.D.
Published in "Chief Surgeon of the Alamo" by R.J. Andrassy, Surg
Gynecol Obstet (1977) 145:913-15.

Amos Pollard, M.D.
1803-1836
by
Richard J. Andrassy, M.D., Flora L. (von) Roeder and Anthony Shinn

★ QUITE OFTEN ONE HEARS the statement that Texas is not only a state but also a state of mind. Who first said it or where it was said is unknown to this writer; however, the attitude toward Texas as a state of mind certainly precedes statehood. Most early Texans and Texas heroes seem to have adopted this philosophy shortly after immigrating to this vast frontier, but others seem to have developed it even before they arrived here!

A Yankee physician named Amos Pollard was very possibly one of the latter. Born in Massachusetts, he grew up in New Hampshire, was educated in Vermont, practiced medicine in New York for about six years and then, leaving his wife and daughter behind, came to Texas. Being a physician, Pollard was unlikely an adventurer for the sake of adventure, but he certainly seemed to sense the excitement necessary to draw one to an area as vast as Texas and to make him willing to become a citizen of a new country in order to practice frontier medicine until his own early death in Texas' struggle for independence.

When Stephen F. Austin successfully settled his first three hundred Americans between the lower Brazos and Colorado Rivers (1822-23), a new cultural mentality was germinated that would entice both New World and Old World personalities to share the struggles of those willing to put down roots in this vast, empty province.

The Mexican revolution of 1810 in which she declared her

independence from Spain reversed the large amount of Spanish progress made in Texas the preceding century. The troops were now commanded by General Joaquin de Arredondo, who either executed or exiled one thousand people, approximately one-third of the Texas-Spanish population. Much of the improved farmland around Béxar (San Antonio) and in East Texas reverted to wasteland. Travelers crossing Spanish Texas faced the risk of starvation, and for some years food was scarce even at Béxar. An underpopulated Texas was a worry for the few colonists who continued to reside there. There were thirty thousand untamed Indians but fewer than four thousand Europeans, odds that threatened to wipe out this small population.

Connecticut-born Moses Austin had emigrated to Missouri when it was a Spanish province. He successfully settled families from the United States there and was considered an excellent Spanish subject. When Upper Louisiana entered the Union in 1804, he returned to American citizenship and became a principal stockholder of the Bank of St. Louis. However, after he was wiped out in an ensuing economic crash, he thought he could repeat his earlier success by following the Spanish frontier and found himself at San Antonio de Béxar in the fall of 1820.

Although General Arredondo had worked long and hard to stamp out Anglo-Americans in Texas, the fact remained that the Indian danger would never end until the country between Béxar and the Sabine was colonized. Austin was granted his wish to settle Americans in Texas by being given the right to settle three hundred families, but he never lived to see it. His son, Stephen F. Austin, carried on with the project. During the summer of 1821, he explored the country and identified the area to which he would bring these first settlers. The Brazos bottomland was perfect for a plantation economy as well as being outside of dangerous Indian country.Upon returning to the United States to advertise for settlers, young Austin already found applicants awaiting approval. They appeared perfectly willing to take an oath to become Spanish citizens, which later was changed slightly to meet the circumstances of Mexican independence. That was about as far as they were required to go, because they were closer to the United States geographically, economically, and culturally than they were to Mexico. That is how commerce was generated and how they conducted their daily lives, based on a typically Protestant work ethic and an independent spirit. In other words, they wanted to be left alone.

In a ten-year period, after Austin's success in settling this area, the tone was probably already set for developing the unique Texas personality. For it was in this small but determined population that more progress was made----chopping down trees, clearing land, breaking soil, raising crops, having children, and building towns—than had been made in three hundred years of Spanish settlement. Austin's colony had expanded to the point whereby, in ten years, fifteen hundred American families had come to Texas. A few families from Northern Europe had just begun to trickle into the area also. Headquarters was San Felipe de Austin.

The Mexican Constitution of 1824 theoretically had made the former Spanish provinces into sovereign states. Texas and Coahuila were a combined state with its capital at Saltillo. An act in 1824 provided that when the Texas population grew sufficiently, this northern colony would be granted a definite measure of independence. More colonization was opened and new impresarios came on the scene. These included Missouri-born Green DeWitt, who brought four hundred families to be located on the Guadalupe, San Marcos and Lavaca rivers. Headquarters was Gonzales. Another settlement led by Mexican-born Martín de León conflicted with DeWitt's, creating some hard feelings that eventually were soothed by Austin's mediation. This new settlement was also on the Guadalupe with its headquarters at Victoria near Goliad.

There were others, not nearly as successful as the foregoing but which nevertheless brought settlers. There also were freelancers, frontiersmen or loners who came over the border alone and staked out independent claims. By 1835, nearly twenty thousand Anglo-Americans and their slaves and Northern Europeans outnumbered Spanish-speaking inhabitants by five to one, all practicing a United States lifestyle and value system rather than that of Mexican Texas. The stage was set for a cultural clash.

As early as 1830 the Mexican government began to tighten up on the essentially totally independent existence of the Texans. Ethnic differences was the underlying problem, but clear-cut authority under Mexican terms was the more evident clash. Left to themselves, Anglo Texans could remain loyal citizens, but too much authority brought back the same rebellious attitude that too much British authority had created in North America two generations earlier. Mexico had decided to stop new immigration, and this meant stopping the economic growth that new settlers would bring. Customs and duties began to be levied, and down south the military was becoming stronger and stronger as the Republic of Mexico wavered.

Military presence was everywhere in Mexico, and Texans hotly resented it although they were not targeted as being in a state of insurrection. Austin and DeWitt managed to continue to bring in legal immigrants, and individual immigration also continued. Conflict over the subject within the Mexican government itself created outrageous conditions, and young American hotheads were drawn to the excitement. By 1832 it appeared that open rebellion might occur, but conditions in Mexico so confused the issues that rebellion did not break out for another three years.

During this time Austin had been imprisoned in Mexico for bringing a plan to the nation's capital that would grant Texas self-government within the Republic of Mexico, repeal of taxes, supply new land titles, etc. He was confined there in January 1834 and was not released until January 1835. In April, General Antonio López de Santa Anna Pérez de Lebrón took over the government. In October 1835, the Constitution of 1824 was officially voided, and the president and national congress held absolute powers.[1]

When he returned to Texas, Austin was ready to issue a call for help. He was ready for Texas to defend itself. Santa Anna had sent his brother-in-law, General Martín de Perfecto de Cós, to keep order in Coahuila. Cós in turn sent Captain Francisco Castañeda to capture a small cannon in Gonzales which had been sent for defense against Indians some years before. Here is where Amos Pollard more or less enters the picture, although he obviously had been in Texas for at least a year or more.

Amos Pollard was a descendant of Thomas and Mary Farmer Pollard, who in about 1692 had immigrated to Billerica, Massachusetts, from Coventry, Warwickshire, England. The relocation of each succeeding generation of Pollards of Amos' direct lineage, always a bit westward, may be a clue to his attraction to a new location. The immigrant Pollards' son William married Martha

Wheeler of Concord, and they moved from Billerica to Lancaster, where he was one of the founders of Bolton, a split off of Lancaster.[2]

Amos Pollard's grandfather, also named William, was a son of the former and was a veteran of the American Revolution. He was born in the Bolton section of Lancaster and married Hannah Whitcomb, also of Bolton, on October 17, 1762.[3] He served as a Sergeant in Captain Artemus How's Company of Militia which marched on the alarm of April 19, 1775, and was discharged May 3 after fifteen days of service. He also saw service as a second lieutenant in Captain Dan Nurr's (Nourse's) 8th Co., 2nd Worcester Co. Regiment of the Massachusetts Militia. He had been commissioned on March 20, 1776.[4]

The William Pollard family moved to Ashburnham from Bolton around 1770. The town is located thirty-three miles north of Worcester and fifty-five miles northwest of Boston, near the New Hampshire border. William became a "respected citizen" of the town, having been elected as a town assessor in 1780, 1783, and 1792. In 1775 the town inaugurated the Cushing Academy, giving its youth a permanent high school without tuition from resident pupils. A committee of town citizens supervised the school, and William Pollard was chosen to be on that committee. His son Jonas, Amos Pollard's father, was the youngest of William Pollard's eight known children. Jonas was born in Ashburnham on March 5, 1779.[5]

Jonas Pollard married Martha Martin of Westminister, and their son Amos was born in Ashburnham on October 29, 1803, the oldest of seven children. William Pollard died on May 10, 1808, in Ashburnham, and in about 1810, approximately two years later, Jonas and Martha and two sons moved to Surry, New Hampshire. The other five children were born in Surry.[6] In 1811 Jonas Pollard bought a homestead there and constructed much of a road known for a long time as "Pollard's Road." He renovated his house and called it the "Half Way House," a tavern located between Walpole and Keene. Martha joined an old Congregational Church served by the Reverend Perley Howe, Pastor.

Near the road was a spring of cold water where Jonas Pollard supposedly "concealed his jug of toddy, which was for the ostensible purpose of keeping good humor among his workmen, but he visited it frequently in his anxiety over the progress of the work and his interest in good order." This use of spirits seems to be corroborated by a letter written by him in 1850 to a relative in Wisconsin (probably his second daughter who lived with her husband, Leander Crain, at Menasha) in which he said he'd left off drinking whiskey because it was so bad.[7]

Amos Pollard's mother died in Surry on November 15, 1826, at age forty-eight. His father remarried in Walpole, New Hampshire, a widow named Phebe Cross at age fifty-four. Sometime after this marriage, they migrated to Northeastern New York State. Jonas' name shows up on the 1850 New York Federal Census in Lewis, Essex County, and his death is recorded in the Lewis, New York, Cemetery record as December 25, 1864, at age eighty-six. An obituary in the Essex County *Republican* stated that the second Mrs. Pollard died March 6, 1873. The three Pollard sons were favored by their father; they received an education, all apparently first going to school in Surry. The girls were sent to work early.[8]

In October 1824 Amos was a senior studying medicine at the Middlebury College and Vermont Academy of Medicine. Quarterly expenses included $20 tuition, $1.50 room rent, $1.50 repairs and other incidental expenses. Students boarded with private families at a rate of $1 to $1.50 per week. Lectures for the Medical College were held at Castleton, south of Middlebury, and included fees for all the courses at $40, a $3 matriculation fee, and a $2 graduation fee. The pre-requisites for an examination for the degree of Doctor of Medicine included three years study in the office of a regularly educated physician and attendance upon two courses of lectures. The time occupied in attending lectures was considered a part of the three years. The candidate had to be twenty-one years old and of good moral character.[9]

In the October 1825 catalog Pollard is again listed as a senior, his residence having changed to Greenbush, Rensselaer County, New York, across the Hudson River from Albany. Rules for graduation had changed somewhat. They were to:

A. Pass a satisfactory examination before the Faculty and Delegates from the Vermont Medical Society,

B. Deliver and defend a written dissertation on some medical subject, to the approbation of the Faculty and Delegates,

C. Obtain certificates from the Treasurer that the candidate has paid into the Treasury the graduation fee, and either paid, or secured to be paid the prescribed lecture fees.[10]

The address given in Greenbush, New York, is where he obviously lived for a time and possibly married before moving to New York City. Inasmuch as he was required to study under a practicing physician, he probably was doing this during his time in Greenbush. "One of the earliest physicians in Greenbush was Dr. Jacob S. Miller, who located there about 1820 and for many years was the leading physician in a large territory. He subsequently moved to New York."[11]

Dr. Pollard also moved to New York. His name appears in the city's directories between 1828 and 1834 as follows:

1828-29	246 Spring Street
1829-31	137 Delancey
1831-33	117 Madison
1833-34	113 Madison[12]

The 1830 Federal Census also lists him as living in New York City as a married man. At that time he had no children. He had married Fanny Oeella, and sometime before he left for Texas they had one daughter named Oeella who died about 1907.[13]

As was the case of many other Americans attracted to the country called Texas, it seems very probable that Pollard was attracted by accounts of opportunities there which frequently appeared in the metropolitan press.[14] He was about thirty years old at this time. He may have been discouraged where he was because of abolitionist riots and cholera epidemics' sweeping the city and decided to try his luck in a totally new environment. Some sources say he left his family in New York and traveled to New Orleans; other sources say he may have left his wife and child there. However, chances are that the former is accurate.

Most early sources say he settled in Gonzales as a land speculator; however, a rather thorough recent study of his movements disputes that. Although the New York Directory lists him in 1834, an entry in Stephen F. Austin's *Register of Families*, indicates that Pollard arrived in Texas on December 23, 1833, giving his occupation as a physician and states that his family had remained in New York. Austin's register also shows that Pollard's application for one-fourth of a league of land (approximately 1,100 acres) was made for him by Asahel C. Holmes, whose own entry in the register is directly above that of Pollard on April 6, 1835, which specifically states that Holmes wanted land between the Brazos and Bernard surveys above Bell. This refers to land north of land granted to Josiah Hughes Bell, who was the founder of the towns of Marion (now called East Columbia) and Columbia (West Columbia) on the west side of the Brazos River.

Mary Austin Holley, a first cousin of Stephen F. Austin on one of her trips to Texas, noted in her diary that, while visiting her brother Henry and his family on her second day in Texas on Sunday, May 24, 1835, she had dined that day at Dr. Phelps and that a Dr. Pollard was there. Dr. Phelps was the owner of Orozimbo Plantation, on the west side of the Brazos River about twelve miles northeast of Columbia and across the river from Henry Austin's Bolivar Plantation.

A quote made in Benjamin Lundy's *Life, Travels and Opinions,* written in his journal at Béxar on August 30, 1834 states, "I met today Dr. Amos Pollard, lately of New York but now of Columbia, Texas. He is a decided friend of our cause." Perhaps the strongest argument that Pollard's actual residence in Texas was Columbia is from the Brazoria County probate records. There is a legal document dated "19th day of September 1836" in the probate file of Dr. Pollard which shows that "Leman Kelcey and Josiah T. Harrell both of the County & Jurisdiction of Brazoria in the said District at held and Bound unto Benjamin C. Franklin Judge of the district of Brazos" in the amount of $2,000. The document also states, "The Condition of the above obligation is such that whereas the above bound Leman Kelcey has been appointed by the said Benjamin C. Franklin Judge as aforesaid to administer the estate of Amos Pollard deceased late of the said District——as curator for the benefit of the absent heirs."[15]

The above seem to be pretty good indications that Pollard was not a resident of Gonzales but rather was there as a member of the detachment of volunteers which originally had set out for the Lavaca River to intercept the force commanded by General Cós but diverted to Gonzales a day after the battle. He co-signed along with seven others the following message to P.W. Grayson at Columbia.

> You will receive important dispatches by the Bearer
> that Col. Ugartachea and probably Gen. Cós—are
> now on their march here, with all their forces to take
> the Gun if it is not delivered. You will see by Ugar-
> tachea's letter to you, he proposes a sort of compro-
> mise. That will give us an opportunity to entertain him
> a little while, upon the suggestion that you are sent
> for, until we can get in more men. We who subscribe
> this, request you earnestly to come on immediately,
> bringing all the aid you possibly can—we want pow-
> der and lead. Do all you can to send on instantly as
> much as possible.

Pollard was among the army of approximately three hundred Texans who marched for San Antonio de Béxar on October
13 to attack the Mexican garrison there. And on October 23,
Austin, commander-in-chief of the Texas Army, issued orders
to Col. John H. Moore, "You will announce the appointment
of Doctr. Pollard as Surgeon of the Regiment and Doctr.
Richardson as Surgeon of the Staff."[16]

This army then, although it did not look much like one,
began its march to San Antonio. Along the way, it picked up
more men. General Cós, whose regular army would have been
better off fighting the Texans in the open fields, pulled his men
into the city. He wanted reinforcements before he would fight.
His reluctance created shortages as his army rapidly ate up its
provisions and its morale sank. The Texans were also in a state
of confusion. They had gone to Gonzales when the crops were
in and the farmers had nothing else to do; therefore, they were
just as content to hunt Mexicans as squirrels. However, they were
only there for two months; after one month they were restless
and by early December were thinking about spring planting.

On November 25 Austin left to seek American aid, and
Colonel Edward Burleson replaced him. The next day General
Cós lost fifty of his men in what was called the "grass fight"
when he sent these unfortunates out to forage for desperately
needed hay. This was not enough to encourage the Texan army
which lacked artillery. They were hesitant to assault the Alamo

presidio without artillery support. Additionally, the late fall
weather turned bad, there was insufficient clothing, inasmuch as
many of the men who had come in late summer had no coats
with them. Food was not only bad but also irregular. There was
no organized commissary or service support of any kind.

By December, most of the Texas militia had deserted the
siege; however during this time, a new body of reinforcements
was swelling the Texas ranks. When news of war reached New
Orleans and traveled up the Mississippi, many American frontiersmen were interested. Frontiersmen from Appalachia were
a tough breed; they loved the idea of adventure and that's where
many of Texas near future heroes, including Sam Houston and
Davy Crockett, came from.

Although at first this new group pouring into Texas swelled
the ranks, the numbers of Texans leaving caused the total to
shrink back again. Despite the fact that by December 3 the
Americans from outside outnumbered the Texans, the whole
army actually did number between three and five hundred.
However Burleson, in consultation with his officers, agreed to
abandon the siege and on December 4 orders had been issued to
retreat to Gonzales. But old Ben Milam, who believed that the
disheartened Mexican force could be easily seized, called for
volunteers to storm the Alamo. It began the next morning. The
Mexican army which had been divided into two areas was no
match for the American frontiersmen, who had been taught to
take cover and shoot to kill. On December 10, 1835, General
Cós surrendered 1,105 officers and men and the Alamo.[17]

Following the successful taking of the fortress, Drs. Samuel
Stivers and Amos Pollard submitted the following report to the
Governor and Council.

Names	Killed	Wounded
Col. B.R. Milam	killed	
Francis Harvey	do	
E.F. Pulham		Severely wounded
James McGehee*		do do
G.B.Logan		do do
Thos W. Wardright		Leg amputated
John Cook		mortal

George Alexander	do
Outlaw	Slightly wounded
Saml G.	Severely wounded
Lieut Ge	do do
Dr. Mitchison*	do do
Capt. John W. Peacock	do do
Alexander Abrams	do do
Wm Thomas	do do
James Noland*	do do
James Mcass	do do
Erastus Smith	Slightly wounded
John Cornel	do do
John Hall	Severely wounded
John Beldon	do do
Dr. Grant**	Slightly wounded

    * later died in the Alamo
    ** Commander of the Matamoros Expedition
We the undersigned having had special charge of the hospital at Bejar from the commencement of the siege at the said Bejar up to the present date, do hereby certify the foregoing to be a true statement of the number killed and wounded at the above siege.

On December 27, Dr. Pollard submitted a revised list which included John West, severely wounded, James Bell slightly wounded, John Cook and George Alexander as having died of wounds, as well as a John Peacock. Dr. Stivers was another surgeon working with Dr. Pollard at the time up to the first report. He did not appear again in the affairs of Texas.[18]

What this meant to the Texas residents was that it was over. It was time to go home to the farm. General Burleson had left, turning his command over to Col. Frank Johnson. There was a kind of overconfidence among the Texans. Troops now controlled not only the Alamo but also the mission at Goliad further south. An attempt to form a government was slow going, inasmuch as these self-reliant people who had successfully colonized Texas had not needed government to show them the way. There were no leaders who had been trained to take on such a role, and most of the average people were not too interested in having any. Commands of the remainder of what had been the army changed frequently, at one time having as many as four commanders at the same time.

Mexican President and General Santa Anna, enraged at the defeat of his brother-in-law at Béxar, rode north on about January 20. His army in northern Mexico totaled about 6,019 men. His intent was that every colonist who had taken part in the rebellion was to be executed or exiled and those who had not would be sent back to the interior; never again would a North American be permitted to enter Texas.[19]

Col. James C. Neill was in command of the Alamo forces at that time. He saw that something needed to be done and decided to attempt to procure a donation of $5,000 to the cause of Texas by Harry Hill of Nashville, Tennessee. He departed about February 12, leaving Col. James Bowie in nominal command. Bowie became ill shortly thereafter.[20]

The Mexican army arrived at the Rio Grande in mid-February. Santa Anna had damaged his army by pressing forward so hard and was somewhat underarmed. When he arrived in San Antonio, he was surprised to find that the Alamo fortress was defended, although there was only a force of 150 men. They had guns but not sufficient powder, although they were well supplied otherwise, having taken away the townspeople's supplies and cattle.[21]

There is no known record of where Dr. Pollard went after the successful taking of the Alamo or if he left. However, it is known that on January 16, 1836, he was in San Antonio because he was on a committee with James Bowie and five others to draft resolutions upholding the governor in a controversy which the governor was having with a group of malcontents bent on deposing him. Three letters written by Dr. Pollard to Governor Henry Smith a few weeks before the battle of the Alamo are as follows.

Bejar, Jan. 16th, 1836

Excellent Sir: I have but a moment to write you as I am so busy in regulating the Hospital. Things have been in the worst possible state here as you are aware. I hope and have reason to believe they will soon become much better. I ought to have written by the express but knew not when it started. I have only to say that we are much in want of money and that some could be collected on goods that are being brought into this place and the Commandant will do it, yet he is ignorant of the rate of duties established by the government. Were he in possession of that knowledge he would avail himself of it now as there are goods here and he talks of charging but four per cent. I am interested in this you will see for the Hospital is in great want of a little money. We shall endeavor to elect as many of our countrymen as possible from this jurisdiction—what the prospect is I have not yet been able to learn. I think we have now an excellent opportunity to completely conquer our most formidable foe our internal enemy—the Mexican tory party of the country. I hope every friend of his country will be diligent at his post and from the righteousness of our cause we cannot but succeed. I am your Excellency's Humble servant, Amos Pollard.

Bejar, Jan. 27th, 1836

Most excellent Sir: I perceive that the tory party have bought up your council and instead of being an assistant to you as intended they have usurped the government to themselves; but the people will not stand this—you will see by our resolutions here that we are determined to support you at all hazards. I did hope that the provisional government would continue till we could establish another and a more firm one. This we shall endeavor to do in March and God grant that we may create an independent government. Should we be previously invaded I hope that the council will come back from its corrupt course and meet the exigencies of the country. Reports say that troops are now on their way. Reply my Dear Sir on every support that my feeble efforts can give you in endeavoring to rescue the liberties and establish the Independence of our adopted country I am your obt. Servt, Amos Pollard.

Hospital Bejar Feb. 13th, 1836

Excellent Sir: I am glad to learn that you are in good
health and spirits. Be assured Sir that the country will
sustain you. We are unanimous in your favor here and
determined to have nothing to do with the corrupt
council. It is my duty to inform you that my department is nearly destitute of medicine and in the event
of a siege I can be very little use to the sick under such
circumstances. I have plenty of instruments with the
exception of a trephining-case, some catheters and an
injection syringe which would complete this station.
I write you this because I suppose the Surgeon general
not to be in the country and we are threatened with a
large invading army. Four Mexicans are to represent
this Jurisdiction in the convention although we might
with great ease have sent the same number of Americans, had it not been that a few of our people through
Mexican policy perfectly hoodwinked headquarters,
making them believe that it was unjust to attempt to
send any other than Mexicans, thereby exerting all that
influence to the same end. Perhaps I have said enough.
However, I intend that those representatives shall
distinctly understand, previous to their leaving, that if
they vote against independence, they will have to be
very careful on returning here. I wish Gen. Houston
was now on the frontier to help us to crush at once
both our external and internal enemies. Let us show
them how republicans can and will fight. I am your
obt. Servt. Amos Pollard, M.D. Surgeon. P.S. Some
method should be devised to neutralize Fannin's influence. A.P. Addressed: To His Excellency Henry
Smith, Governor of Texas. Endorsed: Amos Pollard
to Govr. Smith, Feby. 13th, 1836.[22]

Ten days later the siege began. Shelling began from both
quarters, but inside the fortress, life was still somewhat normal
if anxious. On the second day of the siege, Jim Bowie, whose
shared command had been taken over totally by William B.
Travis because of his extensive illness, was able to sit up on his

cot, "thanks to the work of Dr. Pollard." The fire around which a number of the men, including Dr. Pollard, and women stood watching a beeve being barbequed reflected the variety of people who stood together at this critical juncture in history. Young Lieutenant Colonel William Barrett Travis had been ordered by Governor Smith to cease recruiting duties in the regular army and to assist Colonel Neill. The young firebrand lawyer from Alabama had raised his voice in Southeast Texas some months earlier, and this brought him to the attention of the elder Texans. There were some who even said Travis started the war at Anahuac in 1832 for which he was imprisoned for fifty days. Later he practiced law at San Felipe and became extremely popular.[23]

Travis shared command with Bowie, but on February 23 Bowie, seriously ill with pneumonia, surrendered the command to Travis. The next day, Travis wrote his famous message to the people of Texas.

> Commandancy of the Alamo
> Bexar, Feby 24th, 1836
> To the People of Texas and All Americans in the World
> Fellow Citizens and Compatriots:
> I am besieged with a thousand or more of the Mexicans under Santa Anna. I have sustained a continual Bombardment and cannonade for 24 hours and have not lost a man. The enemy has demanded surrender at discretion, otherwise, the garrison is to be put to the sword, if the fort is taken. I have answered the demand with a cannon shot, and our flag still waves proudly from the wall. I shall never surrender or retreat. Then, I call on you in the name of Liberty, of patriotism, and everything dear to the American character, to come to our aid with all dispatch. The enemy is receiving reinforcements daily and will no doubt increase to three or four thousand in four or five days. If this call is neglected I am determined to sustain myself as long as possible and die like a soldier who never forgets what is due his honor and that of his country.
> VICTORY OR DEATH.
> William Barret Travis
> Lt. Col. Comd't[24]

On March 2, a Constitutional Convention, meeting at Washington-on-the Brazos, 140 miles east of the Alamo, unanimously adopted a Declaration of Independence. They had been at it since February 28. Delegates selected to represent Béxar included Lorenzo de Zavala, Don Francisco Ruiz, Don Antonio Navarro, Erasmo Seguin who was ill, Gaspar Flores who died on his way to Washington, Jesse Badgett, Sam Maverick, Jim Bonham and Amos Pollard, the latter two of whom elected to stay with Travis. This day was also Gen. Sam Houston's (Commander-in-Chief of the Texas Army) birthday, and it was one of the most difficult days of his life. Travis' first urgent message arrived two days earlier, and Houston had to choose between the future survival of all Texans through political structure or the immediate plight of the small army defending the Alamo. He obviously decided on the former, and the embattled soldiers never knew they were fighting for the Republic of Texas.[25] On March 3, 1836, Travis addressed his last letter to the Council at Washington.

> I shall have to fight the enemy on his own terms. I will
> . . . do the best I can . . . the victory will cost the enemy
> so dear, that it will be worse for him than defeat. I hope
> your honorable body will hasten reinforcements . . .
> Our supply of ammunition is limited . . . God and
> Texas. Victory or Death.[26]

Three days later on Sunday, March 6, at nine o'clock, it was over. Ironically, on that same day, James C. Neill, Col. Comdt. Of the Post of Béxar, wrote to Horace Eggleston.

> GONZALES: Received of Horace Eggleston a Set of
> medicine of amount of Ninety Dollars which said
> medicines I have this day purchased from him for the
> use of the post of Bexar.[27]

It was a bit late!

Who or what influenced the educated New Englander, Amos Pollard, to leave the most established area of the United States and come to a large, empty foreign state where a few thousand farmers had set down roots and which was on the brink of being joined by some of the notarious adventurers of the American Appalachian frontier? The adventurers had all had marital problems or tragedies, early adulthood riddled with controversy, and seemed to be drifting into this series of events in Texas in search of a cathartic in the form of a new life.[28]

Inasmuch as so little is known of Pollard's wife, one wonders if this match was somehow marred early on. It is said that she died soon after the tragic death of her husband. Their only daughter, Oeella Pollard, who died in 1907, is only known in that she willed a portrait of her father to her second cousin, Fanny Oeella Chafin, who in turn, willed it to Mrs. Edward H. Johnson of Fort Dodge Iowa, a Pollard descendant. It was hanging in her living room in 1932. The portrait was photographed in 1927, and a copy was sent to Maurice J. Pollard by Mrs. Johnson.[29]

Endnotes

1. The preceding history of Texas is taken from T.R. Fehrenbach, *Lone Star, A History of Texas and Texans* (New York: Collier Books, 1968), 130, 134-35, 138, 146, 147, 151, 168-70, 172-73, 183-85.

2. M.J. Pollard. *The History of the Pollard Family of America* vol. II (Dover, New York, 1964), 200-201.

3. F.W. Bailey (ed). *Daughters of the American Revolution*. Patriot Index of Early Massachusetts Marriages—Prior to 1800, 735.

4. Secretary of the Commonwealth. *Massachusetts Soldiers and Sailors of the Revolutionary War* vol. 12 (Boston: Wright & Potter Printing, 1904), 506.

5. E.S. Stearns. *History of Ashburnham, Massachusetts 1734-1886 With a Genealogical Register of Ashburnham Families.* (Ashburnham 1887), 17, 231-32, 347, 852.

6. F.B.Kingsbury. *History of the Town of Surry, Cheshire County, New Hampshire* (Boston: New England Historical Society, 1994).

7. Pollard, *Pollard Family*, 44, 233; D.R. Proper. "Surry Man at the Alamo." *Keene* (NH) *Evening Sentinel* (July 11, 1967).

8. Proper, "Surry Man at the Alamo."

9. Catalogue of the Officers and Students of Middlebury College and Vermont Academy of Medicine, October 1824.

10. C.J. and J.R. Choquette. "Ashburnham to Alamo," Manuscript, Daughters of the Republic of Texas Library, Alamo, San Antonio, Texas.

11. G.B. Anderson. *Landmarks of Rensselaer County* (Syracuse, New York: D. Mason & Co., 1897), 407.

12. Choquette, "Ashburnham to Alamo."

13. Pollard, *Pollard* Family, 44.

14. D.R.Proper. "You Know About Davy Crockett, but Have you Heard of Dr. Pollard?" *Keene* (NH) *Sentinel* (February 24, 1981).

15. H. Livingston. "The Texas Residency of Amos Pollard." *Alamo Journal* (February 1995).

16. P.I. Nixon. *The Medical Story of Early Texas, 1528-1853.* (n.p: Mollie Bennett Lupe Memorial Fund, 1946), 169-70.

17. Fehrenbach, *Lone Star*, 195-98.

18. W.O. Chariton. *100 Days in Texas, the Alamo Letters.* (Plano, Texas: Wordward Publishing, Inc., 1990), 46, 87.

19. Fehrenbach, *Lone Star*, 202, 205.

20. P.I. Nixon. *A Century of Medicine in San Antonio* (San Antonio, 1936), 57-58.

21. Fehrenbach, *Lone Star*, 206.

22. Nixon, *Century of Medicine*, 55-56.

23. L. Tinkle. *13 Days to Glory.* 2d Ed. (College Station: Texas A&M University Press, 1986), 92, 108-11.

24. Fehrenbach, *Lone Star*, 208.

25. Tinkle, *13* Days, 188-89.

26. Fehrenbach, *Lone Star*, 211.

27. Chariton, *100* Days, 317.

28. Fehrenbach, *Lone Star*, 210.

29. Pollard, *Pollard Family*, 43-44

Biographical Sketch of Authors

Richard J. Andrassy, M.D., is the A.G. McNeese Professor and Chairman, Department of Surgery at the University of Texas-Houston Medical School. He is Chief of Surgery at Hermann Hospital and Chief of Pediatric Surgery at the M.D. Anderson Cancer Center. Dr. Andrassy is a graduate of the Virginia Military Institute and the Medical College of Virginia. His general surgical training was obtained at the Wilford Hall. U.S. Air Force Medical Center in San Antonio, Texas and pediatric surgical oncology training at the University of Southern California Children's Hospital of Los Angeles. He is a member of the Texas Surgical Society, American Surgical Association, the Southern Surgical Association, American college of Surgeons, the American Pediatric Surgical Association, and the American Academy of Pediatrics. His primary clinical interest is in pediatric surgical oncology.

Anthony Shinn is a graduate of West Virginia University. He is a retired geologist from Pennzoin Corporation. He has collaborated with Dr. Andrassy in the Department of Surgery on several medical historical manuscripts.

Flora L. (von) Roeder is a graduate of North Texas State University in Denton, Texas. She is the Editor of the Department of Surgery, University of Texas-Houston Medical School and a member of the San Jacinto Chapter, Daughters of the Republic of Texas. She has published in *The New Hand Book of Texas*, Texas State Historical Association and is the State Editor of the Texas German Society *Reporter*.

Joseph Henry Reuss, M.D., F.A.C.S.
1867-1919
by
James E. Pridgen, M.D., F.A.C.S.

★BORN IN THE POST-CIVIL WAR era in the coastal city of Indianola, Texas, Dr. J. H. Reuss became the organizational chairman of the Texas Surgical Society as well as an outstanding community leader and Texas pioneer. He made many contributions in each of these fields during his lifetime and has numerous firsts to his credit. He was known for his superior professional ability, tireless energy and personal magnetism. A glimpse into the history of the frontier Texas towns before the turn of the century helps us appreciate the accomplishments as well as the hardships of this early Texas doctor who had no medical school available, no long distance consultations and no nearby hospitals except the four he built himself.

Joseph Henry Reuss was born January 16, 1867, in "The Queen City of the West," Indianola, Texas, a close rival of Galveston during the Civil War Era. His father, Doctor Joseph Martin Reuss, was graduated from the University of Wurtzburg Medical School in Germany and moved to Indianola, by way of Galveston where he married Miss Gesine Stubemann, in 1845 with Prince Solms' Braunfels Colony in company with a number of other intellectuals. He left his home in Bavaria along the Reuss River because of the changing political scene in Germany in that decade and arrived in Texas just before it had joined the Union. He distinguished himself in the treatment of patients during the epidemics of yellow fever and cholera and wrote papers on these subjects, which were published in 1876 in Philadelphia.[1] His personal friendships with Texans of this day included such figures as Governor John Ireland, Gustav

Doctor Joseph Henry Reuss in 1918 at the age of fifty-one.

Schleicher and Ashbel Smith, and he also rendered outstanding service in Shae's Battalion of Hood's Brigade defending Indianola, where he treated both Confederate and Union soldiers on a massive table in his drug store. A gavel made from this table was presented at the April 1973 meeting of the Texas Surgical Society in Galveston. His brother, Doctor Augustus Reuss, was a brilliant surgeon in the Franco Prussian War who died at the Nimitz home in Fredericksburg upon returning to the United States.[2]

The Reuss Family Coat of Arms dates back to the first Crusade, 1096 AD in which it was first worn by Sir Knight Crusader Johan Von Reuss.[3] A map of Germany made in 1390 shows the principality of Reussen where his ancestors lived and the Reuss River near Lucerne. One of Doctor Reuss' ancestors, Johan Stephan Reuss, painted by Cranach, was President of the University of Vienna in 1510, shortly after Columbus discovered America.[4]

Indianola was founded in 1844 and was an instant success in spite of early hardships. It was the deepest water port on the Texas Coast and handled more tonnage than Galveston in the 1870s. Steamships traveled non-stop between Indianola and New York City. Lots there sold for $4,000 each when Texas had only 50,000 population.[5] It was the "mother" of West Texas and supplied over thirty-four military forts in Texas.[6] In 1849 the first cattle shipped from Texas were shipped from the port of Indianola. In the prerailroad days of 1856, the exciting innovation in military circles was the Texas Camel Corps. Seventy-five camels were landed at Indianola through the recommendation of Jefferson Davis prior to his becoming the president of the Confederacy. The caravans traveled south to the mines of Northern Mexico, east to San Antonio, and out west. General Robert E. Lee, in his earlier years, gave a strong commendation to the Camel Corps.[7] Indianola suffered three very severe hurricanes and, like legendary Atlantis, was completely destroyed by the sea in 1866. Only a few cement cisterns and a cemetery remain today, containing many markers with prominent San Antonio names.

In 1685 LaSalle, seeking the mouth of the Mississippi River by way of the Gulf of Mexico, landed in the Indianola area, explored it widely, and built Fort Louis in honor of his benefactor, King Louis XIV of France. A statue of LaSalle with a historical note may be seen in old Indianola today. This is the United States' first claim to Texas by way of the Louisiana Purchase. Recent excavations of this old fort produced his cross among other identifiable objects. This cross hangs in Grace Episcopal Church in nearby Port Lavaca, Texas.[8] In 1995 researchers from the Texas Historical Commission, excavating near Indianola in twelve feet of water, delivered a cannon and part of the hull of a ship. This major archaeological discovery has been identified as *La Belle*, the flagship of LaSalle which had been buried in a sand bar for three hundred years.[9] LaSalle used the well-known map of Pineda to explore the Matagorda Bay area; Alfonso Alvarez Pineda had explored the Texas Coast in 1519 and produced an outstanding map used by most explorers who followed him. The map is housed in the Spanish archives in Seville, Spain; [10] Garay was his benefactor. He landed on many places on the Texas Coast, becoming the first European to explore the Texas Coast, but he reported no surgical accomplishments. Pineda's navigator, Anton Alaminos, had made two previous trips to the New World with Columbus, another with Ponce de Leon and one with Cardova; therefore, he supplied much valuable information.[11] Another famous explorer familiar with Pineda's work was Cabeza de Vaca, who was shipwrecked off Galveston Island in 1528. He washed ashore, was captured by the Indians, and wandered along the Texas Coast including the area near Indianola for the next six years. In 1534 he escaped near Corpus Christi during the "tuna" (prickly pear) feast. He then traveled along the Guadalupe River through the area of DeWitt County (Cuero is the county seat) on his unparalleled journey to Mexico City and back to Spain.[12] In 1535 he performed the first recorded operation by a white man on this continent.[13]

In 1875 the Reuss family, along with many others, moved inland seventy miles on the then new C.W. Morgan Railroad to Cuero, Texas, and led another pioneer effort in founding this town. From 1866 to 1895 over ten million cattle were driven up the Chisholm trail, beginning near Cuero, the largest movement of animals under control of men in all history.[14] Many homes in Indianola were disassembled, boards numbered, and then rebuilt in Cuero where they can be seen today. The Reuss Drug Store, established in 1845, was moved from Indianola to Cuero

Reuss Drug
Store built in
1875 in Cuero,
Texas

in 1875 and is today the oldest drug store in Texas in continuous
operation by the same family.

After his pioneer background years in Indianola, Doctor Joe
Reuss began his schooling in Cuero at the German English
School. He entered the University of Texas in 1883, the year it
opened, was graduated in 1886, and in 1889 was graduated from
the Medical College of Physicians and Surgeons of Columbia
University in New York City. Following this he served a one
year's internship at St. Luke's Hospital in New York and observed surgery at the old Presbyterian Hospital there.[15] His close
friend and mentor was the famous New York surgeon Theodore
Gaillard Thomas, for whom he named his eldest son.

In 1891 he began practice with his father in Cuero and
organized the Salome I Hospital, the first of four hospitals he
was destined to organize.[16] By 1892 he had developed a large

practice and performed the first appendectomy in Southwest Texas.[17] In 1897 Doctor Reuss helped organize the Salome Hospital II, used by a number of doctors for years. In 1900 he became a member of the State Board of Medical Examiners and served for many years. He married the prominent Miss Meta Reiffert in 1896. Subsequently they had three children: the late Doctor Gaillard Thomas Reuss, who practiced in Dallas; Anita, who lived in Cuero; and Helen Burns, who lived in Cuero in the Reuss homestead and was the mother of John Arthur Burns, Joseph Henry Burns and Mary Helen Hooks. In this homestead a wood carving by his friend and the well-known Swiss wood craftsman, Peter Mansbendel, was hung over the fireplace by Doctor Reuss which reads, "Verstehen und verstanden werden, Machen unser Gluck auf Erden," which means, "To understand and to be understood makes our happiness on earth."

Mansbendel made the restoration of the handsome doors of the Spanish Governor's Palace and Mission San Jose in San Antonio, which earlier had been destroyed. The Union Building at the University of Texas in Austin contains many examples of his work, including the coat of arms of Cabeza de Vaca in the Latin American Library.[18]

Doctor Reuss worked very hard in Cuero, day and night. By 1904 he decided to move to Dallas in order to limit his practice to surgery. He was a handsome gentleman and very popular with everyone both in and out of the medical profession. He wore a gray morning coat before noon and a black coat in the afternoon. He had a very courtly manner, drove a team of spirited white horses harnessed to his new buggy, and was a charismatic figure much beloved by all. The evening before he left Cuero, the Cuero Band arrived at his home along with other friends to pay their respects. The *Cuero Daily Record* of 1904 stated, "It is with a feeling akin to bereavement to have him leave us, but the promise of a better business field are the just rewards to his unresting energy and high ordered genius."[19]

In Dallas he organized the Marsalis Sanitarium to accommodate his surgical practice and also became Medical Director of the Southwestern Life Insurance Company. The Marsalis was a private sanitarium especially designed for obstetrical surgical and gynecological cases. His surgical slate was kept in the operating suite of the Marsalis and showed the list of operations for each

Salome Hospital built in 1897 in Cuero, Texas

The Marsalis Sanitarium built in Dallas in 1906 was the third hospital
organized by Doctor Reuss

day. He continued to increase his span of close and influential friends in Dallas. However, by 1911 his father and brother had died and responsibilities in Cuero required his return.[20] After returning to Cuero he wanted additional postgraduate training and decided to go to Europe. The night before he left Cuero his friends and the Cuero Band came once again to bid him "Bon Voyage" because he loved music very much. The band played a few numbers, the crowd swelled from his home into his yard and from there into Reuss Boulevard. Many of his friends began a street dance which lasted until a late hour.

Doctor Reuss made every effort to remain current in medical education and took frequent postgraduate courses in this country, such as his period of study at the New York Polyclinic in 1891. For his postgraduate education this time he chose to spend a year in the teaching hospitals of Berlin and the Allgemeine Krankenhaus in Vienna, where the impact of Billroth's work could be felt everywhere. Reservations for his return voyage were made on the *Titanic*, but fortunately he was delayed and returned to Cuero a week later, April 20, 1912, after the sinking of this largest vessel afloat on her maiden voyage across the Atlantic.

What was the quality of life in Cuero in 1912? Why did Dr. Reuss pursue his postgraduate education so diligently? The majority of the German intelligentsia from Indianola settled in Cuero during the 1870s along with similar people from the Green DeWitt Colony. Interest in literature, music and other cultural accomplishments was at a high level. Cuero, with a population of less than five thousand, furnished the second highest number of students of the cities represented by students attending the University of Texas in 1883. Medically, by 1912 it had become the surgical referral center from the Gulf Coast to San Antonio; Cuero maintained this reputation for fifty years due to the influence of the Reuss and Burns families. The infamous days of the Taylor-Sutton Feud were replaced by the world famous Turkey Trot. The development of the unique Cuero turkey industry with the accompaning Turkey Trot Celebration is an interesting bit of history in which doctors Reuss and Burns participated and will be briefly described.

In 1872 Gustav Schleicher, a German engineer, surveyed the present town site of Cuero and also surveyed the route to a new

The list of operations for the day was printed on this
surgical slate in the Marsalis Hospital.

The translation of Mansbendel's wood carving hung over Doctor Reuss'
fireplace is "To understand and to be understood
makes our happiness on earth."

The Cuero Turkey Trot of 1916 shows ten thousand turkeys parading in front
of the famous old Muti Hotel.

branch of the Gulf, Western Texas and Pacific Railroad from
Indianola to Cuero. Because of the repeated storms taking place
in Indianola, a major migration of citizens to Cuero occurred
including Dr. Reuss' family. Their homes were loaded on the
railroad to be rebuilt in Cuero where many can be seen today.
Schleicher was known as the founder of Cuero and later became
a United States Congressman. Although cotton farming and
ranching were the main industries in the 1880s, almost every
farm family raised turkeys for the Thanksgiving and Christmas
markets. Due to the mild winters and lack of severe rains, the
turkeys were easy to raise and the demands of the fall turkey
market grew rapidly. Trucks were not available at this time, and
farmers drove their flocks on foot into Cuero to market. Flocks
of turkeys from outlying areas were joined by flocks closer to
town, and by the time they reached the city, thousands of
Thanksgiving turkeys might be seen marching into town.

   After the turn of the century, wealthy capitalists from the
east came to Cuero during the winter to enjoy the hunting and
fishing in the comfort of the cold weather. They became fasci-
nated with the huge flocks of turkeys brought to market each

year. In 1912 twelve thousand range turkeys were herded into Cuero from nearby ranches and collected in a staging area on a hill behind Doctor Reuss' home. Texas Governor O.B. Colquitt and his staff led the parade the next day with many floats and bands followed by twelve thousand turkeys. Some thirty thousand spectators viewed the parade and later described this spectacle to their friends, and the newspapers advertised this unique production widely. Advertisements ran in New York City, Chicago and Los Angeles about this three-day celebration and developed national interest. In this era the turkey industry reached its peak and Cuero became known as the Turkey Capital of the World.[21]

Mr. Jim Howerton, publisher of the local newspaper *The Cuero Record*, promoted the idea of a civic festival centering around the parade of turkeys. A popular dance of the day was called the "Turkey Trot" and was adopted as a name for the festival. In 1912 the first Turkey Trot Celebration also took place. A king and queen called Sultan and Sultana were chosen from the citizens of Cuero and reigned over a coronation of princes and princesses who came from neighboring cities and subsequently from as far away as San Antonio, Austin, Dallas and Corpus Christi. The social attire of the day at that time was tuxedos, stove pipe hats and tails for the men who accompanied the ladies in their beautiful dresses. Doctor Reuss and his arch competitor, Doctor John Burns, were intimately involved in these celebrations, since each was president of the Chamber of Commerce during this time.

Doctor Reuss' father was a great inspiration to him as a doctor and an outstanding leader who loved music, practiced good medicine and published scientific papers. Doctor Reuss himself had an inner drive to become the best surgeon he could be. His arch competitor in Cuero, Doctor John W. Burns, who built his hospital two blocks from Doctor Reuss' home, also had a great influence on him. Before and after the turn of the century when one of them traveled to Europe to obtain new postgraduate training, the other soon made a similar medical trip bringing back even more recent medical information to Cuero patients. In his later years, Doctor Burns told me in confidence that he would not have been such a good doctor if it hadn't been for his competitor, Doctor Reuss.

At the age of forty-four,
Doctor John W. Burns built
the Burns Hospital in Cuero,
Texas.

During the eight years from 1904 to 1912, in which Doctor Reuss was away from Cuero, the medical affairs of the Salome Hospital were ably directed by Doctors Burns and Kirkham. Doctor John W. Burns was one of the most highly educated doctors in Texas at this time.[22] He later became a member of the Judicial Committee of the American Medical Association and also became President of the Texas Medical Association. He took postgraduate training in New York City in 1892, 1893, 1894, 1897, and in Vienna in 1899, 1902, and 1908; thereafter, he paid yearly visits to large clinics in this country. His father, Columbus Burns, was the first white child born in the Green DeWitt Colony in 1826. Doctor Burns later built a beautiful sixty-five bed hospital in Cuero. Many doctors, including my father Doctor J. H. Pridgen, were associated with him there for many years. Doctor Burns and his son, the late John Gillett, were active members of the Texas Surgical Society. His other son Arthur, an internist, married Doctor Reuss' daughter Helen. Their three children were Mary Helen Hoops, John Arthur Burns, and Joe Burns. In 1959 John Burns, Sid Cockrell and I packed and transported his library of some twenty-five hundred volumes and seven thousand journals to San Antonio to await the building of the medical school.

Doctor Frederick W. Kirkham received his medical education in England with his good friend Doctor James E. Thompson, the first President of the Texas Surgical Society. Doctor Kirkham's son, Doctor H.L.D. Kirkham, of Cuero and Houston, was the thirteenth President of the Texas Surgical Society and the first non-founding member to become president. He had many talents, including playing golf, serving as a first violinist with the Houston Symphony, portrait painting, and making hooked rugs.[23] He married the prominent Frida Buchel of Cuero whose father, Otto Buchel born in Indianola, became owner of the Buchel Bank, the largest bank in Cuero and DeWitt County. His daughter Doris Kirkham continued to visit her Cuero friends and relatives for many years.

An interesting commentary to Doctor Reuss' widespread medical reputation was the summons he received at Shanghai Pierce's final illness. At the time of his death Pierce was the best-known and most colorful cattle baron in South Texas. He owned thousands of acres of land, an enormous number of cattle, timber, rice lands, and a railroad as well as other interests. At the age of nineteen he left his home in Rhode Island and sailed as a stowaway on a ship from New York to Indianola. Shanghai made his fortune from ranching in the Indianola area from 1853 to the 1870s, the golden years of Indianola. Then he moved his headquarters near Wharton, established Pierce, Texas, and extended his fortune. A call went out to Doctor Reuss to come to consult at his last illness. It was, however, to no avail; Pierce died in his home of a cerebral hemorrhage at 3:00 a.m. Christmas night 1900.[24]

In 1912 Doctor Reuss became Chief Surgeon for the San Antonio to Aransas Pass Railroad and began to rebuild his large practice in Cuero with his tireless energy, professional ability and personal charm. Four years later, in honor of his father, he built the Reuss Memorial Hospital and Nurses Training School[25] on Reuss Boulevard next to his beautiful home.

In 1914 he became a member of the American College of Surgeons.[26] He was also a member of the first Board of Medical Examiners for Texas and later President of DeWitt County Chapter of the American Red Cross during World War I.[27] He

Reuss Memorial Hospital, Cuero, Texas, built by Doctor J.H. Reuss in
1916 to honor his father

was an active member of the Knights of Pythias and the Episcopal Church, Cuero, Texas.

During 1914 and 1915 Doctor Reuss served as one of the
founders of the Texas Surgical Society and was elected chairman
of the Founders' Group. Although consideration of a state
surgical society had been discussed for several years, it was not
until the annual session of the Texas Medical Association in May
1914 that steps were taken toward the organization of such a
society. Doctor Reuss was appointed as a committee of one to
interrogate representative men throughout the state for their
consideration. As a result of favorable replies, he called a meeting
to discuss this question in October 1914 at the Tremont Hotel,
Galveston, Texas.

After his election as Chairman of the Founders' Group, he
made many accomplishments during his ten-month tenure. Under his direction, the Founders held the original six organizational meetings, committee and general sessions, and the following activities took place.

1. The Society was named the Texas Surgical Society.

2. The Constitution and By-laws were written and adopted.

3. Charter memberships and "Practice Limited to Surgery" were defined.

4. The first charter members were selected.

5. Sound groundwork was established upon which the Society could be formally launched into action. Doctor Reuss became known as the organizational chairman of the Texas Surgical Society.

Doctor Reuss was elected Vice-President in 1915 and 1916. He was also elected to a three-year term on the Council in October, 1917, thus being an officer or a councilman for the six years from 1914 until his death in September 1919. At the six scientific meetings he attended prior to his death he presented the following three papers.

1. Some Postoperative Abdominal Complications, October 18, 1915, San Antonio, Texas.

2. Complete Atresia of the Upper Third of the Vagina of Multipara at Full Term, April 24, 1916, Dallas, Texas.

3. A Comparison of the Closed or Old Method of Treating Fractures with that of the Open or New Method, October 8-9, 1917, Houston, Texas.

Doctor Reuss also had many community interests. He was elected president of the Cuero Commercial Club and led this organization in its successful campaign for good roads. He used the *Texas A & M Bulletin* to demonstrate that the cost of hauling per ton per mile was twice as high in Texas as in the rest of the United States because of Texas' poor roads.[28]

Doctor Reuss died September 17, 1919, at the age of fifty-two, while attending a meeting at the Rice Hotel in Houston to obtain the passage of road bonds for DeWitt County. His microscope and Reuss Surgical Library were presented to the University of Texas Medical Branch at Galveston to honor the Texas Surgical Society at the Spring Meeting, 1973.[29] Among the firsts he accomplished in his lifetime are:

1. Organization Chairman of Texas Surgical Society, 1914.

2. Built the first real hospital in Southwest Texas, 1892.

3. Performed the first appendectomy in Southwest Texas in 1892.

4. One of the first members of the American College of Surgeons, 1914.

5. Initiated the first Eastern and European Post-graduate training in this area.

6. Member of the first board of Medical Examiners for Texas.

7. President of DeWitt County Chapter of American Red Cross.

8. First Physician President of Chamber of Commerce in this area.

9. Passed the first major bond issue for roads in DeWitt County.

10. First in the hearts of very many patients on whom he continues to cast his shadow to this day.

He was a highly educated gentleman, an excellent surgeon and an outstanding community leader who pioneered in many fields. Upon his death, the Cuero newspaper stated, "The usefulness of a professional man is not marked merely by his learning and skill, his proficiency in medical practice; but also by his character, both private and professional; his honorable adherence to medical ethics and his personal integrity and prudent benevolence. When a physician combines these characteristics, it is with great pleasure that we record his life's work."[30]

ENDNOTES

1. J.M. Reuss. "Report on Yellow Fever Epidemic of 1867, Indianola, Texas." *Yellow Fever and Malarial Diseases,* Greensville Dobell, ed. (Philadelphia: Medical Publication, 1876), 49-52.

2. F.W. Johnson. *A History of Texas and Texans* (Chicago: The American Historical Society, 1916), 1242-44.

3. Ferdinande Seeger. Personal letter March 1919, genealogical researcher, 400 East 93rd Street, New York, quoting Feyerabend, *Geschichte Den Kreuzzuge* (Frankfurt, 1583) and Helms, *Erneenests and Vernachentes Wassenbuch* (Nurenberg: Ritten und Adelspersonen, 1699).

4. Lucas Canach. Portrait of Johann Stephan Reuss in *German Painting,*

The Old Masters, Alfred Werner, ed. (New York: McGraw Hill Book Company, 1964), 42.

5. Lelia Seligson. "A History of Indianola. *Indianola Scrapbook,* G.F. Rhodes, ed. (Austin: San Felipe Press, 1974), 23-27.

6. Brownson Malsch. *The Mother of Western Texas* (Austin: School Creek Publishers, Inc., 1977), 112-29.

7. Chris Emmett. "The Big Bend." *Texas Camel Tales* (Austin: Steck-Vaugh Company, 1969), 138-43.

8. Seligson, "History of Indianola," op. cit.

9. Roni Morales. "LaSalle Shipwreck." *The Medallion* (Austin: Texas Historical Commission, Special Issue, September 1995), 1-11.

10. John Farmer. "Pineda Sketch." *Southwest. Historical Quarterly* 63 (1960), 110-14.

11. P.J. Fock. "Early Exploration of the Coast of Texas." *Our Catholic Heritage in Texas, 1519-1936* (Austin, Texas: Knights of Columbus Historical Commission, St. Edwards University, 1936), 4-13.

12. C. Covey. "Cabeza de Vaca's Adventures in the Unknown Interior of America, A New Translation with Annotation" (New York: Collier Books, 1961), 68-85; C.E.Castaneda. "The Narvaez Expedition, 1526-1535." *Our Catholic Heritage in Texas* (Austin: Von Boeckmann-Jones Co., 1936), 1:69-70; W.CFoster. "Spanish and French Explorer in the DeWitt County Area." *The History of DeWitt County Texas* (Dallas: Curtis Media Corporation, 1991), 3-6.

13. R.S. Sparkman. *The Texas Surgical Society. The First Fifty Years* (Dallas: privately printed by Carl Hertzog, 1965), 1:3-5, 3:17-22; J.E.Thompson. "Sagittectomy—The First Recorded Surgical Procedure in the American Southwest, 1535." *New England Journal of Medicine* 289 (1973), 1403-1407.

14. Chisholm Trail Historical Marker, Cuero, Texas.

15. J.A. Burns, Personal Letters of 1972.

16. O.E. Hall, Jr. *Historical Record Commemorating 100th Anniversary of Founding of Cuero, 1872-1972* (Smithville, Texas: Tex-Print Corporation, 1972), 1-15.

17. G.V. Brindley. "One Hundred Years of Surgery in Texas." *Texas State Medical Journal* 49 (1953), 288-94.

18. Paul Wakefield. "Pioneer In Art, Peter Mansbendel." *Under Texas Skies* 4 (September 1953), 1, 2.

19. James Howerton. "Dr. J.H. Reuss Leaves Cuero." *The Cuero* [Texas] *Daily Record* (October 1904), 4.

20. L.B. Hill. *Dr. Joseph H. Reuss in Greater Dallas and Vicinity, Selected Biography and Memoirs,* vol 2 (Chicago: The Lewis Publishing Company, 1909), 190-91.

21. Jack Howerton. "The Cuero Record Centennial and Turkey Trot Souvenir Edition 1872-1972," vol. 78 no. 249 (Cuero, Texas: The Cuero Publishing Company), 1-88; Frank Sheppard."Cuero." *The History of DeWitt County Texas* (The DeWitt County Historical Commission: Curtis Media Corporation, 1991), 88-93.

22. H. Taylor. "Deaths, Dr. John W. Burns." *Texas State Journal of Medicine,* vol. 35 (1939), 151-52.

23. H.L.D. Kirkham, Mrs. Personal Letter of 1977.

24. C. Emmett. *Shanghai Pierce: A Fair Likeness.* (Norman, Oklahoma: University of Oklahoma Press, May 1955).

25. F.F. Eberhardt. Lutheran Hospital, Reuss Memorial Bulletin (Cuero, Texas: The Cuero Publishing Company, 1918), 1-28.

26. G.W. Stephenson American College of Surgeons Letter January 1973 to Mrs. Cynthia Robinson, University of Texas Medical Branch, Galveston.

27. H. Taylor. "Deaths, Dr. J.H. Reuss." *Texas State Medical Journal*, vol. 15 (1919), 229-30; F.M. Kunethka. *History of War Activities of DeWitt County Chapter of American Red Cross*, (Cuero, Texas: Cuero Publishing Company, 1917), 1-65.

28. Kunethka, *History of War Activities*, op. cit.; Sparkman, *Texas Surgical Society*, op. cit.; Brindley, "One Hundred Years," op., cit.; W.B. Thorning. Minutes of the Texas Surgical Society, October and November 1914; W.B. Thorning. *Transactions of the Texas Surgical Society* (1923-1924), Houston, Texas; B.K. Coghlan. "Gravel Roads." *Bulletin of the Agricultural and Mechanical College of Texas*, vol. 1, Bulletin 7 (Austin: Von Boechmann-Jones Company, 1915), 1-24.

29. H.H. Berner. "Reuss Surgical Library Dedicated in Galveston." *The Cuero Record* (March 31, 1973), 1.

30. James Howerton. "Dr. Joseph H. Reuss Dies". *The Cuero Daily Record* (September 1919), 1.

BIOGRAPHICAL SKETCH OF AUTHOR

DR. JAMES E. PRIDGEN was born October 21, 1918 in Cuero, Texas, one block from Dr. Joe Reuss' home. He lived in Cuero until 1946, with absences for education and World War II, and has been close friends with Dr. Reuss' relatives on a continuing basis to this day.

Dr. Pridgen was raised in the hospital of Dr. John Burns with whom his father was associated. Dr. Reuss and Dr. Burns were archrivals and each had remarked privately he would never have been as good a doctor if it weren't for his competition.

Dr. Pridgen was graduated from the University of Texas, Tulane Medical School, interned in Richmond, Virginia, and served in a battalion aid station in Germany during World War II. He then served a five-year surgical fellowship at the Mayo Clinic obtaining a Master of Science Degree in Surgery. Since then he has practiced surgery in San Antonio. He has helped with the founding of the Southwest Texas Medical Center and served as Chief of Surgery and Chief of Staff at Methodist Hospital, Clinical Professor of Surgery at the Medical School, and Chief of Staff at University Hospital. He was president of International Medical Assembly, San Antonio Surgical Society, Texas Surgical Society, Priestley society, and Vice President Western Surgical Association. He was an active surgical consultant for twenty-five years at Brooke General Hospital and Wilford Hall Hospital; he was a Governor of the American College of Surgeons and is a member of the Southern Surgical Association.

Civic activities include serving on the boards of the Alamo Council of Boy Scouts and the American Cancer Society. He was a past chairman of the Board of Alamo Heights United Methodist Church and was an active member of the San Antonio Rotary Club and San Antonio Symphony Society.

In 1946 he married Betty Rabb, who was graduated from the University of Texas and attended Julliard School of Music, and they have enjoyed music through the years. They have three children and six grandchildren, and all enjoy relaxation on the Pridgen ranch near Cuero and the Texas Gulf Coast.

ACKNOWLEDGMENTS: I would like to thank Doctor Reuss' daughter, the late Mrs. Helen Reuss Burns of Cuero, and his grandson, Mr. John Arthur Burns of Houston, for their assistance.

The only known photograph of Jerome B. Robertson

Jerome Bonaparte Robertson, M.D.
ca. 1813-1890
by
R. Maurice Hood, M.D.

★JEROME BONAPARTE ROBERTSON was one of the rare individuals who successfully served as a physician, as a civil servant in the political world, and as a soldier. He was small to medium in stature yet dynamic as a leader, particularly as a combat officer in the Confederate Army.

His father, Cornelius Robertson, immigrated to America from Aberdeen Scotland in the 1770s. At first he resided in Maryland and for a short time in Versailles, Kentucky.[1] He married Clarissa Hill Keech, a widow, at Port Tobacco, Maryland, in 1803. This union produced five children, Jerome being the fourth and youngest son. Cornelius amassed a fairly large estate in terms of land and slaves but lost most of his assets in the financial crisis of 1819 and died the following year.

The destitute family, in order to survive, bound out the boys to local tradesmen as apprentices. Jerome at age eight was bound out to learn the trade of a hatter and moved with his master to St. Louis. After five years of this apprenticeship, Jerome, now about fifteen, acquired some education and joined a thespian society. He remained in St. Louis until he was eighteen. He had acquired enough money to buy out the last three years of his contract as an apprentice. He had little desire to continue as a hatter and decided that he wished to become a physician.

He was befriended by Dr. W.W. Harris of Yellowbanks, soon to become Owensboro, Kentucky. Dr. Harris apparently decided that Robertson had potential and began to give him formal instruction in literary subjects and in medicine. Jerome became Harris' office assistant. With Dr. Harris' assistance he enrolled in the Medical School at Transylvania College during the years 1834 and 1835. He was graduated in 1835 and returned to Owensboro to enter practice.[2]

At this time the Texas Revolution was attracting national attention and Jerome Robertson, along with hundreds of other young Americans, answered President Burnet's call for help. He immediately immigrated to the new state and joined the First Regiment of Kentucky Volunteers under Colonel Charles H. Harrison. The regiment was mustered in at Louisville in August 1836. Delayed in New Orleans for several weeks, the volunteers had a slow trip to Texas. Finally, transportation was engaged in a somewhat dilapidated steamer. After a strenuous nineteen-day trip, the regiment landed at Velasco in September. Captain J.T. Holmes of Robertson's company was promoted to major and Jerome was elected captain in his stead. The Battle of San Jacinto had been fought several months earlier---before the regiment's arrival---but they elected to remain in the service of Texas.

Thomas J. Rusk, Secretary of war, assigned Robertson's company to the Texas Army of the Southwest under the command of General Felix Huston. Huston was a flamboyant from Mississippi who made quite an impression on Dr. Robertson, so much so that he named his son after him. Sam Houston did not approve of a standing army and the entire army was furloughed. Without his military rank and military activity, Robertson decided to resume the practice of medicine. He returned briefly to Kentucky in 1837 but returned to Texas the same year in December and settled in Washington County at Washington-on-the-Brazos.[3]

Robertson married Mary Elizabeth Cummings on March 4, 1938. The couple had three children, Felix, Julia Ann, and Henry Bell who died in infancy. His wife came from a wealthy and respected family in Kentucky.

Dr. Robertson became ill in 1838 and moved to a farm six miles from his home and farmed while continuing to practice medicine. His health improved and the family soon moved to Independence where there were better educational opportunities for his children. This was to be the Robertson home for the next thirty-four years. He intermittently practiced medicine when not engaged in military or public service.

He was always interested in military matters and soon became a member of a local militia group which was often

The Robertson family home in Independence

involved in recurring Indian campaigns. Dr. Robertson made an average of two excursions each year against either the Indians or the Mexicans. He became a regimental commander in one of these campaigns in 1839-1840 and was well recognized both as a military man and as a physician. Robertson was always an ardent soldier and developed real leadership capabilities. It is difficult to determine what his primary profession was.

He entered public service and was appointed coroner of Washington County in 1838-1839, mayor of Washington-on-the-Brazos in 1839 and in 1840, and postmaster in 1841, 1842 and 1843. He was elected state legislator from 1847 to 1849 and proved to be an able and efficient member of the House. He was elected state senator in 1849 representing Washington, Burleson, Milam and Williamson counties. During his senate years he served on the Committee for State Affairs and was appointed as Chairman of the Committee on Public Debt. At this time, he advocated preparation for war with the north.[4] After 1849 Robertson was inactive in public service until he was elected as a delegate from Washington County to the Secession Convention.

Dr. Robertson was an enthusiastic secessionist and was one of the overwhelming majority that took Texas out of the Union.

He also served on an interim Committee of Safety.[5] Robertson was one of a committee of five men appointed by the Convention president to inform Governor Houston on March 2, 1861, that "The state of Texas is and has been from the 2nd day of this month a free and sovereign and independent state."[6]

Texas called for two thousand volunteers to enter the Confederate army. Jerome Robertson, with the courage of his convictions, agreed to raise a company in Washington County. He accomplished this task easily and was elected captain of the company which they named "The Texas Aids." They were soon named Company I of the Fifth Texas Infantry Regiment.[7] This regiment, along with the First and Fourth Texas regiments, was sent to Richmond. There the Eighteenth Georgia Regiment was added to the Texas units and became a brigade, under Louis T. Wigfall, named The Texas Brigade. John Bell Hood soon replaced Wigfall and developed the brigade into a first-class fighting unit that was to be forever remembered as Hood's Texas Brigade.

Robertson was promoted to lieutenant colonel of the regiment and on July 2, 1862, was promoted to colonel commanding the Fifth Texas. The fighting doctor led the regiment in the desperate battles of Gaines Mill, Malvern Hill, Second Manassas and Freeman's Ford. The colonel was wounded in the shoulder at Gaines Mill and received an injury to the hip during the Manassas battle.[8] Despite his wounds, Robertson insisted on leading the regiment during the invasion of Maryland by Lee's army. The hot, dry march proved too much for the wounded doctor and he collapsed at Boonesboro Gap. He was confined to an ambulance and missed the battle of Antietam. His conduct at Gaines Mill was recorded as gallant.[9] Although the battle of Second Manassas represented a great victory for the South, the Fifth regiment sustained their highest loss of the entire war. There were 261 officers and men killed, wounded or missing out of the 512 men engaged.

John Bell Hood was promoted to major general and given a division to command. Jerome B. Robertson, having proved his military prowess and leadership capabilities, was promoted to brigadier general commanding the Texas Brigade on November 1, 1862. Robertson had difficulty controlling the independent Texans when they were not in battle. He led the now-famous unit in the battles of Fredericksburg, Suffolk, Gettysburg,

Chickamauga, Wauhatchie and Knoxville. He was wounded for the third time at Gettysburg and temporarily gave up his command to Brigadier General John Gregg.

General Robertson's career had an unwarranted and unpleasant termination in the winter of 1863-64. General James Longstreet had a favorite, Brigadier General Micah Jenkins, whom he wished to place in command of the Texas Brigade. Jenkins was a bitter rival of Brigadier General Evander Law and disliked Robertson as well.[10] In a dishonest action, he preferred charges against both generals for purely fabricated accusations of failure to carry out their duties during the battle of Knoxville. This action by Longstreet was also an attempt to lay the blame on subordinates rather than accept the responsibility for his own failure. There was no doubt that Robertson and Longstreet were at odds, and before attempting to carry out his orders Robertson made an uncharacteristic outburst against Longstreet.[11]

The appointment of Jenkins was unpopular with the Texas Brigade. The court martial made scapegoats of the two generals for a failure of Jenkins and Longstreet. They were relieved of command, but General Bragg canceled the proceedings and returned both men to duty.[12]

This proved to be only a temporary respite, for Longstreet again preferred charges against Robertson after a minor fray at Bean's Station. The subsequent court martial findings were against General Robertson, and he was reprimanded and permanently removed from command. This charge is thought by all historians to have also been a fabricated accusation.

Robertson left the Army of Northern Virginia and the brigade who loved and respected him. His farewell address was a touching oration. He had led the brigade longer than any other commanding officer and had led them in the majority of its major battles. The brigade had built an unequaled reputation as one of the greatest infantry units of the war. On several instances the intervention of the brigade literally turned defeat into victory. There is little doubt that the Texas Brigade was Lee's favorite unit. Its casualties were among the highest sustained by any unit in either army; approximately six thousand men had served in the brigade, but only 621 half starved, barefooted and ragged men were left to surrender at Appomattox.

Jerome Robertson continued in the Confederate forces after

leaving Lee's army and was assigned to command the Reserve Forces of Texas under General John B. Magruder. Robertson, preferring combat duty, was transferred to the command of General Maxey Gregg, but the Confederate forces surrendered before he received a command. He was paroled at Houston July 12, 1865. It is of curious interest that, in spite of his being a physician, there is no record to indicate that he ever acted in the role of a doctor during his military service. His son Felix also served in the Confederate army and rose to the rank of brigadier general, the only native Texan to achieve the rank of general and the youngest brigadier in the army in 1864. General Robertson and his son were the only father-son pair to hold the rank of general in the Confederate army. General Felix Robertson died April 20, 1928, in Waco, the last survivor of the general officers of the Confederacy.

In 1865 Dr. Robertson returned to Independence and resumed the practice of medicine. His mother had died in 1864 and his wife, Mary, was only to live until 1868. His youngest son had also died in 1859. All of these members of the family were buried in the cemetery at Independence. With his war record and his civil service prior to the war, he was cast into a leadership role in his community. He was subjected to considerable abuse and indignity by the Federal Army and by carpetbag officials after the war. At one point the CSA buttons were publicly cut from his coat.

He was active in the Texas Medical Association and was active in seeing to the welfare of the numerous Confederate veterans who came to him for help. He treated many of them at his home and provided temporary shelter for many of his destitute comrades-in-arms. Dr. Robertson, following the death of his wife in 1868, moved to Waco to be near his son Felix. He became interested in the Masonic Grand Lodge and held several offices. He was one of the organizers of the Hood's Texas Brigade Association. Annual reunions were held, and Robertson's appearance always produced prolonged cheering and the Rebel Yell. He was elected president eleven times and, finally, life-time president until his death. His fellowship and relations with the brigade veterans was a close one with deep commitment.

Dr. Robertson gave up the practice of medicine following the death of his wife and entered semi-retirement. There is no indication that he practiced medicine after moving to Waco.[13] He was appointed by Governor Coke to the Bureau of Immigration in 1874 and served until 1876. He continued efforts to encourage immigration for several years. He was appointed immigration agent for the Texas Central Railroad from 1877 to 1878.

Robertson married Mrs. Henly Hook, the daughter of a lawyer, the niece of Governor Coke, and the widow of Professor Hook of Bethany College in Virginia. He maintained his membership in the local medical association and in the Texas Medical Association. He engaged in several businesses in Waco and was in partnership with his son.

He developed a malignancy of the face in late 1880 and his health rapidly deteriorated. He suffered horribly from the cancer. He died at 8:30 p.m., January 7, 1890, at the age of seventy-six. His body, dressed in his Confederate uniform and wearing his decorations, lay in state at the home of his son. General Tom Harrison and two veterans of the Army of the Republic of Texas sat near the coffin. It is recorded that hundreds of local citizens and veterans filed past to pay their last respects.

It was planned that General Robertson be buried in Independence. A funeral procession escorted the casket to the railroad station. The pallbearers were all members of the Texas Brigade. Included in the procession were the mayor and city council members, members of the Masonic Grand Lodge, members of the Pat Cleburne Camp of the United Confederate Veterans, representatives of the Central Texas Medical Association, the Texas Medical Association and the McClennan County Medical Association, Waco Bar Association members, the Texas Veterans Association, McClennan County Veterans Association, Mexican War Veterans, and the Waco Police Force.[14] Dr. Robertson's son, General Felix H. Robertson, Dr. T.H. Mott his son-in-law, and his grandson Felix H. Robertson, Jr. accompanied the body to Independence where it was interred.

Felix Robertson, for unknown reasons, had the bodies of his father, his mother Mary E. Cummings Robertson, and his grandmother Clarissa Hill Keach Robertson moved to Waco and reburied in Oakwood Cemetery. Until 1965 the gravesites were neglected, forgotten, and even their location lost. Colonel Harold B. Simpson, Director of the Confederate Research Center at Hill College and historian of the Texas Brigade, undertook a project to locate and refurbish the gravesites. This search was

The rededication of the graves of the Robertson family by Colonel
Harold B. Simpson. Courtesy of the Confederate Research Center, Hill
College, Hillsboro, Texas

successful and the graves suitably marked and rededicated in an
impressive ceremony.

Jerome B. Robertson was not a large man physically. He was
a patriot who was willing to risk his life fearlessly for the cause
he believed in so ardently. He proved to be an outstanding leader
of men and was privileged to command one of the greatest
military units in American history. Although wounded three
times, he did not permit these injuries to keep him from command and combat. He was noted for the care and compassion
for his troops under his command. This characteristic was so
obvious that his soldiers referred to him as "Aunt Polly." He
continued to minister to them for years after the war.

As a physician, he was kind and caring to those whose care
he undertook. Little is known of the details of his medical
practice for he left no records of note; however, he was held in
high regard by his colleagues. He had a single medical publication, "The West and Southwest as a Health Resort." He was
active in the Texas Medical Association in its formative years.

Jerome Bonaparte Robertson, soldier, patriot, citizen, public servant and physician, deserves to be remembered.

ENDNOTES

1.Conlon Collection of letters and papers in the possession of Mrs. Mildred F. Conlon of Chicago, Ill., the great-granddaughter of General Jerome B. Robertson.

2.Ibid.

3.J.B. Robertson. *Touched With Valor, Civil War Papers and Casualty Reports of Hood's Texas Brigade,* Harold B. Simpson, ed., with a biography of General Jerome B. Robertson, Intro. and Bio. by H.B.S. (Hillsboro, Texas: Hill Junior College Press, 1964), 3.

4.Donald C. Everett (ed). *Chaplain Davis and Hood's Texas Brigade* (San Antonio: Principal Press, Trinity University, 1962).

5.Ernest W. Winkler (ed). *Journal of the Secession Convention of Texas* (Austin: The State Library, 1861).

6.Robertson, *Touched With Valor,* op. cit.

7.Roster of the 5th Regiment Texas Volunteers, August 1861. Washington, Confederate Collection. National Archives.

8.Lid S. Johnson. *Texans Who Wore Gray* (N.P.), 86-87.

9.Everett, *Chaplain Davis,* op. cit.

10. Douglas S. Freeman. *Lee's Lieutenants,* vol. III (New York: Scribners, 1944), 404.

11. A.V. Winkler. *The Confederate Capitol and Hood's Texas Brigade* (Austin: Eugene Von Boeckman, 1894), 151; *The War of the Rebellion: Official Records of the Union and Confederate Armies,* Series 1, vol. 31 (Washington: Government Printing Office 1880-1901), 466-67; H.J. Eckenrode and B. Conrad. *James Longstreet, Lee's Warhorse* (Chapel Hill: University of North Carolina Press), 276; Jeffrey D. West. *James Longstreet, The Confederacy's Most Controversial Soldier, A Biography* (New York: Simon and Schuster, 1993), 336, 360.

12. West, *James Longstreet,* op. cit.; *Official Records of the Union and Confederate Armies,* op. cit.

13. P.I. Nixon. *The Medical Story of Early Texas* (San Antonio: M.B. Lupe Memorial Fund, 1946), 355.

14. *The Day* (newspaper), Waco, Texas (January 8, 1890).

Additional Reference: Harold B. Simpson. *Hood's Texas Brigade, Lee's Grenadier Guard* (Waco, Texan Press, 1970).

The author wishes to acknowledge that the primary source of most of the information is found in the biographical study of Jerome B. Robertson by Col. Harold B. Simpson in *Touched with Valor, Civil War Papers and Casualty Reports of Hood's Texas Brigade* written and collected by General Jerome B. Robertson, and from personal conversations with Colonel Simpson and from two of his lectures on this subject.

BIOGRAPHICAL SKETCH OF AUTHOR

(see page 59)

A photograph of Dr. Schilling at his microscope in his office in his later years.

Nicholas T. Schilling, M.D.
1845-1919
by
Drew Davis Williams, M.D.

★NICHOLAS SCHILLING WAS BORN in Bavaria, Germany, on November 28, 1845. His parents, John and Annie Schilling, immigrated to America when he was a small child and settled in Maryland. Nothing is known of his early life or education. He enlisted in the Union Army on March 3, 1861, and served as a private under Captain Lewis Zimmerman in Company K, Coles Regiment, Maryland Volunteer Cavalry. He was discharged June 28, 1863, at Harper's Ferry.

After the war he enrolled in the Chicago Medical College, later to become Northwestern University Medical School, and received his degree in 1872. He came to Texas in 1874 with the intent of going into practice but did not have enough money to set up an office in Cedar Bayou. He was the only doctor listed in Cedar Bayou in Harris County.[1]

He went to work in a brick factory along the banks of Cedar Bayou. Shortly afterward he saved the life of an accident victim who was a fellow worker at the brick yard.[2] This episode attracted community attention and finally enabled him to begin medical practice in a lean-to in the back of a general store along the shore of Cedar Bayou, a waterway at the upper end of Galveston Bay in the location that was to become Baytown.[3]

Schilling married Linna E. Gaillard on October 31, 1883, and built a home on the banks of the bayou on fifty acres of land he bought from a Kingsley family. A son, John, was born in 1885 and a daughter, Annie, came along in 1887.[4] Dr. Schilling practiced out of his home until 1890.

Mrs. Linna Gaillard Schilling

He built an office very close to his home in 1890 and practiced in this office building until his death on September 20, 1919. His son John also became a doctor and a trained surgeon. He left his father's office after the death of his father to set up a practice in Houston, Texas. Dr. Nicholas Schilling's single daughter lived in the old home place on Cedar Bayou until her death in 1966.[5]

Dr. Schilling and his family were very unusual people. They kept meticulous records of everything they did and never threw anything away. After the death of her father, Annie kept everything as before, and the building sat unused from 1919 until her own death on February 8, 1966.[6]

Dr. Schilling's office building was built by himself and local workmen. One of his notes later found in the building contained the names of the workmen, the hours worked, the type of work done, and the payment. The named workers were J.S. Brooks, Sam Brooks, A. Hanson, Gordon Braun, George Wright and Willie Miller.[7]

The building is a two-story, board and batten structure built mainly of long-leaf yellow pine with some cypress. It was originally built on piers but was placed on concrete blocks after it was moved to Anahuac. There were three rooms downstairs. One small room contained a pot-bellied stove; a second room served as Dr. Schilling's pharmaceutical storeroom where he kept and compounded his medicines. This room is lined with shelves for various bottles and containers. The pharmaceuticals give us an insight into the pharmacology unavailable to doctors

Dr. Schilling's office, now a museum in Anahuac, Texas

a hundred years ago. While the contents have dried up or degenerated, the labels tell their story. Some of the drug companies are still in business today. A sink was connected to a water supply from a cistern.

The third and larger room was used for his practice and contained instruments, splints, bandages, and other supplies in addition to a dental chair. Upstairs was a large attic room, reached by a stairway, which contained Dr. Schilling's books and journals. The house was painted barn-red with a lighter trim.

The most dramatic remains of this medical genealogical treasure house are to be found in the Chambers County Archives. File cabinets are literally packed with Dr. Schilling's small, almost identical notebooks containing all his medical notes. While time has deteriorated these records somewhat, they are generally neatly written and are still easy to read. As we peruse these records, we repeatedly come across the names of pioneers in Chambers County who sought the services of this physician for a variety of problems. Doctor Schilling's life and practice are detailed in these notes, although they are not always complete as is typical for rapidly written notes of this type. At times the notes leave us wondering if he intended to return to write more, and very frequently new sentences are begun without any punctuation marks. Some abbreviations of medicines leave considerable uncertainly as to what was actually used, and the notes are somewhat cryptic on occasions. Spelling was also not always accurate.

These records reveal an ability to examine a patient physically with minimal laboratory tests and no x-rays or other elaborate diagnostic tools other than a keen ability to observe physical and mental signs and symptoms. The "hands on" approach to diagnosis and treatment inform us that a skillful physician can tell much without elaborate testing. The records also sadden us as we see many disease processes, easily recognized and cured today, which in those days cost much in human suffering and death because of the absence of modern medicine, diagnostic and therapeutic tools.

On September 5, 1888, Mrs. Sollomon Barrow, whose home was frequented by both Dr. Ashbel Smith from the "Evergreen" Plantation at what is now Baytown close to the Fred Hartman Bridge and by Amos Barber of "Barbers Hill,"

> Has a loose cartilage in the right knee first gave her trouble about 3 years ago and about a year ago it slipped out and she returned it did not trouble her till yesterday she reached over forward and it slipped out to the inside and near the patella she always slipped it back without much trouble but this time she did not get it back right it hurt her very much the pain was about like a cramp. We gave her chloroform and tried to replace we could not detect anything out of place in the joint but she complained of pain as much after as she did before we gave her the chloroform. We will give her, a bottle of Liniment (white) and som morphine powders to take to relieve pain and keep a bandage on the knee—to keep it quiet."[8]

This example sounds very much like a fractured medial meniscus. In another example, on April 26, 1889, Mr. H.H. Gillette

Was taken with severe pain in the left side on Tuesday the 23rd. he coughs som and spits ups bloody mucus Pneumonic expectoration, the left side lower part of lung is dull to percussion more resonant higher up but on the back at the lower angle of the shoulderblade ther is some cours mucus rales and we finde a dry blowing sound in the upper right lob, he has been nauseated som has much thirst and vomited som bullious matter. We left him some Muriate Ammonia cough mixture and quinine capsules. To take the first two hours apart and the second or capsule 4 hours apart. We left at 2 AM 27 and returned at 2 PM and find him wet with perspiration tongue coated with a thick white [large area unable to read] has terpentine applied to the chest it burnt rather severe and he cut up about it for quite a while but after he quieted he went to sleep and when he woke up we gave a dose of Muriate ammon. and Digitalis and some beef soup the Temperature was 100 at 5:30 he was quite wet with perspiration and rather drowsy—at 5:40 we gave him a little more soup—during the night he was very restless and had high fever with much opression and this morning The 28th Sunday he is quite sore the left side is not expanding much is dull the breathing is don by the right lung, the P.100. Mr. Kipp and Mr. Mitchell were up with him during the night the Kidneys act and he has thirst the temperature is still 100—along about 12 o'clock we find the Pulse intermittent the pulse was weak and would skip a beat every 20 to 30 beats we gave him a dose of Whiskey every hour for 3 doses and gave him a dose of Belladonna. He is resting som also seems som weaker than he has been yet and has spells of greater opression—we had a poultice placed on the left lung and applied Croton oil to get up som counter irritation along with the Iodine. At 4 oclock he complained of severe pain in the side clear down to the hip. The skin was dry we gave him a dose of about 1/12 gr Tartar Emetic and 15 drops Tincture of Opium with 1 drop of Ext. Belledonna—at about 5 30/ The skin was hot Temperatur

101 —som friction sound on left side also over the region of the breast the Pleura and the Pericardium [another short section is unreadable] at 6/00 we place blister plaster on the side below the nipple. A little before 8 pm we gave a dose of murial ammonia and 1 Drop Ext Belladonna—At about 10 P.M. the hands got cool and he was restless and more delerious we gave him Toddy in a full dose then a spoonful every half hour at 11:30 the kidneys acted—and he slept som longer breathed free. At about 5:30 A.M. 29th we removed the blister plaster and opened it and used a Poultice over it we gave a teaspoonful of strong Toddy every half hour during the night. When he was not sleeping at about 10 oclock A.M. we find the temperature 100 under the right arm the tongue is coated and red around the edges and is dry. The P. 110 is quite rapid and weak we gave him some more toddy in double size of his usual doses and applied a fly blister to the right side of the chest at 10:45 we gave a dose of nux vomica and Toddy. he is sinking rather fast in strength and minde—we also gave a dose of quinine and calomel early this morning. At 11 R 3 7 at 12:20 he got quite restless and his hands and feet cold the breathing is more shallow, we raised him up in bed on more pillows and got him quieted down he went to sleep for a few minutes. We sent to have Dr. Geo. Smith to see him advised more whiskey in form of eggnog—teaspoonful every 5 minutes he at first could not swallow it but after a few trials he got it down. At 3:15 he began to gasp for breath and died in half an hour[9]

The notebooks contain a day and night vigil, for an infant, that began on November 21, 1893 and culminated in the death of the child thirteen days later. A short course of antibiotics today would probably convert such an ordeal into a brief afternoon visit to the doctor's office. The prolonged care of such a child would not have cost more than $25, during a period when land in that area is known to have gone for as little as twenty-five cents an acre. The books of Dr. Schilling's practice contained literally thousands of such cases.

Shelves of pharmaceuticals in Dr. Schilling's office as can be seen today, one hundred years after their use.

A photograph showing more detail of pharmaceuticals.

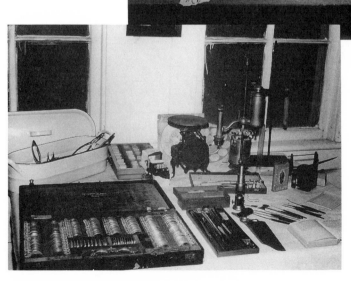

Lens case and instruments from Dr. Schilling's office.

One of the hundreds of identical notebooks in which Dr. Schilling recorded his cases in extreme detail.

Dr. Schilling's notebook open to the death note he wrote after the death of Ashbel Smith.

Even though this author has not seen any documentation as to his training, Dr. Schilling was a founding member of a major surgical organization. Another physician who practiced in this area was required by circumstance to practice general medicine; Dr. Ashbel Smith, who was the first Surgeon General of the Republic of Texas having been appointed to that position by his drinking companion President Sam Houston, was an extremely well trained physician and surgeon having had post graduate training in France. It is noted that settlements and social advancement did not occur as early in the southern portions of the United States when compared with the eastern seaboard. In 1800 and shortly afterward, the pirate Jean Lefitte was still rolling his barrels over Galveston Island. Dr. Ashbel Smith wrote the first medical treatise in 1839 in Texas when he took care of the yellow fever epidemic in Galveston, practicing medicine in a "hospital" which was little more than a shack. It was there that Dr. Smith tasted the "Black Bile" and narrowly missed its association with mosquitoes.

Dr. Smith fought and was an officer on the side of the Confederacy and also cared for Sam Houston's son who fought for the Confederacy while his father, Governor and former U.S. Senator and President of the Republic of Texas, refused to support the Southern cause and was removed as governor of Texas for refusing to sign the oath of allegiance to the Confederacy. Many historians regard Sam Houston as one of the bravest and most independent thinking men to ever live in the South. John F. Kennedy chose him as one of his profiles of courage. And yet Sam Houston trusted the life of his son, as well as the life of his wife on whom Smith performed breast surgery, to this strong supporter of the confederacy. Columnist Lynn Ashby of the *Houston Post* spoke of Dr. Ashbel Smith.

> He was a Connecticut Yankee who became a General in the confederate Army. Between battles he read Latin and for his own amusement in 1881 he gave the commencement address at the Texas Medical School and Hospital in Galveston completely in Latin. He helped start the University of Texas Medical College at Galveston and what became the Texas Medical Association.

This great man's practice also included patients along the shores of Cedar Bayou.

Dr. Nicholas Schilling, the Yankee, was called to the home of Colonel Ashbel Smith, the Rebel, on January 18, 1886. After his service in the Civil War it is said that Smith frequently used the title "Colonel," possibly in deference to those young men who served under him and lost their life. The notes in the care of this great physician are delineated on three pages of the progress notes of Dr. Nicholas Schilling beginning with the caption "Col. Ashbel Smith" and listing, as with his other patients great and humble, the medications that were administered and the responses, and culminating in the statement, "he died at 1:17 o'clock am January 21, 1886. The heart stopped acting and he passed off without a struggle, Mr. J.C. Massey being with him at the time." Dr. Nicholas Schilling did not enjoy the public honor that followed Dr. Ashbel Smith but contributed just as much though in a different way. While Dr. Nicholas Schilling did not enjoy the political influence and high positions of leadership, it is doubtful that any physician in this country has left such a profound legacy of personal and profession effects and records of a nineteenth-century medical practice as that which can be seen in the office of this great pioneer in Anahuac, Texas.

The following letter could easily be related to the Second World War or perhaps to any war. However this is a letter from an old Civil "war buddy," Calmar McCune of Stromsburg, Nebraska. Both of these gentlemen were in their seventies, and the letter was written in 1919 barely six months before the death of Nicholas Schilling. These two gentlemen fought on the side of the Union in the Civil War.

> I was glad to get your letter of March 16 and to know that good health and thankfulness abounded the Schilling domicile. I only wish that I could say the same for the McCune home. Mrs. McCune is far from well and feels more discouraged than she has ever felt. The specialist has diagnosed her trouble as hardening of the arteries leading from the heart. At times she becomes very weak and is deprived of her accustomed outdoor exercise which has been the very breath of life to her.

She is to have another examination by another specialist tomorrow. Naturally I can't feel very comfortable with her in her present condition. Your son may get home sooner than you expected when you wrote. I see that the Germans have been invited to meet with the "Peace Council" on the 25th. If there are no very serious disagreements peace should be proclaimed soon and then the Americans can come home as rapidly as ships can be provided to bring them. I am sure you folks will be glad to welcome him. With the experience gained in the field he will be better equipped than ever for his life work.

I note that you hanker for the 'good old days.' They are gone, my dear old friend, just as our youth is gone, never to return. As to the graft of the present day we must not forget that there was plenty of it during and following the [Civil] war-as much probably in proportion to opportunity as now. The curse of the human race is selfishness and greed. We could have the millennium tomorrow if all men would adopt the doctrine of fair play which is only another name for the 'golden rule.' Modern industrialism has given to greed greater opportunities for plunder thus made it more dangerous. It must therefore be curbed by force or persuasion or it will result in a universal uprising that will destroy modern civilization.[10]

The State of Texas placed a permanent metal plaque in front of the restored office of Dr. Schilling. Dr. Nicholas Schilling was an effective, faithful physician who spent his life in service to his patients. Probably, he was no different than many other doctors of his time. The important features of his life are the voluminous notebooks which detail his medical practice in an unsurpassed record which gives us a clear picture of the profession of medicine in a rural environment in the later part of the nineteenth century. Likewise, his preserved office and pharmacy give an accurate record of the equipment and drugs used at the time.

Dr. Nicholas Schilling has achieved a place in the medical history of Texas.

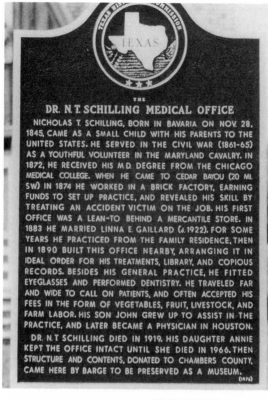

THE

DR. N. T. SCHILLING MEDICAL OFFICE

NICHOLAS T. SCHILLING, BORN IN BAVARIA ON NOV. 28, 1845, CAME AS A SMALL CHILD WITH HIS PARENTS TO THE UNITED STATES. HE SERVED IN THE CIVIL WAR (1861-65) AS A YOUTHFUL VOLUNTEER IN THE MARYLAND CAVALRY. IN 1872, HE RECEIVED HIS M.D. DEGREE FROM THE CHICAGO MEDICAL COLLEGE. WHEN HE CAME TO CEDAR BAYOU (20 MI. SW) IN 1874 HE WORKED IN A BRICK FACTORY, EARNING FUNDS TO SET UP PRACTICE, AND REVEALED HIS SKILL BY TREATING AN ACCIDENT VICTIM ON THE JOB. HIS FIRST OFFICE WAS A LEAN-TO BEHIND A MERCANTILE STORE. IN 1883 HE MARRIED LINNA E. GAILLARD (d. 1922). FOR SOME YEARS HE PRACTICED FROM THE FAMILY RESIDENCE, THEN IN 1890 BUILT THIS OFFICE NEARBY, ARRANGING IT IN IDEAL ORDER FOR HIS TREATMENTS, LIBRARY, AND COPIOUS RECORDS. BESIDES HIS GENERAL PRACTICE, HE FITTED EYEGLASSES AND PERFORMED DENTISTRY. HE TRAVELED FAR AND WIDE TO CALL ON PATIENTS, AND OFTEN ACCEPTED HIS FEES IN THE FORM OF VEGETABLES, FRUIT, LIVESTOCK, AND FARM LABOR. HIS SON JOHN GREW UP TO ASSIST IN THE PRACTICE, AND LATER BECAME A PHYSICIAN IN HOUSTON.

DR. N. T. SCHILLING DIED IN 1919. HIS DAUGHTER ANNIE KEPT THE OFFICE INTACT UNTIL SHE DIED IN 1966. THEN STRUCTURE AND CONTENTS, DONATED TO CHAMBERS COUNTY, CAME HERE BY BARGE TO BE PRESERVED AS A MUSEUM.

(1976)

The metal plaque placed in front of the office of Dr. Nicholas Schilling.

ENDNOTES

1. Medical and Surgical Register of the United States and Canada, Fifth revised edition 1898.

2. George Ellender (born in 1888 and acquaintance of Dr. Schilling), personal interview with Villamae Williams, Baytown, Texas, October 16, 1975.

3. Roberta West, personal interview with Villamae Williams of Baytown, Texas, a friend and companion of Miss Annie Schilling, daughter of Dr. Nicholas Schilling.

4. Chambers County Archives. Schilling, Nicholas T. Papers, notes, 1980.

5. Mrs. Edward L. Scott of Baytown, Texas, telephone interview October 14, 1975. Mrs. Scott was a patient of Dr. Nicholas Schilling.

6. West, interview, op. cit.

7. Schilling, Chambers County Archives, op. cit., Notes, Labor on building.

8. Amos Papers. A collection of unpublished papers 1836-1910 of the Amos Barber family. Original is in the files of the Chambers County Archives, Office of the Chambers County clerk, Anahuac, Texas.

9. Nicholas Schilling, Notebook, April 26, 1889 (in Dr. Schilling's office).

10. Calmar McCune, Personal letter from Stromsburg, Nebraska, to Dr. Nicholas Schilling, 1919.

BIOGRAPHICAL SKETCH OF AUTHOR

DR. DREW DAVIS WILLIAMS completed thirty-five years of general surgical practice at Baytown, Texas, in 1995. He has served as president of the Singleton Surgical Society and the Houston Surgical Society (1994) and was secretary-treasurer of the Texas State Board of Medical Examiners from 1985 until 1988, being elected unanimously, and served as president of the agency in 1988-90. He is board certified by the American Board of Surgery and the American Board of Quality Assurance and Utilization Review Physicians. He has served as president of Medical Staff and chairman of the Surgery Department at San Jacinto Methodist Hospital in Baytown and was liaison for the Commission on Cancer to the hospital for almost ten years. He is a senior member of the Texas Surgical Society. He has membership in the Texas Medical Association and Southern Medical Association and served twice on the executive board of the Harris County Medical Society at Houston, where he was chairman of the Council of Medical Specialties representing the presidents of twenty-one medical specialty societies with a total of five thousand physicians. He has been president of the East Harris County Medical Society and the Baytown Chapter of the American Cancer Society. He is a member of the Texas Medical Foundation and serves as a review source for other federal groups.

In his genealogical activities, he is a Life Member of the Sons of the Republic of Texas, past president and present secretary-treasurer of the Major White Chapter of the Texas Society of the Sons of the American Revolution, member of the Descendants of the Colonial Clergy and the Somerset Chapter of the Magna Charta Barons Society, the Colonial Order of the Crown (lineal descent from the Emperor Charlemagne) and the Sovereign Colonial Society Americans of Royal Descent.

He has membership in Phi Kappa Phi Scholastic Honor Society and has been listed since 1990 in Marquis *Who's Who in America* and *Who's Who in the World*. He has authored articles in multiple fields and delivered hundreds of lectures in medicine, religion and a few in politics.

He served on active duty during the Cuban Conflict as a Naval Flight Surgeon and was a commissioned officer in both the U.S. Naval Reserve and the United States Public Health Service retiring as a lieutenant commander from the Navy.

He is a 32d degree Scottish Rite Mason and Knight Templar of the York Rite and a member of the Arabia Shrine and Baytown Shrine Club. His membership includes the Gideons International, the Democratic Party and membership and lay minister of the Church of Christ.

He presently works full time as an instructor in the Department of Preventive Medicine in the University of Texas Medical Branch and as a Medical Director for the Department of Corrections. He and his wife of forty years live in Baytown as he writes his memoirs and harasses his five grown children-three school teachers, one computer programmer and one manager for a computer firm. Most of all he enjoys gardening and spoiling his three grandchildren.

Ashbel Smith at age seventy-three.
Courtesy Archives Division, Texas State Library.

Ashbel Smith, M.D.
1805-1886
by
Martin L. Dalton, M.D.

★ FEW MEN HAVE HAD THE OPPORTUNITY and the capacity to make the contributions to Texas as did Doctor Ashbel Smith. A listing of his contributions as compared to almost any other Texan would almost certainly place him in a unique position. Arriving in Texas at the age of thirty-two, Dr. Smith literally dedicated the remainder of his adult life to Texas. He has been described as a scholar, linguist, diplomat, soldier, statesman, scientist, physician, editor, writer, farmer, rancher, philosopher, educator and humanitarian. Clearly, an examination of this great man's life is a cheerful duty that should be performed by every Texan.

Ashbel was born to Moses Smith, Jr., and his second wife, Phoebe Adams Smith on August 13, 1805, in Hartford, Connecticut.[1] As was customary, the first born son received a biblical name, and the unusual name "Ashbel" was selected from the Bible (the Ashbelites were one of the tribes of Benjamin). Ashbel was a frail child and early in life developed a lifelong susceptibility to pulmonary and gastrointestinal illnesses. The fortunate aspect of this trait is that he developed a love of reading during these enforced confinements indoors that engendered the scholarly activity that was to characterize his life. After completing his early education at the Hartford Grammar School, he entered the Yale School of Liberal Arts and received his degree and Phi Beta Kappa key in 1824. Unable to decide on his life's calling at the tender age of nineteen, he accepted a teaching position in Salisbury, North Carolina, and remained there until 1826. He decided to study medicine and returned to Yale, where he received his M.D. degree in 1828.

Later that same year, he returned to Salisbury to practice medicine. Despite the development of a large and successful practice, he decided that he needed additional surgical training. At that time, Paris was the premier surgical training center, and in late October 1831 he arrived there and was privileged to study under Baron Guillaume Dupuytren, Baron Dominique Jean Larrey and Rene Laennec.[2] He attended lectures and observed numerous operations at the Hotel Dieu, the Necker Hospital and the Ecole De Medicine. Not only did Ashbel hone his surgical skills, but he also used the time to perfect his French which, unknown to him at the time, would be extremely useful in his later service to Texas as Minister to France. While in Paris he also made some outstanding American connections by spending a great deal of time with Samuel F. B. Morse and James Fenimore Cooper. He also became attracted to Cooper's daughter, Susan.

Ashbel returned to Salisbury, North Carolina, in September 1832 and resumed his medical practice. Once again his practice was extremely successful; he enjoyed a generous income and acquired both property and slaves. He continued to entertain thoughts of matrimony with Susan Cooper, but in 1835 he met the real love of his life, Mary Louisa Phifer. He proposed marriage to Mary, but her response was ambiguous. Unfortunately, later that year, Mary gave Ashbel a definite "no" which led to moderate depression and a general unhappiness with his life in Salisbury. Following this disappointment, Ashbel decided on a lengthy trip through the southeastern United States and spent a great deal of time in New Orleans where he met many individuals en route to Texas in the spring of 1836. One of his new friends, James Pinckney Henderson, a fellow North Carolinian, was soon appointed Secretary of State of the new Republic of Texas. It was Henderson who persuaded Ashbel to come to Texas. He arrived in Houston on May 9, 1837.[3] It was extremely good fortune that one of the first people he met was the President of the Republic, Sam Houston. Ashbel actually moved into the log cabin which served as the presidential home and shared the same bedroom with Sam Houston. In the summer of 1837, when Houston suffered a serious illness, Dr. Ashbel Smith was his physician. Perhaps in repayment for this favor, as well as his high regard for Ashbel, Houston appointed him as Surgeon General of the Texas Army on June 7, 1837.[4] With his characteristic penchant for organization, the new surgeon general proceeded to organize thoroughly the medical affairs of the Army of the Republic of Texas. During this military interval, Ashbel wore a "made-to-order sword to be carried on horseback" and was described as "short in stature and long in dignity."[5] He has also been described as an "unusual man . . . only five feet two inches tall and of ugly countenance."[6] In his capacity as surgeon general, Smith also became good friends with many other prominent Texans of the time, including Mirabeau B. Lamar, Anson Jones and David Burnet. This group of friends founded the Philosophical Society of Texas in December 1837 and Ashbel Smith was elected first vice president.

In early 1838 Ashbel was sent to Washington, D.C., by President Houston to purchase medical supplies for the Texan Army. He had an audience with President Martin Van Buren and also met with Senator John C. Calhoun. Returning to Texas, he supported Martin Van Buren for the presidency and, upon Lamar's election, Smith was reappointed surgeon general. Shortly thereafter, the first of several reactionary episodes occurred in the life of Ashbel Smith. His tempestuous demeanor and his quick temper led him to inflict a horse whipping on a fellow physician, Senator Stephen H. Everitt. The politically engendered debate centered upon Dr. Everitt's calling Dr. Smith a liar, which precipitated the use of the horsewhip. Fortunately, he resisted using his Bowie knife and pistol. Shortly thereafter, to avoid further embarrassment to President Lamar, Smith resigned as surgeon general.[7]

Out of office and no doubt dejected and disappointed, Ashbel sought solace in Galveston where he moved his medical practice in 1839. Opportunity and excitement seemed to follow him, and his move to Galveston was no exception. In September 1839 an epidemic of yellow fever broke out in Galveston and Dr. Smith was involved from the outset. Although he failed to recognize the importance of the mosquito vector, he did realize the city of Galveston was remiss in not paying more attention to basic cleanliness. Ashbel Smith observed and treated numerous cases of yellow fever, and his clinical description of the disease process was incredibly accurate and precise. He later published his experiences.[8] This was the first significant medical publication to originate in Texas.

Ashbel Smith continued his successful practice in Galveston and began to think of Galveston as his home. He acquired several additional slaves and built a log house on Galveston Bay which he called "Headquarters." Meanwhile the capitol had been moved to Austin and, following the two-year term of Mirabeau B. Lamar, Sam Houston was once again elected president and took the oath of office in December 1841. At this time, the principal concern of President Houston was the relationship of Texas with England and France. Simply stated, if annexation with the United States did not materialize, the future of the Republic of Texas lay in the procurement of strong relations with England and France. Seeking a knowledgeable and intelligent minister with fluency in the French language, Houston turned to the only logical candidate, his old friend, Ashbel Smith.

Ashbel reluctantly relinquished his practice and comfortable living in Galveston and sailed for England March 15, 1842. Surprisingly, he encountered a virulent anti-Texas mood in England stemming primarily from anti-slavery political activity. The British and Foreign Anti-Slavery Society was enjoying tremendous popularity; slavery had been abolished many years earlier in England. As minister to both England and France, Smith shuttled back and forth between London and Paris. He met with Lord Aberdeen, Foreign Secretary, and was eventually presented to Queen Victoria. President Houston, sensing that Ashbel might be intimidated by British tradition, conferred knighthood of the Order of San Jacinto on Smith, who became "Sir Ashbel." Eventually, the efforts of Minister Smith met with success, and on June 24, 1844, Lord Aberdeen proposed that the British and French governments "unite with Texas in a Diplomatic Act that would ensure peace and settle boundaries between Texas and Mexico and guarantee the separate independence of Texas."[9] Once the full ramifications of this significant treaty were known to President Houston, he directed Secretary of State Anson Jones, who was also the President Elect of the Republic of Texas, to instruct Smith to conclude the "Diplomatic Act" as soon as possible. For reasons that remain unclear, Anson Jones did not convey this instruction to Ashbel Smith. Consequently, the "Diplomatic Act" was never consummated.[10]

In December 1844 Anson Jones became President of the Republic of Texas, appointed Ashbel Smith as his Secretary of State, and ordered him home. Smith returned to Texas in February 1845 to find "annexation fever" in full swing throughout the Republic. On February 28, 1845, the US congress passed a joint resolution for the annexation of Texas. President Jones was not opposed to annexation but felt that, prior to making a decision, every effort should be made to explore the possibilities of a lasting treaty with England and France which would guarantee the independence of the Republic of Texas. With this in mind, he quickly dispatched Ashbel Smith to London on May 1, 1845.[11] Smith also visited Paris once again, but both the English and French had perceived that the opportunity for the "Diplomatic Act" was lost and that Texas would soon be annexed to the United State of America. On December 29, 1845, President James K. Polk signed the act of annexation and Texas became the twenty-eighth state. Because of his perceived secret negotiations with England and France, Ashbel Smith was out of favor with his fellow Texans and on at least one occasion was burned in effigy. He was present in Austin on February 19, 1846, when President Anson Jones turned over the Republic of Texas to the Governor of Texas, James Pinckney Henderson.

Mexico was quick to react to the annexation of Texas, and the Mexican War began in May 1846. Ashbel quickly joined the Texas Volunteers and served under General Zachary Taylor.[12] Shortly thereafter, on a hot day in July, he suffered an "apoplectic" seizure, followed by generalized weakness. He requested leave and returned to "Headquarters" on the Galveston Bay. During his convalescence, he visited Washington and had an audience with President Polk and then went to Hartford to spend some time with his parents. He also visited Salisbury and found time to propose to an old acquaintance, Margaret Johnston, who refused. Ashbel was certainly not a bachelor by choice.

Dr. Smith resumed his medical practice in Galveston early in 1847. He attempted to limit his practice to surgery and performed surgical procedures on some famous Texans. He did a "breast amputation" on Margaret Houston, the wife of Sam, and a hemorrhoidectomy on John Hemphill, the Chief Justice

Evergreen Plantation, the home of Ashbel Smith on Galveston Bay.
Courtesy Archives Division, Texas State Library.

of the Texas Supreme Court.[13] Later that year, another yellow
fever epidemic struck Galveston; this time Ashbel was not so
lucky and acquired the dreadful disease himself. During his
recuperation at "Headquarters," he purchased some adjoining
acreage from the "Evergreen" plantation of his neighbor, Moseley Baker. Eventually, after the death of Baker, Ashbel combined
"Headquarters" and "Evergreen" into his own plantation which
he then called "Evergreen."

In January 1848, Ashbel and nine other Galveston physi-
cians formed the Medical and Surgical Society of Galveston.[14]
This organization would prove to be the precursor of the Texas
Medical Association. Later in 1848, Smith attended the third
annual meeting of the American Medical Association as an
official delegate. In June 1848 he was appointed to the US
Military Academy Board of Visitors by Senator Sam Houston.
He participated in the annual examinations at West Point and
gave the commencement address to the graduating class of 1848.
While in New York, he was asked to speak on yellow fever at
the meeting of the New York Academy of Medicine. Continuing

in this scholarly vein, Ashbel Smith delivered the annual address to the Yale Chapter of Phi Beta Kappa in August 1849.

Not all of the activities of Ashbel Smith during this period were scholarly—many involved his interest in investments. In 1838, in his capacity as surgeon general, Ashbel came to know Gail Borden, the Customs Collector at Galveston. The men maintained contact for many years and, in 1850 after Mr. Borden had patented his "meat biscuit," Ashbel Smith became a principal investor. The idea of the meat biscuit was to supply preservable food for travelers and the military. In 1851 Dr. Smith represented Texas at the Great Council Exhibition in London and served on a committee that awarded a gold medal to Gail Borden for his invention of the meat biscuit.[15] Shortly thereafter, the US army rejected a contract to supply meat biscuits and Ashbel decided he no longer could continue to invest with Mr. Borden. This was most unfortunate, because shortly thereafter Gail Borden perfected evaporated milk and thereby made a fortune in an enterprise which Dr. Smith did not share. This proved to be a lifelong disappointment to Ashbel Smith.

Following his participation in the Great Council Exhibition at the Crystal Palace in London, Ashbel returned to the United States in October 1851. Early in 1852 he was asked to be superintendent of the first state fair of Texas. The fair was held in Corpus Christi in May and was moderately successful. In June 1852, through the influence of Senator Houston, Ashbel Smith was elected vice-president of the Committee on Organization for the National Convention of the Democratic Party. In January 1853 he attended the organizational meeting for a state medical association held in Austin.[16] Ashbel Smith was instrumental in drafting the constitution and by-laws of the Texas Medical Association at that meeting.

Interwoven with all of his political and international activities, Dr. Smith continued to practice medicine in Galveston and to supervise the day-to-day activities of his ever-enlarging plantation. In 1855 he was elected as a representative from Harris County to the Texas Legislature. Significantly, he was placed on the "Slaves and Slavery Committee" because of his well-known view that the United States did not have the power to regulate slavery in the states. After the election of Abraham Lincoln in 1860, the sentiment in Texas was overwhelmingly in favor of joining the newly formed Confederate States of America and on March 2, 1861, Texas seceded from the Union. Despite his age of fifty-five, Ashbel enlisted and was appointed Captain of the Bayland Guards. The Bayland Guards were assigned to the Second Texas Infantry who ultimately saw action at Shiloh and Vicksburg. At Shiloh on April 6, 1862, newly promoted Lieutenant Colonel Ashbel Smith led a charge in which half of his men were wounded or killed and he was shot in the right axilla.[17] This resulted in an extremely painful wound and he was sent to a hospital in Memphis for recuperation. He ultimately returned to Texas to recruit additional volunteers for the Confederacy and was promoted to colonel in December 1862. In April 1863 he was involved in the siege of Vicksburg, where the Confederates were outnumbered ten to one. The siege of Vicksburg ended in surrender on July 4, 1863, to General U.S. Grant. The men of the Second Texas were paroled and Ashbel was able to return to Texas only to learn that his close friend and confidant, Sam Houston had recently died.

In August 1864 Colonel Smith assumed command of the confederate troops on Galveston Island only to be involved once again with a yellow fever epidemic. He became quite ill, probably with recurrent malaria rather than yellow fever, and was fortunate to survive. In May 1865 he was appointed a commissioner to represent the State of Texas in peace negotiations with the Union Army in New Orleans. In October 1865 he took the oath of allegiance to the United States, received amnesty and returned to Harris County where he was elected once again to the House of Representatives of the State of Texas. Doubtless, his cool demeanor and keen intellect were instrumental in steering Texas through the difficult period of reconstruction following the Civil War. He also felt that the time had come in his life when he should resume his role as gentleman farmer. He began to experiment with all sorts of livestock and numerous agricultural ventures, including the culture of grapes and potatoes. He also set up a winemaking enterprise which was moderately successful. In 1871 he planted cotton, which proved to be extremely successful, and gained quite a reputation as an agricultural advisor to his fellow Texans.

Having been spurned by several suitors, Ashbel began to think less and less about matrimony. However, his love for children continued and he was pleased to assist in the founding of the Bayland Orphans Home for Children of Confederate Soldiers. He became the physician for the orphanage, which was across Galveston Bay from Evergreen. Ultimately he was attracted to eleven-year-old Anna Allen, whom he moved to Evergreen because she needed eye treatment twice daily. Eventually she became a permanent resident and referred to him as "Uncle Ashbel."

Anna Allen, age eleven, adopted by Ashbel Smith in 1873. Courtesy University of Texas at Austin

In 1874 Ashbel Smith was elected to the Harris County School Board and, at the first meeting of the Board, was elected superintendent. This began the last major phase of his long and productive life, during which he made numerous valuable contributions to education in Texas. At the venerable age of seventy, Ashbel was asked to deliver a speech at the annual meeting of the Galveston Historical Society on December 15, 1975. This address, "Reminiscences of the Texas Republic" was published the following year by the Historical Society of Galveston.[18] This is probably the most significant of all his publications. This first-hand account of the history of the Republic of Texas is an extremely valuable reference. Certainly no one knew the principal participants any better than Ashbel Smith. He dealt fairly with each of the principals, and if there is a fault it is his tendency to overlook the character flaws that characterized many of the early Texans. During this time, and commensurate with his advancing age, he

Bust of Ashbel Smith which stands in front of the original medical school building at the University of Texas Medical Branch in Galveston. The Ashbel Smith Building is affectionately known as "Old Red" due to the crimson coloration of its exterior brick wall. Courtesy the Moody Medical Library, The University of Texas Medical Branch at Galveston.

dedicated more time to his plantation than to his medical practice. He became quite an authority on all of the planted crops in Texas as well as in raising horned cattle, pigs, sheep and goats. He contributed frequently to the agricultural literature in journals such as the *New England Farmer* and the *Boston Ploughman*. He represented Texas at the Paris International Exposition in 1878. Upon his return, he unfortunately suffered yet another attack of fever, most likely malaria.

Dr. Smith became President of the Board of Trustees of the Texas Medical College and Hospital in Galveston and was asked

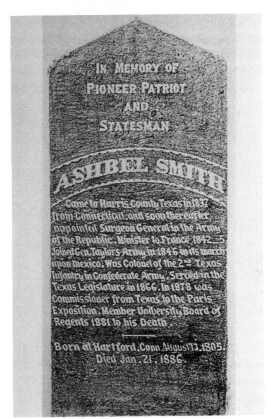

Gravestone marker of Ashbel Smith at the State Cemetery in Austin. Courtesy Texas A&M University Press.

to present the diplomas at the 1880 graduation ceremony. This was repeated in 1881. Despite his prior views on support of slavery, he encouraged the legislature to establish a school for "colored youth." In 1876, the Texas Legislature established the "Agricultural and Mechanical College of Texas, for the Benefit of Colored Youths,"[19] eventually renamed "Prairie View State Normal School." Similarly, in the same year the Texas Legislature established the Agricultural and Mechanical College of Texas at Bryan. However, it was not until 1881 that the University of Texas was established. Shortly thereafter, Governor Oran Roberts selected Austin as the site of the University of Texas and appointed Smith to the Board of Regents. The Board elected Ashbel Smith its president, and he was able to exert his influence to locate the Medical Division of the University of Texas in Galveston. Unfortunately, a decade would pass before these plans came to fruition.

Ashbel Smith was elected President of the Texas Medical Association in 1881 and used his presidential address in 1882 to further the cause of the University of Texas and its medical branch.[20] Subsequently, in November of that year a cornerstone was laid for the University of Texas. The University of Texas officially received students on September 15, 1883. A single student, Samuel Clark Red, was graduated in 1885. Smith as President of the University of Texas Board of Regents was truly joyful that he had lived to see this significant event in the history of Texas.

Ashbel grew weaker with increasing illnesses and the frailty accompanying his advanced age, and he was unable to attend the Texas Medical Association meeting in April 1885. For the remainder of his life, he was primarily secluded at Evergreen. His terminal illness began in early January of 1886 and his physician, Dr. Nicholas Schilling, diagnosed "bronchopleurisy." Ashbel Smith expired January 21, 1886, on a Thursday morning at 1:00 a.m. in his bed at Evergreen. Dr. Schilling stated "the heart stopped acting and he passed off without a struggle."[21]

Ashbel Smith's body lay in state in the Armory Hall in Houston prior to a train trip to Austin where his body once again lay in state for several days prior to burial at the State Cemetery in Austin.[22] His principal biographer, Elizabeth Silverthorne, summarized the many paradoxes of his life, "The Yankee Rebel, the hot-tempered diplomat, the gregarious loner, the idealistic politician, the home loving rover, the bachelor father, the slave owning humanitarian, and the peace loving soldier."[23]

ENDNOTES

1. W.P. Webb (ed.). *The Handbook of Texas* vol. 2 (Austin: The Texas State Historical Association, 1952), 620.

2. E. Silverthorne. *Ashbel Smith of Texas* (College Station: Texas A&M University Press, 1982), 8, 13, 20.

3. Ibid., 38.

4. Ashbel Smith Journal, April, May, 1837.

5. P.I. Nixon. *The Medical Story of Early Texas 1528-1853* (Austin: Mollie Bennett Lupe Memorial Fund, 1946), 430.

6. A.E. Rodin and A.O. Singleton, Jr. "Two Early Leaders: Medical Branch." *Texas Medicine* 63 (1967), 112-16.

7. Silverthorne, *Ashbel Smith*, op. cit., 54.

8. A. Smith. *Yellow Fever in Galveston, Republic of Texas, 1839* (Austin: University of Texas Press, 1951).

9. Silverthorne, *Ashbel Smith*, op. cit., 73, 93.

10. J.D. Lynch. "Life and Character of Dr. Ashbel Smith." *Daniel's Medical Journal* 1(10)(Austin 1886), 441-55.

11. A. Jones. *Memoranda and Official Correspondence Relating to the Republic of Texas, Its History and Annexation* (Chicago: The Rio Grande Press, 1966), 456.

12. Lynch, "Dr. Ashbel Smith," op. cit., 449.

13. Silverthorne, *Ashbel Smith*, op. cit., 107, 111.

14. Nixon, *Medical Story*, op. cit., 466.

15. J.B. Frantz. *Gail Borden, Dairy Man to a Nation* (Norman: University of Oklahoma Press, 1951), 212.

16. P.I. Nixon. *The History of the Texas Medical Association 1853-1953* (Austin: University of Texas Press, 1953), 8.

17. Silverthorne, *Ashbel Smith*, op. cit., 150.

18. A. Smith. *Reminiscences of the Texas Republic: Annual Address Delivered Before the Historical Society of Galveston December 15, 1875* (Galveston: Historical Society of Galveston, 1876).

19. Silverthorne, *Ashbel Smith*, op. cit., 194.

20. Nixon, op. cit., 97.

21. Nixon, op. cit., 231.

22. Lynch, "Dr. Ashbel Smith," op. cit., 455.

23. Silverthorne, *Ashbel Smith*, op. cit., 232.

BIOGRAPHICAL SKETCH OF AUTHOR

(see page 209)

James E. Thompson, M.B., B.S., F.R.C.S. (England).

James E. Thompson, M.B., B.S., F.R.C.S. (England)
1863-1927
by
Walter B. King, M.D.

★THE 1965 PUBLICATION OF *The Texas Surgical Society, The First Fifty Years* documented Dr. Thompson's influence on the formation of the Texas Surgical Society and described his term as its first president. The Society had only a newspaper copy of the first presidential address and no record of any other until Dr. A.O. Singleton's presentation in 1932. The original copy of Dr. Thompson's address with notes in his handwriting was discovered in his personal papers. A presidential address by Dr. K.H. Aynesworth of Waco in 1927, given as a memorial to Dr. Thompson, was also found. It was a beautiful tribute to his friend and teacher and was a valuable source of information. A copy is now in the archives of the Society.

Recorded information about James E. Thompson dates from before 1721 when a John Thompson owned a salt mine near Northwich, Cheshire, close to Manchester near the west coast of England. Taxes on salt greatly affected the history of the British Empire. Later, the River Weaver, which runs through Northwich, was made navigable so barges could transport salt to Liverpool and other ports. Dr. James E. Thompson's father, John, and his brothers took advantage of this situation and added a shipyard to the salt business. This combination prospered and the family home, "Riversdale," was built on the River Weaver near Northwich.

Originally, the mines produced rock salt, but in later years they were able to extract salt from the brine. A nearby mine

Presidential address read before first meeting of The Texas Surgical Society in San Antonio Oct 19, 1915

J E Thompson

Label of Thompson's Presidential Address.

owner sank a shaft underneath the Thompson property. Of course, this was many years before the slant-well scandal in East Texas, but it shows how few things there are that are original. John Thompson tunneled a trespassing shaft and obtained an inexhaustible supply of brine.

When the shipyard began to make steel ships, a younger Thompson brother was in charge of the riveting. The agents from Lloyd's Insurance inspected the six or seven ships being built and found that lead rivets had been used in all the hard-to-get-to places. The ships were condemned and the Thompson business became bankrupt.

John and Mary Thompson had eight living children. James E. Thompson, the youngest, was born at Riversdale on May 21, 1863. He learned to speak "correct" English without effort because he heard no other. Books which his ancestors had read were his daily companions. The old custom of an evening by the fireside with good literature was a part of the home life of his childhood. Culture and intellectual development came to him from the daily association in his home. He learned to love and appreciate the beauties of good literature, to enjoy music and sports, and to value intellectual and refined society.

His medical studies began at Owens College, Manchester, in 1881. His father wanted him to enter the family business and had consented to help him with his professional education, but the bankruptcy changed these plans. James went through medical school on scholarships and no sleep, which he described as "burning the candle at both ends." Many times he did not have enough to eat. The long hours of work without proper nutrition impaired his health and he developed pulmonary tuberculosis. This illness was a decisive factor in many of his future undertakings.

He was awarded numerous gold medals and scholarships. A cash award accompanied each. His family's financial condition made these necessary. He obtained a Bachelor of Medicine and of Surgery from the University of London, whose outstanding professors included the noted anatomist, Daniel J. Cunningham.

James was House Surgeon at the Royal Infirmary at Manchester in 1886. Following a trip to Calcutta as Ship Surgeon in 1888, he spent a year in Europe studying with the world's greatest surgeons, including Dr. Billroth. He passed the examination for Fellowship in the Royal College of Surgeons in England in 1889 and was then accepted as Resident Surgeon of the Manchester Royal Infirmary. This was a much-sought-after, busy, surgical teaching position. Tom W. Jones and Walter Whitehead were his superiors. As all eager residents do, Dr. Thompson kept a record of his operations. The list of cases shows that the "night-fighters" were busy in those days also; forty-four stab wounds and eleven cut throats were recorded.

At this time his future seemed bright. It was the beginning of the golden age of surgery in England. It was becoming a required custom that surgery be done only by those who had successfully passed the examination for Fellowship in the Royal College of Surgeons. James E. Thompson had obtained the highest surgical qualifications conferred in the United Kingdom.

In 1881 the Texas State Legislature again began plans to establish a University with a Medical Department. Austin was selected by popular vote as the site of the main university and the first class entered in 1883. Galveston was chosen as the site for the Medical Department. Funds to build a medical school did not materialize for another five years and operation did not begin until 1891, eight years after the main university.

The minutes of the University of Texas Regents for June 17, 1891, show that twenty-five dollars were appropriated to advertise existing teaching vacancies in medical journals in the United States and Europe. An advertisement appeared in *The British*

Medical Journal on June 27, 1891. This described the well-equipped building and the golden opportunity for those who would exchange the barren pavements of London for the riches of the Great West. Nine professors were to be chosen and the average salary was to be three thousand dollars a year. As a result of this notice the Board of Regents received a document labeled:

Letter of Application and Testimonials in Favour of:
James Edwin Thompson
M.B., B.S., (Lond. University with honors)
F.R.C.S. (England)
Resident Surgeon Manchester Royal Infirmary
Late Resident Surgeon, Guest Hospital, Dudley

Included were glowing testimonials from Drs. Walter Whitehead and Thomas W. Jones of England, Dr. Anton Von Eiselberg of the Billroth Clinic in Austria, and Dr. Edward Meyer of Paris. The record states that Dr. Thompson was selected by the Board of Regents for the Chair of Surgery from a list of eminent applicants.

The minutes of the Board of Regents on August 26, 1891, lists Dr. J.M.T. Finney as Professor of Surgery and Chemical Surgery at the Medical Branch. Dr. Finney did not accept this position and mentioned this fact to Dr. Singleton many years later. Dr. Finney's autobiography stated that he considered himself too young and inexperienced and decided to stay at Hopkins. Although Johns Hopkins Hospital had been established, the Medical School did not open until 1893, two years after the Medical Branch in Galveston.

Dr. James E. Thompson accepted the Chair of Surgery and Chemical Surgery at a salary of three thousand dollars a year. *Daniel's Texas Medical Journal* in October 1891 listed the information about Dr. Finney and Dr. Thompson. The original faculty members were:

Dr. J.F.Y. Paine, Professor of Obstetrics & Gynecology and Dean.
Dr. Seth M. Morris, Professor of Chemistry and Toxicology.
Dr. William Keiller, Professor of Anatomy.

Dr. Edward Randall, Professor of Materia Medica & Therapeutics.

Dr. Allen J. Smith, Professor of Pathology.

Dr. Albert G. Clopton, Professor of Physiology.

Dr. Hamilton West, Professor of Principles and Practice of Medicine & Clinic Medicine.

Dr. James E. Thompson, Professor of Surgery.

Dr. J.F.Y. Paine was the first faculty member elected. As Dean, he helped recruit the other members. Of the original faculty, Drs. Keiller, Morris, Randall, and Thompson served for thirty-five years or more.

Why did Dr. Thompson leave England? Why would a man with such a brilliant record break family ties and leave a secure position in his beloved England to accept a position in a newly founded, but as yet unorganized, medical school in the uncivilized part of the world called Texas? Dr. Thompson did not have funds to buy a practice in London and would have had to depend on the slow process of establishing a practice in Manchester. His pulmonary tuberculosis was arrested at this time, but his health was not good. His position as Resident Surgeon was considered quite an accomplishment, but it was a low rung on the ladder toward the top. Although he had considerable responsibility, the income was low and his finances had not recovered from the strain of his education. The salary of three thousand dollars a year seemed a solution to his financial problems. The decision to apply for the Texas position was made after careful consultation with his superiors.

As a young man, his father had made a journey to the United States and, no doubt, his stories of the new land had made an impression on James, but it was also believed that the climate of Galveston would benefit his pulmonary condition. Dr. Keiller, also a victim of tuberculosis, accepted a position in Galveston because of the climate.

The official announcement of the School of Medicine in 1891 stated that the completed college building would contain commodious and comfortably arranged amphitheaters, laboratories, dissecting rooms, museum, and numerous other apartments useful for medical teaching. The laboratories would be fully equipped with every appliance requisite for instruction in

First faculty

accordance with modern methods. The new John Sealy Hospital, located next to the School, was described as a well-equipped
hospital. It was noted that the cost of living need not exceed five
dollars per week.

It has been stated that Dr. Thompson brought modern
surgery to Texas. He was the first surgeon in Texas to limit his
practice to his specialty. What was the status of surgery in Texas
in 1891? What did Dr. Thompson find when he arrived in
Galveston on that Sunday morning, October 18, 1891? Sailing
vessels and steamers were anchored in the harbor. The towering
grain elevators and wharves covered with bales of cotton showed
that it was one of the nation's busy ports. This island city of
thirty thousand was connected to the mainland by the railway
causeway and a causeway built for wagons. An old beach hotel
was standing, but no seawall offered protection from storms.
There were two hospitals, St. Mary's and the new John Sealy
Hospital, and there was the just-completed University of Texas
Medical Branch.

In a 1925 Commencement Address, Dr. Thompson described his arrival in Galveston.

John Sealy Hospital

I was young and enthusiastic. I must have been endowed with the spirit of a pioneer to have traveled so far to assume new responsibilities and afterwards to have worked so steadfastly and hopefully with my colleagues during the early years of our struggle to create a new School of Medicine in the South.

Despite the glowing descriptions in the bulletin, he found that the school was scantily furnished and almost void of equipment. The library was, "A bare room littered with journals thrown higgled-piggledly in disorderly heaps on the floor."

While still in England, he had heard of the appointment of the Scotch Anatomist Dr. William Keiller and was eager to meet him. Dr. Thompson described this meeting, "As I approached, he raised his head and I saw that he was almost as young as I was and that he had penetrating blue eyes and a brown beard. He spoke to me with a Scotch accent and my heart warmed to him." This was the beginning of the close association that was to last for nearly forty years. Dr. Keiller's Anatomy Department was to become world famous, but at that time had no equipment, no

Original Medical School building ("Old Red")

articulated skeleton, and no prepared dissection.

Finances were a big problem. For many years, the Chair of Surgery had an annual appropriation of only fifty dollars, but Dr. Thompson was enthusiastic about his faculty associates and stated,

> During the first ten years of the School's life, we needed all of our courage. Sustained by hopes of the future, we stood firmly shoulder to shoulder, facing many disappointments. Starved physically by want of equipment and mentally by want of a library, cut off from the educational influences of learned society by our geographical position, and sometimes despairing of the future, we struggled on, spending our days teaching, proud in the belief that we were educating doctors just as capable as those coming from the best schools in the Country.

This was the status of the Medical Branch. What were the conditions in the state? Texas and the South were slowly and painfully recovering from the terrible effects of the Civil War. Only Galveston, Houston, San Antonio, Ft. Worth and Dallas had hospitals. A few of the smaller towns had railroad hospitals. All were poorly equipped. Most of the surgeons had been graduated from schools with two courses of six months each. Their preliminary literary qualifications did not extend beyond the ability to read and write. Only a few doctors, such as Cupples, Paschal and Hadra, were well educated.

In 1886 the Special Committee on Surgery, headed by Dr. George Cupples, submitted its famous report to the Texas Medical Association. This listed 4,293 operations performed by 138 Texas surgeons. Most of these operations were not performed in hospitals. They were proud that the mortality rate for 2,080 major operations was only 16 percent. However, the mortality rate for splenectomy was 100 percent, for herniotomy 6 percent, and for abdominal hysterectomy 92 percent. Certainly there was need for improvement.

This was the year that Ernst von Bergmann introduced steam sterilization and the aseptic period of surgery began. Although general and local anesthesia permitted longer and more complex procedures, the mortality rates were prohibitive until infections could be prevented. Numerous advances in pathology and physiology had accumulated a great storehouse of information which surgeons were suddenly able to use once the aseptic principle had been mastered. What part was Dr. Thompson to play in helping Texas surgeons to join in this advance?

James E. Thompson's training in England and Europe was the type considered ideal by Halstead. He patterned the Hopkins program after the methods observed in England and Europe. With Thompson's background and zeal for teaching, his presence was soon felt. The State Medical Association was organized in 1853, but the Surgical Section was not very progressive. By 1893 Dr. Thompson was taking an active part in the presentation of papers and carefully planned discussions. He was a frequent speaker at County, District, and State Meetings. These talks were considered highlights of the programs.

Dr. Thompson published over eighty articles. A number of completed but unpublished ones are with his personal papers. His studies on a hare-lip and cleft palate, the surgical approach to the long bones, and surgery of the neck received international recognition. His first article on cleft palate and hare-lip was published in 1900, the second in 1901. This subject was of special interest all of his life. The last article was published a few months before his death. A wide range of other subjects, including those requiring anatomical research and accurate embryological knowledge, were also covered. Several of these were published in sections over a period of years. The final contributions were masterpieces of description and information. The illustrations were for instruction and not for display. Many he drew himself, but he did not hesitate to use the services of others when they would serve best. Dr. Keiller collaborated with him on much of his work.

Although Dr. Thompson contributed to the advance of surgery in Texas through his writing, his lectures and discussions had an even greater impact. He had the ability to adapt his clearness of expression and finality of statement to the level of junior students as well as to the senior class or a gathering of surgical specialists.

Dr. Singleton stated that he was at his best while teaching. His tremendous enthusiasm and flow of language describing his clear thinking made him so magnetic that even the dullest students never slept in his classes. In the classroom and at the bedside, he constantly hammered into his students scientific principles based on embryology, anatomy, and pathology as applied to clinical findings.

Although over one thousand doctors received their basic surgical training from Dr. Thompson, only a few surgeons received their post-graduate training from him. All of these were outstanding men. His closest associate was his successor, Dr. Albert Singleton, who carried on in the tradition of his teacher.

Dr. Thompson not only became the Professor of Surgery in 1891, he also became one of Galveston's most eligible bachelors. He deserted these ranks when he married Miss Eleanor Roeck on May 16, 1896. After a courtship, he proposed to her while taking a buggy ride on East Beach. After stating his case, he told her that he wanted her to give it careful consideration and to take all the time she wanted, as long as he had the answer by the next afternoon. Following the wedding, they visited his family in England. They returned to the house he had built at 33rd and

Broadway. A home was established that became a social center where hospitality was dispensed with a lavish hand. The Thompsons were blessed with eight children, four boys and four girls. Contrary to statements by some former students, the children were born at this home and not under the British flag in Canada. As the family grew, the house was enlarged to accommodate them. A classical scholar and blessed with a brilliant and well-trained mind, his wide knowledge in the fields of literature and art was passed on to his family. The dinner table was a forum for the classics as well as current events. A copy of *Phyfe's Ten Thousand Words Often Mispronounced* was by the table. As the children grew older and formed their own opinions, the discussions were sometimes superseded by a general argument. The children's friends were welcomed and the home was the center of culture and refinement.

Each summer until his parents died, Dr. and Mrs. Thompson, their children and the maid visited them in England. After his parents' death, a house was bought at Lake Simcoe, north of Toronto. As soon as school was out, the family and servants would travel by train to the Canadian playground to escape the Texas heat. Dr. Thompson usually managed to have important business that prevented his traveling at the same time as the main group.

Dr. Thompson was an avid fisherman and it was a much-sought-after treat for students and associates to accompany him. In later years, he spent the summers in the high, dry climate of Wyoming, with fishing as his main recreation.

Dr. Thompson was especially fond of children. He loved his own children and their friends and spent hours reading his favorite books to them. He joked, talked, and suffered with each of his pediatric patients. He was a typical grandfather with his grandchildren and made a habit of coming to breakfast early to prolong his visits with them. His letters to his children reveal his remarkable personal interest in, and devotion to, all details of his family's life. The sons John, James, Fred and Edward were sent to the British-type Upper Canada College in Toronto because languages were included in the grade school curriculum. They then attended the University of Texas and all four were graduated from the Medical Branch. The girls attended private school in Galveston and Baldwin School in Pennsylvania.

A great many stories have been told about this distinguished gentleman from England. A few are recorded below to try to complete the image of this great man. Dr. Howard Dudgeon, one of his first assistants, described him as

> of medium height and build, had gray eyes, and a closely cropped beard. He dressed neatly and tastefully, usually wearing navy blue or English tweed. He moved quickly and spoke decisively and had a good sense of humor . . . he was no judge of horses. He normally drove one that could have served better on a farm.

Dr. Thompson was described by some as being aloof and difficult to know, but Dr. Dudgeon disagreed with this and explained that Dr. Thompson was nearly "face blind." He could not remember names or faces. He regretted this and said that he knew that many of the old students thought he high-hatted them. It was one of Dr. Dudgeon's duties to look out for former students visiting the school or hospital and to remind Dr. Thompson of their names.

Dr. Thompson was a very fair grader. He would not mark off much for a mistake if the rest of the answers indicated that the student knew the material. On an oral examination, he made every effort to coax the answer from the student.

Despite the popularity of the complex combinations of drugs before the days of specific therapy, Dr. Thompson used only two or three medicines. As many know, this principle was carried on by his successor, Dr. A.O. Singleton.

Dr. Dudgeon told of assisting Dr. Thompson in doing a radical mastectomy on the wife of a prominent Galveston business man. The operation was performed in the home with the family doctor, Dr. Fly, watching. After the operation was successfully completed, the family asked Dr. Thompson his fee. He said, "Fifteen hundred dollars." Dr. Fly was then asked his fee, and he replied, "Three thousand dollars." The patient's husband could not understand this discrepancy. Dr. Fly said, "You are familiar with the work on the wharfs. The longshoremen are not paid as much as the foreman." This closed the discussion. Dr. Fly later became a bitter enemy of Dr. Thompson.

The beautiful English and appropriate diction with molded sentences which characterized the Thompson lectures have been described. He also gained the reputation of being a master of profanity in the operating room. Nurses who worked with Dr. Thompson referred to him as "Old Hellfire and Damnation." "T.C.S." was the code name for "Thompson Cuss Sponges" and was an accepted term. A student nurse almost disrupted an operation by asking him what the letters meant. One of the most repeated stories involved an assistant supervisor in the operating room who had instruments laid out for a hare-lip case. He tried two or three scalpels and was not satisfied. He then picked up a hemostat. The lock was worn and did not hold. He turned to the nurse and said, "None of these instruments are worth a 'dom' today. Just throw them out the window and get some fresh ones." Without hesitation, the nurse picked up the entire tray and threw them out the window of the old amphitheater. Dr. Thompson hesitated a moment and then turned to the class and said, "The operation will be delayed a short time until I get some fresh instruments."

Although he terrified some of the nurses, most of those who worked with him in the operating room worshipped him. They explained that the profanity was simply a safety valve to let off steam and they just ignored it.

His planned discussions were highlights of any meeting he attended. In the early days of prostatic surgery, a Dallas surgeon reported a large series without a single mortality. Dr. Thompson rose with dignity and said, "Sir, you are a dom liar" and sat down.

Dr. Thompson's part in the formation of the Texas Surgical Society has been well documented. He presented the first presidential address in San Antonio in 1915. This was printed in the San Antonio paper. He explained the importance of surgery being done by trained men. He also discussed the faults of hospitals and advocated many reforms, including the keeping of permanent records and rigid qualifications for staff membership. This stirred up a hornet's nest. A County Medical Society and a District Medical Society passed resolutions condemning the address and asked the State Medical Association to take action against the Texas Surgical Society. The reaction was similar to the response to Dr. Paul Hauley's discussion which appeared in the *U.S. News & World Report* in 1953. One of the most vicious attacks came from his old enemy, Dr. Fly, who wrote, "Dear Sir, You have spoken authoritatively as the head of the 'Texas Surgical Exclusive Society'." He then launched an avalanche of personal, irrelevant questions, which are too lengthy to relate here. His closing paragraph stated, "We have been taught in Julius Caesar that all *Gaul* is divided into three parts, but, after reading your address, I am persuaded that this was a mistake, and that all *gall* is concentrated in the 'Texas Surgical Exclusive Society'." Dr. Thompson made another address to this Society in 1916, while he was still in office, to answer his critics and explain the position of the Society.

It has been said what a genteel, classical scholar Dr. Thompson was. Shortly after the founding of the American College of Surgeons, Dr. Thompson's old enemy, Dr. Fly, introduced false evidence in the Galveston County Medical Society Meeting, accusing Dr. Thompson and Dr. Randall of fee-splitting. The two doctors were able to prove their accuser's guilt, and a motion was made to expel Fly from the society. Dr. Fly then charged down the aisle with a cane pointed at Dr. Thompson. Dr. Keiller stepped into the aisle and wrenched the cane from his hand. This proved to be a loaded gun. Dr. Thompson then subdued Dr. Fly by hitting him and knocking him down. This was such a genteel society!

Dr. Thompson was reported to have taken out first citizenship papers when he arrived in Galveston. Assuming that his papers had been finalized, he voted in each election and was commissioned in the Army Medical Corp Reserve in 1912. During a feud with the Regents in 1917, Governor Jim Ferguson vetoed the University of Texas appropriation bill and demanded the dismissal of Dr. Thompson because he was an alien. The House of Delegates of the Texas Medical Association passed a resolution against this dismissal and a state-wide protest developed against the governor. The impeachment of Governor Ferguson settled this problem. The records show that Dr. James E. Thompson was then naturalized on June 19, 1917.

Dr. Thompson, bothered by poor health for many years, caught cold on a fishing trip with his son Jim in November 1926. He had a febrile episode for several days then went back to work. Dr. Thompson, assisted by Dr. Violet Keiller, was doing a Kraske operation for carcinoma of the rectum when he was

per Faculty

writer.

NOTED SURGEON IS GIVEN LL.D. DEGREE

Professor of Surgery In Texas U. Med. School Honored

₂ made and everything ₂ for the opening of ₂ssion Monday morning rding to Dean ,W. S. the summer school. hapel will be held at day morning and regis- summer term will be- ly after chapel. After ng, chapel will be held week from 11:30 to ind attendance will be

₂ work is scheduled to Tuesday morning, June

professoors will be summer faculty among ₂endent Cobb of the and Principal E. T. f the Waco Public

UDENTS ARE I SCHOLARSHIPS

arships in Baylor Uni- been awarded for next g to Dean W. S. Allen ships pay tuition in the one year and are award- n the basis of the stu-

;iving the scholarships Strickland, the Bennett Miss Edna Haney, the Scholarship; and Edwin Richard Byrd Burleson

est Class in History

The honorary degree of LL.D. was conferred upon Dr. J. E. Thompson, one of the most eminent surgeons in America, by Baylor University this morning when honorary degrees also were conferred upon two other dis- tinguished men.

Dr. Thompson has been a Texan since 1891, in which year he landed in Galveston, coming from his Eng- lish home. He has been in Galveston ever since, where he is professor of surgery in the medical school of the University of Texas. He practices surgery in Galveston at John-Sealy Hospital.

Northwich, Cheshire, England, claims the birthplace of Dr. J. E. Thompson, and England also gave him his education, his medical work being done in Owens College, Univer- sity of London. Dr. Thompson re- ceived the Bachelor of Medicine de- gree in 1887, and the Bachelor of Surgery degree in 1888. In 1888, he was made a Fellow of the Royal Col- lege of Surgery.

O. S. Lattio

heaped upon il throttle every the expansion · ment."

O. L. Bode dent of the A sided during evening. J. W. ed president t the evening.

The graduat ly admitted in tion when M secretary, pre package to J. dent of the ai ing unwrappe the Senior clas Collier respoi class and pled the sentiment E. C. Hank toastmaster of A benedicto closing the gi Three meml one of the clai of '05, everal, many of the ¡ at the banque

NOTED AI HONOR/

Commence Awar E

Article from the Baylor *Lariat*.

seized with a peculiar sensation of numbness and tingling on one side of his face and one arm. Jim was called from the clinic to take his father home while Dr. Keiller finished the operation. A diagnosis of sub-acute bacterial endocarditis was made. He had a series of small embolic phenomena over subsequent weeks and months and a large one in the final days of his illness when he succumbed to the disease on April 8, 1927. He was attended by his friends, Drs. Randall and Stone. It was at Dr. Stone's sugges- tion that a vaccine was made from the strep viridans isolated from Dr. Thompson's blood. Jim was given increasing doses of the vaccine. Serum was then extracted from his blood and given to Dr. Thompson. This was a dramatic effort but not successful. It is ironic that penicillin, which was discovered in his native England, could have saved his life.

University of Texas Medical Branch.

The autopsy confirmed the diagnosis of sub-acute bacterial endocarditis, superimposed upon rheumatic mitral valvular disease. His lungs were entirely clear except for a few healed scars. Maybe that Galveston air wasn't so bad.

Dr. Stone knew Dr. Thompson first as a teacher, later as a colleague and friend, and finally as a patient. He stated that the loss to the Medical School, to the medical profession, and to surgery in particular was one of great magnitude. There was no one of his stature at that time in medical education in this part of the country. Fortunately, he had trained some young assistants to continue his work.

Dr. Thompson received many honors. He was a member of the Founders Group of the American College of Surgeons, Vice President of the American Surgical Association, President of the Southern Surgical Association, Vice President of the Texas Medical Association, and the first President of the Texas Surgical Society.

When Baylor University conferred the degree of Doctor of

Laws on Dr. Thompson in 1925, Dr. S.P. Brooks emphasized the great qualities of Dr. Thompson as an instructor of young men. Other qualities and accomplishments were enumerated, but it was the teacher whom the oldest institution of learning in Texas admitted to its most honorable and famous few.

Dr. Thompson described the struggle of the first faculty to establish a new medical school in the South. Certainly, their dreams have come true.

The over eighty published articles of Dr. James E. Thompson, several written in conjunction with Dr. V.H. Keiller, span the period from 1892-1926 and can be found in such publications of the era as *Daniel's Medical Journal*, *International Medical Magazine*, *Medical News*, *Journal of the American Medical Association*, *Medical Chronicle*, *Annals of Surgery*, *Texas Medical News*, *Texas State Journal of Medicine*, and in the *Transactions of the Texas Medical Association*, *Texas Academy of Science*, *Southern Surgical Association*, and the *American Surgical Association*.

BIOGRAPHICAL SKETCH OF AUTHOR

WALTER B. KING, M.D., was born in Seguin, Texas, on February 13, 1916. He attended Waco, Texas, public schools and was graduated from Waco High School in 1933. He attended Baylor University, was graduated with a B.A. degree in 1936, then was graduated by the University of Texas Medical Branch in Galveston in 1940.

Graduate education began with internship at Kansas City General Hospital in Kansas City, Missouri, in 1940-1941. He entered the U.S. Army in 1941 and advanced to the rank of major. He served as battalion surgeon of the 46th Engineers in the Southwest Pacific and later was assigned to Walter Reed Army Hospital 1944-1945.

After discharge from the service he returned to the Medical Branch in Galveston for a one-year residency in pathology 1946-1947 followed by a four-year residency in general surgery 1946 to 1950. He spent the rest of his career in private practice in Waco. He was affiliated with Hillcrest Baptist Hospital in 1950 and with Providence Hospital also in 1950. He is a member of the McLennan County Medical Society, Texas Medical Association, Southern Medical Association, The American Medical Association, The American College of Surgeons, Southern Surgical Congress, The Singleton Surgical Society and The Texas Surgical Society where he is currently the Archivist. He has been honored by being elected:

Chief of Staff, Providence Hospital, Waco, Texas
Chief of Staff, Hillcrest Baptist Hospital, Waco Texas

Secretary, Singleton Surgical Society
Secretary, Texas Surgical Society
President, Texas Surgical Society
President, McLennan Medical Society
President, North Texas Chapter, American College of Surgeons

He is the author of nine surgical papers and served as Associate Editor of *The Texas Surgical Society----The First Fifty Years*, Robert S. Sparkman, Editor.

Index

Adams family, 61
Adams, Edwin, 61
Allen, Anna, 342
Alling, E.L., 16
Anahuac, Tex., 213, 214, 216, 219, 322, 330
Andrassy, Richard J., 273-290
Augustine, H.W., 138
Austin, Henry, 213
Austin, Moses, 250, 274
Austin, Stephen F., 213, 273, 276
Austin, Tex., 44, 63, 69, 139, 141, 152
Aynesworth, K.H., 349

Baker, Moseley, 340
Barber, Amos, 324
Barksdale, James G., 133
Barrow, Mrs. Sollomon, 324
Bartlett, Elisha, 13
Bastrop Co., Tex., 123
Bastrop, Tex., 124, 126, 152
Baylor, R.E.B., 235
Bennett, John, 191
Bettina, Tex., 175, 176
Bibb, Dr., 114
Blanton, William, 133
Blocker, Truman, xiii
Boerne, Tex., 188, 190
Borden, Gail, 341
Bradburn, Juan Davis, 213, 214, 216
Bradford, George, 241
Brady, J.T., 114
Brady, W., 114
Branham, Henry, 231
Braun, Gordon, 322
Brazoria Co., Tex., 101, 105
Brazoria, Tex., 203, 204, 213
Briggs, J.R., 71-72
Brook, George M., 141
Brooks, J.S., 322
Brooks, S.P., 365
Brooks, Sam, 322
Brooks, W.B., 63
Brown, Dr., 125
Brown, Jeremiah, 202
Brown, John Henry, 240
Brownsville, Tex., 143, 145, 146
Buckley, Samuel B., 238
Burleson, Edward, 125, 142, 282
Burns, John Arthur, 302, 309
Burns, John W., 301, 302
Burt, Dr., 69

Caldwell Co., Tex., 123, 125, 126
Caldwell, Matthew, 125
Calloway, Dr., 95

Canby, E.R.S., 46
Carhart, Agnus Gould, 21
Carhart, Charles Wheeler, 21
Carhart, Daniel Sutton, 9
Carhart, Edward Elmer, 16, 21
Carhart, Ethel, 21
Carhart, Hallie Rogers, 21
Carhart, John Wesley, 8-27
Carhart, Louis Henry, 16
Carhart, Margaret Martin, 9
Carhart, Mathilda, 21
Carhart, Minnie T., 16, 21
Carhart, Nina B., 21
Carhart, Theresa Mumford, 10, 21
Carothers, A.E., 153
Castell, Count, 175
Castro, Henri, 41-42
Cedar Bayou, Tex., 321
Cerna, Daniel, 32
Cerna, David, 28-39
Cerna, Dolores De La Garza, 31
Cerna, Matilda Lorenz, 31
Chambers Co., Tex., 219, 323
Chase, J.C., 64
Childs, Henry, 13
Childs, Timothy, 12-13
Civil War, 4, 6, 21, 46-49, 61-62, 72, 144-46, 182, 233, 236-37, 314-16, 342
Clarendon, Tex., 16
Clark, Alonso, 13
Cleburne, Pat, 46
Clopton, Albert G., 32, 353
Coleman, W.L., 107
Columbia, Tex., 280-81
Cook, James H., 181
Cuero, Tex., 294-96, 298-302
Cummings, A.J., 48
Cupples, Alexia Bourland, 41
Cupples, Carnelia, 41, 42
Cupples, Charles, 42, 47-48
Cupples, George, viii, 4, 40-60, 69, 73, 151, 180, 187, 188, 253, 264, 267, 357
Cupples, Jane, 42
Cupples, Robert, 41

Dallas, George M., 204
Dallas, Tex., 155, 296-97, 357
Dalton, Martin L., xiii, 201-209, 335-47
Daniel, Fannie R. Smith, 63
Daniel, Fannie, 63
Daniel, Ferdinand Eugene, 61-78, 263
Daniel, Gertrude, 63
Daniel, Hester Jordan Adams, 61
Daniel, Josephine, 64, 74, 76
Daniel, Marie, 63

Daniel, Minerva Patrick, 62
Daniel, R.W.T., 61
Darwin, Charles, 239
Davis, E.J., 146-47
Donley Co., Tex., 21
Dorset, Dr., 113
Dowell, Alep, 80
Dowell, Frances Dalton, 80
Dowell, Greensville, 79-122
Dowell, James, 80
Dowell, Laura Baker Hutchison, 84
Dowell, Sarah Z. White, 83-84
Dudgeon, Howard R. Jr., 227-245, 360

Eagle Pass, Tex., 32
Everitt, Stephen H., 337
Ewing, Alexander, 203, 215, 216

Fenner, E.D., 61
Fentress, James, 123-29
Fentress, Mary O. Hardeman, 123
Fentress, Thomas Hardeman, 125-26
Ferguson, Jim, 362
Fielding, Dr., 114
Finley, Carlos, 106
Finney, J.M.T., 352
Fischer, Dr., 48
Flint (medical school teacher), 61
Fly, Dr., 360, 362
Ford, Addie Smith, 145
Ford, Elizabeth, 131
Ford, Harriet, 131
Ford, John Salmon (Rip), 130-49, 237
Ford, John, 131
Ford, Louise Lewis, 138
Ford, Mary Davis, 133
Ford, William, 131
Fort Worth, Tex., 63, 357
Foster, John, 90

Galveston, Tex., 62-63, 81-83, 107, 109-
	10, 153, 175-76, 207, 211, 219-20,
	222, 233, 329, 227-38, 340, 244,
	353, 357
Gillett, H.H., 324-26
Gonzales Co., Tex., 80
Gouley, Dr., 98
Granbury, Hiram, 46
Green, Thomas, 47
Gross, Samuel D., 98, 202, 207
Grumbles, John H., 141
Guerin, Camille, 42
Guerin, Joseph, 42

Haddock, George C., 17
Hadra, Auguste Beyer, 151
Hadra, Berthold Ernest, 150-69, 357
Hadra, Emma Weisselberg, 152, 155
Hadra, Frederick, 151, 155
Hadra, Ida Weisselberg, 152

Hadra, Ida, 152, 155
Hadra, James Marion, 152, 155
Hadra, Josephine, 165
Hadra, Sedana, 152
Halsted, William Stewart, 3
Hamilton, Jack, 48
Hanson, A., 322
Hardeman, Monroe, 125
Hardeman, Thomas B., 123
Hardeman, W.P., 147
Harrington, Dr., 155
Harris Co., Tex., 321, 342, 243
Harris, W.W., 311
Harrison, Charles H., 312
Hays, Jack, 44, 125, 139-40
Heintzelman, S.P., 143, 144
Henderson, James P., 206, 336, 339
Herff, Adolph, 191
Herff, August F. Jr., 171, 191
Herff, August, 191
Herff, Christian Samuel von, 171
Herff, Eleanora Freiin von Meusbach,
	171
Herff, Ferdinand Ludwig, 4, 50, 170-99
Herff, Ferdinand P., 190
Herff, John B., 190, 191
Herff, Mathilde Kingel-Hofer, 175, 177-
	78, 180, 181, 190-91
Hicks, Marshal, 262
Highsmith, Samuel, 139
Hockley, Colonel, 216, 217-18
Holmes, Asahel C., 280
Holmes, J.T., 312
Hood, R. Maurice, xiii, 1-7, 41-60, 61-78,
	123-29, 131-49, 211-25, 311-19
Hood, William F., 211-225
Hooper, Richard, 135
Houston, Sam Jr., 241
Houston, Sam, 138, 139, 144, 201, 203,
	204, 215, 216, 217-18, 233, 236,
	312, 336-37, 338
Houston, Tex., 152, 207, 233, 357
Hudspeth, Dr., 112
Hull, Amos C., 202
Huston, Felix, 125, 312

Independence, Tex., 312
Indianola, Tex., 291, 293-95, 303

Jones, Anson, 200-209, 216, 338-39
Jones, Mary Smith McCrory, 204
Jones, Sarah Strong, 201
Jones, Solomon, 201
Johnston, Albert Sidney, 46

Keep, Nathan Cooley, 4
Keiller, Violet, 362-63, 365
Keiller, William, 352, 355, 358, 362
Kennon, Bill, 191
Kennon, William, 191

King, Walter B., 349-66
Kirkham, Frederick W., 302, 303
Knox, Orman, 115-16
Koch, Robert, 2-3
Krause, Robert Bernard, 29-39

Labadie, Agnes Rivera, 220
Labadie, Antoine Louis, 211-12
Labadie, Charlotte Berthe Raume, 211,
    219-20
Labadie, Charlotte, 220
Labadie, Joseph, 220
Labadie, Julia Seymour, 220
Labadie, Mary Cecelia, 220
Labadie, Mary Norment, 214
Labadie, Nicholas D., 203, 210-25
Labadie, Sarah, 220
LaGrange, Tex., 21, 23
Lampasas, Tex., 18, 20-21
Lee, Robert E., 144, 182, 293
Liberty Co., Tex., 214
Lincecum, Addison, 234
Lincecum, Gideon, 74, 226-45
Lincecum, Hezekiah, 228
Lincecum, John, 234, 235
Lincecum, Lucullus, 233-34
Lincecum, Lycurgus, 232
Lincecum, Lysander, 239
Lincecum, Sally Bryan, 229, 239
Lincecum, Sally Hickman, 228
Lincecum, Sarah Matilda (Mrs. William
    P. Doran), 234, 235, 240
Linnville, Tex., 124
Lister, Joseph, 2-3, 4, 6
Littlefield, George W., 84
Logan, William M., 214, 215
Long Point, Tex., 233, 241
Long, Crawford, 4
Lumley, Susie, 183-84

Mansbendel, Peter, 296
Markoe, Dr., 98
Matagorda Co., Tex., 123-24
McCulloch, Ben, 46, 125
McCulloch, Henry, 125, 142, 147, 148
McCune, Calmar, 330-31
McDonald, J.S., 44
McFee, Arthur S., 247-71
McNeill, Joseph P., 79-122
Medical Schooling, 19th Century, 4-5,
    12, 212, 243
Merry, Samuel, 212
Middleton, Dr., 95
Miller, Robert, 152
Miller, Willie, 322
Mitchell, Alice, 21-23
Mitchell, T.J., 61
Morris, Seth M., 352
Morton, W.T.G., 3-4
Mumford, John H. & Mary, 10

Nacogdoches, Tex., 213
Neighbors, Robert S., 140
Nelson, Allison, 142
Nelson, Thomas, 91
New Braunfels, Tex., 174-75, 179
Nixon, Pat Ireland, vii, 4

Odin, Jean Marie, 212

Paine, J.F.Y., 352-53
Parker, Willard, 13
Paschal, Agnes, 252
Paschal, Augustus, 252-53
Paschal, Francis Roach, 253
Paschal, Frank, 53, 74, 246-71, 357
Paschal, Franklin, 252-53
Paschal, George H. Jr., 262
Paschal, George, 257
Paschal, Ladie Napier, 255
Pasteur, Louis, 2-3, 6, 50, 80
Penrose, Thomas A., 48
Peter, Ferdinand, 191
Phelps, Dr., 280
Phifer, Mary Louisa, 336
Pierce, Shanghai, 303
Pitchlyn, John Jr., 230
Pitts, Billy, 142
Pollard, Amos, 272-90
Pollard, Fanny Oeella, 279
Pollard, Jonas, 277
Pollard, Martha Martin, 277
Pollard, Phebe Cross, 278
Prairie Lea, Tex., 124, 125, 126, 128, 129
Price, Sterling, 46
Pridgen, James E., 291-309

Raines, Dr., 72
Randall, Edward, 353, 362, 363
Rankin, Dr., 112
Red, George P., vii
Red, Samuel Clark, 346
Reuss, Anita, 296
Reuss, Augustus, 293
Reuss, Gaillard Thomas, 296
Reuss, Gesine Stubemann, 291
Reuss, Helen (Burns), 296
Reuss, Joseph Henry, 291-309
Reuss, Joseph Martin, 291
Reuss, Meta Reiffert, 296
Riggs, John M., 3
Roberts, Adam Alsen, 140
Roberts, O.M., 148
Robertson, Clarissa Hill Keech, 311
Robertson, Cornelius, 311
Robertson, Felix, 312, 316, 317
Robertson, Henly Hook, 317
Robertson, Jerome B., 310-19
Robertson, Julia Ann, 312
Robertson, Mary Elizabeth Cummings,
    312, 316

Roeder, Flora L. (von), 273-90
Roemer, Ferdinand, 175
Ross, Sul, 46
Rowe, Ed. B., 169
Rusk, Thomas J., 219, 312

San Antonio, Tex., 23, 32, 37, 42-43, 46,
    50, 153, 179-80, 182, 189, 247-51,
    253, 257, 267-69, 357
San Augustine, Tex., 134, 138
San Felipe, Tex., 214, 275
Sandy Point, Tex., 80
Saunders, W.B., 31
Sayers, Joe, 126
Schilling, Annie (dau), 321, 322
Schilling, John & Annie (parents), 321
Schilling, John (son), 321-22
Schilling, Nicholas T., 320-33, 346
Schleicher, Gustav, 175, 298, 300
Scott, A.C., 154-55
Semmelweis, Ignaz Phillip, 2, 50, 178
Senn, Nicholas, 154-55
Servoss, George L., 74
Shelburn, Dr., 113
Sheldon, Daniel, 202
Sherman, Sidney, 215
Sherman, Tex., 17, 63
Shinn, Anthony, 273-90
Sibley, Henry Hopkins, 46-47
Simpson, Harold B., 317-18, 319
Simpson, James Y., 4
Sims, J. Marion, 154
Singleton, A.O. Jr., 151-69
Singleton, Albert B., 83
Singleton, Albert O., 349, 358, 360
Smith, Allen J., 188, 353
Smith, Ashbel, 41-42, 83, 153, 234, 324,
    329-30, 334-47
Smith, Moses Jr., 335
Smith, W.R., 82
Smock, Henry, 141
Solms-Braunfels, Prince Karl, 175, 179,
    291
Sparkman, Robert S., vii-viii, xiii
Spiess, Hermannn, 175, 177
Spillman, James, 213
Steele, William, 46
Stembridge, Vernie A., 171-99
Stivers, Samuel, 282-83
Stone, Dr., 363-64
Stoneman, George, 144, 145
Stout, W.B., 207

Tandy, Charles C., 9-27
Tankersley, J.H., 142
Taylor, Joseph, 44

Texas Medical College, 63, 83, 153, 189,
    243-44, 344, 351-56
Texas State Medical Association, 44-46,
    50-51, 64, 69, 71-72, 73-74, 77, 80,
    109, 155, 159, 187, 191, 204, 253,
    263, 264-65, 304, 316, 317, 340,
    341, 346, 357, 361
Texas Surgical Society, 265, 291, 293,
    302, 304, 305, 349, 361-62
Thomas, Dr., 115
Thomas, Theodore Gaillard, 295
Thompson, Edward, 359
Thompson, Eleanor Roeck, 358
Thompson, Fred, 359
Thompson, Henry, 98
Thompson, James E., 153-54, 265, 303,
    348-66
Thompson, James, 359, 362-63
Thompson, John, 349
Thompson, John, 359
Thompson, Mary, 350
Throckmorton, James W., 238, 240
Tobin, W.G., 143
Travis, William B., 203, 286-87

Van Buren, Professor, 98
Venable, Charles S., 191
Victoria, Tex., 124,
von Humboldt, Alexander, 172, 173,
    177, 179
Von Muesebach, Ottfield Hans, 179
Von Rehfuss, Dr., 172

Waco, Tex., 155, 316
Wallace, "Big Foot," 181
Walthall, Walter, 258, 261
Warren, John Collins, 3-4
Washington-on-the-Brazos, Tex., 203,
    206, 312, 313
Watkins, Dr., 112
Wells, Horace, 3
West, H.A., 32
West, Hamilton, 353
White, John H., 83
Wilkerson, C.H., 95-96, 117, 118
Wilkes, William O., 165
Williams, Drew Davis, 321-33
Wolf, W.M., 191
Wolf, William M. Jr., 191
Wright, George, 322

Yandell, Dr., 62
Young, Hugh Hampton, 53, 54, 255-56

Zavala, Lorenzo de, 203